SO-AGF-258

Cover photo: Harbor Court Hotel, Baltimore, MD
See listing on page 96.

They were chosen, both for their elegant decor and because they possess an ambience like that of a fine residence.
—Washington Post

Thank you, Pamela for your unerring good taste for quality and for your talent in telling us about it.
—Peter Balas, President
International Hotel Association

It is indeed very good and full of fascinating addresses for people who travel as much as we do.
—Duchess of Bedford

My schedule is so hectic that when I can steal a few days for myself, they are very precious to me. I always choose small, out-of-the-way places, which give me and my family privacy, while providing excellent service and luxury accommodations.
—Donna Karan

The elegant ones make staying in hotels a little more bearable. The elegant ones don't seem like hotels at all.
—Philip Glass

All the best for a sure success.
—Valentino

. . . devoted to pleasing the most discriminating. The photos put you on the scene while the text and side notes offer explicit answers.
—Los Angeles Times

Elegant Small Hotels makes a seductive volume for window shopping. . . . Handsomely illustrated. Hotels that provide the atmosphere of a fine residence: beauty in design, color and furnishings, fresh flower, luxurious toiletries and linens. Other considerations are select business and physical fitness facilities, excellence of cuisine and concierge services.

—Chicago Sun Times

I stay at the Huntington because it is quiet and elegant like home. I know all the people and there are no ladies in the lobby with purple hairdos.

—Alistair Cooke

*If elegant small hotels are your thing—and whose aren't they?—check out **Elegant Small Hotels**. . . . Details 168 such establishments, complete with celeb comment on many of them.*

—Elle

*The entries for each hotel include rates, service and facilities available, as well as a short description of the **style and mood** of the establishment.*

—San Francisco Chronicle

Every great hotel in this guide is unique . . . handsome photographs.

—Hideaways International

*The switchboard operator knows your name, the people at the desk say welcome back when you come through the door, and they try to give you your favorite room if you've stayed there a long time, and its fine to have dinner in the dining room if you're there alone. My favorite is the Hotel Bel Air because that's where I spent my honeymoon. . . . We all **know** small hotels are sexy because they **are** small and intimate.*

—Helen Gurley Brown

What I love about managing a fine, elegant small hotel is the same that makes me choose these houses for staying: Elegance and efficiency, smallness and smoothness, accuracy and actuality and that personal touch I like so much to feel.

—Count Johannes Walderdorff

Congratulations Pamela! Looks good. Cheers and all best regards.

—Herb Caen

A sweet collection of great hotels.

—Gavin McLeod

My enjoyment of the elegant small hotel lies in its uniquely personalized service. This smaller scope also affects my role as designer, for I am allowed the freedom to draw upon my residential design knowledge. This approach would be impossible in a larger establishment.

—Valerian Rybar

It's a great adventure to read.

—Roger Horchow

Breaking the rules was the challenge: to create charm by giving up overdone effects, pompous details, nostalgic fake Louis'. . . to attract attention with almost invisible details; these little things grow on you during your stay . . . and cast a spell.

—Andree Putman

Let me tell you that we are proud to collaborate with you, and it will be a pleasure to welcome you in France.

—Pierre Cardin

One of the rewards of designing small high quality hotels is that they often are the culmination of a greater sense of interest from the owner and the operator, and therefore provide us, the designer, with a more personalized direction. It also offers us an opportunity to promote the specialized field of hotel design to a higher level of professionalism and excellence. This in turn influences the level of sophistication and appreciation of the general public who previously experienced this design only in high and residential work.

—James Northcutt

A small hotel is your home away from home.

—Caroline Hunt Schoelkopf

There is less chance of running into people you know, so there is more time for the actual purpose of being there.
—Bill Graham

The author and Peter Duchin, who wrote the introduction, make a very persuasive case for staying at small elegant hotels . . . these hotels lived up to the author's description. Fortunately the author covers a range of rates from afford-able ($50) to expensive ($300) and more.
—St. Louis Post-Dispatch

Pamela Lanier offers up a wish-book for the most luxuri-ous small hotels (less than 200 rooms) in America.
—Dallas, Texas News

. . . unique places with exquisitely appointed rooms, inter-esting architecture, luxurious ambiance and excellent food and service. "Small" translates into fewer than 200 rooms.
—Cincinnati Enquirer

"Small" is fewer than 200 guest rooms, "elegant" refers to decor as well as attitude. . .In a book which differs from the usual guides.
—Midwest Book Review

A collection of 168 fine hotels is described . . . A page is devoted to each hotel, with a description of the accommoda-tions and facilities plus information on dining rates, credit cards, and other items of interest.
—Chicago Sunday Sun-Standard

. . .inviting descriptions of each hotel, along with detailed lists of the services offered.
—Milwaukee Journal

From the Huntington in San Francisco to the Pierre in New York, these hotels cater to a choosy clientele devoted to their particular charms and personal services, seductively described here.
—Banana Republic Travel Bookstore

Services, facilities and amenities nation-wide. . .Available in retail outlets.

—Travel Age West

. . . detailed information about small hotels in the U.S.

—San Francisco Examiner

If you are looking for exquisitely appointed guest rooms in a small hotel, inspired architecture, luxurious ambiance and extraordinary personal service then this is the book for you.

—Book Passage

Each hotel is described in detail with a side listing that includes everything . . . this is an excellent guide for the traveler who is looking for European style tradition in the U.S.

—The Armchair Traveler

A valuable source for the discriminating traveller seeking a luxurious lodging in the European tradition. . . . In addition to exquisite decor, they offer an elegance of atmosphere, accomplished only through the meticulous attention to detail so rare in contemporary life.

—Innsider

America's finest! . . . An abundance of places to stay; that rival any European hotel in warmth, charm and service.

—The Horchow Collection

Biggest is not always best. . . . If you can afford to be choosy.

—Dallas Magazine

If you've enjoyed the charming personalized hotels of Europe, you will love Pamela Lanier's selection of . . . outstanding hotels here at home. The information and photographs will allow the discerning traveller to choose from among the best. . . .

—Traveller's Bookstore

Elegant small hotels have always fascinated me. This connoisseur's guide describes the atmosphere and individual style of selected hotels. . . . Detailed listings of all services, facilities and amenities.
—Travel Briefs—Station WLOO, Chicago

. . . as a resource on elegant, somewhat smaller hotels, this is a good one. Good descriptions, photographs, and all practical data are included.
—Going Places

It happens I always stay at a fine small hotel when given the choice. I'm familiar with quite a few of your selections and must commend you upon the realistic assessments you provide.
—Tom Shane

Dignified and classy.
—Publish

Lanier Publishing has facilitated the
planting of nine trees for every tree used
in the production of this book.

ELEGANT
SMALL HOTELS™
A CONNOISSEUR'S GUIDE

PAMELA LANIER

The interactive version of this book
may be found on the Internet
(www.elegantsmallhotel.com)
E-mail: elegant@TravelGuideS.com

A division of the Travelguides.com Network

A *Lanier* Guide
▲

HUNTINGTON CITY-TOWNSHIP
PUBLIC LIBRARY
200 W. Market Street
Huntington, IN 46750

Other books from Lanier Travel guides

Cinnamon Mornings and Chocolate Dreams
Bed & Breakfast—Australia's Best
Family Travel & Resorts
Condo Vacations — The Complete Guide
All-Suite Hotel Guide — The Definitive Directory
Golf Resorts — The Complete Guide
Complete Guide to Bed & Breakfast Inns & Guesthouses International
Sweets & Treats from America's Inns

Copyright @ 1986–2006
Lanier Publishing International, Ltd.
Cover Copyright @ 1986–2006
Lanier Publishing International, Ltd.

There's a Small Hotel by Rodgers & Hart. Copyright @ 1936 by Chappell & Co., Inc. Copyright renewed. National Copyright secured. All rights reserved. Used by permission.

Design by Laura Lamar
Production Coordinators: J.C. Wright, John Richards, Russell Rottkamp

Editor: Russell Rottkamp

Library of Congress Cataloging-in-Publication Data
Lanier, Pamela
    Elegant small hotels: a connoisseur's guide/Pamela Lanier.
        p.   cm.—(A Lanier guide)
    ISBN 1-58008-724-8
    1. Hotels, taverns, etc.—United States—Guidebooks.   2. United
States—Guidebooks.   I. Title.   II. Series.
Library of Congress Cataloging in Publication data is on file with the publisher.

First Edition September 1986
Nineteenth Edition August 2004
Twentieth Edition August 2005

Published by Lanier Publishing International, Ltd.
Drawer D
Petaluma, CA 94953 USA
707-763-0271
707-763-5762 (Fax)
Email: Elegant@TravelGuideS.com

American Hotel
& Motel Association
ALLIED MEMBER

Distributed to the trade by Ten Speed Press
P.O. Box 7123
Berkeley, CA 94707

Printed in Canada on recycled paper

All information in this book is subject to change without notice. We strongly recommend that you call ahead and always verify the information in this book before making final plans or reservations. The author and publisher of this directory make no representation that it is absolutely accurate or complete. Errors and omissions, whether typographical, clerical or otherwise, do sometimes occur and may occur anywhere within the body of this publication. Hotels in this guide have been charged a listing fee to help defray the costs of compiling the guide.

This book is lovingly dedicated to the memory of John Muir. Very special thanks to Sarah Morse, Lauren Childress, Marianne Barth, Venetia Young, Mary Kreuger, Jay Clark, Katherine Bertolucci, Mary Ellen Callahan, Marjorie Silverman, Harriet Choice, Jeremy Dove, Frank Waldrop, Sally Carpenter, Sartain Lanier, Carol Delattre, Lorraine Strain, Ann Chandler, Judy Johnson, Mariposa Valdes, Molly Mosier, Karen Aaronson, Danielle Palmer, Stephen High, Cliff Burdick, and the staff of Ten Speed Press.

*"There's a small hotel,
with a wishing well,
I wish that we were there
together . . ."*

—Rodgers and Hart

Contents

INTRODUCTION

. . . And then there was the time that my band (eight men and one woman) and myself travelled all day changing planes twice to get from New York to a small town in the West where we had to play that night. It had been *that* kind of travelling day—replete with rudeness, abruptness, computer mixups and a complete lack of attention or care for the individual. So somehow it didn't really surprise us when we found upon reaching our ultimate destination that all our instruments and other bags had been mis-routed and sent to Kalamazoo, Chattanooga or some other strange Indian-sounding city. This meant that only those of us who had carried our clothes on board (something I've learned to do) had anything to wear that evening and only me on piano (it doesn't travel with us, thank God) and the trumpet player (who had carried his instrument with him) had anything to play that night—a most unlikely duet! What to do? One could rage uselessly at the cipher in back of the airlines desk, or one could attempt to be cunning.

Opting for the second alternative, I remembered that we were staying in an elegant small hotel which had a reputation for service and attention to the individual; so with fading hope I called the hotel. I was immediately switched to a polite concierge whom I belabored with our seemingly insoluble problem. He listened attentively, asked intelligent questions (a first that day, I'll tell you) and told me to come directly to the hotel and see him there. When we arrived and assembled numbly around his desk, we found that this wonderful man had done the following: he had contacted the local music store which was standing by to hear the specifications of the instruments we needed and would deliver them to the job on time: he had contacted the local evening wear store, which was waiting to hear our sizes and would deliver to the hotel; he had contacted the airlines and traced our bags; he had pre-registered us in our rooms; and finally, he had set up a private room for us in which he had arranged to serve us dinner before we left for the job. Furthermore, it all worked!

Believe me, I need no further inducement to stay in elegant small hotels for the rest of my days. When I travel, which I do a great deal of the time (we played in 41 states in the last three years). I really do appreciate those wonderful qualities that can be found in these hotels: politeness, attentiveness and really an old-fashioned attention to detail and to the needs of the client. Sadly, these qualities are quite lacking in everyday life as we prepare for the 21st century. I'm glad to see, though, that these hotels are returning to a sense of service and style . . . I just hope that with the publication of this book my band and I will be able to get reservations whenever we need them!

—*Peter Duchin*

GUIDE NOTES

This book is sorted by USA first, by state and within each state, by city or town. Hotels are listed in alphabetical order within each city. International properties appear next listed alphabetically by country or area.

If you are among those discerning travelers who understand that the essence of the good life is quality, this book is designed especially to enhance your travel enjoyment.

To identify the most elegant small hotels in the world today, we have used the following criteria:

When we say "small," we generally mean fewer than 200 guest rooms; in fact, the typical hotel selected for inclusion in this guide has approximately half that number. We have found that small hotels are best able to offer the high staff-to-guest ratio enabling a genuine concern for each guest's comfort and pleasure.

By "elegant," we mean decor—and also something more. If a hotel is to be one's "home away from home," its atmosphere should be like that of a fine residence. The feeling should be reflected not only in design, color and furnishings, but also in those little touches that *really* matter; fresh flowers, nightly turndown (with a chocolate!), overnight shoeshine, luxurious toiletries and oversized towels . . . all the myriad details that add up to the intangible quality we call elegance.

For us to even consider a particular hotel, it must first have met the foregoing standards. Other factors we have kept in mind, while separating the exceptional from the merely first-class, relate to individual traveler's needs. For example . . .

If you conduct business while traveling, such facilities as secretarial service on call, teleconferencing, and Internet access, and perhaps an appropriately-sized meeting or conference room, will be essential.

If you are among the growing number of people to whom physical fitness is a personal must, your hotel should provide in-house facilities such as swimming pool, tennis, spa and massage room, and perhaps weight training equipment. Many of our recommended hotels also arrange guest privileges at prestigious private country clubs and health centers.

If you are among those travelers for whom fine cuisine is a top priority, we agree completely. We have chosen our hotels with excellent dining in mind, and we often include a description of a representative dinner recently served at the hotel. The words "Dress Code" in any listing show that coat and tie are appropriate. We have also indicated when a hotel's dining room is for guests only.

Whether you travel for business, pleasure, or a bit of both, each elegant small hotel described in this guide deserves a special place in your plans and your memories.

This guide encompasses five types of elegant hotel accommodations:

Grand Luxe Hotels: Each of these world-class hotels projects an incomparable aura of tradition and grace. A few of the services provided are superb restaurant and room service, an attentive but very discreet staff with full concierge services, and a sumptuous atmosphere of well-secured luxury.

City Center Hotels: Designed especially for the business traveler, each of these hotels offer a comfortable, inviting environment where an executive may return each day to lodgings ideally appointed to satisfy business, personal and recreational needs. Special emphasis is placed upon conference facilities and services for executives.

Outstanding Resorts: The quick weekend trip or brief resort holiday is becoming the new vacation style of the ultra-busy. From a wide range of possibilities, we have selected our resort recommendations with regard for their luxurious ambience, excellent cuisine and sporting facilities. Most also offer excellent conference facilities and are perfect for combining recreation and business meetings in beautiful surroundings.

Affordable Elegance: Though one normally expects elegant lodgings to come at higher-than-ordinary rates, we have discovered a select few that offer some of the best of both worlds: comfortable, well-appointed rooms, excellent restaurants and access to sports facilities, with many of the essential amenities associated with Grand Luxe hotels—at surprisingly reasonable prices. Please bear in mind, though, that throughout the world, the very top quality accommodations carry a correspondingly steep price.

Wonderful Country Inns: Those great small hideaways we all dream about, the perfect place for restoring body and soul (and romance!) cosseted by a caring staff in a gracious and restful ambiance.

For different styles in affordable elegance, please check our most recent editions of *The All-Suite Hotel Guide* and *The Complete Guide to Bed and Breakfasts, Inns and Guesthouses in the United States and Worldwide*, both by Pamela Lanier.

We have indicated room rates showing the price range of the lowest-priced double-occupancy room. Unless otherwise noted all prices are in U.S. dollars.

We have noted many amenities provided. Other services and sundries are often available. When you call to book reservations, ask whether the hotel offers those you desire.

We have indicated when a hotel will not accept pets, or when pets are accepted only under special conditions. An additional deposit is often required. In establishments that do not permit pets, the concierge can make arrangements with the best local kennel.

Children are accepted when accompanied by their parents except where otherwise noted. There is no additional charge for children under a certain age; the age varies among hotels.

Most hotels have at least some rooms designed to accommodate the handicapped. We have noted the number of rooms so equipped. Hotels with only a few handicap equipped rooms should be booked well in advance.

An important key to getting the most out of your Elegant Small Hotel experience is to allow the concierge to assist you whenever possible. The hotels described in this guide are small enough to permit a degree of personal attention rarely encountered in modern life. Accordingly, the function of the concierge is to cater to the individual needs (and whims) of each guest. Rather than attempt a detailed description of services and amenities the concierge can arrange—which would leave no space in this guide for the hotels themselves— we have presented "A Concierge's Day," the viewpoint of one outstanding concierge, on the following page.

Every attempt has been made to be absolutely current. Some information contained in this guide has been provided by the hotels' management, and management policies may change. If you feel that anything in this book is even slightly inaccurate, please inform us so we can put it right in future editions.

We appreciate reader comments, including any hotel we have overlooked which you feel deserves to be included.

—*Pamela Lanier* August 2005

A CONCIERGE'S DAY

"I am absolutely certain we can have the car and driver here in twenty minutes, sir. I only need to know what sort of car and what sort of driver you would prefer. And yes, I expect your day in the wine country will be splendid; the weather is perfect."

The 20-minute wait for the special car and driver to arrive will not be wasted. The concierge first calls ahead for luncheon reservations at a spot that normally requires two weeks' notice. Next, he will call the wineries for any special considerations that might be possible for his guest. After all, everything must be the best. (It will soon become evident that perfect weather is the only thing the concierge has not arranged—the sunshine being courtesy of a somewhat higher power.)

The larger day's work begins for the concierge at this small Nob Hill hotel (the Huntington) in San Francisco with a review of the arriving guest list and of their special requests noted in his log. He opens that delicious document with the same excitement felt by a maestro opening the score of a beautiful symphony.

Appreciating that not everyone who travels in America is yet fully acquainted with the full range of services he can provide, the concierge will promptly call each guest within minutes of arrival to extend a personal introduction and a warm invitation to take full advantage of his skills and resources. To him and his hotel, every guest is a Very Important Person.

The concierge next turns his attention to a couple at his desk, eager to begin a day of sightseeing. Shopping, museum-hopping and general about-towning are the plan, with a lovely lunch along the way. The concierge will not only point them in the right direction, but also enhance their day with helpful hints and local insights.

The couple will return with happy faces and tired feet, to swap a few stories with the concierge and then retire for a nap or workout followed by tea.

Afterward they will consult the concierge once again to plan an evening grand finale to a delight-filled day. Knowledgeable and sensitive to his territory, he can advise them concerning matters of cuisine, attire, entertainment, transportation and adventure; then he will make the necessary arrangements.

You see, living vicariously is the route to concierge heaven. As the concierge plans the guests' daytime and evening activities with them, striving to maximize their pleasure, and as he takes the necessary measures to bring the plan to reality, and as he hears guests tell of their experiences afterwards, he feels something beyond professional pride. He actually enjoys it.

—Jeremy Dove

[*Special thanks to Marjorie Silverman, First Vice President of Les Clefs d'Or, for her help on this project.* —P.L.]

THE BOULDERS

The dramatic and innovative architecture of The Boulders blends with the prehistoric boulder formations and harmonizes with the natural beauty of the surrounding Sonoran desert foothills. Navajo rugs and southwestern Indian pottery accent the subtle desert-hued decor.

160 individual casitas and 39 villas are scattered throughout the 1,300-acre resort. Rooms have viga ceilings, horno-style corner fireplaces, private patios, and such special touches as quality toiletries and fluffy bathrobes.

Outdoor sports abound: 36 holes of golf on courses designed by Jay Morrish, 8 plexi-cushion all-weather tennis courts, 3 swimming pools, bicycling, marked hiking trails and nature paths. There is also the Sonoran Spa and Rock-Climbing Clinics.

The concierge will gladly arrange a hot-air balloon ride, desert Jeep trip, or spectacular flying tour of the Grand Canyon. Five dining rooms offer a full range of outstanding cuisine. The Latilla features Grand American Cuisine as well as a diverse and tantalizing main menu and irresistible continental pastries. It also affords a stunning view of waterfalls and the impressive rock formations for which the resort is named. The light and airy Palo Verde features southwestern cuisine characterized by local ingredients and dramatic presentations. The Boulders Club serves both lunch and dinner. The Cantina del Pedregal features inspired Mexican cuisine. The Bakery Cafe is also available for breakfast, lunch and dinner.

For large groups there are 7,000 square feet of meeting rooms including a 5,600-square-foot ballroom. Together, the meeting spaces can accommodate up to 450 persons.

Address: 34631 N Tom Darlington Rd, PO Box 2090, Carefree 85377
Phone: 602-488-9009
800-553-1717
Fax: 602-488-4118
Room Rates: casitas 175–560
Suite Rates: villas 325–113
No. of Rooms 160
No. of Suites: 39
Credit Cards: Most Credit Cards accepted
Attractions: El Pedregal Art galleries, Heard Museum North, Specialty shops, Restaurants, Day trips to Sedona/Oak Creek Canyon, Fly or tour Grand Canyon, Jeep tours, In January – Boulder Fest
Services & Amenities: Valet service, Car rental available, Parking, Gift shop, Tennis & golf pro shop, Baby-sitting, Laundry service, Card/game area, Cable TV, 2-line telephone, CD player, Hair dryer, Robes, Complimentary newspaper and toiletries, Complimentary coffee & tea
Restrictions: Handicap-equipped facilities
Concierge: 7:30 a.m.-7 p.m.
Room Service: 6:30 a.m.-10 p.m.
Restaurant: Latilla Restaurant, 7 a.m.-9:30 p.m. & Sunday Brunch, Palo Verde, Boulders Club, Cantina del Pedregal, The Bakery Cafe
Bar: Discovery Lounge
Business Facilities: Full service business center
Conference Rooms: 11 rooms, capacity 450 – 7000 sq.ft.
Sports Facilities: 8 tennis courts, 36 holes of golf, 3 pools, Sonoran Spa, Biking, Hiking/Nature path, Rock climbing clinic
Location: 15 miles north of Scottsdale, 33 miles northeast of Phoenix

INN AT EAGLE MOUNTAIN

Guests at the stunning architecturally designed Inn at Eagle Mountain, awarded AAA Four Diamond status, enjoy dramatic daytime views of Red Mountain and 50 miles of desert terrain and nighttime city lights from their private deck or patio. This Santa Fe adobe-style resort is located on a 6-acre site bordering the Eagle Mountain Golf Course in Scottsdale.

High ceilings, and custom-designed southwest décor grace each room, along with a kiva fireplace and 25-inch cable TV. Baths have their own telephones, robes, and Jacuzzis. Every guestroom has a work center with 2 phone lines, computer and modem setup.

The lobby is a Navajo-style kiva building with a stone floor, six-foot skylight, and stained glass doors.

Amenities include Eagle Mountain's 18-hole championship golf course, a large pool, outdoor spa and a conference center designed for meetings of up to 40 people. The continental breakfast features bagels, muffins, fruits, juices, coffee and tea.

The Inn is close to Scottsdale, Frank Lloyd Wright's Taliesen home, and beautiful lakes and desert terrain.

Those who are committed to walking lightly on the land will appreciate the care that went into the environmental aspects of the facility, with recycling, water conservation, and protection of native plants.

Address: 9800 North Summer Hill Blvd, Fountain Hills 85268.
Phone: 480-816-3000 800-992-8083
Fax: 480-816-3090
Email: info@innateaglemountain.com
Web site: http:// www.innateaglemountain.com
Room Rates: 109–209
Suite Rates: 159–279
No. of Rooms: 42
No. of Suites: 11
Credit Cards: Most Credit Cards accepted
Attractions: Eagle Mountain Golf Club on-site, Scottsdale ¼ mile away, "Out of Africa" 5 miles, Taliesen (Frank Lloyd Wright's winter home) 5 miles, Lakes 10 miles
Services & Amenities: Parking, Gift shop, Gas fireplaces, Private decks and balconies, Whirlpool spa tub, Cable TV, VCR, Telephone, Radio, Complimentary USA *Today*, Room service, Complimentary deluxe continental breakfast
Restrictions: No pets allowed, 2 rooms handicap equipped, Children under 12 stay free in parent's room
Concierge: 10am-9pm, days vary
Restaurant: Golf Club Grill, lunch and cocktails until sundown; Cafe Vu
Bar: Seasonal
Business Facilities: Message center, Copier, Audio-visual, Fax, Modems, Every room has a work center
Conference Rooms: 3 rooms, capacity 15, 15, 40
Sports Facilities: Outdoor swimming pool, Whirlpool, Massage, Complete exercise & tennis club nearby (small fee)
Spa Services: Adjacent Day Spa
Location: Fountain Hills, East suburb of Scottsdale

BRIAR PATCH INN

Nestled along the lush banks of Oak Creek, the Briar Patch Inn invites you to nurture your relationship with nature. At the base of the surrounding red rock mountains, the spring fed waters of Oak Creek create a healing, magical oasis, a quiet blending of 9 acres and 18 cottages.

The cottages, furnished with Southwest charm and Native American arts, are designed for comfort in rustic ambiance. Fireplaces, shaded patios, and privacy lure you to relax and enjoy the moment or a good book from the ample library. To help you relax, massages are offered in your own cottage setting or in the open air creekside gazebo.

Healthy breakfasts of fresh home baked breads and muffins, crunchy homemade granola, yogurt, fresh fruits and juices, quiche, eggs in the shell, coffee and herbal teas can be enjoyed by the fireside in the lounge, or on a tray at your cottage, or best of all, at the creekside. In the summers, the music of Lyra (violin and classical guitar) brings the feeling of Old World charm to breakfast.

Hiking the mountain and canyon trails, exploring Indian ruins, fishing for rainbow or German Browns, birdwatching and sighting the bald eagle on the creek patio each spring are all highlights for the nature lover.

"It is a corner of paradise, where the river is the maestro, nature the musician, and all together they play a peaceful harmony at the Briar Patch."

Address: 3190 North Highway 89A, Sedona 86336.
Phone: 928-282-2342 888-809-3030
Fax: 928-282-2399
Email: briarpatch@sedona.net
Web site: http://www.briarpatchinn.com
Room Rates: 175–335
Suite Rates: 199–335
No. of Rooms: 18 individual cottages
No. of Suites: 8
Credit Cards: Visa
Attractions: Grand Canyon, Hope and Navajo Indian reservations, Meteor Crater, and Petrified Forest all within a 2-hour drive, Hiking, Fishing, Birdwatching, Indian ruins, galleries, Jeep tours, horseback riding, golf, restaurants, shopping, music and art festivals
Services & Amenities: Parking, Gift shop, Baby-sitting service, Library, Card/game area, Kitchen facilities, Wood burning fireplaces, Decks, Radio/CD players, Individual climate controls, 6 cabins-cable TV, Coffee makers w/comp coffee & tea, Comp.shampoo & conditioner, Comp. breakfast buffet
Restrictions: No pets allowed, Children welcome, 1 cottage handicap equipped, 2 night minimum on weekends
Concierge: 8 a.m.-8 p.m.
Room Service: Limited
Business Facilities: Message center, Copiers, Fax
Conference Rooms: 1 room, capacity 49
Sports Facilities: Massage service available, Swimming hole at Oak Creek
Spa Services: Open air creekside Gazebo where we offer private massages for 1 person, or for 2 persons side by side. Available year round. Also offered in the cottages.
Location: 3 miles north of Sedona

SOUTHWEST INN AT SEDONA

The Southwest Inn at Sedona is set on an acre in the heart of "Red Rock Country." Near the ancient Anasazi and Sinagua Indian ruins, with their mystical pictograph and petroglyph sites, this is an area known as the adventure capital of Arizona. The completely non-smoking inn offers an array of spacious rooms and suites, and a staff that takes pride in offering particularly warm personal service.

The Inn's award-winning décor is the ultimate in Santa Fe style, with nine-foot ceilings, fireplaces, lodge-pole furniture, and southwest fabrics and wall décor. Among the many thoughtful appointments are in-room coffee makers, refrigerators, and hair dryers. After peaceful nights, guests awaken to the splendor of breathtaking red-rock vistas.

A complimentary sumptuous continental breakfast of freshly baked muffins, bagels, Belgian waffles, hard boiled eggs, fruit, juices, teas and coffees is served daily in the breakfast room, which is flooded with natural light and open to the spectacular views. Weather permitting, guests may choose to eat breakfast al fresco, either on their own deck or patio, or on the outdoor viewing deck.

Concierge service is provided to help guests plan their days, and to arrange reservations at a wide selection of nearby restaurants, many of which are within walking distance. In addition to the numerous restaurants and shopping opportunities, guests can explore ancient ruins, learn the ways of Native Americans, play golf, and enjoy horseback riding, hiking, and the many other outdoor activities and tours available. Guests of the Southwest Inn at Sedona have the option to pay a fee for privileges at the nearby Sedona Racquet Club, which is a complete health club with tennis courts.

The Inn's heated pool (seasonal) and spa (year 'round) provide a place for those who choose to simply soak or sun poolside, and for others, relaxation after more strenuous activities.

True to its reputation for being "The" place to stay in Sedona, the Inn was voted "The Best Place to Stay" in Sedona 3 years in a row by *Sedona Spectrum* magazine. We are known for our wonderful friendly staff.

Address: 3250 W Highway 89A, Sedona 86336.
Phone: 928-282-3344 800-483-7422
Fax: 928-282-0267
Email: info@swinn.com
Web site: http://www.swinn.com
Room Rates: 119–239
Suite Rates: 189–259
No. of Rooms: 24
No. of Suites: 4
Credit Cards: Most Credit Cards accepted
Attractions: Ancient Native American ruins, Sedona's restaurants, theatres and galleries, 10 minutes to Oak Creek Canyon, Ballooning, Jeep and other tours, Indian gaming casino, Sedona Cultural Park, Verde Canyon Railroad, 2 hours to Grand Canyon
Services & Amenities: Complimentary deluxe continental breakfast and newspaper, 25" cable TV & VCR, Refrigerators, Coffee makers, Phones with free local and 800 calls, Fireplaces, Patios or decks with views, Whirlpool baths, Optional turndown service, Complimentary toiletries
Restrictions: No pets allowed, No smoking, 2 rooms handicap equipped
Concierge: 8 a.m.-9 p.m.
Restaurant: Complimentary deluxe continental breakfast served daily in the Breakfast Room. Breakfast includes bagels, Belgian waffles, muffins, fruit, juice, cereal, yogurt, etc.
Business Facilities: Internet Cafe & FREE in-room wireless Internet, modem hookups, Copier Fax, Internet Cafe
Conference Rooms: Deluxe conference room–board room style–seats 12
Sports Facilities: Outdoor swimming pool & whirlpool spa, Exercise rm, Sedona Racquet Club privileges $25/day, Hiking

TANQUE VERDE RANCH

Tanque Verde Ranch is one of America's old time cattle and guest ranches. Today's resort quality Ranch is recognized as one of the last luxurious outposts of the Old West! This historic ranch, founded in 1868, is located on 640 spectacular acres in the lush desert foothills of the Rincon Mountains, adjacent to the Saguaro National Park and Coronado National Forest. Miles of scenic horseback riding and hiking trails offer ranch guests the opportunity to explore the rugged and unique Sonoran desert of the Old West. While secluded and surrounded by the natural desert, the ranch is just minutes from all that Tucson has to offer in the way of shopping and sightseeing!

The present-day lobby recreates the ambiance of the Old West with its high adobe walls, beam ceiling and saguaro rib struts. The 74 authentically decorated rooms and suites are fully air-conditioned and offer beautiful desert and mountain views. Most rooms are spacious and have adobe fireplaces and outside private patios. Larger suites and smaller, cozier rooms are also available. The rooms are scattered over a lovely hillside, capitalizing on the spectacular views, and offering plenty of peace and quiet at the end of a busy day. The flavor of the region is evident in the Main Dining Room where one can savor a breakfast of French Toast with prickly pear cactus jelly or a dinner of mesquite charred duck à l'orange.

Horseback opportunities abound at Tanque Verde, where rides lead out into the desert, through spectacular canyons, along historic cattle trails or high up into the mountains. Riding lessons are included as well. This historic ranch features five tennis courts, indoor and outdoor pools and hot tubs, saunas, fitness center, a lake for fishing and other activities such as guided hiking, mountain biking and nature walks that allow you to enjoy that famous Arizona sun! For an additional fee, championship golf is available nearby and soothing massages, body treatments, manicures and pedicures may be enjoyed in the luxurious La Sonora Spa!

Address: 14301 E. Speedway, Tucson 85748.
Phone: 520-296-6275 800-234-3833
Fax: 520-721-9426
Email: dude@tvgr.com
Web site: http://www.tvgr.com
Room Rates: 290–495
Suite Rates: 385–565
No. of Rooms: 74
No. of Suites: 23
Credit Cards: Most Credit Cards accepted
Attractions: Saguaro National Park, Coronado National Forest, Arizona Sonora Desert Museum, Pima Air & Space Museum, Kitt Peak National Observatory, San Xavier del bac Mission, Bisbee Copper Mine, Kartchner Caverns, Colossal Cave, historic Tombstone, Nogales (Mexico).
Services & Amenities: Three delicious meals a day and all of the scheduled ranch activities are included in the nightly rates! Library, Laundry services (fee), Baby sitting (fee), Care hire (fee), Gift shop open daily. Fully supervised children's program for kids ages 4-11.
Restrictions: No pets allowed; 5 rooms handicapped accessible
Restaurant: Main dining room– Breakfast, Lunch and Dinner
Bar: Doghouse Saloon - open daily 5-11pm
Business Facilities: Color copier, full scale conference facilities
Conference Rooms: 3 rooms, capacity of the largest is 150
Sports Facilities: Indoor & outdoor pools, 5 tennis courts, horseback riding, hiking, biking , nature walks, golf (fee)
Spa Services: The La Sonora Spa offers soothing massages and body treatments, spa foot treatments, pedicures and manicures.
Location: 18 miles east of Tucson in desert foothills

BEVERLY HILLS HOTEL

The Beverly Hills Hotel presides majestically above Sunset Boulevard in its second decade of impeccable service and unparalleled beauty welcoming luminaries, royalty, legends and leaders from around the world.

Privacy, tranquility and a true residential ambiance are the hallmarks of this hotel situated on 12 lush acres of tropical gardens with private walkways through groves of orange blossoms, coconut palms, oleanders, bougainvillea and citrus garden and exotic flowers.

Guests luxuriate themselves in any one of the hotel's 194 suites or rooms. Uniquely decorated, individual bungalows have private patios and evoke the feeling of a private residential environment.

A competition-size pool, Jacuzzi, individual cabanas, a patio with lounge chairs and festive umbrellas, the Cabana Club Cafe and lush garden surroundings make guests feel as though they are miles away from a city. The private cabanas are equipped with phone and fax for conducting business poolside the Beverly Hills Hotel way. The hotel also features tennis courts and a fully equipped exercise room with televisions strategically placed, affording guests entertainment while they work out. Jogging trails wind throughout the beautiful grounds.

Under the guidance of Executive Chef Greg Waldron, the hotel's restaurants offer myriad dining options. The Polo Grill has its own entrance and is open nightly for dinner. Diners may choose from delectable culinary delights including Duck Breast Marinated in Soya and Honey served with Fig and Celery Salad and Sea Bass Tournedos with Potato Crust and Sea Urchin Ragout. Other options include the world-famous Polo Lounge, the more casual Fountain Coffee Shop, the Cabana Club Cafe poolside, and the Tea Lounge located adjacent to the lobby.

Address: 9641 Sunset Blvd, Beverly Hills 90210
Phone: 310-276-2251
800-283-8885
Fax: 310-281-2905
Web site: http://www.thebeverlyhillshotel.com
Room Rates: 380–470
Suite Rates: 820–5,000
No. of Rooms 203
No. of Suites: 37
Attractions: Most famous hotel in Beverly Hills, Bungalows, Sunset Boulevard
Services & Amenities: 3 Multi-line telephones, Cable TV and VCR, CD/cassette stereo sound system, Private safe, Private bar, Walk-in closet, Choice of 4 complimentary newspapers, Suites have kitchens & dining rooms, fireplaces, Jacuzzi tubs and private balconies, Valet service
Restrictions: Children under 12 free in parent's rooms, 9 rooms handicap equipped
Concierge: 24 hours
Room Service: 24 hours
Restaurant: The Polo Lounge, 7 a.m.-1:30 a.m., Dress code for dinner
Bar: The Polo Lounge, 7 a.m.-1:30 a.m.
Business Facilities: In-room plain paper fax machines, Data port, In-room voice mail, Message center, Copiers, Modems
Conference Rooms: 3 rooms, capacity 1000
Sports Facilities: Outdoor swimming pool, Whirlpool, Massage, Aerobics videos, Weight training, Fully-equipped fitness
Location: 12 miles from LAX

POST RANCH INN

Described by *Travel & Leisure* as ". . .the most spectacular hotel on the Pacific coast," this innovative California resort was created by eco-sensualists who enjoy relaxing on the edge of the world. Designed by G.K. "Mickey" Muennig, Post Ranch Inn is an architectural tribute to environmentally friendly guestrooms nestled 1,100 feet above the Pacific Ocean. With a full-time massage crew, a private Jacuzzi lined with Indian Raja slate in each room, designer bathrobes and an in-house Tarot Card Reader, guests experience a private, casually elegant retreat atmosphere.

The 30 guestrooms are carefully concealed in the landscape, so that even out to sea the ridge line looks natural. Built of natural wood and stone, the rooms offer the requisite luxury and amenities—fireplaces, state-of-the-art music systems and large, customized spas. televisions are not provided so not to interrupt the peace of this retreat. Each room has been constructed to provide guests with dramatic and breathtaking views of forest, mountains or sea.

The intimate Sierra Mar restaurant is perched on the cliffside, offering spectacular views through its tinted floor-to-ceiling glass walls. Prix fixe four-course meals are served each night, with a vegetarian entree. The wine cellar of 10,000 bottles and over 4,000 different labels has won the *Wine Spectator* Grand Award. A continental breakfast buffet is included in the room rate.

The Post Ranch is designed primarily for adults who wish to relax, regenerate their energy and nurture relationships. Also, the cliffside terrain makes the Inn unsafe for children.

Voted #1 resort in California by *Fodor's Travel Guide*.

Address: PO Box 219, Hwy 1, Big Sur 93920.
Phone: 831-667-2200
800-527-2200
Fax: 831-667-2824
Email: res@postranchinn.com
Web site: http://www.postranchinn.com
Room Rates: 485–935
No. of Rooms 30
No. of Suites: 0
Credit Cards: Visa
Attractions: The Post Ranch is a wildlife reserve, close by are beaches, gift shops, galleries, Monterey Aquarium and Carmel 45 minutes drive, Henry Miller Library
Services & Amenities: Complimentary breakfast buffet & reception beverages, Valet service, Parking, Gift shop, Library, Comp. newspaper, exercise and nature activities, Robes, Private decks, Fireplaces, A/C, Jacuzzis, CD library
Restrictions: 2 night min. on wkeds, $100/night 3rd. per, 2 rms handicap equip, Min. Age 18, pets not allowed,
Concierge: Activities Director
Room Service: 7:15 a.m.-10 p.m.
Restaurant: Sierra Mar Restaurant – Complimentary Buffet Breakfast 8-10:30 a.m., Dinner 5:30-10 p.m. nightly; Snacks, picnic baskets and light lunch daily noon – 4 p.m.
Bar: Sierra Mar Bar noon until closing
Business Facilities: Message center, Fax, Audio-visual, Meeting supplies, Copies
Sports Facilities: Exercise equipment, Guided hikes, Yoga, Star gazing lectures
Spa Services: Spa program w/ massage and herbal facials
Location: 30 miles south of Monterey, nearest airport Monterey or San Jose International

INN AT DEPOT HILL

Originally constructed in 1901, this stately turn-of-the-century railroad depot has been lovingly transformed into a sophisticated seaside inn with all of the amenities of a top-flight European hostelry. Located near a sandy beach along the Monterey Bay, the Inn overlooks the jewel-box village of Capitola-by-the-Sea, a charming cluster of shops, restaurants and galleries.

Each guestroom at the Inn has been painstakingly decorated to evoke a singular time, place, and state of mind. Guests may choose from a variety of distinctive suites and rooms which have been lovingly decorated to create the ultimate getaway retreat. The Railroad Baron Suite, for example, boasts a large indoor soaking tub, domed ceiling, red/gold fabrics, and luxurious amenities. The Portofino Room, modeled after an Italian Coastal Villa, is lavishly appointed with a large canopy bed, private patio, and outdoor whirlpool tub. Rooms feature fireplaces, private entrances and patio gardens, private outdoor hot tubs, video and audio equipment, white marble baths, two person shower, and such amenities as bathrobes, hair dryers, feather beds and fresh roses.

Guests can also enjoy the Inn at Depot Hill's garden, parlor and dining room. The garden, landscaped in the classical mode, is full of roses, azaleas, ferns and colorful trumpet vines surrounding a reflecting pond. A herringbone brick patio and pergola are the perfect setting for a morning cup of coffee or afternoon tea. The dining room features a clever trompe l'oeil, a scene that creates the illusion of the dining car of a train. Sumptuous breakfast dishes such as Cinnamon Apple Strudel, Raspberry Cream Crepes and Peach Stuffed French Toast are complemented by the ambiance of the room.

Known for their first-class service and accommodations, the Inn at Depot Hill is a secret getaway retreat that shouldn't be missed.

Address: 250 Monterey Ave, Capitola-by-the-Sea 95010.
Phone: 831-462-3376 800-572-2632
Fax: 831-624-2967
Email: DepotHill@InnsbytheSea.com
Web site: http://www.innatdepothill.com
Room Rates: 200–385
Suite Rates: 350–385
No. of Rooms: 12
No. of Suites: 6
Attractions: Walking distance to beach, numerous restaurants, shops, and art galleries; Situated between Golf Courses; 15-20 minutes south of Santa Cruz Beach Boardwalk and Steam Railroad
Services & Amenities: On-site parking, Library, Fireplaces, Balconies, Cable TV/VCR, Telephones, Audio cassette player, Radio, Complimentary toiletries, newspaper and in-room refreshments
Restrictions: 1 room with handicapped access, No pets allowed
Concierge: 8 a.m.-10 p.m.
Restaurant: Complimentary breakfast served in rooms, dining area, or patio
Bar: Complimentary tea, wine, hors d'oeuvres, and dessert
Business Facilities: Fax, Modems
Conference Rooms: 1 room, capacity 10
Sports Facilities: Whirlpool, Sailing nearby
Location: Monterey Bay Coast

LA PLAYA HOTEL

Local residents have known this Mediterranean-style villa as the "grand lady of Carmel-by-the-Sea" ever since artist Chris Jorgensen built it for his bride in 1904. Now it's grander than ever. A resort since the 1920s, La Playa was acquired in 1983 by the Cope family (owners of San Francisco's incomparable Huntington), who have done extensive restoration and renovation to make it Carmel's only full-service resort.

The subtly exquisite decor accents pale pastel walls and upholstery with custom hand-loomed area rugs, paintings by contemporary artists, and the Cope family's extensive collection of California antiques and heirlooms. Rooms afford views of the garden, the ocean, or residential Carmel. Handcrafted furnishings incorporate La Playa's mermaid motif in hues of soft rose and blue. The baths have marble floors and inlaid decorative tile. La Playa's five guest cottages offer the luxuries of a private vacation home. Complete with kitchens, wet bars, fireplaces, terraces, and patios, La Playa's cottages are ideal for a private getaway or family outing.

The Terrace Grill's gorgeous terrace is a perfect spot to watch the sunset. The wood-paneled interior of the restaurant provides a cozy dining atmosphere. An extensive California wine list and a fine collection of old Ports and Sherries set the stage for tempting cuisine. If you can pull yourself away from La Playa's lush formal gardens and heated swimming pool, there are myriad recreational options in the area, including Pebble Beach, Spyglass, and Carmel Valley Country Club golf courses. The boutique shops and galleries of Carmel Village are just four blocks from the hotel.

For the meeting-minded, a conference coordinator is on the premises and complete business facilities are available.

Address: Camino Real & Eighth, PO Box 900, Carmel 93921
Phone: 831-624-6476
800-582-8900
Fax: 831-624-7966
Email: info@laplayahotel.com
Web site: http://www.laplayahotel.com
Room Rates: 165–325
Suite Rates: 325–550
No. of Rooms 73
No. of Suites: 7
Attractions: 2 blocks to beach, Shopping, 17 Mile Drive, Pt. Lobos, Carmel Mission, Monterey Bay Aquarium, 11 nearby golf courses.
Services & Amenities: Valet service, Off-street parking, Babysitting service (available on request), Color TV, Radio, Hair dryer, Iron & ironing board, Shampoo, Conditioner, Hand lotion, Bath gel.
Restrictions: No pets allowed, Handicapped access to 3 rooms
Concierge: 9 a.m.–5 p.m.
Room Service: 7 a.m.–11 p.m.
Restaurant: Terrace Grill Restaurant, 7 a.m.– 10:30 a.m., 11:30 a.m.-2 p.m., 5 p.m. – 10 p.m.
Bar: Terrace Grill Lounge, 10 a.m.-midnight
Business Facilities: New Business Center w/multiple phone/modem lines and basic business equipment, Audio-Visual equipment
Conference Rooms: 5 rooms, capacity 10-150
Sports Facilities: Heated outdoor swimming pool.
Location: Residential Carmel

QUAIL LODGE RESORT & GOLF CLUB

Situated on the Central California Coast just minutes from Carmel-by-the-Sea, Quail Lodge is located beyond the fog on the sunny side of Carmel. Guests enjoy the best of both worlds: cool ocean breezes and lots of sunshine.

The Resort is nestled on 850 acres of lush fairways, oak-studded meadows, 10 sparkling lakes and green hills where wildlife abounds. The resort conveys an inviting ambiance, a peaceful retreat for discerning travelers.

In addition to its natural beauty, guests enjoy such pleasures as a championship 18-hole golf course, 3 tennis courts, a fitness room, spa and Wellness Center, 2 swimming pools and miles of hiking and jogging trails. A special enticement is The Covey Restaurant, which features California Contemporary cuisine inspired by the abundance of fresh ingredients from valleys and bays, and one of the finest collections of Central California wines on the Monterey Peninsula and around the world

Quail Lodge's 97 guestrooms and suites offer a multitude of comfortable amenities. Each room features a complimentary refreshment center, private deck or patio overlooking one of the Resort's ten lakes, the golf course or lush gardens. Window seat, spacious bathrooms with marble baths and shower stalls, feather beds, plasma TV's and high speed Internet access.

Shopping is a highlight in Carmel's chic boutiques. Guests may also like to visit Steinbeck's Cannery Row, the Monterey Bay Aquarium or famous 17-Mile Drive.

Address: 8205 Valley Greens Dr, Carmel 93923.
Phone: 831-624-2888 888-828-8787
Fax: 831-624-3726
Email: info@quaillodge.com
Web site: www.quaillodge.com
Room Rates: 225–435
Suite Rates: 325–825
No. of Rooms: 97
No. of Suites: 14
Credit Cards: Most Credit Cards accepted
Attractions: Wildlife Refuge, 17 Mile Drive in Pebble Beach, Big Sur, Monterey Jazz Festival, Monterey Bay Aquarium, Winery tours, hiking
Services & Amenities: Parking, Airport transfers available, Laundry service, Baby-sitting service, gift shop, Library, AM/FM radio, plasma televisions, In-room movies, Hair dryer, Bathrobes, Refrigerator complimentary refreshment center, dialy newspaper, turn down service
Restrictions: No pets
Concierge: 7am-11pm
Room Service: 7 a.m.-10 p.m.
Restaurant: The Covey, is open for breakfast 7 days a week from 7am-11am, and opens for dinner at 6pm until 10pm, Edgar's, the luxury sports bar, is open daily from 11am-10pm.
Bar: The Covey Lounge & Deck-11am-10pm; Edgar's, a luxury sports bar, open 11 am-10pm
Business Facilities: Message center, Admin. assistance, Translators, Copiers, Audio-Visual, Computer
Conference Rooms: 6 rooms, capacity 15-220
Sports Facilities: Outdoor swimming pool, Fitness Center, Tennis, Croquet and Bocce, Golf, Hiking, Full health spa
Spa Services: 2000 square foot European spa with four indoor treatment rooms, and three outdoor treatment suites.

BERNARDUS LODGE

Nestled on verdant acres with stately pines and California oak trees, surrounded by a vineyard and the Santa Lucia mountains rising majestically in the background, Bernardus Lodge is a premier luxury resort that combines the simple elegance of fine country living, with the high quality of service and luxury amenities found in only the choicest European hotels. Here, discriminating travelers experience the finest accommodations, cuisine, viti-culture, spa services and recreational venues in a singular environment.

Acclaimed chef, Cal Stamenov, has created cuisine that is distinctively California Natural and the menu is designed to take you on an exciting gastronomical journey that will tempt your palate and keep you wanting more. *Wine Spectator* magazine has awarded Marinus since 2001 The Grand Award for the generous, balanced wine list that was created to enhance the innovative California Natural Cuisine.

Carmel Valley enjoys moderately warm temperatures year round with an average high of 73 degrees in the summer. September and October offer the best weather of the year with an average high of 81 degrees.

Address: 415 Carmel Valley Rd., Carmel Valley 93924.
Phone: 831-658-3400 888-648-9463
Fax: 831-659-3529
Web site: www.bernardus.com/bl
Room Rates: 275–685
Suite Rates: 525–1870
No. of Rooms: 57
Credit Cards: Most Credit Cards accepted
Attractions: Major attractions close to the resort include wine tasting and antique shopping in Carmel Valley Village, The Monterey Bay Aquarium, Cannery Row, Carmel-by-the-Sea, 17-Mile Drive, Carmel Mission Basilica, Point Lobos State Reserve, and Golf.
Services & Amenities: All rooms include a stone fireplace, French doors, private deck, double bathtub, Feather bed, complimentary wine pantry, remote cable TV, CD players, coffee makers, fresh flowers, plush robes, hair dryers and WI-FI
Restrictions: No Pets
Concierge: 7am–11pm
Room Service: 7am –10pm
Restaurant: Marinus serves Dinner nightly, 6pm to 10pm. Wickets serves Breakfast daily, 7am to 10:30am, Lunch from 11am to 2:30pm, and Dinner from 2:30pm to 10pm.
Bar: Wickets Bistro serves cocktails 11am -Midnight
Business Facilities: High Speed Internet Guest Rooms
Conference Rooms: 4 meeting rooms–4,000 sq ft of flexible meeting and banquet
Sports Facilities: Workout Facility, Croquet, Bocce Ball, Swimming Pool, Two Tennis Courts
Spa Services: The Spa is a haven designed for pure indulgence and luxury pampering. The spa offers 8 treatment rooms and uses indigenous herbs, flowers and oils for a peaceful and pampering enviroment.
Location: On 22 acres in Carmel Valley. 15 minutes from Carmel-by-the-Sea.

GOLDEN DOOR

Crossing a long, camellia-shaded wooden footbridge at the Golden Door, guests enter a serene, luxurious destination spa closely patterned after Japan's historic Honjin travelers' inns. Inside, one of the finest Japanese-style gardens in the world weaves through the Golden Door's many sheltered courtyards, creating a sense of peace and beauty unmatched in the spa world.

Known for its complete attention to the needs of mind, body, and spirit, the small yet hugely famous "Door" cultivates an atmosphere of serenity and congeniality coupled with the most personalized instruction and service found in the spa world.

Only 39 guests a week partake of fitness classes, hikes, beauty treatments, distinguished guest lecturers and class leaders, and world-class cuisine created by Golden Door's master chefs. Most of each meal's ingredients come direct from a 3-acre organic garden on the grounds. A full-time nutritionist gives advice and recommendations.

Primarily a women-only spa ("Founded by a woman for women"), the Golden Door makes an exception for men during five annual men-only weeks, as well as four annual coed weeks.

All guests enjoy private single rooms, even during couples' weeks. Each generously sized accommodation becomes a peaceful, deeply comfortable retreat, complete with garden view and deck, flitting hummingbirds, and sumptuous furnishings. Guests receive a freshly laundered set of spa exercise wear daily, plus a beautiful flowered Japanese yukata (robe) suitable for wearing to meals and around the grounds.

The outside world seems far away from the 377-acre site with its many mountain trails. Each day's combination of vigorous activity and unabashed relaxation and pleasure melts stress and renews stamina: sunrise walks, labyrinth meditation, whirlpool spas, pool exercise, body contouring, steam baths, herbal wraps, massages, facials, hair treatments, tennis, meditation, and much more. Guests choose from more than 80 different fitness classes and activities in a given week, and are encouraged to do as much or as little as they like during their stay.

By the end of the week, staff members and new friends feel like family, and the body fairly hums with a youthful new energy.

Address: 777 Deer Springs Road, Escondido 92069.
Phone: 760-744-5777 800-424-0777
Fax: 760-471-2393
Email: reservations@goldendoor.com
Web site: http://www.goldendoor.com
Room Rates: 6,750 week
No. of Rooms: 39
Credit Cards: Most Credit Cards accepted
Attractions: Always temperate in climate with mountain breezes
Services & Amenities: Valet service, Boutique, Library, Laundry service, newspaper, CD player w/ radio, Hair dryer, Makeup lights, Complimentary skin care products, complete set of spa clothing daily. Complimentary transportation to and from the San Diego airport.
Restrictions: No pets allowed, Not appropriate for children under 17
Concierge: Yes
Room Service: 6 a.m.-11 p.m.
Sports Facilities: Tennis courts, 3 pools, 377 acres, 4 gyms (including weight training), yoga pavillion
Spa Services: Full-scale luxury spa—fitness classes, hikes, beauty treatments, distinguished guest lecturers and class leaders. Primarily a women-only spa but 5 annual men-only weeks, and 4 annual coed weeks.
Location: Rural area; Guests are requested to remain on premises during their stay.

CARTER HOUSE VICTORIANS

Built in 1986, the Hotel Carter is modeled after Eureka's Old Town Cairo Hotel. The Carter House is a renovated 1880s Victorian residence. The lobby of the brand-new Victorian Hotel Carter features unshaded windows, ceramic urns, oriental rugs, and antique pine furniture imported from England. Each afternoon, guests enjoy complimentary wine and appetizers before a crackling fire in the lobby's marble fireplace.

Rooms are decorated in a salmon and ivory color scheme with bleached pine antiques. Original contemporary artwork and fresh flowers add a tasteful touch. The queen-size beds with comforters and overstuffed lounge chairs are reminiscent of a Victorian bed and breakfast, but these accommodations have all the modern conveniences: desks, telephones, clock-radios, and cable TV in the armoires. Spacious modern bathrooms are done in black and white tile. Many have whirlpool baths.

At the Hotel Carter's Restaurant 301, tables are formal, with white linens, fresh flowers, and crystal candlestick holders. Live music enhances the romantic ambiance and a large selection of fine regional wines is available. A typical five-course dinner might begin with cabbage leaf stuffed with smoked salmon and cream cheese, followed by homemade soup and a refreshing sorbet. The entree might be rock Cornish game hen with sage sauce, or seasonal fresh fish. All are served with fresh vegetables and sprigs of herbs and edible flowers, many grown in the hotel's own gardens. For the finale, try one of the Hotel Carter's award-winning desserts.

The Hotel Carter is located at the gateway to Eureka's Old Town, with its charming brick-and flower-lined streets, art galleries, antique shops, and boutiques. It is also only two blocks from Humboldt Bay and the Marina. Before sitting out in the morning to explore, be sure to savor the homemade muffins and tarts offered with the complimentary continental breakfast.

Address: 301 "L" St, Eureka 95501.
Phone: 707-444-8062 800-404-1390
Fax: 707-444-8067
Email: reserve@carterhouse.com
Web site: http://www.carterhouse.com/
Room Rates: 250–495
No. of Rooms: 30
Attractions: Fort Humboldt, Sequoia Park and Zoo, Old Town Eureka, Humboldt Bay harbor cruises, Lost Coast, Humboldt Redwoods State Park
Services & Amenities: Valet, Laundry, Baby-sitting service w/prior arrangements, Wine & Gift shop, Breakfast included, Cable TV, Radio, Whirlpool baths, Complimentary toiletries, Complimentary wine & hors d'oeuvres in evening, cookies & tea for turndown
Restrictions: No pets allowed, 22 rooms handicap equipped
Concierge: 7 a.m.-6 p.m.
Restaurant: Restaurant 301 6–9 p.m. (until 9:30 p.m. on Fridays and Saturdays)
Bar: Full cocktail service
Business Facilities: Message center, Copiers, Small conferences
Conference Rooms: 2 rooms, capacity 35
Sports Facilities: Privileges to Adorni Center (fee)
Location: Northern border of Old Town, Quiet residential-commercial-artist's quarters

MADRONA MANOR WINE COUNTRY INN & RESTAURANT

Planning a drive through the Sonoma County wine country? Madrona Manor in Healdsburg is a must.

Built in the 1880s by a wealthy San Franciscan, and fully restored a century later, Madrona Manor achieved National Historic Registry status in 1987. A visit here is a step back in time.

The original Victorian Mansion offers eight romantic guestrooms, all with fireplaces. The remainder of this 8 acre romantic hideaway features five suites with fireplaces and separate sitting rooms and eight elegant rooms are located in the Carriage House. The two luxurious new School House Suites each have a Jacuzzi tub for two.

Accommodations are uniquely furnished with Victorian antiques. All have private baths. No televisions interrupt the secluded peace of this retreat. The pleasures are those of earlier times: fresh flowers from the garden, freshly baked cookies in every room, and a vast kitchen garden which supplies the restaurant with fresh herbs, fruits and vegetables throughout the year.

Ahh, how those Victorians did enjoy meals! Breakfast at the Manor is a bountiful style buffet. The restaurant under Chef Jesse Mallgren, formerly of Stars in San Francisco, Syzygy of Aspen, has the highest overall restaurant ratings in the Zagat Survey for 2003 and 2004 in Sonoma County. Dinner offers a choice of a la carte, seven, and nine course Chef's tasting menus. *Wine Spectator* magazine calls the Madrona Manor both the Grande Dame of Sonoma restaurants and of Victorian Inns.

Because the Manor is not open for lunch, its four charming Victorian dining rooms and outside Palm Terrace can cater business meetings all days, as well as business dinners at night. The Manor offers some audio-visual equipment at no cost, and can arrange for other equipment as needed for groups who must step beyond the 19th century.

Address: 1001 Westside Rd, Healdsburg 95448.
Phone: 707-433-4231 800-258-4003
Fax: 707-433-0703
Email: info@madronamanor.com
Web site: http://www.madronamanor.com
Room Rates: 175–420
Suite Rates: 265–480
No. of Rooms: 22
No. of Suites: 5
Credit Cards: Visa
Attractions: Sunday afternoon concerts in the Plaza, Wine festivals, 30 minutes to Calfornia Redwoods, 70 wineries within 30 minutes, Live Jazz on the Veranda in Summertime
Services & Amenities: Fireplaces, Complimentary buffet breakfast and toiletries, In-room massage, Individual climate controls
Restrictions: No pets, Children over 12 are welcome. No smoking indoors
Concierge: 8 a.m.-8 p.m.
Restaurant: Seating 6–9 p.m. Monday–Sunday, April through December. Wed to Sun in Jan, Feb, Mar. Lavish Victorian Christmas decorations and live caroling during Dickens Dinners throughout December.
Bar: Fully licensed bar
Business Facilities: Copier, Fax, Administrative Assistance, Audio-visual by prearrangement
Conference Rooms: Four conference rooms, outdoor terrace. Private dining rooms
Sports Facilities: Outdoor heated swimming pool on site. Tennis, golf, fishing, hiking and cycling nearby
Location: In the heart of the Sonoma wine country, 1 mile west of downtown Healdsburg

LA VALENCIA HOTEL

An ornate 1926 Spanish Mediterranean-style building enhanced by a year-round kaleidoscope of fresh flowers and greenery inside and out, La Valencia is just a seashell's throw from the Pacific. Stroll the oceanfront lawn, relax on the beach or the sundeck, swim in the surf or in the hotel's heated swimming pool. At the foot of the hotel grounds is the famous Cove in Scripps Park.

The lobby area features European furnishings, antique oriental screens and carpets, painted ceilings, art works, and a grand piano. Guestrooms are individually decorated with pastel hues in traditional California style. A favorite suite, in a frosted bronze, coconut milk, and chantilly green color scheme, affords a sweeping postcard-pretty view of the ocean and the hotel's flower garden from a private balcony as well as from the spacious living room.

The Sky Room restaurant serves outstanding haute cuisine. The restaurant, intimate and elegant, is located on the 10th floor and has 12 tables, each with a spectacular ocean view. Mauve colors, Wedgewood china, crystal, silver, fresh flowers and roses on the tables create a special atmosphere that is known as the "Most Romantic Restaurant in San Diego."

The Whaling Bar & Grill, with its publike ambiance reminiscent of an English pub, is the place to see and be seen in La Jolla. The Whaling Bar is cozy and serves American Grilled Cuisine. The Mediterranean Room Restaurant offers views of the Pacific Ocean, or dine outside on the beautiful Tropical Patio adorned with Palms and flowers.

The Ocean View Terrace, offering breakfast and lunch in the open air with the best ocean view dining in La Jolla.

Address: 1132 Prospect St, La Jolla 92037.
Phone: 858-454-0771 800-451-0772
Fax: 858-456-3921
Email: info@lavalencia.com
Web site: http://www.lavalencia.com
Room Rates: 305–725
Suite Rates: 600–3500
No. of Rooms: 115
Credit Cards: Most Credit Cards accepted
Attractions: Beach, La Jolla Cove, Ellen Browning Scrippts Park, Hot air ballons, Bay cruise, Temecula, San Diego, Palomar Mountain, Fashion shows, Sailing
Services & Amenities: Ocean/garden views, Daily housekeeping and turndown service, Morning paper, La Valencia bath amenities, Color TV/VCR, Minibar, In-room coffee maker, Plush terry bathrobes, Compl. shoe shine, Whirlpool tubs, balconies/terraces, bidets
Concierge: Available
Room Service: 24 hour
Restaurant: The Sky Room, The Mediterranean Room, The Whaling Bar & Grill and Cafe La Rue
Bar: The Whaling Bar, La Sala
Business Facilities: Flexible meeting spaces, Conference Coordinator, Wetbar, Private bathrooms, Automatic screen
Conference Rooms: 3 rooms, capacity up to 200
Sports Facilities: Bike rentals and tours, Walking, Jogging
Spa Services: Spa facilities
Location: Sits in the heart of downtown La Jolla

THE BED & BREAKFAST INN AT LA JOLLA

This romantic historic Inn can boast of being the one and only official Bed & Breakfast Inn in La Jolla Village by the sea, as well as being the loveliest in San Diego. Designed by the "Cubist" architect Irving Gill in 1913 and home to the John Philip Sousa family in the 1920's, the Inn exudes European charm with wood burning fireplaces in some of the select rooms. A full gourmet breakfast by candlelight is served daily in the dining room. Bask in the sun on the bouganvilla draped, second floor patio, or relax with a cup of tea and a good book in the light and airy library. Order a picnic basket for two and enjoy a romantic evening watching the sun set from the La Jolla cliffs or take a leisurely stroll along the beach and explore the wonders of the tide pools.

Stroll into the Village for a relaxing dinner at one of the many fine restaurants, then browse among the galleries, antique stores and designer shops. The Museum of Contemporary Art is just steps from the Inn.

A block from the beach, in the heart of La Jolla's marvelous shops, restaurants and art galleries, the Inn is only minutes from San Diego's many other attractions such as Del Mar Race Track, Mexico, Sea Port Village, Old Town, Sea World, the Zoo, Wild Animal Park, Gas Lamp District, numerous theaters and the enchanting Balboa Park.

The garden, a lovely oasis with hummingbird feeders, loquat trees, dappled sunlight and a lyrical fountain, is especially cozy in the early morning with the rich aromas of Colombian coffee and French pastries filling the air. So take a break from the ordinary and experience a more relaxing and gracious style of travel. There are fresh flowers throughout the Inn and in all of the guestrooms to embrace the senses; fresh fruit and fine sherry to soothe a weary body; and the beauty of the nearby sea to heal the soul. Some rooms with ocean view.

Voted "San Diego's Best", and showcased in *Los Angeles Times*, *Travel and Leisure*, *New York Times*, *Glamour* magazine, *Cooking Light* and *Country Inns*. The Inn abounds in priceless antiques. Hardwood floors with one of a kind Oriental and European area rugs and original works of art and antique prints add to the luxurious décor and European ambiance.

Enjoy being their guest.

Address: 7753 Draper Ave, La Jolla 92037.
Phone: 858-456-2066 800-582-2466
Fax: 858-456-1510
Email: bedbreakfast@innlajolla.com
Web site: http://www.innlajolla.com
Room Rates: 179–299
Suite Rates: 359–399
No. of Rooms: 13
No. of Suites: 2
Credit Cards: Most Credit Cards accepted
Attractions: Enjoy the Stephen Birch Aquarium, Sea World, San Diego Zoo, Sea Port Village, Balboa Park, Lego Land, Wild Animal Park, Old Town, Gas Lamp District Downtown, Mexico, Wineries in North County, the Del Mar Racktrack, Whale Watching and much more.
Services & Amenities: Limited free parking; Car hire, Beauty shop, House doctor (can be arranged). Some fireplaces, balconies, and Cable TV. in select rooms. Wireless Internet. Phones/dataports, Gourmet breakfast. Robes, Hair dryers, Complimentary toiletries.
Restrictions: No pets allowed but accommodations can be arranged. Not recommended for children under 12
Concierge: On staff
Restaurant: Wine & appetizer buffet reception with hors d'oeuvres 5–6 p.m., Sweet treats available throughout day in dining room - homemade chocolate biscotti & chocolate chip cookies / tea and coffee .
Business Facilities: Fax and copier
Conference Rooms: Space for small corporate and executive meetings
Sports Facilities: Public tennis courts, Fitness centers, and golf nearby. Snorkeling, Scuba diving, Windsurfing.

SURF & SAND RESORT

Where the waves of the Pacific meet 500 feet of pristine white sand on California's Laguna Beach shoreline, lies the Surf & Sand Resort. Here, a magnificent oceanfront location combines with luxurious accommodations, dedicated personal service, distinctive dining, and a soothing spa to create a relaxing, romantic getaway.

Every guestroom at the Surf & Sand includes a private balcony with a breathtaking view of the waves crashing on the beach below. Guestrooms themselves are elegant retreats with plantation shutters covering expansive windows, custom furnishings, spacious baths and all the amenities you need to really get away.

Adding to the relaxing ambiance is the Aquaterra Spa, offering an array of treatments enhanced by the healing, therapeutic properties of ocean and earth. These natural essences are combined with aromatic botanicals in a range of massages, skincare and body treatments to provide each guest with a spa experience artistically designed just for them by experienced practitioners.

Throughout the resort, guests are never far from the soothing waves and stunning views of the Pacific, as even the airy Splashes dining room features windows opening to the sea. Guests may also choose to dine al fresco on palm shaded patios, or to enjoy the romance of dinner served on their room's balcony, accompanied only by a spectacular sunset.

Surf & Sand's location, just minutes from Orange County's John Wayne Airport and within an hour's drive of both Los Angeles and San Diego, affords a wealth of recreational activities. At the resort itself, guests may pass the day lounging by the oceanfront pool and on the beach itself, or take advantage of the fitness and yoga studios for an invigorating workout. Beyond the resort, options range from strolling through the galleries and boutiques of Laguna Beach to shopping at South Coast Plaza to championship golf and more.

With a beautiful location and the excellent amenities and service that have made it one of just 128 hotels in the world to be granted membership in Preferred Hotels & Resorts, Surf & Sand Resort is an ideal escape.

Address: 1555 South Coast Highway, Laguna Beach 92651.
Phone: 949-497-4477 800-524-8621
Fax: 949-494-2897
Email: surfreservations@jcresorts.com
Web site: http://www.surfandsandresort.com
Room Rates: 290–460
No. of Rooms: 165
No. of Suites: 13
Attractions: Renowned Laguna Beach art galleries within strolling distance of the resort, annual summer Arts Festival, legendary Pageant of the Masters, unique shopping from fine antiques to handmade pottery.
Services & Amenities: All rooms oceanfront w/private balconies & plantation shutters, in-room safe, stocked mini-refrigerator, TV w/full cable service, stereo w/CD player, complimentary newspaper, valet service.
Restrictions: No pets allowed, Children welcome, 7 rooms handicap equipped
Concierge: 7am-8pm, Fri-Sat til 9
Room Service: 7am-8pm, Fri & Sat. til 9pm
Restaurant: Splashes Restaurant serves contemporary cuisine in an ocean-view dining room and terraced patios over the sand. 7 a.m.–11 p.m. Monday–Saturday, 7 a.m.–9:30 p.m. Sunday.
Bar: Splashes Lounge 11:30am-midnight, til 1 a.m. Fri–Sat
Business Facilities: Small business center with Internet access on property, full-service imaging lab services available
Conference Rooms: 10,000 sq ft; 10 rooms all with windows; groups from 10–250
Sports Facilities: Aquaterra Spa; expanded fitness facility and yoga studio, ocean beach and other recreational activities
Spa Services: Aquaterra Spa offers a full range of massages, skin care and body treatments.

WINE & ROSES HOTEL & RESTAURANT

Nestled in the heart of Lodi Wine Country, Wine & Roses provides a comfortable and relaxing environment set among seven acres of towering deodar trees and serene botanical gardens.

Relax . . . and indulge in the simplistic elegance of our Vintner Suites and Garden Rooms, each offering breathtaking views of lush gardens from spacious verandas. These luxurious and spacious rooms have the look and charm of the Old World with all the essentials of the modern world. You can also experience the heritage presented in the Historic Inn. A beautiful, charming and romantic estate that began its existence in 1902. It includes seven beautifully appointed guestrooms including a honeymoon suite.

Savor . . . the essence of fresh, local ingredients flavored to the season in an ambiance of comfort and elegance. Drink and be merry as you are serenaded in the piano bar near a warm fire or on the outdoor patio on a summer afternoon. We feature "Regional California" cuisine prepared by professionally trained chefs using an abundance of fresh herbs and local produce from the San Joaquin Valley and only the finest ingredients. We take pride in serving from an extensive list, including wines from the Lodi Appellation.

Heal . . . your mind, body, and spirit by experiencing a therapeutic or pampering massage and facial, each designed to revive the senses and rejuvenate the soul. For the ultimate relaxation of body and mind, all of our massages integrate the power of fragrant pure essential oils. Our aromatherapy oils are distilled from plants, herbs and flowers and blended with the highest quality grape seed oil.

Motivate, inspire and create . . . as you are surrounded by a calming and natural setting where all your desires are happily met with unique and professional facilities, dining and service. We offer event coordination, business services, audio-visual, exceptional cuisine (from our Banquet kitchen), local winery tours and tastings, and much more.

Address: 2505 W Turner Dr, Lodi 95242.
Phone: 209-334-6988 877-310-3358
Fax: 209-371-6049
Email: info@winerose.com
Web site: http://www.winerose.com
Room Rates: 169
Suite Rates: 275–325
No. of Rooms: 36
No. of Suites: 4
Credit Cards: Most Credit Cards accepted
Attractions: Located in the heart of Lodi Appellation–with over 40 local wineries, tours and special events throughout the year
Services & Amenities: Complimentary Gourmet Continental Breakfast, Laundry, Cable TV, Radio, Telephones, Complimentary newspaper, Suites have wet bar and CD player, Some rooms have fireplace and balconies/decks, Dataports, Voice Mail & Business Services
Restrictions: Pet room upon availability ($25 p/pet p/night), Children welcome, 2 rooms handicap equipped
Room Service: 7 a.m.–9 p.m.
Restaurant: Breakfast 7 a.m.–10 a.m., Lunch 11:30 a.m.–1:30 p.m., Dinner 5:30 p.m.–9 p.m., Champagne Sunday Buffet Brunch 10 a.m.–2 p.m.
Business Facilities: Complete conference and wedding facilities
Conference Rooms: 3 rooms, patio and pavilion, capacity 350
Spa Services: Spa services including therapeutic treatments, aromatherapy, pampering treatments and products. Grand Spa opening in October 2005!
Location: In the Lodi Wine Country

HOTEL BEL-AIR - LOS ANGELES

The *Zagat Guide* named Hotel Bel-Air "Top Hotel in California" in 2004, simultaneously declaring its restaurant "Most Popular Hotel Restaurant in Los Angeles." *The Tatler*, London's top society magazine, proclaimed it "Hotel of the Millennium." While the accolades pour in, as they have for over 50 years, Hotel Bel-Air continues to do what it does best: maintain an internationally renowned oasis of elegance and charm.

Discretion reigns so supreme that first-time visitors may have difficulty spotting the hotel's street signage. Once inside, to reach the hotel proper, guests cross a covered bridge that spans the signature Swan Lake, home of four pure white Polish mute swans.

The famous bridge serves as a gateway to a haven of natural beauty. Hotel Bel-Air boasts 12 acres of densely landscaped grounds reminiscent of a private arboretum. Over 200 botanical species thrive here, among them plants rarely seen in Southern California. The pink blossoms of the largest known silk floss tree in North America drape high above the koi pond in the Chalon Courtyard.

Hummingbirds nest in the redwoods and tree ferns. Colorful fruit trees, scarlet trumpet vines, and multihued azaleas and roses—plus over 10,000 tulip, iris, and daffodil bulbs—create a continuous symphony of color. From this enchanted glade rise the hotel's bell tower and pink mission-style buildings and bungalows—seemingly worlds away from the metropolis, yet actually just minutes from Beverly Hills, Westwood, and Century City.

Address: 701 Stone Canyon Rd, Los Angeles 90077
Phone: 310-472-1211
800-648-4097
Fax: 310-476-5890
Email: info@hotelbelair.com
Web site: http://www.hotelbelair.com
Room Rates: 385–550
Suite Rates: 725–3500
No. of Rooms 52
No. of Suites: 39
Attractions: Rodeo Drive in Beverly Hills, Getty Center, Beaches, Santa Monica Pier, Melrose Avenue, Hollywood walk of fame, Universal Studios – all a short drive from the Hotel.
Services & Amenities: 24-hour room service, Complimentary tea service delivered to your guestroom upon arrival, Complimentary daily one-way shared car service to select areas, Complimentary shoe shine, Complimentary daily newspaper.
Restrictions: Handicapped access to 2 rooms
Concierge: 24 hours
Room Service: 24 hours
Restaurant: Californian cuisine provides mouthwatering temptations at breakfast, lunch, dinner, and Sunday brunch in the dining room and on the outdoor Terrace. Afternoon Tea served daily (except Sunday)
Bar: 11 a.m.- 12:15 a.m. (weekday) 1:15 a.m. (weekend last call)
Business Facilities: Complimentary laptop use, high speed Internet
Conference Rooms: Pavillion Room, Garden Room, Executive Boardroom
Sports Facilities: Outdoor swimming pool, Golf & Tennis arranged
Spa Services: For optimum privacy, all spa services are arranged in the comfort of the guestroom or suite.

SUNSET MARQUIS HOTEL

Hard to believe this is West Hollywood, these secluded suites and villas are so private, and the Whiskey Bar so strict with its admissions, that one need never be reminded of the throngs of celeb-watchers and velvet-ropers that beset most of LA's other hot spots. This exclusive atmosphere, and possibly the state-of-the-art recording studio in the basement, are the keys to the Sunset Marquis's rock star appeal. Unlike some rock-and-roll hotels, this one's décor avoids retro kitsch and glam decadence, opting instead for an understated modern style, all clean lines and rich earth tones and the low-lying two-story villa construction takes some of the fun out of heaving television sets out windows.

So as much as the buzz about this place may center on its music industry connections, this is no Chelsea, no debaucherous rock dormitory. Today's rock stars are more traveling business-people than tortured artists, so it's sensible that their favorite hotel would be perfect for their colleagues in other less glamorous industries. Soundproof windows ensure that unless you're cutting an album, you won't hear noise from the studio or, for that matter, the pool, and everything today's harried business traveler requires is close at hand, from 24-hour room service and extensive health and fitness facilities to a business center and airline ticket desk.

Guests gain access to the Whiskey Bar, and to be frank, that's the only way most of us could ever make it past the doorman. The benefit, of course, is that it's one place in Hollywood that you won't have to rub elbows with sightseers from the Valley or Orange County.

Address: 1200 North Alta Loma Rd, Los Angeles 90069.
Phone: 213-657-1333 800-692-2140
Email: information@ sunsetmarquishotel.com
Web site: http:// www.sunsetmarquishotel.com/
Room Rates: 355–2100
Suite Rates: 355–2100
No. of Rooms: 8
No. of Suites: 104
Credit Cards: Most Credit Cards accepted
Attractions: Located on a quiet residential cul-de-sac off of Sunset Boulevard, and is very private indeed; once off the compound, however, all the sights (and shopping) of Hollywood are close at hand, including the bizarre and legendary nightlife of the Sunset Strip.
Services & Amenities: 24-hour in-suite room service, indoor and outdoor dining, two heated swimming pools and private cabanas, state of the art recording studio/screening room, multi-lingual concierge staff, hotel/airport transfers, valet and self-parking, high speed Internet
Restrictions: Must be 21 to register, Cancellation is required 24 hours in advance
Concierge: Multi-Lingual
Room Service: 24 hour in room service
Restaurant: What's a great stay without great food? The Sunset Marquis Hotel and Villas has a delectable selection of gourmet fare 24-hours a day. Our menu has everything to satisfy your cravings.
Bar: The Whiskey Bar
Business Facilities: Business Center is available
Sports Facilities: Dry Sauna, Whirlpool, Weightroom and Cardiovascular Equipment
Spa Services: We can order spa services direct to the privacy of your own suite or villa.

THE STANFORD INN BY THE SEA

Each of the Stanford's wood-paneled rooms has French doors leading to a deck from which to enjoy the sunset over the Pacific. Traditional furnishings grace rooms in tones of mauve, burgundy, and blue. A fireplace laid with real wood enhances the romantic ambiance.

Nothing is left to chance. You are welcomed with a bottle of wine, cold drinks in your room's refrigerator and the inn's own blend of organic coffee ready to brew. A compact stereo/CD system is tuned to classical, while a VCR and DVD players awaits a recent release from the inn's library.

And for the pet owner, pets are welcomed, with areas to walk them. A special seating area in the lobby is available to owners and their dogs during breakfast or dinner. The staff provides treats, food and water bowls, blankets to protect furniture, and even pet beds.

Breakfast is included, and is served in the inn's dining room cooked to order from organic ingredients. After a day's exploring, join other guests in the expansive lobby for Afternoons at the Inn offering a complimentary selection of cheeses and hors d'oeuvres. An outstanding selection of wines by the glass is also available.

Dinner at The Ravens features vegetarian and vegan cuisine and has received national acclaim in the *Vegetarian Times*. The menu is inspired by the Stanford's California Certified Organic Farm and includes pizza, calzones, raviolis and signature dishes such as Sea Palm Strudel, Tofu and Wild Mushroom Wellington, and Baked Cashew Encrusted Tofu.

If you have never tried yoga, you might sign up for classes for just yourself and your partner. The inn's Massage in the Forest offers bodywork in Esalen, Shiatsu, Thai and other techniques. You can canoe or kayak from the inn's Catch A Canoe & Bicycles, too! or take a mountain bike and explore coastal trails and backroads.

Address: PO Box 487, Hwy 1 & Comptche Ukiah Rd, Mendocino 95460.
Phone: 707-937-5615 800-331-8884
Fax: 707-937-0305
Email: info@stanfordinn.com
Web site: www.stanfordinn.com
Room Rates: 215–295
Suite Rates: 345–450
No. of Rooms: 31
No. of Suites: 10
Attractions: The Mendocino Art Center and other galleries, Big River, The beautiful Mendocino coast where the Wine Country meets the Pacific Ocean.
Services & Amenities: Parking lot, Game area, Laundry, Exercise room, VCR, DVD players, CD player, Radio, Fireplaces, Balconies, Refrigerators, Coffee makers & gourmet coffee, Complimentary toiletries and full breakfast, Wireless High Speed Internet access
Restrictions: Pets welcome
Concierge: 8:30 a.m.-11 p.m.
Restaurant: The Ravens, breakfast–7:30-11 a.m., dinner–5:30-9 p.m. Serving organic, vegetarian and vegan cuisine, the Ravens has received national acclaim from *Vegetarian Times*.
Bar: Wine and beer available with meals
Business Facilities: Message center, Computers, Admin. assistance, Copiers, Audio-visual, Teleconferencing
Conference Rooms: 3 rooms, capacity 50–100
Sports Facilities: Indoor pool, Whirlpool, Sauna, Mountain bikes, Canoe & kayak rentals avail., Massage, Work-out room
Spa Services: Body work, varieties of massage and yoga are offered guests at Massage in the Forest.
Location: South of Mendocino's historic district

HOTEL PACIFIC

The Monterey Peninsula's luxury hotel is a graceful adobe structure in the heart of the historic district, adjacent to California's First Theater and directly across from the Monterey Conference Center. The lobby of the Hotel Pacific features original artwork, distinctive artifacts, antiques, handcrafted tile floors and a warm fireplace.

The Hotel Pacific is Monterey's only all-suite hotel. Each guest suite is a 560-square foot executive suite, complete with gas log fireplace, custom furniture in rich earth tones, goose-down feather beds, remote-control color TV and VCR, CD players, fresh-ground coffee and brewer, and spiced cider. Custom cabinetry houses a refrigerator and honor bar. A tiled desk area separates the living area from the sleeping room. The spacious bathrooms feature separate showers and tubs, scales, TV, telephone and Aveda toiletries as well as handmilled soaps. Each room has a private patio or terrace, some with a view of the hotel's lavish garden courtyards with spas and hand-carved fountains.

Special services for guests include complimentary continental breakfast, afternoon tea, and nightly maid service and turndown with chocolates. The hotel's meeting rooms will accommodate an intimate board meeting or a conference for 40 participants.

Walk outside this tranquil hideaway and find yourself in the heart of downtown Monterey. You can visit Monterey Bay Aquarium, peruse Carmel galleries and shops, appreciate Carmel Mission Basilica, hang out on Fisherman's Wharf, and walk, run, bike or drive 17-Mile Drive. Nearby sporting facilities include 18 world-famous golf courses, a jogging and bike trail, riding, sailing, scuba diving, fishing, and whale watching.

Address: 300 Pacific St, Monterey 93940.
Phone: 831-373-5700 800-554-5542
Fax: 831-373-6921
Email: reservations@innsofmonterey.com
Web site: http://www.hotelpacific.com
Suite Rates: 179-429
No. of Suites: 105
Attractions: Monterey Conference Center, Monterey Bay Aquarium, Cannery Row Carmel galleries and shopping, Wine Tasting, Fisherman's Wharf, Golf courses, Whale watching, Kayaking, Laguna Seca Raceway.
Services & Amenities: Parking ($14 per day), Drycleaning and laundry, Nightly maid service, Cable TV, VCRs, Honor bar, CD players, Phone and TV in bath, Robes, Complimentary newspaper, Aveda toiletries, continental breakfast and afternoon tea social
Restrictions: No pets allowed, 3 rooms handicap equipped.
Room Service: 11 a.m.-10 p.m.
Business Facilities: Voice mail, Copiers, Fax, Audio-visual available by special arrangement
Conference Rooms: 3 rooms, capacity 40
Sports Facilities: Golf, Riding, Sailing, Jogging and bike trail, Scuba diving and fishing nearby, Whirlpool
Location: Historic downtown Monterey, Pacific Ocean, 6 miles to Monterey airport

SPINDRIFT INN

In 1927 the Ocean View Hotel, then the only hotel on Monterey Bay, opened as an ornate and opulent contender for the San Francisco carriage trade. In later years, as the area's fishing and canning industry flourished, the grand hotel deteriorated to a shadow of its former splendor. The once exclusive Ocean View Avenue was renamed "Cannery Row," the setting for John Steinbeck's novel of the same name. As the fishing industry declined in the 1970s and the last operating cannery was converted into an aquarium, Cannery Row underwent major restoration and redevelopment as an historic district.

In 1985 the original Ocean View Hotel reopened its doors after renovation as an intimate 42-room luxury hotel surpassing even its own past glory. The hotel was given a new name—the Spindrift Inn.

The hotel is located directly on the beach, in the heart of Cannery Row and only two blocks from the Monterey Bay Aquarium. The lobby is a four-story atrium focusing on a fireplace flanked by large candelabras. A 20- x 30-foot sculpture in 22-karat gold leaf is mounted above the lobby on the atrium wall.

Each romantic guestroom features a wood-burning fireplace, down comforters and pillows, draped or canopied feather beds, oriental carpets over hardwood floors, and built-in armoires. Half of the rooms feature spectacular ocean views. Baths are done in marble with brass fixtures and handcrafted tile floors. Afternoon tea, wine and cheese are served daily in the lobby. Silver tray continental breakfast is delivered each morning to your room. Room service is available.

The Spindrift Inn made history when it became the first hotel ever to win two first-place awards for excellence in the same year at the prestigious Gold Key Awards co-sponsored by the American Hotel and Motel Association and The Designer West Magazine. The Spindrift Inn won for Best Guestroom and Best Hotel Lobby/Reception Area.

Address: 652 Cannery Row, Monterey 93940.
Phone: 831-646-8900 800-841-1879
Fax: 831-646-5342
Email: reservations@innsofmonterey.com
Web site: http://www.spindriftinn.com
Room Rates: 239–449
No. of Rooms: 42
Credit Cards: Visa
Attractions: Monterey Bay Aquarium, Fisherman's Wharf, Cannery Row, Carmel, Carmel Mission Basilica, Galleries and shops, Big Sur, Whalewatching, National Steinbeck Center
Services & Amenities: Valet service and parking, Drycleaning and laundry, Turndown service, Complimentary continental breakfast w/newspaper, afternoon wine & cheese reception, Cable TV, VCRs, Radio, CD players, Honor bar, Fireplace, Phone in bath, Robes, Comp. toiletries
Restrictions: Children under 12 stay free, No pets, handicapped access to 2 rooms
Room Service: 11am–10pm
Business Facilities: Copiers, Fax
Sports Facilities: Riding, Sailing, Golf, Jogging and bike trail, Scuba diving, Fishing, Sauna, Horseback riding
Location: Historic Cannery Row, 1 mile from downtown and Conference Center

MONTEREY BAY INN

The Monterey Bay Inn is a luxurious retreat where newly remodeled guestrooms and lobby take their design cues from the natural beauty of the Monterey Bay Marine Sanctuary. A short stroll down Cannery Row finds you at the Monterey Bay Aquarium, in the midst of lively restaurants, eclectic shops and a variety of recreational activities. Guest will enjoy our sister restaurant, The Sardine Factory, Monterey's premier seafood restaurant and lounge. Guestrooms feature plush king feather beds with elegant 310 thread-count Pima cotton bed linens for an extra touch of luxury. Spacious bathrooms provide sophisticated comfort, with fine linens, marble floors, double lavatory granite vanities, Aveda bath products, make-up mirrors, and handheld hair dryers. Your private balcony provides the perfect setting to experience the invigorating ocean air and enjoy a complimentary continental breakfast for two which is served to your room.

Address: 242 Cannery Row, Monterey 93940.
Phone: 831-373-6242 800-424-6242
Fax: 831-373-7603
Email: reservations@innsofmonterey.com
Web site: http://www.montereybayinn.com/
Room Rates: 229–339
No. of Rooms: 47
Attractions: Monterey Bay Aquarium, Cannery Row, Monterey Conference Center, Carmel galleries and shopping, Carmel Mission Basilica, Fisherman's Wharf, Golf courses, Whale watching, Kayaking, SCUBA diving, Wine tasting, Laguna Seca Raceway
Services & Amenities: Plush feather beds and pillows, Aveda bath products, DVD players with a new 27" TVs, locally inspired DVD's, stereo CD players, cordless phones, laptop computer safes, wireless Internet, and evening turndown service, self parking $13 per day.
Restrictions: No pets allowed, 2 night min. stay on most weekends
Room Service: 11am–10pm
Restaurant: Our sister restaurant, the Sardine Factory, is Monterey's premier seafood restaurant and lounge featuring extraordinary cuisine and a world-renowned wine list along with warm and gracious service.
Business Facilities: Wireless Internet, voicemail, copy, fax
Conference Rooms: 2, up to 14 people maximum
Sports Facilities: Golf, Riding, Sailing, Jogging and bike trail, Scuba diving and fishing nearby, Whirlpool
Spa Services: To sooth the mind and body, indulge in a relaxing spa service in our soothing massage room or in the comfort of your own guestroom. The rooftop, bay-view hot tub is the perfect hideaway.
Location: Perched on the water at the quiet end of historic Cannery Row.

LA RESIDENCE

Embodying the distinctly French ambiance of the vineyards, architecture and climate of Napa Valley's acclaimed Carneros region, La Residence is set amid oaks and pines and surrounded by world-famous vineyards. Two new ponds with water jets surrounded by French Plain trees, lawns and gardens complete the French country style.

The 23 rooms and suites of the newly remodeled Mansion and recently built French Barn are lovingly decorated in French Country style with European antiques and designer prints in individual color themes. French doors, European bed linens, baths for two, private verandas or patios, and fireplaces are among the pleasures of La Residence. The residence buildings, outdoor pool and Jacuzzi spa are surrounded by two acres of gardens and heritage oaks. There are 3 additional suites in the new "Cellar House".

When they are not busy baking fresh bread for breakfast, innkeepers David Jackson, Craig Claussen, and their staff eagerly assist in planning activities such as wine tours, bicycle tours past wildflowers and wineries, and site-seeing excursions, all beginning at the inn's doorstep.

The innkeepers are also your hosts for evening wine and cheese sampling on the veranda-or by the fire in cool weather-and for breakfast at antique pine tables for two, with piano accompaniment. For dinner, the acclaimed Bistro Don Giovanni is a short stroll away, and other fine restaurants, antiques and art galleries are nearby.

Address: 4066 St. Howard Lane, Napa 94558.
Phone: 707-253-0337 800-253-9203
Fax: 707-253-0382
Email: reservations@laresidence.com
Web site: http://www.laresidence.com/
Room Rates: 225–265
Suite Rates: 275–375
No. of Rooms: 23
No. of Suites: 8
Credit Cards: Visa, MasterCard, American Express, Discover, Most Credit Cards accepted
Attractions: World-famous Napa Valley vineyards and restaurants, Wine tasting tours, Shopping, Antiques, Art galleries, Biking, and Driving the beautiful Napa Valley.
Services & Amenities: Radio, Babysitting service by arrangement, Telephones, CD player, Most rooms have fireplaces, Complimentary toiletries, Complimentary breakfast, afternoon wine and hors d'oeuvres.
Restrictions: No pets allowed, 1 room handicap equipped
Concierge: noon–8 p.m.
Room Service: 8 a.m.–8 p.m.
Business Facilities: Message center, Audio-visual, Teleconferencing, Fax
Conference Rooms: 1 room, capacity 15
Sports Facilities: Swimming pool, Spa, Massage by appointment, Nearby golf, tennis and horseback riding
Location: Napa Valley vineyards

CHURCHILL MANOR BED & BREAKFAST

This grand 3-story mansion was built in 1889 and was the first Napa residence listed on the National Historic Registry. Surrounded by an extensive covered veranda and flanked by large white columns, the building rests amid a private-enclosed acre of beautiful trees, expansive lawns and lush gardens. As visitors pass through the massive, beveled-glass doors, they step back in time to a less hurried way of life. The first floor boasts four large parlors, each with a fireplace and magnificently carved redwood moldings and a solarium with an original mosaic floor of over 60,000 marble tiles.

The mansion was refurbished in 2003 and is furnished with fine European antiques, oriental rugs, brass and crystal chandeliers, and a grand piano in the music room. All 10 guestrooms are individually and uniquely decorated. The Edward Churchill room is the original owner's master bedroom and features a magnificent antique French matching 7-piece bedroom set of carved walnut and marble and ample comfortable seating for relaxing. It also features original gold-leaf bathroom and fireplace tiles, a giant bathtub mounted on a mahogany pedestal, a two-person tiled shower, and the original pedestal sink.

A complimentary, bountiful breakfast including homemade muffins, nut breads, croissants, a generous fruit platter, and daily egg entrees, is served each morning, either in the solarium overlooking the garden or outside on the veranda. Each evening there is a two-hour Napa Valley varietal wine-and-cheese reception, and each afternoon freshly baked cookies, coffee and tea are available for snacking. Croquet and tandem bicycles are provided complimentary to guests to enhance the Victorian charm of a stay at Churchill Manor.

Churchill Manor is an ideal place for a romantic wedding or reception for any festive occasion. The inn hosts weddings each year with in-house catering, equipment and coordination. Hot-air ballooning, COPIA, the Napa Valley Wine Train, mud baths in nearby spas, gourmet restaurants, shopping, tennis, and golf are among the many recreational activities available.

Address: 485 Brown St, Napa 94559.
Phone: 707-253-7733
Fax: 707-253-8836
Email: be@churchillmanor.com
Web site: http://www.churchillmanor.com
Room Rates: 155–275
No. of Rooms: 10
Credit Cards: Most Credit Cards accepted
Attractions: Napa Valley wineries, COPIA, Hot-air ballooning, Mud baths, Art galleries, Gourmet restaurants, Shopping, Horseback riding, Napa Valley Wine Train
Services & Amenities: Packages available, TV Lounge, Card/game area w/VCR/movies, Music room w/grand piano, Sunroom, Veranda, 10 rms – fireplaces, 5 rms – 2 person showers, 8 rms – antique bathtubs, Private baths, Radio, Telephones, Complimentary full breakfast, snacks, wine/cheese
Restrictions: No pets, 1 handicap equip room, 2 night min. Saturday, Children over 12 only unless booking entire inn
Concierge: 9 a.m.-9 p.m.
Restaurant: Breakfast–8:30 a.m.-10 a.m., and dinner by prior arrangement
Bar: Main parlor for evening wine and cheese
Business Facilities: Complete wedding and catering services
Conference Rooms: 1 room, capacity 45
Sports Facilities: Croquet, Tandem bicycles, Nearby health club privileges, 5 golf courses nearby
Location: Old Town Napa, Abajo National Historic District

THE MARTINE INN

This gracious palace was built in 1899 high atop the cliffs of Pacific Grove overlooking the rocky coastline of Monterey Bay. Don Martine and his staff attempt to create for you the ease and grace of being a guest of the very wealthy 100 years ago. This gracious palace was built in 1899 high atop the cliffs of Pacific Grove overlooking the rocky coastline of Monterey Bay. Don Martine and his staff attempt to create for you the ease and grace of being a guest of the very wealthy 100 years ago. Innkeeper and veteran antique collector, Don Martine, has carefully filled this Victorian-turned- Mediterranean mansion with his extensive collections of pewter and sterling silver, vintage automobiles and early California art.

The inn's twenty four guestrooms are filled with an impressive sampling of furniture designs including American Victorian and lyrical Deco styling. An example of the attention to details are the fresh roses and other flowers in each guestroom. The Edith Head Room, for example, contains a nine-piece 1920s walnut bedroom suite which once graced the costume designer's home, and the McClatchy Room has a massive Eastlake inlaid walnut and mahogany suite. Some rooms have spectacular views of waves crashing against the rocks and/or wood-burning fireplaces. In the morning guests awake to a newspaper placed outside their door and a full breakfast served on Old Sheffield silver, porcelain, Victorian-style crystal and lace.

Possible activities may include reading in the library, sunbathing in the enclosed landscaped courtyard, whale watching from the parlor or sitting rooms, playing pool in the game room or lounging in the spa. There is also a display of Don's vintage MGs from the 1920s through the 1950s. Guests who choose to venture outside may stroll 4 blocks to the Monterey Bay Aquarium and Cannery Row, or walk, jog or bike along the 15-mile coastal recreational trail.

Throughout the day guests can enjoy complimentary coffee and tea with snacks. Guests may relax at the end of the day with wine and hors d'oeuvres served each evening in the parlor.

Address: 255 Ocean View Blvd, PO Box 330, Pacific Grove 93950.
Phone: 831-373-3388 800-852-5588
Fax: 831-373-3896
Email: don@martineinn.com
Web site: http://www.martineinn.com
Room Rates: 139–329
Suite Rates: 329–359
No. of Rooms: 24
No. of Suites: 3
Credit Cards: Visa, MasterCard, Discover
Attractions: Whale and Sea Otter watching, Aquarium, Cannery Row, Antiquing, 17 Mile Drive, Carmel, Fishermans Wharf, Bicycling, Horseback Riding, Golf, Tennis, Diving, Kayaking, Monarch Butterflies, Big Sur, Historic Buildings, Steinbeck Center, Laguna Seca, Wineries
Services & Amenities: Full breakfast, Offstreet parking, Vintage auto display, TV Lounge, Card/game area, Library, Billiard room, Babysitting service, 15 fireplaces, Jacuzzi, Refrigerators, Clock Radio, Hair Dryer, Robes, Newspaper, Toiletries, Fresh Fruit, Fresh Flowers
Restrictions: No pets (will arrange boarding), 1 room equipped for handicapped, 2-night minimum with Saturday
Concierge: 8 a.m.-10 p.m.
Room Service: 8 a.m.-9:30 p.m.
Restaurant: The Parlor, 8 a.m.-10 a.m. for breakfast, 5:30-7 p.m. for wine hour, Lunch, Dinner and Receptions available for groups of 20 or more
Business Facilities: Message center, Copier, Audio-Visual, Teleconferencing, DSL connections available
Conference Rooms: 6 rooms, capacity 6-25
Sports Facilities: Whirlpool, Massage, Aerobics/weight training nearby, Golf–Pebble Beach (5 min), Sailing, Tennis ne
Location: Butterfly Town U.S.A. (Monarchs), Nearest airport is Monterey

SEVEN GABLES INN

It's hard to imagine a more picturesque and romantic location than that of Seven Gables. The waves crashing along the rocky shoreline, the sea otters frolicking just offshore, the whales spouting, the surrounding mountains lit up by the sunset ... these are the images seen from each guestroom of this century old Victorian inn.

Such natural beauty is complimented on the inside by a unmatched array of museum-quality European, Asian and American antiques. A bountiful breakfast, enjoyable afternoon wine and hors d'oeuvres, outstanding guest service and the comfort of all private baths combine to make Seven Gables, truly, one of the most outstanding inns in California.

Seven Gables Inn is personally managed by our family. We opened our home to guests in 1982. Since then, we have anticipated the wishes of our guests, and we endeavor to make your holiday one that you will always remember.

Your Hosts, Susan Flatley Wheelwright & Ed Flatley

Address: 555 Ocean View Blvd, Pacific Grove 93950.
Phone: 831-372-4341
Email: susan@pginns.com
Web site: http://www.pginns.com
Room Rates: 175–385
Suite Rates: 385–485
No. of Rooms: 14
No. of Suites: 1
Credit Cards: Visa
Attractions: 17-Mile Drive, Cannery Rowand the MontereyBay Aquarium, Carmel-by-the-Sea, Point Lobos and Big Sur, world famous golf courses in Pebble Beach, Old Fisherman's Wharf, Whale watching
Services & Amenities: Our rates include a bountiful breakfast, afternoon wine and hors d'oeuvres, evening turn down service, evening milk and cookies and, of course, outstanding customer service.
Restrictions: Non smoking, please no pets
Concierge: Absolutely!
Location: On the very edge of Monterey Bay

LIGHTHOUSE LODGE & SUITES

Nestled among the Monterey pines just one block from the Pacific Ocean lies The Lighthouse Lodge & Suites.

The "Suites" property offers comfort and luxury at its finest. This 31 unit boutique Cape-Cod style village is the Monterey Peninsula's best kept secret. Each "Suite" includes five-star king-size bedding with down pillows, in-room fireplaces, over-sized Jacuzzi tubs with plush robes, mini-kitchenettes with stocked honor bars, large screen televisions with cable and remote, and the latest releases on our pay-per view movie system.

For large families, groups or entertaining, there is the "Executive Residence." This beautifully appointed 1400 sq. ft. home can sleep six adults, and comes complete with three bathrooms, three marble fireplaces, a gourmet cooking kitchen and full size laundry facilities. Sit back and enjoy the tranquility the fully fenced and landscaped backyard has to offer, not to mention the roof top deck that is perfect for taking in the evening central coast sunset.

Awaken each morning to your complimentary chef prepared breakfast. Afternoons include an evening hospitality reception where guests can relax and enjoy a bountiful array of hors d'oeuvres and a complimentary pool side BBQ.

The Lighthouse Lodge and Suites is a golfers paradise with world famous courses nearby. Adjacent to the property is Pacific Grove's own 18 hole oceanside golf course and only one mile to Pebble Beach.

Whether your travel is for romance, relaxation or business, the "Suites" are proof positive that big things do come in small packages.

Address: 1150 & 1249 Lighthouse Ave, Pacific Grove 93950.
Phone: 831-655-2111 800-858-1249
Fax: 831-655-4922
Email: lighthouselodge@att.net
Web site: http://www.lhls.com
Room Rates: 79–179
Suite Rates: 228–625
No. of Rooms: 64
No. of Suites: 31
Credit Cards: Most Credit Cards accepted
Attractions: Whale watching, Kayaking, Scuba diving, Fisherman's Wharf, two miles to Monterey Bay Aquarium, 2 miles to John Steinbeck's Cannery Row, 7 miles to Carmel, 1 mile to Pebble Beach, World famous golf courses
Services & Amenities: Garage and parking, Baby-sitting service, Card/game area, Car hire, Complimentary breakfast, Cable TV, Wet bar, Telephone, Some rooms with fireplc & balconies/decks, Individual heat controls, Robes, Complimentary toiletries, In-room coffee
Restrictions: Pets allowed $25 per day, 4 rooms handicap equipped, children 17 and under free with parents
Room Service: 7–10:30 a.m.
Restaurant: Breakfast is served 7-10:30am daily in dining room or call for breakfast in bed in your suite, an evening hospitality reception 3:30-5:30pm daily, poolside BBQ 4:30-6:30pm (weather permitting)
Business Facilities: Full scale conference facilities w/message ctr, admin. assistance, e-mail, copiers, A/V, fax, modems
Conference Rooms: 5 rooms, capacity 70 with banquet facilities
Sports Facilities: Outdoor swimming pool, whirlpool, massage on call, adjacent to golf
Location: One block from Monterey Bay

THE VILLA ROYALE INN

Open-beam ceilings, tile floors, fireplaces, and private patios are among the features guests may find in their quarters at The Villa Royale. Here you will enjoy the atmosphere of a romantic and tranquil country inn, decorated in colors, textures and art reminiscent of different European regions.

Overall, the resort is a series of interior courtyards framed with bougainvillea and shade trees. Asymmetrical gardens with potted flowers, brick paths and bubbling fountains create the intimate atmosphere of a Mediterranean villa.

Rooms, each different, have telephones and cable TV. Many have fireplaces and kitchens. Guests may enjoy 2 pools and a brick-terraced hot tub set among palm trees and desert flowers. A complimentary cooked-to-order full breakfast is served each morning.

Dining at the award-winning Europa Restaurant is a highlight of The Villa Royale experience. Once the Innkeeper's residence, this intimate auberge offers Continental cuisine and an impressive variety of imported and domestic wines, served fireside or under the desert stars.

Tennis, golf and horseback riding are a short drive from The Villa Royale. Palm Canyon Drive, with its shops and romantic nightlife, is within walking distance.

Address: 1620 Indian Trail, Palm Springs 92264.
Phone: 760-327-2314 800-245-2314
Fax: 760-322-3794
Email: info@villaroyale.com
Web site: http://www.villaroyale.com
Room Rates: 95–225
Suite Rates: 185–375
No. of Rooms: 30
No. of Suites: 8
Credit Cards: Most Credit Cards accepted
Attractions: Palm Springs Aerial Tram, Horseback riding, Desert Museum, Desert Jeep tours, Golfing, Tennis, Shopping
Services & Amenities: Complimentary newspaper, Basic Cable TV, Telephones, Radio, Air conditioning, Plush terry robes, in room hair dryers, Complimentary toiletries, Complimentary full cooked-to-order breakfast.
Restrictions: Adult clientele, no pets allowed, no rooms hadicapped equipped.
Concierge: Contact Front Desk
Room Service: 6–9:30 p.m.
Restaurant: Europa, Tuesday-Sunday, 6-10 p.m. Sunday Brunch 11:30-1:30. Closed Monday and Tuesday evenings from June 1 through September 30.
Bar: Same as restaurant
Business Facilities: Copiers, Fax, high speed Internet available in the lobby.
Sports Facilities: 2 outdoor swimming pools, Whirlpool, Massage
Spa Services: In room massage and facial treatments can be arranged either prior to or upon arrival.
Location: Palm Springs

THE WILLOWS HISTORIC PALM SPRINGS INN

Built in 1924 and embraced by Mount San Jacinto, the striking architecture of this Mediterranean Villa set against the hillside creates a dramatic effect. Mahogany beams, frescoed ceilings and the mountain waterfall that spills into a pool just outside the stone-floored dining room delights visitors and creates a memorable atmosphere.

The Willows has been meticulously restored to its former grandeur, refinement and elegance. *Country Inn* magazine named it "One of the 10 best inns in the country." All eight rooms are beautifully appointed with antique furniture, sumptuous linens, luxurious baths and modern amenities. Several rooms have a working fireplace, hardwood floors, private balcony, garden patio and/or mountain and garden vistas. Rooms are decorated individually so that each room has its own unique character. The Loft Room, for example, is charmingly complemented by vaulted ceiling, Italian burled walnut antique furnishings, a two-person claw foot tub in the bathroom, as well as a fireplace which is enhanced by cascading water outside the windows. These romantic rooms conjure up images of times past and times to be had.

Each night's stay at The Willows is followed by an extensive gourmet breakfast, which will tempt even the most discerning palate. Specialty dishes include cilantro-rolled omelets served with fresh avocado and salsa, pumpkin waffles topped with apple-cider syrup, caramelized poached pears, sides of chicken apple sausage and praline bacon, an assortment of pastries, and more. The Willows also serves afternoon hors d'oeuvres and wine to celebrate yet another leisurely day.

For the curious guest, The Willows boasts a magical hillside garden which leads to secluded lookouts where one may contemplate the "sun-bleached land, the pale mysterious desert" or the star splashed night sky above the still mountains.

The Willows beckons visitors to its superb setting and tranquil atmosphere.

Address: 412 W Tahquitz Canyon Way, Palm Springs 92262
Phone: 760-320-0771
800-966-9597
Fax: 760-320-0780
Email: innkeeper@
thewillowspalmsprings.com
Web site: http://
www.thewillowspalmsprings.com
Room Rates: 295–575
No. of Rooms 8
Credit Cards: Most Credit Cards accepted
Attractions: A short walk to the Desert Museum, restaurants, shopping and theatres
Services & Amenities: Parking, Gift shop, Dining Room w/fireplace, Living room w/fireplace, patio and verandah, Cable television, Telephones,Individual climate controls, CD player, Refrigerator, Complimentary toiletries & newspaper
Restrictions: 1 room with handicapped access, Children over 16 years welcome, No pets allowed
Concierge: 24 hours
Room Service: 11 a.m.-11 p.m
Restaurant: Le Vallauris, across the street, operated separately by Paul Bruggermans, providing room service
Business Facilities: Voice mail, Copiers, Audio-Visual, Fax, Dataports & The O'Donnell House – weddings, meetings, events
Conference Rooms: 1 room, capacity 20 & The O'Donnell House, capacity 125
Sports Facilities: Heated outdoor swimming pool and Jacuzzi, Massage services available. Golf and tennis nearby
Location: Historic old village, 2 blocks from downtown

GARDEN COURT HOTEL

"A world apart, in the center of everything."

The preferred hotel of many guests who travel to the Bay Area, the Garden Court Hotel is located in the heart of Palo Alto's lively downtown district, providing an elegant retreat featuring spacious guestrooms, a highly attentive staff, and the acclaimed Northern Italian cuisine of Il Fornaio.

Mediterranean architecture and an open-air courtyard complete with olive trees and flowers create a lush and restful ambiance. Each of our 62 newly-renovated guestrooms is furnished with many luxuries, such as Aveda bath products and fresh Peet's coffee. Our signature turn-down service includes a fresh gardenia, slippers and a terrycloth robe, an eye mask and aromatherapy lotion, and, in our suites, tea service. High speed Internet access, dual line speaker phones, and a printer/copier/fax provide a convenient way to conduct business. Our staff is pleased to assist with special requests at any time.

Dining at the Garden Court features the award-winning Northern Italian cuisine of Il Fornaio Cucina Italiana, which offers freshly-baked breads, house-made pastas, seasonal menus, and perfectly paired wines and foods.

Our spacious ballrooms and adjoining courtyards or terraces offer an elegant and gracious environment for memorable weddings, family celebrations, and special events. Our large and comfortable meeting rooms feature picture windows, comfortable seating, high-speed Internet access, and audio-visual equipment designed to make doing business a pleasure.

At the Garden Court Hotel, we cultivate your comfort.

Address: 520 Cowper St, Palo Alto 94301.
Phone: 650-322-9000 800-824-9028
Fax: 650-324-3609
Email: ahotel@gardencourt.com
Web site: http://www.gardencourt.com
Room Rates: 299–379
Suite Rates: 369–599
No. of Rooms: 50
No. of Suites: 12
Attractions: Silicon Valley, Stanford University and Medical Center, Stanford Shopping Center, Local wineries; Walking vicinity: Boutiques, upscale shopping and dining, antiques, galleries, beauty salons, barber shops
Services & Amenities: Valet parking, Dry cleaning/Laundry, Cable TV, Bose CD Radios, Twice Daily housekeeping services with turndown, Aveda amenities, Hair dryers, Iron/steamer/boards, Down comforter/pillows, Mini bars, in-room safe, Balconies
Restrictions: Pet friendly (pet fee required), Handicap equipped rooms
Concierge: 24 hours
Room Service: 24 hours
Restaurant: Il Fornaio Restaurant, 7 a.m.-11 p.m. daily, Weekend brunch 9 a.m.-2 p.m.
Bar: 7 a.m. to midnight
Business Facilities: In-room printer/fax/copier, High speed T1 Internet access, 2-line Cordless speaker phone & voicemail
Conference Rooms: 8 flexible, attractive rooms, capacity 10-250
Sports Facilities: On-site fitness center (cardiovascular, strength training, free weights), hiking trails, area jogging map
Location: Active downtown, nearest airports SFO & SJO in epicenter of Silicon Valley

THE INN AT RANCHO SANTA FE

Nestled in the exclusive village of Rancho Santa Fe is a historic inn that was the getaway of choice for the stars of a bygone era. San Diego North County's premier resort destination. Today, lush gardens, winding paths, and the recently renovated Cottages, Dining Room and cozy bar create a new tradition of quiet elegance. Discover signature cuisine, enjoy a round of golf in Rancho Santa Fe, play croquet or splash in the surf at the Inn's own beach house in nearby Del Mar. The Inn is a perfect quiet romantic getaway and a stunning location for weddings, conferences and executive retreats.

Most accommodations are in cottages scattered about the property. Each cottage room has been individually decorated and nearly all have secluded porches or sun decks. Rooms with wood burning fireplaces and kitchens are available, as well as interconnecting suites for larger groups.

The 23-acres are lushly landscaped and bloom almost continuously, providing a verdant backdrop for The Inn's heated pool, Jacuzzi, Spa and three tennis courts.

Enjoy the relaxed charm of another era amidst the sunny splendor of Southern California. The old Inn spot is new again.

Address: P.O. Box 869, Rancho Santa Fe 92067.
Phone: 858-756-1131 800-843-4661
Fax: 858-759-1604
Email: reservations@theinnatrsf.com
Web site: http://www.theinnatrsf.com
Room Rates: 220–360
Suite Rates: 460–895
No. of Rooms: 87
Credit Cards: Most Credit Cards accepted
Attractions: Sea World, San Diego Zoo, Wild Animal Park, La Jolla Museum of Modern Art, Legoland, Del Mar Racetrack.
Services & Amenities: The Inn is just minutes from the beach at Del Mar, Swimming pool and Jacuzzi, Gym, Croquet, Fitness Programs, Spa & Salon services and Complimentary wireless High-Speed Internet. Custom designed, "memory foam" beds topped with Egyptian cotton sheets.
Restrictions: Pets allowed in designated rooms only. Smoking is only permitted outdoors.
Concierge: 7am to 9:30pm daily
Room Service: 7am to 9:30pm daily
Restaurant: Our locals favorite Dining Room features innovative Rancho Cuisine, seating inside our on terrace and serving breakfast, lunch and dinner. Live music most evenings in our cozy Bar.
Bar: 11 a.m.-11 p.m. daily
Business Facilities: Clerical services available
Conference Rooms: 4 rooms, capacity 10-150
Sports Facilities: 3 hard-surface tennis courts, Exercise room, 18-hole golf course nearby
Spa Services: Spa and Salon services on site incuding variety of massage treatments, facials, manicures, pedicures and hair cuts.
Location: 25 miles from San Diego

RANCHO VALENCIA RESORT

The Rancho Valencia Resort is set on 40 acres in a private canyon, lushly landscaped with eucalyptus, palm trees, and colorful bougainvillea. Citrus trees fill the air with the scent of orange blossoms.

Set around a mission-style courtyard, the Resort features terra cotta floors and hand-painted Mexican tiles, complementing the rich hues and stunning landscape. The Resort's suites feature a large, distinctive living room with open-beamed ceilings, fireplace bordered with hand-painted tiles, and French doors opening onto the garden patio. The bathrooms are complete with a walk-in closet, robes and slippers, double sinks, and a separate bathtub and shower designed with paver tiles on the floors and counter tops. The views of the garden and pool are especially spectacular during sunset. Opening of our newest suites, The Grove, took place in April 2002. Larger than the original suites, these also offer private spas on patios, steam showers, and jetted tubs.

Activities abound at the Resort, where guests can enjoy four nearby golf courses, 18 tennis courts, an outdoor pool, croquet, and polo. The deluxe spa facilities offer guests an opportunity to indulge their desires for relaxation. The Resort is also just minutes away from the beaches of Del Mar and shopping in La Jolla. The Stephen Birch Aquarium and Wild Animal Park are nearby, offering exciting activities and behind-the-scenes tours for the Resort's guests.

The Rancho Valencia Restaurant, located at Rancho Valencia Resort, is a wonderfully romantic and elegant restaurant tucked in a private canyon in Rancho Santa Fe. Sitting just off a mission-style courtyard, the restaurant exudes a sophisticated French country charm with its white-washed, open beamed ceilings, yet maintains a California breeziness with an abundance of live palms scattered throughout and fresh flowers on every table. Executive Chef Steven Sumner presents an innovative and imaginative menu featuring California/French cuisine with an Asian influence.

Address: 5921 Valencia Resort, PO Box 9126, Rancho Santa Fe 92067.
Phone: 858-756-1123 800-548-3664
Fax: 858-756-0165
Email: reservations@ranchovalencia.com
Web site: http://www.ranchovalencia.com
Suite Rates: 470–1420
No. of Suites: 49
Attractions: Minutes from beaches of Del Mar and shopping in La Jolla, Close to Stephen Birch Aquarium, San Diego Polo Club, Wild Animal Park—all offering exciting activities and behind the scenes tours for our guests.
Services & Amenities: Orange Juice & newspaper delivered daily, Complimentary valet parking, Complimentary use of fitness center & tennis courts, Laundry, Boutique, Comp. shoeshine, Card/game area, Fireplaces, 3 telephones per room, Wet bar, Cable TV, VCR/DVD, Radio.
Restrictions: $75 charge per pet per day, Children are welcome, 2 rooms handicap equipped
Concierge: 7 a.m.-11 p.m.
Room Service: 24 hours
Restaurant: Rancho Valencia Restaurant, 7 a.m.-10 p.m.
Bar: Rancho Valencia Bar, 11 a.m.-10 p.m., Classical guitarist on Fri. & Sat.
Business Facilities: Message center, Admin. assistance, E-mail, Copiers, Audio-visual, Teleconferencing, Fax, Modems
Conference Rooms: 2 rooms
Sports Facilities: Outdoor pool, Croquet, Whirlpool, Sauna, Massage, Weight training,18 hard-tru tennis courts, Putting
Spa Services: A full menu of spa services are offered in the privacy of your suite.
Location: Fairbanks Ranch in private canyon of Rancho Santa Fe

RANCHO CAYMUS

Rancho Caymus Inn, located in the village of Rutherford in the heart of the Napa Valley, was built in Spanish Hacienda style, designed to capture the rustic spirit of Early California. The Early California atmosphere is established with hard-wood floor and wood beam ceilings in all 26 rooms, and further experienced in all the details from hand carved furnishing, wrought iron lamps, stained glass windows and hand-thrown stoneware basins.

The inn, owned by the Flora Springs Winery, affords both the seclusion of its walled gardens and close proximity to the quaint towns of Yountville and St. Helena. There are 5 different styles of suites to choose from, most with wood-burning fireplaces and private patios or balconies, some with king size beds and whirlpool Jacuzzi tubs.

All choices of rooms include a "Hacienda continental breakfast" served in the dining room or "al fresco" in the garden courtyard. At dinner time, guests of the inn need look no further than outside their front doors to the La Toque Restaurant located at the inn. The award-winning, gourmet cuisine of the La Toque Restaurant has been featured in such publications as The Wine Spectator, Gourmet and W magazines.

This is the perfect place for winetasters! There are approximately 30 wineries within 5 minute drive of the inn, including the inn owner's Flora Springs Winery who offer special tastings for Rancho Caymus guests. For those who do not want to go wine tasting, there are lovely shops and relaxing spas in nearby towns. For the more adventuresome, hot air balloon flights are available, leaving from the steps of the inn. Many other outdoor activities can also be arranged.

Address: 1140 Rutherford Rd, PO Box 78, Rutherford 94573.
Phone: 707-963-1777 800-845-1777
Fax: 707-963-5387
Email: frontdesk@ranchocaymus.com
Web site: http://www.ranchocaymus.com
Room Rates: 205–300
Suite Rates: 305–440
No. of Rooms: 26
No. of Suites: 5
Credit Cards: Visa
Attractions: Located in the center of the Napa Valley, with-in a five minute drive to dozens of world famous wineries, gourmet restaurants and health spas.
Services & Amenities: Complimentary continental breakfast, Some rooms with fireplaces, and balconies, All rooms have TV, Radio, Wet bar, Individual climate control, Refrigerators, Private baths with shower-tubs, Complimentary toiletries
Restrictions: No pets allowed, 2 rooms handicap equipped, 2 night minimum for weekends
Concierge: 10 a.m.-7 p.m.
Restaurant: La Toque Restaurant, dinner only
Sports Facilities: Nearby tennis and golf
Location: Downtown

HUNTINGTON CITY-TOWNSHIP
PUBLIC LIBRARY
200 W. Market Street
Huntington, IN 46750

RANCHO BERNARDO INN

In weather-perfect San Diego, Rancho Bernardo Inn offers a complete resort getaway featuring luxurious accommodations, world-class recreation, exceptional dining and AAA Four-Diamond service. The Inn's Old World elegance is complemented by the warmth of genuine hospitality.

Guestrooms are secluded throughout the property, with buildings connected by pathways through lush, manicured gardens. Each room is a spacious retreat featuring custom furnishings and artwork, and a patio or balcony overlooking the golf course or gardens.

Guests may spend their days at play on the Inn's 18-hole championship Resort Course, a traditional layout enhanced by the noted design team of Schmidt & Curley to provide a modern challenge. Tennis players will feel right at home at the Inn's twelve-court tennis complex, while those

looking for relaxation will enjoy the array of massages and body treatments at the Spa. Finally, two swimming pools—including one reserved just for adults—and seven hydro-spas are perfect for lounging the afternoon away.

In the evening, choose from two outstanding restaurants. In an elegant dining room, El Bizcocho serves contemporary French cuisine that has earned the Zagat Survey's highest ratings in San Diego. Complemented by an extensive wine list and impeccable service, it should not be missed.

For more casual dining, the Veranda offers a menu inspired by the fresh flavors of Southern Europe. Dine indoors or on the sunny, expanded patio overlooking the golf course. In the evening, an outdoor fireplace sets the perfect mood.

Rancho Bernardo Inn's quiet setting in northern San Diego is convenient to all of the city's attractions, including the Wild Animal Park, SeaWorld, Legoland, the San Diego Zoo, beaches and more.

Address: 17550 Bernardo Oaks Dr, San Diego 92128.
Phone: 858-675-8500 800-542-6096
Fax: 858-675-8501
Email: ranchobernardoinn@jcresorts.com
Web site: http://www.jcresorts.com
Room Rates: 239–578
Suite Rates: 400–850
No. of Rooms: 287
No. of Suites: 58
Attractions: Sea World, San Diego Zoo, Wild Animal Park, Tijuana, La Jolla, beaches, Del Mar racetrack, wineries, Balboa Park, Legoland
Services & Amenities: Valet service, car hire, concierge, airport meet-and-greet services, library, gift shop, children's summer camp
Restrictions: No pets allowed, Handicap equipped rooms available
Concierge: 7 a.m.-8 p.m.
Room Service: 6:30 a.m.-midnight
Restaurant: El Bizcocho serves contemporary French cuisine rated San Diego's finest by the Zagat Survey. The Veranda offers more casual fare indoors or on the expanded terrace overlooking the golf course.
Bar: La Taberna
Business Facilities: Admin. assistance, Copiers, Audio-visual, Business Services Center, Full-scale conference facilities
Conference Rooms: 15 rooms, 15,000 square feet
Sports Facilities: 18-hole championship golf course, complete spa and fitness center, 12 tennis courts, 2 pools
Spa Services: The Spa at Rancho Bernardo Inn offers a complete array of massages, facials and body treatments.
Location: Rancho Bernardo, 25 minutes to downtown San Diego

CAMPTON PLACE HOTEL

The exterior is Spanish revival, the James Northcutt interiors contemporary, and the location the best—just off the fashionable Union Square where San Francisco's financial district, airline offices, art galleries, designer boutiques, department stores, theater district, convention center, and cable cars are all within walking distance of the hotel.

For over two decades Campton Place Hotel in San Francisco has been a refuge for the sophisticated executive traveler, providing the quiet, intimate atmosphere that make guests feel as comfortable as if they were at home. Pear wood, a light colored wood used in many European hotels, sets the tone of the room design, along with other luxurious touches such as Roman shades and furniture upholstered in silk and other fine fabrics. The bathrooms also feature European touches, such as oversized tubs. All rooms are equipped with state-of-the-art soundproof windows, many with window seats overlooking the fashionable shopping area of Union Square.

A destination in itself, the highly regarded Campton Place Restaurant has been named one of the "Top 10 Restaurants in San Francisco" by *Gourmet* magazine. Executive Chef Daniel Humm has received a steady stream of accolades since his arrival at Campton Place Restaurant in May 2003. In February 2004, the *San Francisco Chronicle* named him a Rising Star Chef, and he has been nominated for one of the industry's most prestigious awards, the James Beard Foundation Rising Star Chef of the Year, 2005. Most recently, he was named one of *Food & Wine* magazine's Best New Chefs 2005. The delectable, equisitely varied menu, elegant tableside service and an unsurpassed wine list, provide an unforgettable meal and experience. The award winning cuisine is served in luxurious surroundings that include hand-waxed Italian olive wood chairs upholstered in cream leather, pale sycamore banquettes, cabinets of Macassar ebony inlaid with faux ivory and coco panels and a free-form sculptural hand-blown glass chandelier.

Address: 340 Stockton Street, San Francisco 94108.
Phone: 415-781-5555 800-235-4300
Fax: 415-955-5536
Email: reserve@campton.com
Web site: http://www.camptonplace.com
Room Rates: 340–475
Suite Rates: 575–2050
No. of Rooms: 101
No. of Suites: 9
Credit Cards: Visa
Attractions: Maiden Lane boutique shopping, Union Square major shopping district, near cable car line
Services & Amenities: Valet service, parking, international currency exchange, dry cleaning, complimentary shoeshine, house doctor, bath phone, terry towels and knitted robes, choice of 4 newspapers daily, 3 rooms handicap equipped, pets accepted
Concierge: 24 hours
Room Service: 24 hours
Restaurant: Campton Place Restaurant, 7 a.m.-10:30 p.m. daily, Dress code
Bar: Campton, 7 a.m.-11 p.m.
Business Facilities: Message center, Admin. assistance, Copiers, Word processing available
Conference Rooms: 4 rooms, capacity 96 in rounds
Location: Union Square

HUNTINGTON HOTEL AND NOB HILL SPA

Known for a long-standing tradition of high standards and gracious service, the prestigious Huntington Hotel and Nob Hill Spa, located atop Nob Hill, has been a favorite among visiting dignitaries, nobility, celebrities and discriminating travelers throughout its existence.

Built originally as a residence hotel in 1924, this was the first brick and steel high-rise west of the Mississippi. A guarded secret among society's most elite members since its inception, the family-owned and operated Huntington remains somewhat of a best-kept secret today.

As the doorman admits guests to the lobby, they encounter an understated luxury that is difficult to find in more contemporary lodgings. The spacious, comfortable rooms, each individually decorated by top designers, have a rare, one-of-a-kind feel that is both luxurious and residential. Guests such as Placido Domingo, Luciano Pavarotti, Robert Redford and Paloma Picasso regularly request their own personal favorites from among the 35 elegant suites.

Named for the four railroad tycoons of the 19th century—C.P. Huntington, Charles Crocker, Leland Stanford and Mark Hopkins—The Big 4 Restaurant proves a perfect showcase for its impressive collection of original artifacts, historical photographs, and memorabilia. The dining room is marvelously appointed with leaded glass mirrors and rich, forest green leather banquettes. One step into The Big 4 transports guests to a bygone era of California's wild past. The cozy bar is a San Francisco favorite.

The new Nob Hill Spa at the Huntington is the ultimate urban escape in the heart of San Francisco. The first of its kind in the City, the full service spa and wellness center called in a noted feng shui expert to bring harmony and good fortune to the entire spa. The stunning spa offers a unique array of restorative treatments designed to soothe body and spirit.

Address: 1075 California St, San Francisco 94108
Phone: 415-474-5400
800-227-4683
Fax: 415-474-6227
Web site: http://www.huntingtonhotel.com
Room Rates: 275–445
Suite Rates: 475–1125
No. of Rooms 100
No. of Suites: 35
Attractions: Financial district, Fisherman's Wharf, Pier 39 and Union Square are just blocks away on Cable Car line
Services & Amenities: Valet, Garage & parking, Car hire, Chauffeured limo, Laundry service, House doctor, Baby-sitting service, Individual heat and air-conditioning controls, Radio, Cable TV/VCR's, Audio cassette players, Comp. shoeshine & newspaper, tea or sherry upon arrival
Restrictions: No pets allowed
Concierge: Available
Room Service: Available
Restaurant: The Big 4, 7 a.m.-10:30 p.m., Weekend breakfast, 7 a.m.-11 a.m., Dress code
Bar: The Big 4 Bar, 11:30 a.m.-midnight
Business Facilities: Message & admin. assistance, Copiers, Audio-Visual, Teleconferencing, Fax, DSL Internet Service
Conference Rooms: 4 rooms, capacity 75
Spa Services: New Nob Hill Spa at The Huntington, for reservations call 415-345-2888
Location: Nob Hill near Grace Cathedral, Huntington Park & the Pacific Union Club

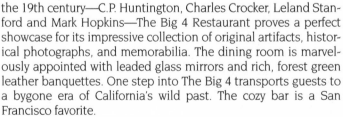

Harbor View Inn, *Santa Barbara, CA* PAGE 44

Meadowood Napa Valley, *St. Helena, CA* PAGE 48

MANDARIN ORIENTAL, SAN FRANCISCO

Towering high above the San Francisco skyline, Mandarin Oriental occupies the top 11 floors of the city's third-tallest building, giving every guestroom spectacular sweeping views. Luxurious amenities and warm atmosphere with attention to detail fill 158 spacious guestrooms and suites. For the third consecutive year, Mandarin Oriental is the only hotel in San Francisco to receive the coveted Mobil Travel Guide Five-Star Award.

Ideally situated in the heart of downtown and one-half block from the California Street cable car line, all of the city's activities are minutes from the hotel. For a gourmet dining experience with uncompromising service, guests may enjoy the award-winning Silks restaurant serving contemporary American cuisine. A perfect beginning or end to the evening awaits you in The Mandarin Lounge for cocktails and light bistro fare.

The hotel offers distinctive meeting and banquet space, all with windows and unique designs for any business meeting or social event. An extensive Business Center is available with a computer workstation and secretarial services. A fitness center with state-of-the art equipment including Cybex, Paramount, Stairmaster, LifeFitness, and flat-screen TVs is available for guest use.

Mandarin Oriental Hotel Group is the award-winning owner and operator of some of the world's finest hotels. The Group operates 18 luxury hotels in key leisure and business destinations, with a hotel under development in New York (opening late 2004) and Toyko (2006). In total, Mandarin Oriental employs almost 9,000 staff in three continents with nine hotels in Asia, six in North America and three in Europe.

Address: 222 Sansome Street, San Francisco 94104-2792
Phone: 415-276-9888
800-622-0404
Fax: 415-433-0289
Email: reserve-mosfo@mohg.com
Web site: http://www.mandarinoriental.com
Room Rates: 275–725
Suite Rates: 1400–3000
No. of Rooms 154
No. of Suites: 4
Credit Cards: Most Credit Cards accepted
Attractions: Near Cable Car line, Chinatown, Embarcadero Center, Union Square, Museums and Theaters, Wine Country tours available through the concierge
Services & Amenities: Valet & garage parking, Car hire, Int'l currency exchange, Compl. shoeshine & newspaper, Baby-sitting serv., Laundry, Iron/Ironing board, Cable TV w/on-command video, Radio, Mini bars, Robes, Hair dryer, Fine English toiletries, High speed Internet access
Restrictions: Handicap equipped
Concierge: 7 a.m.-10 p.m.
Room Service: 24 hours
Restaurant: Silks, one of the finest restaurants in the city, serving contemporary American cuisine with Pacific Rim influence.
Bar: The Mandarin Lounge
Business Facilities: Business Center with Admin. assistance, Copiers, Audio-visual rental
Conference Rooms: 5 rooms
Location: Downtown, Nearest airport is San Francisco International

STANYAN PARK HOTEL

The Stanyan Park Hotel, listed on the National Register of Historic Places, is an elegant, thoroughly restored Victorian Hotel that will take you back to a bygone era of style, grace and comfort. Their thirty-six romantic rooms and suites come in a lovely variety of period decors that will please the eye and provide you with your own quiet little getaway world. All of their rooms are equipped with a color television with cable, direct-dial telephone with data port, and a full, modern bath. The suites all have a full kitchen, dining room and living room.

Although the Stanyan Park Hotel has entirely modern amenities, they offer you touches of past elegance. Please enjoy their complimentary breakfast with croissants, bagels with cream cheese, muffins, fresh juices, fruit, and freshly brewed coffee served every morning. Every evening they offer a tea service with a variety of teas, coffee and cookies.

Stanyan Park Hotel is within walking distance of Golden Gate Park with its De Young Museum, Museum of Natural History, Aquarium, Hall of Flowers, Japanese Tea Garden, and bicycling and horseback riding. The University of California Medical Center, St. Mary's Hospital and the University of San Francisco are within 6 blocks. (Morning shuttle service is available to UC Medical Center.) San Francisco attractions such as Golden Gate Bridge, Chinatown, Pier 39, Ocean Beach and Fisherman's Wharf are easily accessible via public transportation.

Manager John Brocklehurst and staff pride themselves on their attention to the individual needs of all guests. In the heart of busy San Francisco, the Stanyan Park Hotel is a beautiful and quiet getaway.

Address: 750 Stanyan Street, San Francisco 94117.
Phone: 415-751-1000
Fax: 415-668-5454
Email: sales@stanyanpark.com
Web site: http://www.stanyanpark.com
Room Rates: 130–185
Suite Rates: 265–315
No. of Rooms: 30
No. of Suites: 6
Attractions: Golden Gate Park, UC Medical Center, St. Mary's Hospital, Haight-Ashbury, University of San Francisco
Services & Amenities: Cable TV, Telephones, Clock Radio, Hair dryer, Complimentary toiletries, Complimentary breakfast, Tea Service 4-6 p.m.
Restrictions: No pets allowed, 2 rooms are handicapped-equipped, Non-smoking hotel
Concierge: Front desk
Business Facilities: Copiers, Fax
Location: Near Golden Gate Park, 10 miles from SF Airport, 2 miles from downtown SF

HOTEL MAJESTIC

Built in 1902, this magnificient five-story Edwardian structure high atop Cathedral Hill in Pacific Heights was among San Francisco's earliest grand hotels. In the 1980s it was restored to surpass even its original splendor.

The Hotel Majestic's ambiance is one of lush romanticisim, from its Belle Epoque lobby to its individualized accommodations. Most guestrooms have a large hand-painted four-poster canopy bed with a down comforter, feather pillow and fine linens. French Empire and English antiques are blended with custom furniture and soft-hued fabrics. Many rooms have fireplaces, armoires, and clawfoot tubs.

The Avalon Bar, whose specialty is pisco punch, offers happy hour prices. For those who prefer to relax in a health club, guest privileges are extended by the Cathedral Hill Club, which is only half a block away.

A professional multilingual staff with Old World manners will pamper you in the best European tradition at the Hotel Majestic, chosen by San Francisco Focus Magazine and CitySearch readers as one of the city's most romantic hotels.

Address: 1500 Sutter St, San Francisco 94109.
Phone: 415-441-1100 800-869-8966
Fax: 415-673-7331
Email: info@thehotelmajestic.com
Web site: http://www.thehotelmajestic.com
Room Rates: 115–150
Suite Rates: 175–250
No. of Rooms: 58
No. of Suites: 9
Attractions: Boutique shopping on nearby Fillmore and Union Streets, Opera and Symphony 8 blocks away at Civic Center. Japantown with its sushi restaurants and Japanese culture just 4 blocks away.
Services & Amenities: Comp. Cont'l Breakfast each morning, Comp. hors d'ouerves and wine each afternoon, 24hr room service, dinner nightly in Avalon Bar, Valet Parking, newspaper, turndown w/ goodnight cookies, irons/boards, dataport & wireless Internet, hair dryers and dry cleaning.
Restrictions: No pets allowed, 3 rooms handicap equipped
Concierge: 7 a.m.-11 p.m.
Room Service: 24 hours
Restaurant: Complimentary continental breakfast served 7 a.m.–10:30 a.m. each morning. Comp.wine and hors d'ouvres each afternoon from 4 –6 p.m. Bar menu nightly in the Avalon Bar 5pm–9pm.
Bar: The Avalon Bar – 5p.m.–Midnight
Business Facilities: Message center, Admin. assistance, Translators, Copiers, Audio-visual, Teleconferencing
Conference Rooms: 3 rooms, capacity up to 90 ppl maximum
Sports Facilities: Health Facility with indoor pool ½ block away with discount pricing for guests
Location: Pacific Heights section of San Francisco

APPLE FARM INN

The Apple Farm Inn is an experience in traditional hospitality. Guests enjoy what will be remembered as "good old American" virtues: friendliness, cleanliness, honest value, homemade food and cozy rooms. The inn conveys country Victorian charm and provides modern conveniences and all the comforts of a luxury hotel.

The sunny, spacious octagon-shaped lobby is decorated with Ralph Lauren wicker furniture. It allows spectacular views of both the giant sycamores that grace the quiet banks of the San Luis Creek and the beautiful coastal mountains. Each guestroom features a gas-log fireplace and is uniquely appointed with canopy or enamel and brass beds, love seats and wingback chairs.

Service at the Apple Farm Inn is based on the philosophy of warm hospitality. Complimentary wake-up coffee, fresh flowers and plants in every room, three-sheet beds, remote control TVs and breakfast in bed with a newspaper are just some of the ways guests are pampered. Homemade food served with country charm describes the fare at the Apple Farm Restaurant. For dinner, American favorites like chicken and dumplings and turkey with dressing are featured. Fish entrees such as broiled orange roughy and baby salmon are also available. All entrees are served with cornbread and honey butter, and selections for the diet-conscious are available as well. The breakfast menu is extensive (all fresh-baked, of course). The lunch menu includes old favorites such as hot roast beef sandwiches, turkey pot pies, and freshly prepared salads.

The Apple Farm Gift Shop is an experience unto itself. Housed in an exact replica of a two-story country Victorian house, it offers a wide variety of items including decorative accessories, framed prints, glassware, kitchenware, toys, cards and books. The Apple Farm Brand products are the real draw of the shop—apple butter and spreads in canning jars, gift packages in miniature wooden crates, pressed cider and mulled cider spices—are only some of the items. Also worth a visit is The Old Millhouse. This is an operating gristmill with a 14-foot wheel, which harnesses water to power a cider press, grind wheat and make ice cream.

Address: 2015 Monterey St, San Luis Obispo 93401.
Phone: 805-544-2040 800-255-2040
Fax: 805-544-2513
Email: kwykoff@ccaccess.net
Web site: http://www.applefarm.com
Room Rates: 179–349
No. of Rooms: 69
Attractions: Evening carriage rides, Within 10 miles of numerous wineries, 12 miles to fishing village of Morro Bay, 45 miles to Hearst Castle, 2 miles to Performing Arts Center, Millhouse Gift Shop with creekside patio is the perfect spot to relax & enjoy lunch
Services & Amenities: Parking, Gift shop, Fireplaces, Balconies (2 rooms), Cable TV, Radio, Robes, Complimentary toiletries/ newspaper, Complimentary Guest Reception in Garden Room & flower filled patio w/wine, tea and delicious homemade snacks, Massage therapy
Restrictions: No pets allowed, All rooms handicap equipped
Concierge: Front desk
Room Service: Full room service
Restaurant: Apple Farm Restaurant, 7 a.m.-9:30 p.m.
Business Facilities: Message center, Copiers, Audio-visual, Voice mail, Data ports on phones, Meeting space
Conference Rooms: Garden Room & Quilt Room, max capacity, 60 ppl.
Sports Facilities: Outdoor heated swimming pool, Whirlpool, Nearby tennis, Golf, Horseback riding and Sailing
Location: Monterey Street near Highway 101, Close to historic downtown

THE UPHAM HOTEL

In 1871, Boston banker Amasa Lincoln sailed to Santa Barbara and built the Victorian hotel of his dreams with redwood timbers, sweeping verandas, and topped with a cupola. Today, completely restored, The Upham Hotel and Garden Cottages is the oldest continuously operating hotel in Southern California.

Situated on an acre of lovely gardens are seven buildings housing fifty guestrooms and suites, some with gas fireplaces highlight the accommodations all of which include private baths, color cable televisions, radios and telephones. Daily amenities include a deluxe continental breakfast buffet, afternoon refreshments of fruit, wine and cheese, and Oreo cookies with milk in the evening.

Louie's Restaurant, adjoining the hotel lobby, is one of Santa Barbara's finest. This restaurant features innovative California cuisines and serves year-round on the veranda. The Upham is located in the heart of downtown within easy walking distance of restaurants, shops, art galleries and museums.

Address: 1404 De La Vina St, Santa Barbara 93101.
Phone: 805-962-0058 800-727-0876
Fax: 805-963-2825
Email: upham.hotel@verizon.net
Web site: http://www.uphamhotel.com
Room Rates: 165–235
Suite Rates: 245–425
No. of Rooms: 46
No. of Suites: 4
Attractions: Walking distance from restaurants, shops, art galleries and museums
Services & Amenities: Parking, Laundry service, Cable TV, Complimentary newspaper, toiletries, Continental breakfast and afternoon refreshments, Dial up Internet in every room
Restrictions: No pets allowed, 1 room handicap equipped
Concierge: 7 a.m.-11 p.m.
Restaurant: Louie's, Lunch 11:30 a.m.-2 p.m., Dinner 6 p.m.-9 p.m.
Business Facilities: Conference rooms, Copiers, Audio-Visual, Fax, DSL Internet in 2 meeting rooms
Conference Rooms: 3 rooms
Location: Santa Barbara

HARBOR VIEW INN

The Harbor View Inn is Santa Barbara's premier 4-Diamond oceanfront boutique hotel. Located in the heart of Santa Barbara with easy access to the many shops and restaurants that make Santa Barbara so unique. Whether you are planning a romantic getaway, golf vacation or a weekend away with the family, look no further than the Harbor View Inn.

A range of accommodations in our small luxury hotel include 86 spacious, well-appointed guestrooms and 10 luxurious suites. All rooms include a private patio or balcony and added amenities like terry cloth robes, refrigerator, coffeemaker, CD player, personal safe, iron and board, hair dryer and a daily newspaper delivered to your door. Your remote-control TV has cable service with HBO and pay-per-view movies and games. Stay connected with the outside world via complimentary wireless Internet access and voice mail phones.

Eladio's: a Santa Barbara restaurant that both locals and tourists agree has one of the best breakfasts in town. Window tables combine a panoramic view of waterfront palms with an inspired selection of main courses. Offering traditional Italian cuisine for lunch and dinner, Eladio's is sure to please any palate. Breakfast, lunch and dinner are served daily with an extensive regional and international wine list as well as a full bar. We are open every day at 3:30pm for cocktails and light fare.

Address: 28 W. Cabrillo Blvd., Santa Barbara 93101
Phone: 805-963-0780
800-755-0222
Fax: 805-963-7967
Email: sylvie@harborviewinnsb.com
Web site: http://www.harborviewinnsb.com/
Room Rates: 275–425
Suite Rates: 475–795
No. of Rooms: 86
No. of Suites: 10
Credit Cards: Most Credit Cards accepted
Attractions: dining, shopping, golf, kayaking, fishing, whale watching, museums, horseback riding, wine tasting in the Santa Ynez Valley, bike rentals
Services & Amenities: Room service, fitness center, business center, heated pool & jacuzzi, gift shop, conference center, restaurant
Restrictions: 72-hr cancellation policy
Concierge: 24 Hour Service
Room Service: 6:30 am – 9:30 pm
Restaurant: Eladio's – one of the best breakfasts in Santa Barbara. Serving traditional Italian fare for lunch and dinner. Full bar and heated fountain patio.
Bar: Eladio's 7:00 am – 10:00 pm
Business Facilities: Yes
Conference Rooms: Yes
Sports Facilities: Swimming Pool, Whirlpool
Location: Oceanfront/downtown

VINTNERS INN

Set in a 90-acre vineyard, the warm glow of terra cotta walls and tile roofs evoke the mood of southern France, while the California mission detailing reminds you of the Sonoma County wine-making community, redwood forests, and Pacific beaches just minutes away.

The European-style Vintners Inn was patterned after a small village in Provence, with four guest buildings encircling the courtyard fountain plaza. Our newly remodeled rooms are spacious, oversized Provençal French furnishings and fluffly down comforters, featherbeds and pillows enhance your comfort. Rooms feature balconies or patios and some are furnished with wood-burning fireplaces and high beamed ceilings; the bathroom features an oversized oval tub; suites feature jacuzzi tubs and separate showers. The main building leads to tile walkways, a trellis-covered sun deck jacuzzi spa and fitness room. Conference rooms also open to the courtyard and beatifully landscaped areas. The friendly and well-trained staff is ready to assist in the success of your meetings or seminars.

John Ash & Co. is the award-winning and nationally acclaimed restaurant at the Inn, which epitomizes wine-country dining at its best. Chef Jeffrey Madura's commitment to incorporating all that is fresh and wonderful from Sonoma County's wealth of produce, meats, poultry, and seafood is evident in his ever-changing menu. Begin your meal with Crab Cakes or a Warmed Red Cabbage Salad with Laura Chenel's goat cheese, followed by a main entree of Smoked and Grilled Rack of Lamb on a bed of artichoke risotto. Sonoma Chocolate "Stonehenge" finishes your dinner while you savor another Sonoma county wine, perhaps one which began life on the Sauvignon Blanc vines just off your patio.

Spend your day in the Russian River resort area and wind your way to the seal beaches at the coast. Start with an early morning hot-air balloon ride, go antiquing in Sebastopol, or golf one of the local courses. Visit the sprawling orchards and fields by bike, hike the redwood forests, or go boating on Lake Sonoma. You'll be back to Sonoma County and Vintners Inn.

Address: 4350 Barnes Rd, Santa Rosa 95403.

Phone: 707-575-7350 800-421-2584

Fax: 707-575-1426

Email: info@vintnersinn.com

Web site: http://www.vintnersinn.com

Room Rates: 173–268

Suite Rates: 228–308

No. of Rooms: 44

No. of Suites: 6

Attractions: Complimentary wine tasting at Ferrari-Carano Winery, Centrally located amongst luscious Vineyards and Sonoma County Wineries. ½ mile to Luther Burbank Center for the Arts, Antique shopping, Hot air ballooning with pick-up at hotel, Golf, Tennis, Hiking,

Services & Amenities: Valet service, Free Parking, Gifts shop, Fireplaces, Balconies and Patios, DSL access in-rooms, Satellite TV with HBO, VCR's available, radio/CD player, Complimentary local newspaper, Complimentary wine & full breakfast. Weddings on property.

Restrictions: No pets, No checks, 3 rms handicap access, Kids under 6 free w/adults, 2-nite min. Sat stay high season

Concierge: 7 am–11 pm PST

Room Service: Noon–10 p.m.

Restaurant: Award-winning John Ash & Co. restaurant, open 11:30 a.m.-9 p.m. daily, closed Saturday lunch. Sunday Brunch 11 a.m.–2:30p.m.

Bar: Vineyard Lounge at John Ash & Co., 11:30 a.m.-10 p.m.

Business Facilities: Message center, Admin. assistance, Copiers, Audio-Visual, Teleconferencing, Translators w/request

Conference Rooms: 4 rooms, biggest capacity 50 pp

Sports Facilities: Whirlpool, Massage available on-site, fitness equipment and weights on-site. Golf, Hiking, Biking.

THE ALISAL GUEST RANCH AND RESORT

The Alisal Guest Ranch and Resort presides over a 10,000-acre pastoral setting on California's Central Coast. Year-round beauty envelops the 1946-built retreat, whose clusters of one-story cottages sprawl comfortably in the Santa Ynez Valley. The views of the surrounding countryside may be the reason why so many families have made vacations here part of their traditions.

Relaxation and comfort, complemented by attentive service, are high priorities at this resort. Each room boasts a wood-burning fireplace, which guests seem to prefer to television. (TV can be enjoyed in the public rooms when desired.) Two championship 18-hole golf courses will tempt the family duffers, while swimming and other water activities on the Ranch's 96-acre spring-fed lake, tennis, and superb horseback riding over the many trails of this working cattle ranch will keep everyone else busy. Touring the valley is a real treat, too. The town of Solvang is nearby (where fully two thirds of the population is of Danish descent), as well as scenic parks, horse ranches, and wineries.

Business conference facilities are generous, with an array of audio-visual equipment and an accommodating staff in attendance. There are also staff members dedicated to entertaining the children in tow, with day camps classified according to the participants' ages.

Red hues highlight the Ranch Room Restaurant, artfully appointed with western antiques and colorful country quilts adjacent to the spacious picture windows. The fireplace crackles invitingly

while you select a dinner entree by Chef Pascal Gode from the menu, which changes daily. One of tonight's choices may be Fresh Dungeness Crab Cakes with Creole Sauce or Grilled Colorado Lamb Chops with Herbs de Provence and Balsamic Glaze. A featured dessert might be Tulip of Chocolate Mousse with White Chocolate Shavings. Enjoy after-dinner relaxation, conviviality, music and dancing in the Oak Room.

Address: 1054 Alisal Rd, Solvang 93463.
Phone: 805-688-6411 800-425-4725
Fax: 805-688-2510
Email: sales@alisal.com
Web site: http://www.alisal.com
Room Rates: 435–550
Suite Rates: 475–550
No. of Rooms: 36
No. of Suites: 37
Credit Cards: Most Credit Cards accepted
Attractions: Famed Danish village with shops & restaurants, Danish heritage, 21 wineries, Art galleries, Thoroughbred & Arabian horse ranches
Services & Amenities: Parking, Library for adults, Baby-sitting service, Laundry service, Game area, Playground, Gift shop, Ballroom, Music, Summer wine tastings, Vacation packages, Fireplaces, Wet bar, Cable TV, Complimentary newspaper, Refrigerators, coffee makers
Restrictions: 3 rooms with handicap access, No pets allowed
Restaurant: Ranch Room open 7:30 a.m.–10 a.m. and 6 p.m.–9 p.m (breakfast and dinner included in room rate); Sycamore Room open summers (same dining hours as Ranch Room)
Bar: Oak Room, open evenings (live music nightly)
Business Facilities: Message center, Copiers, Audio-Visual, Fax
Conference Rooms: 5 rooms, capacity 150
Sports Facilities: Outdoor pool/spa, Billy Bell-design 18-hole golf & 18-hole River Course, 7 tennis courts, Fishing
Spa Services: In room massages are available through the front office.
Location: Countryside, Solvang 3 mi., Santa Barbara 35 mi.

MACARTHUR PLACE INN & SPA

Once a prestigious address for a 300 acre vineyard and working ranch, the lush 19th century estate has been transformed into a luxurious 64 room hotel and spa.

Each of the Inn's 64 rooms and suites are individually designed with beautiful furnishings, down comforters, custom linens, and original artwork. Ten rooms are located in the property's original residence built in the 1850's. The Inn's 31 luxury suites offer wood-burning fireplaces, king-sized beds, hydrotherapy tubs, wet bars, flat-panel televisions, and DVD players with six-speaker surround sound.

MacArthur Place is set among seven acres of magnificent gardens filled with original sculpture. Flagstone walkways lead guests past hedgerows, fountains and benches to a sparkling swimming pool and whirlpool. The Garden Spa at MacArthur Place offers over 40 different massage, facial and body treatments utilizing the flowers, herbs and plants found in the garden.

Dining is a special experience at MacArthur Place. Located in the Inn's historic barn on the estate, Saddles is the wine country's premier steakhouse and specializes in steaks, chops and fresh seafood. The restaurant also offers a martini bar and award-winning wine list.

MacArthur Place is the perfect place for any company's corporate retreat. There are two suites that are ideal for small board meetings and the Conference Center can accommodate up to 125 people.

Feeling more like a lavish country estate than a hotel, MacArthur Place provides unique special touches to make any stay something memorable.

Address: 29 E. MacArthur St., Sonoma 95476.
Phone: 707-938-2929 800-722-1866
Fax: 707-933-9833
Email: info@macarthurplace.com
Web site: http://www.macarthurplace.com
Room Rates: 225–375
Suite Rates: 299–550
No. of Rooms: 64
No. of Suites: 31
Credit Cards: Visa
Attractions: Walk to historic Sonoma Plaza–shops, galleries, restaurants, California's northernmost mission, 30 wineries nearby. 15 minutes to Napa Valley and 45 minutes to San Francisco.
Services & Amenities: Gift shop, Valet service, Parking, Library, High-speed wireless access, Card/game area, Suites have fireplaces, whirlpool bath and/or balconies, Cable TV, DVD player, Radio, CD player, Comp. wine & cheese each evening, Comp. breakfast buffet
Restrictions: No pets allowed, 3 rooms handicap equipped, Children free in parents rooms
Concierge: 7 a.m.-10 p.m.
Room Service: 7 a.m.-9:30 p.m.
Restaurant: Saddles Restaurant 5:30 p.m.- 9:30 p.m., Martini Bar, Award-Winning Wine List
Bar: Saddles Martini Bar 11:30 a.m.-10 p.m.
Business Facilities: Message center, E-mail, Admin. Asst., Copiers, Teleconferencing, Fax, Modems, Outdoor meeting spaces
Conference Rooms: 6 rooms, capacity 125 (4 boardrooms and two large conference rooms)
Sports Facilities: Outdoor swimming pool, Croquet, Weight training, Giant chess garden & Bicycles
Spa Services: Full-service spa with massages, facials and body treatments

MEADOWOOD NAPA VALLEY

Hike it, bike it, float above it in a hot air balloon. The Napa Valley is meant for exploring. Taste it at over 100 wineries. The Napa Valley is here for you to experience, and Meadowood is in the heart of it all. A private club designed as a playground for the local gentry, this exclusive hotel, nestles among the estates's oak and madrone trees in a private 250-acre valley with a 9-hole golf course, seven tennis courts, two swimming pools, 4.5 miles of hiking trails and a complete Health Spa.

The architecture is New England traditional, as is the lobby with its wainscoting, watercolor prints, huge stone fireplace, antiques, and elegant country feel. Rooms are available on the lawn-view terrace, overlooking the croquet lawns, and in four-suite lodges, which are scattered about the property in a variety of settings. Depending upon your sport preference, you may prefer a lodge poolside, courtside, or on the fairway. Or, for the ultimate in privacy, choose a lodge deep in the woods. The rooms, decorated in soft tones, feature window seats with lots of cushions, beamed cathedral ceilings, remote-control skylights, king-size beds with down comforters, brass lamps, terrycloth robes, heated-tile floors in the bathrooms, plus many other wonderful amenities. Each has a private balcony with a magnificent view of the grounds.

Comfortable and elegant, The Restaurant offers the option of al fresco dining on warm evenings. The menu showcases the natural bounty of the wine country with his California Wine Country cuisine. Meadowood's wine list features a selection from nearly every Napa Valley wine producer.

The resort's executive conference center hosts meetings and special occasions of all kinds in rooms opening onto contiguous outside areas for indoor-outdoor affairs. These facilities, combined with the secluded setting, sporting activities and professional, caring service, make business a pleasure.

Address: 900 Meadowood Lane, St. Helena 94574.
Phone: 707-963-3646 800-458-8080
Fax: 707-963-3532
Email: reservations@meadowood.com
Web site: http://www.meadowood.com
Room Rates: 475–850
Suite Rates: 675–3,850
No. of Rooms: 45
No. of Suites: 40
Attractions: Complete Health Spa, Hiking, Fine dining, Wine Center, Musical events
Services & Amenities: Pro shops, Baby-sitting service, Laundry, TV, Complimentary newspaper, Robes, Musical performances, Complimentary toiletries, Daily newsletter, Complimentary nightly wine reception
Restrictions: No pets allowed, 2 rooms handicap equipped
Concierge: 8 personal concierge
Room Service: 24 hour menu available
Restaurant: The Grill is open 7 a.m.–9:30 p.m.
Bar: In The Grill and The Restaurant Lounge
Business Facilities: Message center, Copiers, Audio/visual, Fax, Computers, High speed Internet access, Teleconferencing
Conference Rooms: 7 rooms, capacity 110
Sports Facilities: State-of-the-art Health Spa, Whirlpool, Outdoor swimming pools, 7 tennis courts, Golf, Hiking trails
Spa Services: Full Service Health Spa and Fitness Equipment
Location: 1 mile east of St. Helena, Equidistant to SFO or Oakland Int'l Airports

THE INN AT SOUTHBRIDGE

Just North of San Francisco, in the center of America's most famous wine growing region, lies the historic town of St. Helena and the charming Inn at Southbridge. Set in a stand of sycamore trees and wrapped around an inviting courtyard inspired by Europe's small town squares, this twenty-one room inn offers a unique destination where guests can savor the pulse and flavor of the Napa Valley.

French doors in the second-floor guestrooms reveal views from the balconies onto the courtyard or the rolling hills beyond. Rich ivory and sage fabrics, cherrywood finishes and white linens reflect the vibrant Napa Valley light. Further touches include fireplaces, down comforters, vaulted ceilings and communications systems for business needs.

The first-floor lobby and living room, with hand-crafted furniture and limestone fireplace, are a congenial gathering place for friends and associates. The adjoining Courtyard Room is the perfect setting for celebrations or business meetings.

Also on the ground floor is Pizzeria Tra Vigne. Pizzeria Tra Vigne offers Mediterranean dishes using superb local ingredients complemented by the wines for which the Napa Valley is world-famous.

Guests at The Inn at Southbridge are a short stroll from Merryvale vineyards with its award winning wines, and St. Helena with its shopping, galleries and Epicurean dining. Other attractions include golf, tennis, croquet, and hiking at nearby Meadowood Resort; winetasting, balloon and glider rides, bicycling, boating and trail rides.

Address: 1020 Main St, St. Helena 94574.
Phone: 707-967-9400 800-520-6800
Fax: 707-967-9486   **Email:** dlynch@innatsouthbridge.com
Web site: http://www.innatsouthbridge.com
Room Rates: 350–525
Suite Rates: 525–625
No. of Rooms: 20
No. of Suites: 1
Credit Cards: Most Credit Cards accepted
Attractions: The Inn is walking distance to St. Helena's fabulous restaurants Tra Vigne, Martini House, Terra, Market, Pinot Blanc, and Cindy's Backstreet Kitchen. Walk to downtown St. Helena for boutique shopping, art galleries, antique shops, and wine tasting.
Services & Amenities: Complimentary continental breakfast, Fireplaces, Juliet balconies, Complimentary in room high speed Internet connection, Cable TV w/DVD, Room service for lunch & dinner, Same day dry cleaning, Wet Bar, Down comforter, and Complimentary toiletries.
Restrictions: No pets allowed, 2 rooms handicap equipped
Concierge: 24 hours
Room Service: 11:30 a.m.-8:30 p.m.
Restaurant: Pizzeria Tra Vigne– 11:30 a.m.–8:30 p.m.
Bar: Pizzeria Tra Vigne, 11:30 a.m.– 8:30 p.m.
Business Facilities: High speed Internet, Fax, Copier, Audio-visual
Conference Rooms: 1 rm, cap 45
Sports Facilities: Privileges at Meadowood Resort, with croquet, tennis and a 9 hole executive golf course.
Spa Services: Hotel guests have complimentary access to Health Spa Napa Valley, a superior day spa offering soothing treatments, a fitness center, eucalyptus steam rooms, an outdoor whirlpool and a lap pool.
Location: 1 block walk to downtown St. Helena

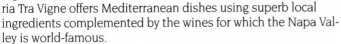

INN ON SUMMER HILL

Nestled between the rolling foothills of the Santa Ynez Mountains and the sparkling Pacific Ocean, just 5 miles south of Santa Barbara, lies the quaint coastal village of Summerland, California—home of the Award Winning Inn on Summer Hill. Experience the warmth and charm of a traditional Bed and Breakfast, New England-style with uncompromising comforts, luxury and service. Exquisitely decorated, each accommodation showcases heirlooms and antiques, original art and a collection of unique furnishings including custom-painted armoires and lounging sofas. In addition to the captivating English country décor, all guestrooms offer spectacular ocean and island views.

Mornings begin with a sumptous gourmet breakfast featuring such delectable entrees as an open faced sandwich of brioche, proscuitto and gruyere topped with poached eggs and served on a bed of mixed baby greens with a mustard wine beurre blanc, or a tiger shrimp and Yukon gold potato omelet served with a vegetable butter nage and garnished with freshly minced chives, or a puffed pastry topped with smoked salmon and eggs, served with a lemon chive butter sauce and garnished with sprigs of freshly snipped dill. A buffet of fresh-baked scones, muffins, coffee cakes, fruit crisp, bread pudding, seasonal fresh fruit, juices, coffees and teas complement the entree of the day.

Afternoon refreshments may include such hors d'oeuvres as caramelized vidalia onions and gorgonzola tarts, roasted vegetable caviar over parmesan palmiers, or gruyere frico tacos stuffed with baby frisee and lemon olive oil vinaigrette, offered with an assortment of beverages including wine.

Before retiring for the night, a mouthwatering homemade dessert is served in the Teapot Room. Some of the guests' favorites include the fresh strawberry and toasted almond tart, cappuccino cheesecake with a chocolate sauce, and a quartet of nuts tart.

Guests enjoy soaking in the sunshine and strolling through Summerland's many antique stores, village shops, as well as walking on the nearby beach or bicycling through the hills and back roads.

Address: 2520 Lillie Ave, Summerland 93067.
Phone: 805-969-9998 800-845-5566
Fax: 805-565-9946
Email: info@innonsummerhill.com
Web site: http://innonsummerhill.com
Room Rates: 215–245
Suite Rate: 325
No. of Rooms: 16
No. of Suites: 1
Attractions: Antique shops, Village shops, Walking on nearby beaches, Bicycling through hills and back roads
Services & Amenities: Ocean & island views, King or queen-size canopy beds, Goosedown comforters, Gas fireplaces, Jacuzzis, Cable TV w/VCR, Stereo/cassette systems with speakers in bedroom & bathroom, Mini refrigerators, Luxurious bathrobes, and more
Restrictions: Two night minimum on weekends, 3 night minimum on holidays, No pets allowed, No smoking
Restaurant: Teapot Room: Gourmet breakfast, afternoon refreshments and homemade desserts included in room rate
Sports Facilities: Outdoor Spa
Location: 5 miles south of Santa Barbara

CAL-A-VIE

Cal-a-Vie has one purpose: to revitalize the body, mind and spirit so that you return home feeling nurtured and inspired!

Nestled away in an expansive and private setting of native landscape just 40 miles north of San Diego, Cal-a-Vie combines the theories of a luxurious European Spa with the American concepts of fitness and nutrition. Your day begins with an invigorating hike or walk, followed by a nourishing breakfast. You are given a schedule of the day's events beginning with fitness classes that include cardio, aerobic, stretch and weight training; sequentially arrange for optimal results. Following a delicious and healthy lunch, you will indulge in some of the finest European Spa and beauty treatments, interspersed with peaceful pursuits such as yoga and stretch. Evenings offer a fabulous meal that is mysteriously low in calories. Afterwards, you can choose to relax in one of our social lounges or have quiet night in the comfort and privacy of your Mediterranean-style villa.

Our 24 guest cottages has been individually decorated to recall the serene luxury of a European country villa: terra cotta roofs, wide wooden plank doors, private terraces with breathtaking views and window boxes full of flowers, and inside, hand-carved furniture covered in floral chintz.

Cal-a-Vie's fitness program, which begins with a personal fitness assessment, is designed to achieve personal goals in stress reduction, relaxation, weight control and toning. Exercise includes hiking on Cal-a-Vie's 200 acres of private trails, aerobic conditioning, pilates, NIA, Cardio Kick Boxing, water sports, and personalized workouts on state-of-the-art equipment. Private Tennis lessons are available on site and golf is available at an adjacent private country club. The day ends with peaceful pursuits such as Yoga, Tai Chi, meditation or a walk in our Labyrinth.

Cal-a-Vie's gourmet spa cuisine is highlighted by herbs and vegetables from the Cal-a-Vie gardens. A weekly cooking class in Cal-a-Vie's kitchen is a fun way for guests to learn the techniques used here.

Cal-a-Vie's beauty therapy program for men and women employs European techniques of thalasso therapy, hydrotherapy and aromatherapy to help restore inner balance and serenity. A week where the day begins with fitness and ends massage, meditation, tai chi or yoga, leaves guests feeling relaxed, content and deliciously pampered.

Address: 2249 Somerset Rd, Vista 92084.
Phone: 760-945-2055
866-SPAHAVEN
Fax: 760-630-0074
Email: info@cal-a-vie.com
Web site: http://www.cal-a-vie.com
Room Rates: 5,395–7 nt, 349
No. of Rooms: 24
Credit Cards: Visa, MasterCard
Attractions: Coastal beaches, San Diego Zoo, Wild Animal Park, Seaworld, Botanical Gardens, Palomar Mountain and Observatory, Temecula Wine Tasting, Stephan Birch Aqurium, Del Mar Fairgrounds and Racetrack
Services & Amenities: 2 guests lounges equiped with satellite TV& VCR. On site boutique. Rooms offer telephones, Radios, Robes, work out clothes, complimentary laundry service of personal items. Complimentary transportation to and from San Diego and Carlsbad Airports.
Restrictions: Minimum age 18 years, 1 room handicap equipped, no pets allowed
Concierge: Yes
Room Service: Yes
Restaurant: "Cal-a-Vie Cuisine" is highlighted by garden fresh herbs and vegetables which are carefully prepared and artfully presented to help revitalize your body while meeting your unique nutritional needs.
Business Facilities: Message center, Copiers, Fax
Conference Rooms: Yes
Sports Facilities: Outdoor pool, Whirlpool, Sauna, Massage, Aerobics, Weight training, One har-tru tennis court, Privil
Spa Services: Facials Hair and Scalp Hand and Foot Massage Ayurvedic Mud Scrub Thalassotherapy Hot Stone Massage Hydrotherapy Aromatherapy Massage Reflexology Magnet Treatment Seaweed Wraps
Location: Semi-rural Vista/ Vistaarea, 40 miles from San Diego

POSTE MONTANE LODGE

With all the warmth and personality of a traditional European Inn, the Poste Montane Lodge has brought Old World charm to the heart of Beaver Creek, Colorado. Beaver Creek Resort is smaller, quieter and more refined than other local ski resorts. It is where you go when you want to get away from it all-but still have it all. The resort is known as a snow rider's paradise, and it keeps that reputation with the most advanced grooming equipment available. Beaver Creek's 1,625 acres also include some of the steepest inbounds terrain located in Colorado.

The resort is no longer a winter destination only. Visitors to Beaver Creek can stroll down quaint walkways that are conveniently linked by escalators to lead you through the village. In the village, you will find a year-round outdoor ice-skating rink, sidewalk cafes and restaurants, colorful boutiques and galleries. The summer season also includes numerous festivals and weekly rodeo performances.

Considered by many to be the jewel of Beaver Creek, the Poste Montane Lodge presides over the pedestrian village in a place of honor. Our lobby doors open onto the village plaza. Next door, the Vilar Center for the Performing Arts provides a world-class calendar of events to enrich your evenings. Did we mention the mountain? The ski lifts are just a stone's throw away.

After a long day on the slopes or a full day of golf, it's comforting to know that a jacuzzi, steam room and sauna await you at the Poste Montane Lodge.

For your convenience, a full-service sporting goods store and a restaurant are located within the Poste Montane Lodge. Keep in mind that our concierge can help you arrange a variety of activities, including your next stay at the Poste Montane. As many of our guests have already realized, we hope that, you too, will become a lifetime "friend of the Poste Montane Lodge."

Address: P.O. Box 5480, Beaver Creek 81620.
Phone: 970.845.7500 1.800.497.9238
Fax: 970.845.5012
Email: pmlodge@eastwestresorts.com
Web site: http://www.postemontane.com
Room Rates: 130–495
Suite Rates: 140–1,225
No. of Rooms: 7
No. of Suites: 17
Attractions: Beaver Creek and Vail Ski Areas, Snowshoeing, Fly Fishing, Biking, Hiking, Golfing, Horseback Riding, Rafting, Rock Climbing, Jeep Tours, The Vilar Center for the Arts, Ford Amphitheater, Glenwood Springs
Services & Amenities: Complimentary Deluxe Continental Breakfast, Heated Underground Parking, Park Hyatt Allegria Spa Health Club Privileges, On-Site Spa, Steam Room, Sauna, and Ski Locker Room, Daily Housekeeping Service, Concierge Services
Restrictions: No Pets Allowed, No Smoking Permitted in the Lodge
Concierge: On-site Staff
Restaurant: The Beaver Creek Village offers a number of world-class restaurants, which are located only steps from the property.
Business Facilities: Business Center with Internet access, Voicemail, Wireless Internet access, Copier, Fax
Sports Facilities: Park Hyatt Allegria Spa Health Club Privileges, Local Ski and Golf Areas
Spa Services: The Park Hyatt Allegria Spa offers full spa services. In room massages are also available.
Location: The Heart of Beaver Creek Village, Colorado

BURNSLEY ALL SUITE HOTEL

Gracious and inviting, the Burnsley All Suite Hotel offers the charming intimacy of a European-style inn—uniquely set in the heart of downtown Denver, Colorado. Rich in history and luxury, each suite of this distinct hotel offers an environment of comfortable elegance. The 17-story Burnsley Hotel was originally built in 1963 and was converted into an all-suite hotel and famous jazz club shortly thereafter. Joy and Franklin Burns bought the hotel in 1969 from an investment group that included singer Ella Fitzgerald and actor Kirk Douglas. In 1983 the hotel was remodeled into a small European Boutique Hotel that characterizes the hotel it is today. The drawing-room style, two-story lobby features shimmering brass, polished Italian marble, oriental antiques and original art, with richly textured furnishings.

Each of the 80 suites are equipped with a living-dining room, fully equipped kitchen and furnished balconies overlooking downtown and the mountains. All suites have been renovated in rich hunter greens, jewel tones of deep burgundys and teals, accenting taupe backgrounds.

Accommodating business meetings and social affairs are the Burnsley's specialties. The Director's Room is adjacent to a beautiful bar and an outdoor private patio, and the richly decorated Boardroom with leather chairs make either of these rooms the perfect meeting place or elegant host to almost any intimate social event.

The Burnsley offers free parking and a complimentary local shuttle service anywhere downtown and in the Cherry Creek shopping area. Each suite is wired with free high speed Internet access. There is a complimentary computer and printer for guest use on the Mezzanine level. Live jazz is popular in the newly renovated lounge on Thursday through Saturday evenings and the newly renovated dining room is open for breakfast, lunch, and dinner.

The Burnsley is conveniently located within a mile of the new Colorado Convention Center and all Denver cultural venues. With its large suites and comfortable furnishings, it is the perfect choice for a weekend getaway, an important business trip, long-term corporate housing, or other extended stays.

Address: 1000 Grant Street, Denver 80203.
Phone: 303-830-1000 800-231-3915
Fax: 303-830-7676
Email: burnsley@rdamanagement.com
Web site: http://www.burnsley.com
Suite Rates: 129–229
No. of Suites: 80
Credit Cards: Most Credit Cards accepted
Attractions: Cultural Museums, State Capitol, 6 Flags Elitch Gardens, Pepsi Center for Nuggets & Avalanche, Invesco Field for Broncos, Coors Field for Colorado Rockies, Shopping at 16th Street mall & Cherry Creek, Dever Zoo, Natural History Museum, Bike paths
Services & Amenities: * Spacious 700 sq ft suites * Free parking * Free van service 5 mile radius (7A-11P)* Private balconies * Free HSIA * Restaurant and Jazz lounge * Close to Colorado Convention Center & Denver Cultural Venues * Reduced Corporate housing for extended stays
Concierge: 24 hours
Room Service: 6:30 a.m.–10:30 p.m.
Restaurant: Breakfast Mon–Fri 6:30am–10am Sat–Sun 7am–11am Lunch Mon–Fri 11:30am–2pm Dinner Sun–Thu 5:30pm–9pm Fri–Sat 5:30pm–10pm
Bar: 11 a.m.-11 p.m.–Weekdays, 5-11 p.m.–Weekends
Business Facilities: Guest computer, Data ports
Conference Rooms: 2 rooms, capacity 12-80
Sports Facilities: Seasonal outdoor swimming pool.
Location: The Burnsley Hotel borders downtown Denver in an historic residential area

CASTLE MARNE A LUXURY URBAN INN

Come fall under the spell of one of Denver's grandest historic mansions. Built in 1889, Castle Marne is considered by many to be the finest example of the work of "America's most eclectic architect," William Lang (designer of Unsinkable Molly Brown's house). Its history glows through the hand-rubbed woods, the renowned circular stained glass "Peacock Window," and original ornate fireplaces.

Your stay at Castle Marne combines Old World elegance and Victorian charm with modern-day convenience and comfort. Each guestroom is a unique experience in pampered luxury. Carefully chosen furnishings bring together authentic period antiques, family heirlooms, and exacting reproductions to create the mood of long-ago charm and romance. The parlor invites you to spend some quiet time nestled with a good book. A romantic interlude, whether a weekend getaway or honeymoon, will be truly unforget-table when spent in one of the luxury suites complete with jetted whirlpool tub.

In the heart of one of Denver's most historic neighborhoods, the inn is just minutes from many fine restaurants, plus the city's finest cultural, shopping and sightseeing attractions.

Awake to the spicy aroma of brewing Marne-blend coffee, homemade breads and muffins. Linger over a complete gourmet breakfast in the original cherry-paneled Formal Dining Room.

Join other guests from 4:30–6 p.m. for Afternoon Tea served in the Parlor, with freshly baked scones, shortbread, lemon curd, raspberry butter and a plenitude of sweets and savory treats. Browse in the library, enjoy the game room, work on the jigsaw puzzle or savor the beauty of a Colorado sunset. Relax your mind and spirit, soak up history—or just soak in a hot tub.

Address: 1572 Race St, Denver 80206
Phone: 303-331-0621
800-92-MARNE
Fax: 303-331-0623
Email: jim@castlemarne.com
Web site: http://www.castlemarne.com
Room Rates: 105–255
Suite Rates: 245
No. of Rooms 9
No. of Suites: 2
Credit Cards: Visa
Attractions: Denver Zoo, Museum Natural History, IMAX Theater, Gates Planetarium, Denver Botanic Gardens, Historic Molly Brown Hse, Denver Art Museum, US Mint, Colorado History Museum, Cherry Creek Shopping Ctr, Downtown 16th Street Mall, Ocean's Journey Aquarium
Services & Amenities: Excellent dining nearby, Gift shop, Card/game area, Comp. newspaper, In-room phones, Radios, Air conditioning, Heat control, Garden, Comp. toiletries, Whirlpool baths, 2 Suites with Jacuzzis for two, 3 rooms with private balconiesw/hot tubs
Restrictions: No pets allowed, Children over 10 welcome
Concierge: Daily
Restaurant: Formal Dining Room – by reservations only complimentary Gourmet Breakfast, Complimentary Afternoon Tea in the Parlor. Inquire about private 6-course romantic dinners, served in formal dining rm.
Business Facilities: Fully-equipped guest office with computer, phone and fax, Message center, Copiers, Audio-visual
Conference Rooms: 1 room, capacity 12
Sports Facilities: Nearby City Park with running paths, Tennis courts, Public golf course
Location: Downtown Wyman Historic District

Boardwalk Plaza Hotel, *Rehoboth Beach, DE* PAGE 60

Lodge and Club At Ponte Vedra Beach, *Ponte Vedra Beach, FL* PAGE 72

ROCHESTER HOTEL

In the tradition of the Old West, The Rochester Hotel will transport guests back to the days of gunslingers and railroad bandits amid Durango's scenic downtown setting.

Built in 1892 and restored in 1994, The Rochester is a beautiful two-story brick Victorian. The many antiques displayed throughout the hotel and its historical surroundings complement the Western motif. During their stay at The Rochester, guests will delight in picturesque views of the mountains, courtyard, and downtown. Each of the luxury guestrooms is uniquely decorated in style true to the Old West and inspired by the many movies filmed in the Four Corners area. Each of the rooms has high ceilings and a private bath. The bathrooms offer either a shower or bath combo and are spacious with stunning granite tile floors. The Rochester prides itself on the King Suite, where guests will enjoy a master bedroom with a king-size bed, a large bath with Jacuzzi, living room, desk, cable TV, and lovely antiques.

Activities abound at The Rochester, where guests are within walking distance of the railroad and many fine restaurants and shops. Nearby parks also offer hiking and biking trails, in addition to exciting river rafting. In the courtyard or on the patio of the hotel guests will find a delightful spot to relax and enjoy the beauty of the area after a day in town.

A delicious breakfast such as chive potato cakes, spinach-and-cheese-stuffed croissants, and scrumptious baked goods can be enjoyed in the landscaped courtyard, old-fashioned train car, or on the patio where guests will enjoy their meal along with the beautiful view.

At The Rochester Hotel, guests will leave behind their everyday lives and step into the historical world of the Old West where every moment is filled with adventure.

Address: 726 E. 2nd Avenue, Durango 81301.
Phone: 970-385-1920 800-664-1920
Fax: 970-385-1967
Email: stay@rochesterhotel.com
Web site: http://www.rochesterhotel.com
Room Rates: 109–189
Suite Rates: 159–320
No. of Rooms: 25
No. of Suites: 7
Attractions: Within walking distance to Durango and Silverton Narrow Gauge RR, Many fine restaurants, shops, Parks nearby, Hiking trails, Biking trails, River rafting
Services & Amenities: Off-street parking, Valet, Gift shop, TV lounge, Card or game area, Baby-sitting service can be arranged, Some kitchens, Some fireplaces, Patio/gardens, Cable TV, Telephones, Clock radios, Individual climate controls, Robes, Complimentary toiletries
Restrictions: Children welcome at $20 per night, Pets accepted at $20 per night, 1 room handicap equipped
Concierge: Noon-5 p.m.
Restaurant: Breakfast served in the Rochester Lobby, 7-9 a.m.
Business Facilities: Wireless Internet, Message center, E-mail, Copiers, Fax, Modems
Conference Rooms: 3 rooms, capacity 10-20
Sports Facilities: 19 miles to snow skiing
Location: Historic downtown, Historic District

STRATER HOTEL

Authentic Victorian elegance with a hint of the Wild West characterize this four-story red brick beauty, as they have since this southwestern Colorado landmark first opened its doors over a century ago. Conveniently located in the heart of downtown Durango, the Strater Hotel has plenty to offer both inside and out. Impressive craftsmanship is a signature of the Strater, which displays a facade of elaborately carved sandstone sills and cornices. Housing the world's largest collection of American Victorian walnut antiques, the Strater faithfully reflects this bygone era of history in comfortable detail.

Walking into the lobby is like taking a trip to yesteryear. One is greeted with an array of antiques including marble-topped tables, ornate mahogany and cherry woodwork, stained and leaded glass, and brass and crystal chandeliers. The guestrooms are all as lush as they are unique. Custom-made rich velvet draperies, hand-stenciled wallpapers, and ornate bed art compliment the other unique pieces of the period in any given room. Constant renovations make this hotel a class act. Meeting and Banquet facilities cater to as many as 150 guests. But the true meeting place, for guests and locals alike, is the Diamond Belle Saloon, which features live honky-tonk piano nightly and saloon girls in traditional costume—traditional, that is, for Old West saloon girls. The Office martini bar is also located within the hotel boasting of rich woods and fine leather furniture. Guests can enjoy turn-of-the-century melodrama and vaudeville in the Diamond Circle Theatre during the summer months.

Durango is located in the Four Corners region (in the heart of Anasazi-land) and ringed by mountains, offering a nice variety of outdoor activities. The Strater Hotel is centrally located in downtown Durango and surrounded by galleries and nightspots. It's also just two blocks from the famous Durango-Silverton Narrow Gauge Train Station, which can take you on an unforgettable day-long excursion into the heart of the rugged San Juan Mountains. Fabulous skiing is available at Durango Mountain Resort Ski Area just 25 miles away, and Mesa Verde National Park is less than an hour away. Perhaps you'd rather try your luck at the Sky Ute Casino, only 20 minutes away. Durango is served by air service from Denver and Phoenix.

Address: 699 Main Ave, PO Drawer E, Durango 81301.
Phone: 970-247-4431 800-247-4431
Fax: 970-259-2208
Email: reservations@strater.com
Web site: http://www.strater.com
Room Rates: 69–285
No. of Rooms: 93
Credit Cards: Most Credit Cards accepted
Attractions: Galleries, Night spots within walking distance, Sky Ute Casino, Durango/Silverton narrow-gauge train, Mesa Verde National Park, Million Dollar Highway, Durango Mountain Resort ski area, White Water Rafting, Hiking, Mountain Biking, Fishing and Golf.
Services & Amenities: Valet service, Free parking, Jacuzzi, Cable TV, Diamond Circle Theatre, Car hire, Radio, Individual heat and air-conditioning, Complimentary toiletries
Restrictions: No pets allowed, Children welcome
Restaurant: Complimentary Continental Breakfast available daily. Lunch is served daily from 11am-2pm in the Diamond Belle Saloon Dinner is offered just two doors down at the Mahogany Grille.
Bar: Diamond Belle Saloon,11 a.m.-closing, The Office martini bar 4pm-closing
Business Facilities: Copiers, Audio-visual, Teleconferencing, Fax, Modems, Admin. assistance
Conference Rooms: 5 rooms, capacity 150
Sports Facilities: Three major golf courses, Skiing, Horseback riding, Rafting, Hiking, Fishing, Ballooning, Kayaking,
Location: Historic downtown Durango, Four Corners area–In the heart of Anasazi land

THE FABULOUS VAILGLO LODGE

The Fabulous Vailglo Lodge opened in 1973. The lodge is run like a private hotel. The hotel is locked every night when the front desk closes, and every guest is given a key to the front door. It is very much like a Swiss inn with exquisite appointments.

White ash paneling and custom-made white ash furniture dominate the décor of this contemporary resort. The lobby has accents of pink Brazilian Juparana granite on the tabletops and fireplace. Complimentary coffee, tea, and Danish cookies are served all day by the fire, welcoming those who have just arrived or just returned from the slopes. The top floor of the hotel is paramount level for selected clientele.

The hotel is adjacent to the slopes, and is also within walking distance of Vail's gourmet restaurants and famous shopping.

In order to preserve its treasured quietude, The Fabulous Vailglo Lodge does not accept groups. The atmosphere is cozy, intimate, relaxed, and very quiet. The hotel caters to a very select clientele, which makes it all the more attractive for the individual or couple seeking a peaceful retreat. The Vailglo is, without question, one of the most unique lodging properties in Vail.

Address: 701 W Lionshead Circle, Vail 81657.
Phone: 970-476-5506 800-541-8245
Fax: 970-476-3926
Email: craigholzf@aol.com
Web site: http://www.vailglolodge.com
Room Rates: 125–280
No. of Rooms: 34
Attractions: Ski-slopes adjacent to hotel, Famous restaurants and shopping within walking distance
Services & Amenities: Valet service, Parking, Free guest laundry, Cable TV, Radio, Individual heat control, In-room safes, Refrigerators, Hair dryers, Robes, Complimentary toiletries and newspaper
Restrictions: No pets allowed, Children under 6 free with parents
Sports Facilities: Outdoor swimming pool, Whirlpool, Skiing
Location: Downtown, Nearest airport is Denver International

HOMESTEAD INN

Critically acclaimed for his "flawless French food" Chef Thomas Henkelmann's contemporary French cuisine is inspired by his classical French training with the renowned Auberge d'ill in Alsace and Aubergine in Munich, his German background and time spent in New York City as Executive Chef of Maurice restaurant at Le Parker Meridien.

The renowned Relais Gourmands 4 star restaurant Thomas Henkelmann and Relais & Chateaux hotel Homestead Inn are nestled on a beautiful piece of land jutting into Long Island Sound aptly named Belle Haven. Grand Victorian homes and modern architectural achievements hug its stand like a sun kissed string of pearls.

It is said the difference between real life and the movies is that real life has bad lighting and no score. All of that changes as one enters the grounds of Thomas Henkelmann and Homestead Inn in Greenwich, CT. Purchased in 1997 by Theresa and Thomas Henkelmann as a showcase for Thomas Henkelmann's incredible cuisine, the existing hotel was a logical extension and a blank canvas for Theresa's design expertise.

Integrating the architecture that defers to the hotel's history and individuality, the Henkelmanns' purposeful and sensitive renovation is a salute to the past while resolutely embracing the new and the now. Art and artifacts from around the globe are seamlessly woven into each room and suite's décor. European in flavor, the hotel speaks to both the artist and the bon vivant. Cement tiles designed and colored by French artist Denis Colomb add tactile appeal to the heated bathroom floors. Each room differs in style and design and all have sumptuous amenities intended to coddle.

A design thread throughout the hotel is the inspired use of color. Brave and bold, it effortlessly blends the old world with the new. Contemporary artists' paintings and forged iron and bronze sculpture reminiscent of Garouste and Bonetti characterize the blend. Artisans' craftworks are called upon to perform their intended function.

The charming gardens, exquisite individually designed and decorated guestrooms, knowledgeable and caring staff and the unparalleled cuisine of Master Chef Thomas Henkelmann creates an experience to treasure for a lifetime.

Address: 420 Field Point Rd, Greenwich 6830.
Phone: 203-869-7500
Fax: 203-869-7502
Email: events@homesteadinn.com
Web site: http://www.homesteadinn.com
Room Rates: 250–395
Suite Rates: 495
No. of Rooms: 18
No. of Suites: 7
Credit Cards: Most Credit Cards accepted
Attractions: New York City–25 miles, Bruce Museum, Luxury Boutique Shopping, World renown restaurant Thomas Henkelmann, Long Island Sound, Financial Centers,
Services & Amenities: Limousine service available upon request, Fili d'oro linens, Originial artwork, Plush robes, Hair dryers, Air conditioning, Cable TV & VCR, Ethernet modem & voicemail, AM/FM clock radio, Newspapers delivered, Bulgari amenities
Restrictions: No Pets, Children under 12 not recommended
Concierge: 24 hour
Room Service: Yes
Restaurant: Thomas Henkelmann-5 Star Diamond, 4 Star Mobil, Relais Gourmands A la carte breakfast, lunch and dinner available. Open Sundays December. Open Thanksgiving, Christmas, Easter
Bar: Yes
Business Facilities: Audio-visual equipment available upon request, complete dining and catering facilities
Conference Rooms: Cottage Conference Center, capacity 20–Breakout room, capa
Sports Facilities: Large park, beach, tennis and golf nearby
Spa Services: In room spa services available
Location: Belle Haven on Long Island Sound

THE INN AT MONTCHANIN VILLAGE

The Inn at Montchanin Village, once a part of Winterthur Museum Estate, exists in a wonderful little world of its own. A world in which time has seemingly stood still. Into this rural vignette are cleverly woven 28 guestrooms and suites appointed with period and reproduction furniture, marble baths and every modern convenience and amenities for the sophisticated traveller.

The unique walkways flow through the historic walled gardens, creating a sense of unity throughout the entire hamlet. The seasonal colors complemented by the use of native plantings, capture the very essence of the Brandywine Valley and its surrounding world-class gardens.

Of the eleven carefully restored buildings dated from 1799–1910, nine were once houses for the workers of the Dupont black powder mills. The original blacksmith's shop is now Krazy Kat's Restaurant. The Dilwyne Barn houses Guest Services and a lounge with an honor bar.

A member of Historic Hotels of America, the Inn is listed on the National Register of Historic Places. Krazy Kat's Restaurant is described as "whimsical dining room with an eclectic menu and an award-winning wine list." Be sure to make a dinner reservation when booking your room.

Address: Rt 100 & Kirk Rd, PO Box 130, Montchanin 19710.
Phone: 302-888-2133
800-COWBIRD
Fax: 302-888-0389
Email: inn@montchanin.com
Web site: http://montchanin.com
Room Rates: 160
Suite Rates: 190–375
No. of Rooms: 28
No. of Suites: 6
Attractions: MUSEUMS: Winterthur Museum & Gardens, Hagley Museum & Gardens, Longwood Gardens, BrandyWine River Museum, Delaware Art Museum, Nemours Gardens & Museum, Delaware Museum of Natural History, Rockwood Museum.
Services & Amenities: Member of Small Luxury Hotels and Historic Hotels of America. All rooms have private marble-baths,kitchenette with refrigerator,ice-maker,coffee-maker and microwave. Complimentary coffee,tea, bottled water and sodas.Free/daily N.Y. times. Daily turndown service.
Restrictions: All buildings are non-smoking, No pets allowed
Room Service: 8 a.m.-9 p.m.
Restaurant: Krazy Kat's, dress code: business casual. *Breakfast*: weekdays, 7-10.am. weekend, 8-11am.
Lunch: Mon-Fri only, 11.30-2pm.
Dinner: Mon-Sun 5.30-9.30pm.
Private dining-rooms available.
Bar: Honor Bar
Business Facilities: Message Center, Copiers, Audio-visual, Fax, Modems, Front desk will assist with all needs
Conference Rooms: 2 rooms, capacity 16 & 35
Sports Facilities: Tennis courts nearby
Spa Services: Spa services available in near-by-area
Location: Heart of Brandywine Valley, 4 miles Wilmington

BOARDWALK PLAZA HOTEL

Step back in time, just steps from the sand—t the oceanfront, full-service Boardwalk Plaza Hotel. The Boardwalk Plaza Hotel has offered the Delaware seaside's only oceanfront, AAA Four Diamond Award-Winning hospitality for more than a decade. Proudly standing over Rehoboth Beach's clean white sand beach and mile-long boardwalk, the fanciful pink-and-white gingerbread facade brings to mind the quainter and gentler Victorian era—yet only hints at the charms to be found inside—Delightful accommodations — an oceanfront restaurant — a soothing spa pool — Four Diamond service. From the doorman who greets you beneath the antique wrought iron canopy to the attentive desk staff that welcomes you in the antiques-filled lobby parlor, the Boardwalk Plaza's staff stands ready to offer you exceptional service and a truly unique beach experience.

Reached via indoor glass elevator and entered from quiet interior hallways, guest accommodations offer the combination of Victorian elegance and thoughtful modern amenities. A wide selection of accommodations is available, each tastefully decorated in the Grand Victorian style—from suites with private balconies to deluxe accommodations which team king-size or poster beds with whirlpool bathtubs. Charming and comfortable Victorian-reproduction furnishings fashionably combine with modern luxuries such as ultrafast T1 Internet access. Accommodations on the adults-only, keyed-access Concierge Level are enhanced by genteel extras such as evening turndown service, plush bathrobes, daily newspaper delivery, morning coffee in the garden (seasonal), a later checkout time and use of the private rooftop sundeck and spa.

All guests are welcome to enjoy a relaxing soak in the heated indoor-outdoor spa pool, located just off the lobby. Little ones are welcome by day; in the evening the lights are lowered and the spa jets activated for adults-only "quiet time." Spa-side drinks and refreshments are available through Victoria's, the Boardwalk Plaza's signature restaurant.

Address: 2 Olive Ave at the Boardwalk, Rehoboth Beach 19971.
Phone: 302-227-7169
800-33-BEACH
Fax: 302-227-0561
Email: bph@boardwalkplaza.com
Web site: http://www.boardwalkplaza.com
Room Rates: 70–359
Suite Rates: 120–499
No. of Rooms: 33
No. of Suites: 51
Credit Cards: Most Credit Cards accepted
Attractions: Beautiful beach and mile-long boardwalk, tax-free shopping at in-town boutiques, antiques shoppes and over 140 outlet stores.
Services & Amenities: 4 Diamond Service! Valet parking (complimentary), bellhops, room service, daily housekeeping, fitness room. Cable TV, VCR & DVD, dual-line telephone, T1 Internet, radio, climate control, in-room coffee; most rooms with balconies, ocean and beach views.
Restrictions: Non-smoking property. Please, no pets. Minimum stays may apply in season.
Concierge: In-Suite Service
Room Service: Full Menu, 7a.m–10 p.m
Restaurant: Victoria's Restaurant, 7 a.m.-10 p.m. daily; private parties for up to 110 by prior arrangement.
Bar: The Plaza Pub–serving drinks and light fare daily.
Business Facilities: State-of-the-art AV, Wireless T1 Internet, Copier, Fax, Teleconferencing
Conference Rooms: 4 rooms, capacity up to 150 , fully catered by Victoria's.
Sports Facilities: Beach on site; Golf, Tennis and Watersports nearby.
Spa Services: Privately arranged, en-suite or at guest's choice of local partner spas.
Location: Oceanfront, on the boardwalk. Near downtown, 3 blocks north Rehoboth Ave.

THE BELLMOOR

Introducing a new standard of excellence in Rehoboth Beach lodging accommodations, The Bellmoor is a family owned and managed stylish inn offering guests the finest in modern amenities while maintaining an aura of tradition and unsurpassed comfort.

The new 78 room inn provides a wide range of extraordinary accommodations from garden rooms to suites in a warm, residential setting. The adults-only Club Level Suites offer unprecedented luxury and privacy, with exclusive elevator access, fireplaces, balconies, wet bar, marble baths and a private library.

The Garden Room is the perfect place to start the day with a complimentary hearty country breakfast overlooking the inn's gardens. Large windows and French doors allow the sun to stream in, bathing the room in a welcome glow. Afternoon refreshments daily. For Club Level Suites, there are drinks and snacks all day.

Recent Awards: Chosen as a 2005 "Dream Weekend" destination by *The Washingtonian* magazine *Delaware Today* magazine named The Bellmoor "Best New Hotel in Delaware." "The Bellmoor offers more residential amenities than you have ever experienced." It is "like vacationing at the seaside manor of a longtime friend." *Southern Living*—"spectacular coastal vacation that won't break your budget."

Address: 6 Christian St, Rehoboth Beach 19971.
Phone: 302-227-5800 800-425-2355
Fax: 302-227-0323
Email: info@thebellmoor.com
Web site: www.thebellmoor.com
Room Rates: 105–395
Suite Rates: 150–495
No. of Rooms: 55
No. of Suites: 23
Credit Cards: Most cards accepted
Attractions: Walk to fabulous boutique shopping, fine dining restaurants and the beach. Golf, tennis, fishing, sailing, birding, antiquing, seashore parks, and 160 outlet stores are nearby.
Services & Amenities: On-site parking, bellman, gift shop, Day Spa, library, guest laundry, comp. newspapers. All rooms have refrigerator, coffee maker, 2-line phone, cable TV & radio, high speed Internet access; wireless Internet in meeting rooms, lobby, sun room and gardens.
Restrictions: Entire property non-smoking, No pets allowed, Children under 6 free, 4 rooms handicap equipped
Concierge: 8 a.m.-8 p.m.
Restaurant: Garden Room–Hearty country breakfast 7:30 a.m.–10:30 am, Afternoon refreshments. Club level–snacks & drinks all day in private library.
Business Facilities: Complete business and conference center, full time conference coordinator, 24 hour copy & fax
Conference Rooms: 5 rooms, capacity 10 -110
Sports Facilities: 2 outdoor pools, hot tub (adults only), full service Day Spa (6 rooms), Massage, Fitness room
Spa Services: Experience total relaxation in The Spa at The Bellmoor, offering over 40 services, including massage, facials, body treatments, nail care, and waxing, to rejuvenate your body and spirit.
Location: 2 blocks from the beach in South Rehoboth

WYNDHAM GRAND BAY HOTEL

If the ultimate in style and a "jet set" social scene appeal to you, you will love the Wyndham Grand Bay.

Guest balconies at the Wyndham Grand Bay view Biscayne Bay or Downtown Miami from the fashionable Coconut Grove area of Miami, Florida. Convenient for sailing on the bay and shopping the designer boutiques of Bal Harbour, the hotel also takes full advantage of Miami's year-round cultural offerings.

The royal treatment begins at check-in, accompanied by fresh Florida orange juice in the terra cotta floored lobby and comfortable designer furniture in the rooms. Perhaps best of all, every room and suite has floor-to-ceiling windows, which open to a spacious balcony.

The comforts of home include fluffy bathrobes, mini-bars, TVs with VCRs, stereo systems with CD and tape players, safes, personal fax machines, and multilingual voice mail. Bathrooms provide hair dryers, custom toiletries, and two telephone extensions. The personal luxuries are hard to beat.

The Grand Bay's public dining pleasures are not to be missed. The world-famous BICE Restaurant is nestled on the mezzanine level overlooking the garden terraces. The BICE offers the finest Italian fare available in Miami. For a light lunch and cocktails, guests gather at the Poolside Bar & Grill. For Mozart, Brahms, and Chopin and an updated afternoon tea, guests may visit the Lobby Terrace, as inviting as an English club with its deep leather sofas and chairs. After hours, guests may relax with live music at The Bar, which rounds out another club-like atmosphere with a light menu, wine and cocktails.

Guests will truly enjoy the Grand Bay's sophisticated blend of service, discretion, luxury, style and class.

Address: 2669 S. Bayshore Dr, Miami, Coconut Grove 33133
Phone: 305-858-9600
800-GRANBAY
Fax: 305-858-1532
Web site: http://www.wyndham.com/hotels/MIAGB/main.wnt
Room Rates: 275–365
Suite Rates: 400–1500
No. of Rooms 177
No. of Suites: 46
Attractions: Shopping, Vizcaya, Key Biscayne, Downtown Miami, Seaquarium, Planet Ocean, Mayfair shops, Cocowalk
Services & Amenities: Valet service and parking, Car hire, Sundry boutique, Beauty salon, Currency exchange, Laundry service, Baby-sitting service, Cable TV, Radio, Robes, Complimentary newspaper & toiletries
Restrictions: No pets allowed
Concierge: 24 hours
Room Service: 24 hours
Restaurant: BICE, 7 a.m.-3 p.m., 6:30 p.m.-11 p.m., Dress code
Bar: The Bar
Business Facilities: Full-scale business center
Conference Rooms: 7 rooms, capacity 20-400
Sports Facilities: Outdoor swimming pool, Exercise room with Sauna, Massage, Weight training, Access to water sports
Location: Coconut Grove, Fifteen minutes from airport, Across from Biscayne Bay

THE PILLARS AT NEW RIVER SOUND

One block from Fort Lauderdale Beach on the Intracoastal Waterway is the lush tropical grounds of The Pillars at New River Sound.

The décor is inspired by a Jamaican plantation style, which a lovely mix of classic and cane, with beautiful fabrics and colors. The 23 guestrooms and suites each contain a custom made designer bed with multiple pillows, elegant bedspreads, and high thread count sheets. The color schemes are variations of tropical shades of green, gold and deep red. The favorite suite is the Intracoastal Suite, situated by the water. It has a Jacuzzi tub and magnificent views of the Waterway from the well-appointed sitting area.

Should you wish to venture from the private paradise of The Pillars, Fort Lauderdale beach has a palm-lined promenade, lovely outdoor cafes and shops overlooking the beach. Las Olas Boulevard beckons with world-class shopping, elegant dining and unforgettable nightlife.

It feels like a beautiful, comfortable home. Its size makes guests feel that the service, the ambiance and the staff are all there just to accommodate them.

Address: 111 North Birch Road, Fort Lauderdale 33304.
Phone: 954-467-9639 800-800-7666
Fax: 954-763-2845
Email: guestservices@pillarshotel.com
Web site: http://www.pillarshotel.com
Room Rates: 205–265
Suite Rates: 295–455
No. of Rooms: 18
No. of Suites: 5
Attractions: Las Olas shops, restaurants, and boutique; Riverfront on the New River - restaurants, entertainment, shops, Air & Sea Show, Ft. Lauderdale Boat Show, Everglades
Services & Amenities: Parking, Valet service, Car hire, Water taxi pick up, 100' dock, Library, Comp. newspaper, Cable TV w/HBO and VCR, Telephones, Radio, Individual air conditioning, Robes, Complimentary toiletries, Some rooms semi-private balcony/deck, wet bar and CD player
Restrictions: No pets allowed, Children over 12 welcome, 1 room handicap equipped
Concierge: 24 hours
Room Service: 24 hours
Restaurant: Max's Beach Place, 12 noon–10 p.m., dress code–casual chic
Business Facilities: Audio-visual and Fax
Conference Rooms: 1 room, capacity 14
Sports Facilities: Outdoor swimming pool, Massage, Dining privileges at Tower Club, Nearby golf, water sports, parasail
Location: Ft. Lauderdale Central Beach

CASA MORADA

Casa Morada is located on the bay in Islamorada, the jewel of the Florida Keys. Tucked away on a quiet side street, Casa Morada is an upscale 16 suite hotel with the informal character of the Caribbean. Guests of Casa Morada enjoy the seclusion of a private tropical island but are only minutes away from some of the best dining and outdoor activities in the Florida Keys.

Casa Morada is a 90 minute drive from Miami International Airport and 90 minutes from Key West. Guests of Casa Morada may also arrive to the hotel by boat.

Stonehouse Development acquired the hotel in August of 2002 and has recently renovated the property. Raymond Jungles, an award winning Key West Landscape Architect known for his lush natural landscapes, has transformed the entire property and added variety of garden spaces, from intimate to group scale. In the center of the property, near the garden suites, a grotto has been created, sculpted from the native limerock.

The highlight of the resort, Casa Morada's private island, has been transformed into a sandy playground. On the Island guests enjoy a spectacular waterside pool, a secluded cabana for lounging and a waterside terrace for breakfast, lunch and poolside beverage service.

All accommodations are suites with private terraces and gardens. Each suite has a stocked refrigerator, DVD/audio CD player, fresh orchids, private library, safe, hairdryer and robes.

Casa Morada is "a cool mediterranean style hideaway. . . ." *Travel and Leisure*, July 2001.

Address: 136 Maderia Rd, Islamorada 33036
Phone: 305-664-0044
888-881-3030
Fax: 305-664-0674
Email: info@casamorada.com
Web site: http://www.casamorada.com
Suite Rates: 229–649
No. of Suites: 16
Credit Cards: Visa
Attractions: Fishing guides, boat rentals, snorkeling and diving – Many of our captains will come to pick you up at our property; scuba, ecotours, sunset cruise on 60' sailing clipper, beaches, tennis, golf
Services & Amenities: All Suites are appointed with various amenities including central air conditioning, cable television, DVD/CD players, direct-dial telephones with modem ports, Stocked refrigerators, fresh orchids, hair dryers and robes.
Restrictions: Pets welcome, children welcome 16 and over, 1 suite handicap equipped
Concierge: 7:00 a.m.–11:00 p.m.
Room Service: 7:00 a.m.–10:00 p.m.
Restaurant: Seaview Terrace – breakfast 7:00 a.m.–10:00 a.m.; Unique selection of wines and beers. Breakfast and Lunch in the Suites and poolside is available upon request.
Bar: Sunset Terrace – Champagne, beer and wine 5:00 p.m. – 9:00 p.m.
Business Facilities: Message center, E-mail, fax
Conference Rooms: 1 room, capacity 6
Sports Facilities: Outdoor swimming pool, massage, kayaks, bicycles, snorkeling, diving, fishing, boating from private
Spa Services: In Suite and outdoor Massage is available. Spa Services, Tennis and Golf can be arranged through the Front Desk.
Location: Halfway between Miami and Key West

HERON HOUSE

In the heart of Historic Key West is the Triple A 4 Diamond rated Heron House, meticulously designed by Key West's most gifted artists and craftsmen specifically for the discerning traveler. Combining artistic sensitivity with open hearts, a genuine sense of caring pervades every aspect of this unique, private retreat. Lacking pretense, this style has been inspired by the informality of the Florida Keys' natural environment, revealing itself in a casually elegant style within which you will feel totally free, welcome, and relaxed.

With gener-
ous private
decks and bal-
conies, guest-
rooms merge
with luxurious
tropical gar-
dens. Interior
and exterior
spaces blend
and flow
together. The
multi-level
decks provide
guests with
space to
lounge and
view the gar-
dens. There is
ample use of
natural materi-
als, and they
have recently
adapted a
waterfall/rain-
forest theme.
Many of the

rooms feature "signature walls" of teak, oak or cedar. Granite baths and tile floors are cool and tropical. The stained glass transoms above French doors create a glow of natural sunlight and sparkling colors throughout the room. Interiors feature original commissioned watercolors from local Keys artisans. New, this year, is a tropical conservatory complete with orchids, streams, waterfalls and a 5,000 gallon tropical fish aquarium.

When it comes to Key West activity, Heron House is just one block from world-famous Duval Street with its epicurean delights, lively entertainment, shopping, and art galleries. Guests may wander away to the beach, which is only four blocks away.

Heron House has always meant attention to fine detail. Whether it is a Honeymoon Special or just a special time away, guests will find Heron House vintage champagne ready to put on ice, bubble bath for the Jacuzzi, robes placed in every room, reef snorkeling and sunset champagne sails. Come and see for yourself.

Address: 512 Simonton St, Key West 33040.
Phone: 305-294-9227 800-294-1644
Fax: 305-294-5692
Email: heronkyw@aol.com
Web site: http://www.heronhouse.com
Room Rates: 129–369
No. of Rooms: 23
Attractions: Historic district, One block from most attractions, Tropical Conservatory on-site complete with orchids, streams, waterfalls, and a 5,000 gallon tropical fish aquarium
Services & Amenities: Off-street parking, Balconies, Cable TV, Telephones, Radio, Robes, Individual air-conditioning control, Wet bar in suites, Whirlpool bath in some rooms, Robes, Complimentary newspaper & toiletries, 2nd story sundeck, Orchid gardens
Restrictions: Limited handicapped access, Children over 16 years of age welcome, No pets allowed
Concierge: 8 a.m.-8 p.m.
Room Service: 9 a.m.-8 p.m.
Bar: Complimentary Wine & Cheese
Business Facilities: Message center, Copiers, Fax
Sports Facilities: Outdoor heated swimming pool, Sundeck, Orchid Gardens
Location: Old Town, Downtown

LA MER HOTEL AND DEWEY HOUSE

Lavishly renovated in 2003, this romantic island retreat with its distinctive turn-of-the-century architecture and gracious seaside setting, embraces sophisticated British Colonial style with an unexpected edge.

Indulge yourself in dramatically decorated garden and ocean-view accommodations, exquisite bed linens, granite wet bars, private balconies and porches, spa tubs, sumptuous continental breakfasts, relaxing afternoon teas and weekday newspapers delivered right to your door.

Unsurpassed quality and attention to every detail combine to assure you of the finest vacation experience Key West has to offer. Key West's only luxury oceanfront bed and breakfasts emanate island elegance against the backdrop of a white sand beach and lush, tropical flora and fauna.

Dewey House, the original home of philosopher and educator John Dewey and its neighbor, the intimate La Mer Hotel are located in the heart of Key West's historic district on the Atlantic Ocean.

Unspoiled. Uncomplicated. Unforgettable.

Come live the dream!

Address: 506 South Street, Key West 33040.
Phone: 305-296-6577 800-354-4455
Fax: 305-294-8272
Email: clbabich@ southernmostresorts.com
Web site: http:// www.southernmostresorts.com
Room Rates: 185–425
No. of Rooms: 19
Attractions: Swimming, snorkeling, sunbathing, shopping, historic sites, city tours, museums and galleries, sailing, glass bottom boat rides, sunset cruises, scuba diving, bike riding, plays and theatre.
Services & Amenities:
Monogrammed bathrobes, Refrigerator, Umbrellas, Complimentary bottled water, Irons & boards, Coffee maker w/coffee, Kitchen/Wet bars, Hair dryer, In room safes. Access to three pools and Tiki Bars at sister property. Dipping pool on site.
Restrictions: Two night minimum on Weekends, Adult exclusive.
Concierge: 8am to 5pm
Room Service: Nightly turn down service
Restaurant: Charging privledges at the oceanfront Duval Beach Club. Open for breakfast, lunch and dinner.
Bar: Poolside tiki bars open 10am–10pm
Business Facilities: Internet access at concierge and Southernmost Tiki bar
Conference Rooms: Located across the street at the Southernmost Hotel
Location: Atlantic Ocean in Key West's Historic District

PIER HOUSE RESORT & CARIBBEAN SPA

This is the place to conch out in Key West. Pier House is located in the heart of Old Town overlooking the Gulf of Mexico. Just footsteps away from the hustle and bustle of Duval Street in the heart of historic Old Town, this 10-acre beachfront resort is in the continental United States' southernmost city.

Rooms are furnished in Caribbean decor with pastel color schemes and floral prints. You may relax in your own whirlpool bath, enjoy the resort's outdoor swimming pool, or indulge in the spa facilities.

Groups, as well as individual travelers, will appreciate the resort's Caribbean Spa. There are twenty-two guestrooms, including two suites, and four conference rooms right in the spa building, making it the perfect place for a group that wants to include fitness on its agenda.

The Caribbean Spa offers such programs as "stretch breaks," quick ten-minute programs of stretching exercises conducted by a trained fitness specialist, during a day of heavy meetings. Other classes can be tailored to the group's schedule. For instance, an early morning fitness walk through Old Town would combine a workout with some sightseeing fun.

The resort also offers excellent wining and dining opportunities. One Duval, perhaps Key West's finest place to dine, has indoor or outdoor seating overlooking the Gulf of Mexico. For a more casual breakfast or lunch, explore The Market Bistro with its sidewalk tables on Front Street, or The Beach Bar & Grille with fabulous views of the Gulf.

The Chart Room Bar reflects Key West in the days of Papa Hemingway, while Havana Docks Sunset Deck offers the island's most spectacular sunset views.

Address: One Duval St, Key West 33040
Phone: 305-296-4600
800-327-8340
Fax: 305-296-7569
Email: info@pierhouse.com
Web site: http://www.pierhouse.com
Room Rates: 200–460
Suite Rates: 355–1800
No. of Rooms 142
No. of Suites: 16
Credit Cards: Most Credit Cards accepted
Attractions: Ernest Hemingway House, Audubon House, Conch Tour Train, Old Town Trolley, Sloppy Joe's, Mel Fisher's Museum, Historic Seaport District, Water Sports
Services & Amenities: Cable TV, In-room movies, WebTV,Coffee Maker, Hairdryer,Full-Serice Spa, Fitness Center, Beauty and Barber shop, Gift shop, Baby-sitting service, In-room coffee maker, Balcony or patio, Private beach, Pool with whirlpool, Valet Service
Restrictions: No pets allowed, 7 rooms handicap equipped, Children under 12 free w/parents w/existing bedding
Concierge: 9 a.m.-6 p.m.
Room Service: 7 a.m.- 12 a.m.
Restaurant: One Duval Restaurant B/L/D waterfront 4-Diamond, The Market Bistro sidewalk cafe B/L, Beach Bar and Grille one the beach B/L, Chart Room Bar
Bar: 4 bars, open 11 a.m.-2 a.m.
Business Facilities: Audio-visual equipment, Teleconferencing, Copier
Conference Rooms: 5 rooms, capacity 15-175
Sports Facilities: Outdoor swimming pool, Full Fitness Center, Beach
Spa Services: The Caribbean Spa is Key West's only full service spa. Massage, facial, body treatments, hair and Nail salon, fitness center.

HOTEL OCEAN

In the heart of the Art Deco Historic District, the Hotel Ocean is an unbelievable destination for an exciting, luxurious, ocean-side vacation.

The accommodations are bright and spacious with an artistic flair that will energize guests and, when accompanied with the personal service, will fulfill all desires. They are appointed in a warm Mediterranean style, with décor that varies from room to room in colors, shapes, and accents. Furnished with 1930s collectibles, original art Deco fireplaces and exquisite bathrooms, the guestrooms are much more than expected. The most fascinating suite is accessed via private elevator, opening its door in the center of the suite to a spectacular terrace facing the Atlantic. The bedroom is decorated with great sophistication and personal touches, featuring a king-size bed that seems to be surrounded by the ocean.

On world-famous Ocean Drive, the Hotel Ocean offers endless excitement, including fashionable boutiques, great restaurants, trendy clubs, museums, art galleries and, of course, the ocean. Hotel Guests can enjoy deep-sea fishing, diving, snorkeling, horseback riding, golf, tennis, a massage, and a private jet trip to a remote island. The Hotel Ocean's attentive staff will make sure your wishes come true.

Hotel Ocean's restaurant, Les 2Fontaines - Lobster Cafe & Bar, is a paradise for seafood lovers, offering a seafood feast with a French twist and an ocean view. The atmosphere is electric and the food is amazing. Mondays feature 2-for-1 Lobster: other delicious dishes include Bouillabaisse, Octopus Ceviche, Lobster Cake and more. . . . The evenings are full of excitement when Les 2Fontaines presents Dixieland, Jazz, and Swing music.

The magnificent service, stunning artistic style, spectacular food, and beautiful setting will create an insatiable desire for guests to return time and again to the Hotel Ocean.

Address: 1230 Ocean Drive, Miami Beach 33139.
Phone: 305-672-2579 800-783-1725
Fax: 305-672-7665
Email: info@hotelocean.com
Web site: http://www.hotelocean.com
Room Rates: 179–260
Suite Rates: 275–647
No. of Rooms: 27
No. of Suites: 19
Attractions: Fashionable boutiques, Great restaurants, Trendy clubs, Museums and art galleries, Theater, Ballet, Cinemas
Services & Amenities: Valet parking and garage nearby, Car rental, Laundry service, Gift shop, Some balconies, Complimentary newspaper, Cable TV, 2-line telephone, VCR, Mini-bars, Individual heat and air-conditioning, Complimentary continental breakfast, Bathrobes upon request.
Restrictions: Very pet friendly, 1 room handicap equipped
Concierge: 24 hours
Room Service: 7:30 a.m.-midnight
Restaurant: Les 2Fontaines– Lobster Cafe & Bar: seafood restaurant, Jazz, Dixieland & Swing music nightly
Bar: Speakeasy Lounge, Raw and Sushi Bar: Noon–midnight
Business Facilities: Overhead projector, Flip chart, Markers, Admin. assistance, Fax, Copiers, E-mail, TV/VCR
Conference Rooms: 5 rooms, capacity 10-380
Sports Facilities: VIP pass to elite gym: Crunch, Golf, Tennis, Aquatic sports, Horseback riding, European or therapeut
Location: In the heart of Art Deco Historic District, the center of hip South Beach

HOTEL NASH

Welcome is the key word at the beautifully restored Hotel Nash in the heart of Miami Beach's Historic Architectural District. Eagerly awaited as South Beach's premier boutique hotel, the Hotel Nash opened in December 1999, with an emphasis on superb comfort, elegant style, and attentive personal service.

The imaginative renovation has resulted in a five-story 28,000 square foot hotel offering 54 rooms, including three luxurious penthouse suites with expansive terraces and ocean and bay views, a city-style terraced duplex, and two pool side cabanas. A serene counterpoint to the lively bustle of Collins Avenue, the Nash lobby is decorated in a handsome palette of sage-green and ivory, and furnished with plush club chairs, historic stone wainscoting, and original terrazzo floors.

A museum-style concierge desk holds an extensive library of classic and unusual DVDs and videos—the only one of its kind in South Beach. The Nash also offers facilities for film and fashion production. Cabanas are ideal for castings, and the garden and pool areas are available for filming.

Modeling the civilized luxury of the South of France in the 1940's, the Nash's self-contained garden evokes a romantic and aromatic Eden, replete with blooming jasmine, star anise, cypresses, bougainvillea, and soaring Norfolk island pines. Each season in the garden yields a different, captivating fragrance. Three soothing spa provide an added balm to the senses.

If there is one chef responsible for putting South Florida on America's culinary map, it is surely Mark Militello. His new restaurant at the Hotel Nash is Mark's South Beach. The chef weaves Caribbean, Californian, Mediterranean and Asian influences into a cuisine that defies easy description, but that's universally acclaimed and uniquely his own.

Address: 1120 Collins Ave, Miami Beach 33139.
Phone: 305-674-7800 800-403-NASH (6274)
Fax: 305-538-8288
Email: info@hotelnash.com
Web site: http://www.hotelnash.com
Room Rates: 155–330
Suite Rates: 195–1,400
No. of Rooms: 54
No. of Suites: 17
Credit Cards: Visa
Attractions: One block from the beach and within strolling distance of some of the best shops, restaurants, and cultural attractions in town, including the galleries and boutiques of nearby Lincoln Road
Services & Amenities: Videos, High-speed Internet access in every room, Rainforest shower heads, Nash customized toiletries
Restrictions: No pets allowed
Concierge: 12:30–9 p.m.
Room Service: 7-11a.m., 12-3p.m., 7-11p.m.
Restaurant: Mark's South Beach–Breakfast 7-11 a.m., Lunch 12-3 p.m., Dinner 7-11 p.m.
Bar: 7 p.m.- midnight
Business Facilities: Modems, Fax, Copiers
Sports Facilities: 3 soothing spa pools
Location: Ideally located in the heart of Miami Beach's landmark Art Deco district

COURTYARD AT LAKE LUCERNE

Overlooking Lake Lucerne, encircling a lush, intimate garden, within walking distance of Orlando's business and financial district and downtown's exceptional shopping and dining, is the Courtyard at Lake Lucerne. Four historic buildings, each of a different era, comprise this unique bed and breakfast getaway.

Fall asleep by the fire in the parlor of the Norment-Parry Inn, and you might awaken to imagine yourself transported to Victorian England as you gaze upon the Dickens collection in the entrance hall cupboard. Or curl up on a tuxedo chair with a Raymond Chandler novel in your apartment at the Wellborn. Savor a cup of coffee in the living room as the morning sun filters through a cobalt blue glass window. Sip wine on the verandah of the I.W. Philips House. A complimentary carafe greets every guest upon arrival. Close your eyes and you can almost hear the sweep of gowns and the clatter of horse hooves on brick. From the abundant front porch of the Dr. Phillipps House, refresh yourself with fresh Florida air after a leisurely stroll around the lake appreciating the native Florida ambiance and the gardens around the property.

More than a place, the Courtyard at Lake Lucerne is another place in time.

Address: 211 N Lucerne E, Orlando 32801.
Phone: 407-648-5188 800-444-5289
Fax: 407-246-1368
Email: info@orlandohistricinn.com
Web site: http://www.orlandohistoricinn.com
Room Rates: 89–250
Suite Rates: 89–250
No. of Rooms: 30
No. of Suites: 14
Credit Cards: Visa
Attractions: Downtown Orlando with shopping and dining, Disneyworld, Universal Studios, Cape Canavaral, Daytona Beach, Thorton Park, Winter Park, Bobb Carr Permoring Arts Center. Islands of Adventure
Services & Amenities: Complimentary continental breakfast, Daily maid service, Cocktail hour, Complimentary wine upon arrival, TV, telephone, clock radio and private bath; Honeymoon suites and all rooms in Dr. Phillips House include oversized whirlpool tubs.
Business Facilities: Services include catering and administrative assistance
Conference Rooms: 1 room, capacity 16
Location: Historic downtown Orlando

HEART OF PALM BEACH HOTEL

We invite you to enjoy the Heart of Palm Beach, a distinguished Palm Beach resort. Surrounded by sun and sea, you arrive at the Heart of Palm Beach resort to try on a lifestyle that can be experienced only at a world-class Palm Beach resort. As you settle into this gorgeous South Florida luxury resort, let the tropical atmosphere sweep you away like an island breeze. The tranquil setting of our Palm Beach resort quickly melts away the worries of the outside world.

The Heart is an elegant Palm Beach resort in the heart of Florida 's most luxurious and magnificent island. Our Palm Beach, Florida resort is located mid-island just a half block from the shores of the Atlantic Ocean. Situated on picturesque Royal Palm Way, we are just minutes away from the world-class shopping of Worth Avenue, the world's leading financial institutions, South Florida 's cultural jewels, a variety of recreational activities, fine dining, and vibrant nightlife. Our ideal location and intimate setting makes the Heart one of the most attractive Southern Florida resorts in Palm Beach .

There is no place quite like Palm Beach. Travelers have been attracted to the Palm Beach landscape for over a century. More than any other resorts in the Heart of Palm Beach has been a winter hotspot for socialites and celebrities. Unique architecture and beautiful Southern Florida resorts augment the beauty of the island. Experience the good life of a Southern Florida resort in beautiful Palm Beach .

Address: 160 Royal Palm Way, Palm Beach 33480.
Phone: (561) 655-5600 (800) 521-4278
Fax: (561) 832-1201
Email: reservations@ heartofpalmbeach.com
Web site: http:// www.heartofpalmbeach.com/
Room Rates: 90–489
Suite Rates: 179–599
No. of Rooms: 86
No. of Suites: 9
Credit Cards: Visa
Attractions: The Palm Beach area has 9 challenging golf courses and a number of tennis facilities nearby. Perhaps our staff could suggest and arrange a Broadway, opera or ballet performance at the Kravis Center for Performing Arts or take in a polo or croquet match.
Services & Amenities: Relax and be pampered, at our new Spa at the Heart. Or lounge by our tropical courtyard pool and enjoy sumptuous cocktails from the Oasis Bar. Enjoy the fabulous dining in our chic Oasis restaurant, or order in room service. Complimentary valet parking.
Concierge: No
Room Service: Yes
Restaurant: The Oasis Grille serves up a dynamic "global fusion" of American and Continental cuisine and has an extensive selection of wines for the most discerning palates.
Bar: The Oasis Bar
Business Facilities: In room high speed Internet access
Conference Rooms: Banquet Room or Poolside Garden Pavilion, up to 200.
Sports Facilities: Heated pool, golf & tennis off-site, fitness membership at Trainers Gym, bicycle & snorkel rental

LODGE AND CLUB AT PONTE VEDRA BEACH

Framed by graceful palms and sand dunes, the Lodge & Club sparkles as one of Florida's most elegant oceanfront resort hotels. Nestled in the charming seaside community of Ponte Vedra Beach, midway between Jacksonville and St. Augustine, this sophisticated resort has been charming guests since its opening in 1989. The resort's distinctive character is echoed throughout its ten seaside acres. A beachside fountain courtyard, classic archways, Spanish tile roof, awnings, trellises and balconies all combine to create the illusion of a seaside European village.

The Lodge & Club is a member of the prestigious Preferred Hotels & Resorts, an upscale collection of the world's finest hotels and resorts. It is also a proud recipient of the distinguished "Gold List Award" presented by *Condé Nast Traveler* as one of the top resorts in North America.

White beaches and the Atlantic surf provide dramatic backdrop for The Lodge's 66 guestrooms and suites. Each richly appointed room or suite features king or queen bedding with triple-sheet luxury, remote-control cable TV, fully stocked honor bar, and the thoughtful addition of a coffee maker. Spacious bathrooms offer full-length terry robes, hair dryers, makeup mirrors, and designer toiletries. Other distinctive features include French doors, fireplaces and oversized jacuzzi bath tubs. The spacious suites offer the added convenience of a kitchenette. Additional services appreciated by all include 24-hour room service, nightly turndown service and a choice of complimentary morning newspapers delivered to the doorstep each morning.

From sunning and swimming to building sand castles or exploring for shells, The Lodge's beautiful beach creates a spectacular playground for all ages. Additional recreational pleasures include 3 heated swimming pools, sailing and biking. An oversized gym features the latest in cardiovascular and resistance machines and provides more than fifty fitness classes a week. Additionally, a steam room, sauna room, jacuzzi and a selection of popular massage services provide for a complete experience.

Address: 607 Ponte Vedra Blvd., Ponte Vedra Beach 32082.
Phone: 904-273-9500 800-243-4304
Fax: 904-273-0210
Email: membership@prresorts.com
Web site: http://www.pvresorts.com/
Room Rates: 220–440
Suite Rates: 340–540
No. of Rooms: 66
No. of Suites: 24
Credit Cards: Most Credit Cards accepted
Attractions: Popular museums nearby as well as boutiques for shopping. Luxury spa available featuring more than 100 pampering services. Beach horseback riding, day trips to historic St. Augustine for antiques, romantic sailboat rides on Atlantic Intercoastal waterway.
Restrictions: No pets
Concierge: Yes
Room Service: 24-hours
Bar: Yes
Business Facilities: Yes
Conference Rooms: Yes
Sports Facilities: Yes
Location: Oceanfront

CASA MONICA HOTEL

First established in 1888, The Casa Monica Hotel holds a fascinating history as one of Henry Flagler's luxurious turn-of-the-century destinations.

Faithfully restored in 2000, the hotel resembles a medieval castle with intricate balconies, hand-painted Italian tile and five majestic tower suites. Romantic ambiance fills the grand lobby, 138 guestrooms and majestic tower suites. 14 luxurious suites, four of which are two and three stories, each are original, while the corner tower houses the four story, three bedroom Kessler Suite.

A highly acclaimed fine dining restaurant—95 Cordova and The Cobalt Lounge, St. Augustine's newest and most elegant lounge, enhance the uncommon experience in the oldest hotel in St. Augustine, America's oldest city. And for casually superb cuisine try the Gourmet Deli-Market.

An elevated 2nd floor outdoor swimming pool is heated in the winter and chilled in the summer. There is also access to the private Serenata Beach Club with 3 swimming pools, beach equipment, complete fitness center, several dining options, meeting and reception rooms. There is also an Activities Staff to coordinate a full schedule of fun.

With more than 12,000 square feet of modern and flexible function space featuring state of the art sound system and audio visual equipment, The Casa Monica has everything for your next business conference.

Address: 95 Cordova Street, St. Augustine 32084.
Phone: 904-827-1888 800-648-1888
Fax: 904-827-0426
Email: casamonica@ grandthemehotels.com
Web site: http:// www.casamonica.com
Room Rates: 119–249
Suite Rates: 249–699
No. of Rooms: 138
No. of Suites: 15
Credit Cards: Visa
Attractions: Oceanfront Beach Club with three pools, workout faicility, oceanfront restaurant and some of the finest beaches in Florida. St. Augustine Beach, some of the finest golf and tennis facilities, 40 annual festivals and events, museums, historic churches, an
Services & Amenities: Electronic key system, sitting areas, 6-channel stereos, 25" color TV, 3 phones w/ voicemail and dataports, in-room safe, iron & board, coffeemaker, hair dryer and makeup mirror, boutique shops, valet laundry, valet parking
Restrictions: No pets allowed, Children up to 18 stay free with parents, handicap rooms available
Concierge: Days and nights
Room Service: 6 a.m.-11 p.m.
Restaurant: 95 Cordova, 4 star restaurant, 6 a.m.-10 p.m., Market at 95 Cordova, sidewalk cafe, recent winner of the prestigious DiRONA Award for distinguished fine dining.
Bar: 11:30 a.m. to midnight
Business Facilities: Complete business center with conference rooms both large and small totalling 12,000 sq. ft.
Conference Rooms: More than 12,000 sq ft of luxurious mtg space
Sports Facilities: Outdoor pool on 2nd floor deck, outdoor whirlpool spa, Access to private Serenata Beach Club w/exerc
Spa Services: Nearby
Location: Historic district of St. Augustine, oldest city in USA

GOVERNORS INN

Located in the center of the Adams Street Commons, Governors Inn is the crowning touch in a bid to restore a sense of history to the heart of the city. Imposing heart-of-pine overhead beams and warm pine paneling help to maintain the charm of the original 50-year-old buildings. Antique furniture, quality reproductions, traditionally patterned wall coverings with chair rails and cove moldings complement the French Country style.

No two of the 40 guestrooms are identical. Each has its own spirit and is uniquely decorated. Antiques are used throughout and armoires act as closets and hide modern amenities. Some rooms feature sleeping lofts, corkscrew staircases, wood-burning marble fireplaces, clerestory windows, a bar or Jacuzzi. The staff provides turndown service, terrycloth robes, valet parking, continental breakfast, complimentary cocktails, newspapers and many personal care amenities.

Governors Inn is fortunate to have one of the capital city's finer restaurants—"Andrew's 228"—within easy walking distance. In addition, guests wishing to dine in the comfort of their own room may order room service from "Andrew's."

Many guests are corporate executives and the hotel's professional staff can help arrange for conferences up to 35 people.

Address: 209 So. Adams St, Tallahassee 32301.
Phone: 850-681-6855 800-342-7717 (in FL)
Fax: 850-222-3105
Web site: http://www.thegovinn.com
Room Rates: 139–229
Suite Rates: 159–229
No. of Rooms: 40
No. of Suites: 8
Attractions: Central City, ½ block north of Capitol building
Services & Amenities: Valet service, Garage and parking, Card/game area, Cable TV, Telephone, Robes, Complimentary newspaper and toiletries
Restrictions: No pets allowed
Room Service: 6 p.m.-10 p.m.
Restaurant: Room service is available through "Andrew's 228" located across the street from Governors Inn
Business Facilities: Message center, Copiers, Fax, Dataports
Conference Rooms: 2 rooms, capacity 10-30
Location: Adams Street Common, Nearest airport is Tallahassee Regional

REGENCY SUITES HOTEL

This classic European Hotel in the center of Atlanta's Midtown brings guests quiet elegance along with friendly service in a homelike setting. With ninety-six well designed and carefully furnished suites that were newly renovated in January 2003, it offers a welcome stay for the business or leisure visitor. All suites feature king, queen, or double/double beds and living rooms with queen-size convertible sofas. Kitchens are equipped with microwave ovens, refrigerators, coffee maker, small appliances, and table service for four people.

Regency Suites Hotel is located in the center of Atlanta's cultural and business district, just 2 blocks from Interstates 75/85. Marta's Midtown Station, conveniently located a few steps away, offers a quick ride to Underground Atlanta, Downtown, the Georgia Dome, World Congress Convention Center, Woodruff Arts Center and Buckhead. Also located nearby are the Georgia Tech Campus and Piedmont Park.

Monday through Thursday evenings guests are offered a complimentary meal at Millenium Cafe directly across the street. In addition, a complimentary breakfast is served daily in the Club Room. Here guests can watch a movie, borrow a book, read the complimentary daily newspaper or just relax with friends.

Guests will also find valet service, covered parking, and on-site laundry. Choice microwavable food is available in the mini-convenience store.

The Executive Board Room offers business guests a professional atmosphere in which to conduct meetings. Furnished with Chippendale-style conference table and chairs, this room can be scaled to accommodate executive meetings for up to 12 people. The accompanying audio-visual center is at your command. Larger meeting space is also available, as is catering.

Address: 975 West Peachtree St., Atlanta 30309.
Phone: 404-876-5003 800-642-3629
Fax: 404-817-7511
Email: sales@regencysuites.com
Web site: http://www.regencysuites.com
Suite Rates: 89-179
No. of Suites: 96
Credit Cards: Most Credit Cards accepted
Attractions: Six Flags, Underground Atlanta, High Museum of Art, Fox Theatre, 4 blocks-Atlanta Symphony's home, Woodruff Art Center, Carter Center, Georgia Tech Campus, Martin Luther King Jr. Center, Atlanta Botanical Gardens, Center for Puppetry Arts, Night clubs
Services & Amenities: Daily Complimentary breakfast, Comp. dinner Monday-Thursday, Valet service, Garage parking, Car hire, Library, Cable TV, VCR, Exercise room, Comp. newspapers, Hair dryers, Complimentary toiletries, Suite service, Non-smoking suites, Phones w/dataports
Restrictions: No pets allowed, 4 suites handicap equipped
Business Facilities: Message Ctr., Copiers, Audio-visual, Overhead, VCR 1/2", Fax, Notary, Computer PC w/Internet
Conference Rooms: 2 rooms, capacity 50, 1 Executive Board Room
Location: Midtown, Nearest airport is Hartsfield International

GREYFIELD INN

The Greyfield Inn is a grand and graceful mansion located on Georgia's largest and southernmost coastal island, Cumberland Island. Built in 1900, and opened as an inn in 1962, Greyfield is furnished today as it was at the turn of the century, with contemporary amenities blended in with the comfort of guests in mind.

Family portraits still hang in the parlor; horsehair chairs flank a massive fireplace. Even the original books, including first editions are in place in the library. There is no check-in desk, no televisions or phones or ice machines or spa services. Just a rambling house with a spacious old verandah, dining rooms, bedrooms on this floor and that, large bathrooms with clawfoot tubs and pedestal sinks. Bedroom windows face massive live oaks or the salt marshes along the Cumberland River.

In true southern fashion, they take great pride in their kitchen. Each morning, awaken to a full and satisfying breakfast which includes fresh-squeezed orange juice and fruit, homemade muffins and breakfast meats, as well as eggs, pancakes or one of the chef's specialties. Midday, enjoy the day's explorations with a satisfying picnic lunch. During cocktail hour each evening, Greyfield serves hors d'ouvres in the Inn's well-stocked bar while sharing stories with fellow guests. Dinner is a casually elelgant affair, served in the glow of candlelight. The nightly entrees feature fresh and creative cuisine, accompanied, if desired, by a selection from the wine cellar.

This grand Carnegie southern plantation is a step back in time. The dedicated staff is there to ensure that the stay on their idyllic, private island is the perfect retreat.

Address: PO Box 900, Fernandina Beach, FL 32035, Cumberland Island 0.
Phone: 904-261-6408 888-241-6408
Fax: 904-321-0666
Email: seashore@greyfieldinn.com
Web site: http://www.greyfieldinn.com
Room Rates: 395
Suite Rates: 450–575
No. of Rooms: 17
No. of Suites: 5
Credit Cards: Visa
Attractions: National Seashore and Wilderness, 18 miles of pristine, undeveloped white sand beach, Wildlife, Wilderness Jeep tours
Services & Amenities: Airport pick up, Shuttle service, Free parking, Gift shop, Library, Robes, Complimentary toiletries, All meals included in room rate
Restrictions: 2 night minimum stay, No pets allowed, Children 5 and over welcome, 1 room handicap equipped
Room Service: Avaliable
Restaurant: Greyfield Inn Restaurant, open breakfast, lunch and dinner; dress code – jackets. Complimentary non-alcoholic beverages and hors d'oeuvres in bar 24 hours daily.
Bar: Greyfield, open 24 hours
Business Facilities: Copiers and Fax
Conference Rooms: 1 room, capacity 22
Sports Facilities: Massage, Croquet, Beach/Ocean, Wilderness Jeep Excursions, Fishing, Hiking, Biking, Boating
Location: Cumberland Island, Georgia

KEHOE HOUSE

William Kehoe was one of Savannah's most prosperous and influential citizens during the late 1800's and early 1900's. In 1892 he built a grand home on Columbia Square befitting his stature in the community. He chose a Renaissance Revival style with terra cotta moldings, iron railings, red brick and Corinthian columns. It remains one of Savannah's most distinctive structures offering the perfect setting for this luxury Historic Inn.

From the moment you walk through the sparkling leaded glass doors you will begin to unwind. An attentive but unobtrusive staff is on hand 24 hours a day to assist throughout your stay. The Kehoe House offers generously proportioned guestrooms. Each is distinct in character and décor. Antique and period reproduction furnishings are dressed with rich designer and custom-made treatments. All rooms are extra spacious, some with private verandahs and separate sitting areas. All of the rooms have private baths with robes, hair dryers, and luxury toiletries.

Each morning our chef greets you with a gourmet, made-to-order breakfast along with Kehoe House specialties including apple-pecan pancakes, banana fosters french toast and designer omelets. Afternoon tea comes at just the right time to take a break from all the sightseeing this beautiful city has to offer. You'll find a selection of beverages, including sweetened ice tea along with lovely desserts. The knowledgeable staff is on hand during the hors d'oeuvre hour (complete with complimentary wine) to assist with suggestions of interest, directions, and reservations. Upon your return from dinner, you'll find your bed turned down, lights low, soft music, and cozy robes awaiting you. Save room after dinner for that special turndown treat!

The Inn is on the National Register of Historic Places and is in a prime location within Savannah's two-mile square Historic District. River Street with all its shops, galleries, and restaurants is only a three block walk from the Inn.

Relax and indulge in a tradition of refined elegance.

Address: 123 Habersham St, Savannah 31401.
Phone: 912-232-1020 800-820-1020
Fax: 912-231-0208
Email: info@kehoehouse.com
Web site: http://www.kehoehouse.com
Room Rates: 249–429
No. of Rooms: 13
Credit Cards: Most Credit Cards accepted
Attractions: Historic District, River Street, museums, theatre, riverfront, ecotours, beach nearby, horse carriages, trolley tours, and much more.
Services & Amenities: Gourmet Breakfast; Afternoon Tea; Evening Wine and Hors d'ourvres; Elevator Access; Cable TV with DVD player; Cordless Telephone; Wireless High-Speed Internet; CD alarm clocks; Bathrobes; luxury ammenities and Lavish Turndown Services.
Restrictions: No pets allowed except service animals, 1 room handicap equipped
Concierge: 24 hours
Room Service: Continental in room breakfast
Restaurant: Our knowledgeable Concierge staff is on hand 24 hours a day to recommend enjoyable dining for your stay. Or venture over to 700 Drayton at the Mansion on Forsyth Park for a total dining experience.
Bar: Complimentary wine from 5–7 pm
Business Facilities: Message center, E-mail, Copiers, Fax, Wireless Internet access
Conference Rooms: 1 room, capacity 65
Sports Facilities: Privleges to Downtown Athletic Club, $10/day
Spa Services: Access to the Posiden Spa at the Mansion on Forsyth Park, where luxury meets relaxation. One mile away at the Mansion, guests can enjoy a variety of spa services, sure to complete your experience.
Location: Historic District

FOLEY HOUSE INN

For travelers who value a sense of place and time, the 100-year-old Foley Inn on historic Chippewa Square has been lovingly and authentically refurbished to reflect Savannah in its Victorian heyday. The parlor glows with the earth tones of brown, green and gold. Two carved fireplaces, a crystal chandelier and fresh flowers remind guests that they are not in some faceless large hotel.

The amazingly quiet rooms in this downtown location are individually decorated with antique English dressers and armoires, lace-canopied four-poster beds, and complemented by sumptuous wallpaper and drapes in Old Savannah's signature colors of peach, crimson and salmon. Many rooms have fireplaces, marble bathrooms with whirlpool baths, and balconies. Guests may enjoy a complimentary movie in their private VCR. The adjacent Carriage House offers simpler rooms at surprisingly modest prices.

Guests enjoy a full Southern breakfast in the parlor or open-air courtyard. The afternoon hors d'oeuvres hour features fresh fruit, cheese, crackers, and wine or lemonade. Owner Beryl Zerwer enjoys providing European-style personal attention that makes guests feel truly special. "That's why I love this business." During the holiday season, she adds a touch of her native New Orleans with a month-long traditional advent celebration.

All the delights of landmark Old Savannah, with its restaurants, theaters and historic riverfront walk, await guests who venture forth to tour the area on foot or by horsedrawn carriage or trolley.

Address: 14 W Hull St, Savannah 31401.
Phone: 912-232-6622 800-647-3708
Fax: 912-231-1218
Email: foleyinn@aol.com
Web site: http://www.foleyinn.com
Room Rates: 215–345
Suite Rates: 345
No. of Rooms: 18
No. of Suites: 2
Credit Cards: Visa
Attractions: Trolley tours, Jazz festivals, Shakespeare in the Park, Riverfront festivals, Antique shops
Services & Amenities:
Complimentary full Southern breakfast, Complimentary newspaper, Cable TV, Telephones, VCR, CD player, Air-contiioning, Complimentary toiletries, Complimentary afternoon tea, cordials, hors d'oeuvres and wine
Restrictions: No pets allowed, no children under 12, No handicap equipped rooms, Non-smoking rooms.
Concierge: 7 a.m.-11 p.m.
Room Service: 8-10 am
Restaurant: Walk to Sapphire Grill. Old Pink House, Savannah Bistro, 45 South,Il Pasticcio, A Vida, and many more
Bar: Complimentary – 600 to 700
Business Facilities: Copiers, Fax, Modems
Conference Rooms: One – handles 16
Sports Facilities: Privileges by special arrangement at Downtown Athletic Club
Spa Services: Spa services in room available by advance notice.
Location: Downtown, Chippewa Square, Historic landmark district

HOTEL HANA MAUI AND HONUA SPA

For untold generations, Hana has existed in splendid isolation and unspoiled beauty. It is considered one of the last true Hawaiian places. The legendary intimate Hotel Hana-Maui is known for "The world's most romantic hideaway," is in the exclusive, secluded Hana area of the island of Maui. 66 accommodations, including 47 sea ranch cottages with ocean views, are scattered throughout 66 acres of landscaped gardens within a 4,700-acre working ranch. These accommodations feature a striking decor of white with natural wood beams and shuttered windows. Plantation ceiling fans whir overhead. Orchids and other tropical plants bloom indoors as well as out. The luxurious baths have sunken tubs, and outside each bath is an enclosed private garden.

The sporting life is in full swing at this resort. Facilities include two swimming pools, tennis courts, a croquet lawn, and a well-equipped riding stable. A full range of water and ranch sports is available at the hotel. Our Wellness Center features programs designed to enhance the quality of life.

The Hotel Hana-Maui Restaurant is a favorite meeting spot for guests and residents alike. The Paniola Lounge features local entertainment Thursdays through Sundays.

The Hana area is rich in Hawaiian lore and replete with visitor opportunities. View the local botanical gardens, enjoy hiking trails in Waianapanapa State Park, Ohe'o Gulch and Hana Ranch. To stay at Hotel Hana-Maui is to experience "the Hawaii that used to be."

Address: PO Box 9, Hana, Maui 96713.
Phone: 808-248-8211
800-321-HANA
Fax: 808-248-7264
Email: info@hotelhanamaui.com
Web site: http://www.hotelhanamaui.com
Room Rates: 425–845
Suite Rates: 995–1625
No. of Rooms 62
No. of Suites: 7
Credit Cards: Most Credit Cards accepted
Attractions: Cultural and Museum Center, Waianapanapa State Park, Kahanu Gardens, Ohe'o Gulch, Waimoku Falls Trail, Ka'eleku Cavern, Ulaini (Blue) Pond, Hamoa beach, Fagan Cross, Hana Bay, Charles Lindberg's Grave, Hana Coast Gallery,
Restrictions: No pets allowed
Concierge: 8 a.m.-6 p.m.
Restaurant: Hotel Hana-Maui Restaurant, 7:30 a.m.-9 p.m., Hana Ranch Restaurant, take-out lunch, casual dinners
Bar: Paniola Lounge, 11:30 a.m.-10 p.m.
Conference Rooms: 2 rooms, capacity 10-40
Sports Facilities: Tennis, Croquet, Practice golf, Horseback riding, Snorkeling, Bikes, Swimming pool, Fishing, Hula
Spa Services: Intimate new Honua Spa offers a relaxing sanctuary overlooking Hana Bay. Nine Treatment rooms including massage suites, steam room, cold plunge pool. Lava rock whirlpool, private gardens, Spa store
Location: Hana Ranch, nearest major airport: Hana Airport

HOTEL INDIGO

On Chicago's Gold Coast stands The Claridge Hotel, a quiet, unassuming part of the neighborhood. Travelers from all over the world choose The Claridge for its comfortable accommodations and close-to-it-all location. The Magnificent Mile, Water Tower Place, Lincoln Park Zoo, River North Art Galleries, Lake Michigan and Chicago's best dining and nightlife are just a few of the nearby attractions.

Your stay at The Claridge will be unforgettable with a comfortable room, including three with fireplaces, mini-bar, in-room cinema, voice mail and turndown service with fresh-baked cookies. We feature continental breakfast, free morning limousine service, morning newspaper and room service, four board rooms, a banquet room, fax and general business services.

You'll enjoy world-class dining at our own Foreign Affairs restaurant, offering the finest international cuisine that changes with the seasons.

Address: 1244 N. Dearborn Parkway, Chicago 60610.
Phone: 312-787-4980 800-245-1258
Fax: 312-787-4069
Email: melissa.duff@ichotelsgroup.com
Web site: http://www.claridgehotel.com
Room Rates: 149–250
Suite Rates: 375–750
No. of Rooms: 161
No. of Suites: 2
Attractions: The Magnificent Mile, Water Tower Place, Lincoln Park Zoo, River North Art Galleries and Lake Michigan
Services & Amenities: Complimentary morning limo service, Valet parking, Valet service, Japan TV, In-room Lodgenet Entertainment, Mini bars, Complimentary daily newspaper, Complimentary continental breakfast
Restrictions: Small, well-behaved pets allowed, Limited handicap access
Room Service: 6:30 a.m.-10 p.m.
Restaurant: Foreign Affairs Restaurant & Cafe
Bar: Lobby bar, 5 p.m.-midnight
Business Facilities: Fax, Computer-ready phone jacks, Duplicating service, Conference calling, Complete AV rental
Conference Rooms: 4 boardrooms, capacity 15, 1 ballroom, capacity 65
Sports Facilities: Numerous health club affiliations
Location: Gold Coast

HOMESTEAD

Ideally located two blocks from Northwestern University, two blocks from the lakefront and two blocks from downtown Evanston, The Homestead provides inviting comfortable accommodations in a lovely European atmosphere. Each of our ninety guestrooms and suites has been individually decorated with traditional décor, guaranteeing every guest a unique experience in charming and comfortable surroundings—whether for a day or a year. With our compliments, freshly brewed hot coffee and tea, fresh fruit and a delicious assortment of freshly baked bagels and breads are served each morning. Our lovely Salon provides a welcome respite for guests and residents who enjoy sitting by the fire with one of our books or challenging a new friend to a game of chess.

The Homestead provides quiet, relaxed ambiance and simple elegance combined with staff who has an exceptional desire to serve.

Address: 1625 Hinman Ave, Evanston 60201.
Phone: 847-475-3300
Fax: 847-570-8100
Email: office@thehomestead.net
Web site: http://www.thehomestead.net
Room Rates: 125–135
Suite Rates: 155–240
No. of Rooms: 30
No. of Suites: 55
Credit Cards: Most Credit Cards accepted
Attractions: Excellent shopping & dining options, museums, art galleries and cultural attractions can be found in walking distance or a short drive away, including . . . Baha'i Temple, Block Museum of Art, Chicago Botanic Garden, Kohl's Children's Museum & Ravinia.
Services & Amenities: Complimentary parking, complimentary continental breakfast, in-room refrigerators upon request, free basic cable, in-room iron and ironing board, on-premise laundry, high speed wireless Internet access upon request
Restrictions: Limited handicap accessibility; Dogs and cats welcome in select apartments.
Concierge: None
Room Service: None
Restaurant: Trio Atelier (847-733-8746). Reservations accepted but not required. Monday: closed Tuesday-Thursday: 5:30-9 p.m. Friday: 5:30-10 p.m. Saturday: 5-10 p.m. Sunday: 5-9 p.m.
Bar: Trio Atelier serves cocktails in our Salon & has an extensive wine list.
Business Facilities: Facsimile, photocopy services, and high speed wireless Internet access is available.
Conference Rooms: Both the Library and the Salon accommodate 20 people.
Sports Facilities: Workout privileges provided by nearby Evanston Athletic Club at reduced rates.
Location: Edge of Downtown

THE CHECKERBERRY INN

The Checkerberry Inn is a gorgeous, 14-bedroom, European-style country inn nestled on a rolling 100-acre private, wooded estate in the heart of Indiana's Amish Country. The Checkerberry Inn is a member of the prestigious "Select Registry" Association; a select group of 400 luxurious inns and bed & breakfasts throughout North America and the UK. The Checkerberry is also the only hotel/restaurant in the state of Indiana listed in Patricia Schultz' New York Times Bestselling Book: 1,000 *Places to See Before You Die* (Workman Publishing, 2003), and has been named "One of the Ten Best Inns Nationwide" by *Inn Review*.

Each room in the Inn has a lovely, individual décor. In-room amenities include: coffee makers with Starbucks coffee, complimentary bath products, cozy chaise lounges, blowdryers, satellite TV, and high-speed Internet access.

The grounds offer an outdoor pool, tennis and regulation croquet court, and a private walking trail through 20 acres of virgin woods. Carriage rides are available in season.

The Inn's restaurant, Citrus, an American Bistro, serves dinner Tuesday-Saturday nights, lunch in season, and breakfast to guests of the inn. The cozy "Library", with its over-sized stone fireplace, is a wonderful room for relaxing, and makes an ideal meeting room for executive retreats.

The beautiful front porch is lined with comfy rocking chairs, perfect for sipping a glass of wine and watching the buggies clip-clopping down the road. Visit the Checkerberry Inn and find out why people say. . . "There's nothing else like it in the world!"

Address: 62535 County Rd 37, Goshen 46526.
Phone: 574-642-4445
Fax: 574-642-0198
Email: karen@checkerberryinn.com
Web site: http:// www.checkerberryinn.com
Room Rates: 100–155
Suite Rates: 175–325
No. of Rooms: 14
No. of Suites: 3
Credit Cards: Most Credit Cards accepted
Attractions: Observe the serenity of the Amish culture as buggies glide slowly by. Shipshewana offers a huge Flea Market/Antique Auction in the summer months. Beautiful parks, lakes & golf courses. Notre Dame is 45 min. away.
Services & Amenities: Incredible on-premise restaurant, pool, croquet court, wooded walking trail, carriage rides, in-room spa services, cont+ breakfast included in room rates, Internet access, CD players, fridges & Jacuzzis in suites.
Restrictions: Sorry, no pets!
Concierge: Yes
Room Service: Yes
Restaurant: Citrus, an American Bistro offers eclectic world cuisine, featuring locally grown, organic ingredients. Full bar with specialty martinis, live music most Friday nights, & outdoor, poolside dining.
Bar: Yes
Business Facilities: Yes
Conference Rooms: Yes
Sports Facilities: Yes
Spa Services: In-room spa services include: Manicures, pedicures, massage, body scrubs, hot stone treatments, hair stylist, reflexology & aromatherapy.

MONT REST B&B

From the moment you walk through the door Mont Rest transports you back to a lost era of grace and beauty. This historic Inn is Iowa's most luxurious bed and breakfast overlooking the Mississippi River in beautiful Bellevue, Iowa.

This prestigious 3-Diamond AAA, 4-star Hotel.com inn was built in 1893. Mont Rest is nestled halfway up a 9 acre wooded bluff overlooking one of the most panoramic views of the mighty Mississippi River.

Sit in a rocker on the front porch and watch eagles catch fish from the Mississippi. We're the perfect setting for a Honeymoon, Anniversary, or just a get-away weekend, and are located near two of the largest gambling boats on the Mississippi.

Choose from twelve luxury suites with whirlpool baths, fireplaces, queen or king size beds with incredible Mississippi River views, and gourmet dinner, dessert & full breakfast.

Special Complete Overnight Package: Evening snacks & desserts, full gourmet breakfast, history & tour. Hot tub access.

Honeymoon/Romantic Getaway Package: (Sunday thru Thursday) includes Riverboat Package & murder Mystery. Special Pricing on Wedding & Honeymoon packages.

All Grown Up Pajama Party: Includes relaxing therapeutic massage, cooking seminar and delicious gourmet lunch, view your favorite romantic movie, guided shopping tour at area stores, fabulous dinner party, fresh flowers and homemade chocolates in your room.

Two Day Historic Stay/Romantic Riverboat Excursion: enjoy the deck top observation veranda, jacuzzi, imported chocolates, fresh flowers, huge country breakfast, boat ride, shopping and sightseeing from Bellevue, IA to Galena, IL

Winter Ski Package: includes a stay in one of our deluxe rooms plus free lift tickets at Chestnut Mountain in Galena, Illinois or Sundown Ski in Dubuque, Iowa. Cross country skiing is also available.

Address: 300 Spring Street, Bellevue 52031.
Phone: 563-872-4220 877-872-4220
Fax: 563-872-5094
Email: innkeeper@montrest.com
Web site: http://www.montrest.com
Room Rates: 135–195
No. of Rooms: 12
Credit Cards: Most Credit Cards accepted
Attractions: State parks, riverboat gambling, golfing, canoeing on the Maquoketa River, theater events in the area, downhill skiiing, dog track, boating, fishing, horseback riding, hiking near Galena Hills.
Services & Amenities: Gift shop, video library, reading library, babysitting service. Nine of our rooms feature fireplaces, five feature balconies/decks. Our rooms are all equipped with radio, cable TV, VCR and telephone. Our facility has one guest kitchen.
Restrictions: No pets please. Smoking not permitted. Limited access for disabled.
Concierge: Yes
Room Service: Yes
Restaurant: We offer private dining to our guests by reservation only. A sample of our menu: Shrimp Scampi, Grilled NY Strip, Grilled Salmon Planks and more. We also offer hors d'oeuvres and dessert with dinner.
Bar: Limited alcoholic services. All non-acoholic beverage for guests available 24 hr
Business Facilities: Fax, Copier and Modems available
Conference Rooms: Yes 1–24 people
Sports Facilities: Outdoor hot tub; Massages by appt., Horseback riding & Skiing-45 min. drive; Golf -5 min. drive
Spa Services: Massages by appointment.
Location: 1½ blocks from Lock & Dam & downtown

INTERNATIONAL HOUSE

This hotel alone has managed to fuse old and new successfully—it is modern without being obnoxious, stylish without being frigid. It is, in fact, one of those most rare things in life, a boutique hotel with soul. In the lobby, ornate pillars and decorative moldings are copied from the original 1906 blueprints, when this building was a bank. Chandeliers are based on 19th century models, and the softly glowing gaslights outside the entrance are copied from 1918 drawings. Every night, the bar holds a welcome ceremony for the spirits with candles, thrift shop seats, and mirrors made of old church windows serve as an altar. And the usual romantic weekend package is given a, ahem, magic spin. A real, live voodoo priestess can be hired for you very own love ceremony. *Complimentary wireless access.*

2 blocks from the French Quarter in the historic Central Business Districtin one of the world's most eclectic cities, it is a hotel like no other.

International House is about a tangible temporary style and an intangible spiritual warmth weaving its way throughout. It's about the welcoming glow of amber light. It's about the lobby ever changing for summer and winter in observance of rich local customs and rituals.

Address: 221 Camp Street, New Orleans 70130.
Phone: 504-553-9550 800-633-5770
Fax: 504-553.9560
Email: reservations@ihhotel.com
Web site: http://www.ihhotel.com
Room Rates: 159–349
Suite Rates: 349–749
No. of Rooms: 119
No. of Suites: 3
Credit Cards: Visa
Attractions: French Quarter, Aquarium of the Americas, River Walk, River Boat Cruises, walking distance to downtown Museums, French Market, Farmer's Market, one block from Street Car Stop, walking distance to renowned restaurants and world class shopping.
Services & Amenities: Fresh LA Wildflowers, Orig Black & White Photographs of Local Jazz Greats, Two-line phones/w VM, Wireless Internet, stereo/cd players with Jazz CD's, Cable TV w/ Comp Movie Channels, Aveda Bath Amenities, Fully stocked Honor Bars, Robes, Non-Smoking
Restrictions: Bookings over 5 rooms must contact hotel directly
Concierge: Services Available
Room Service: 7am-11pm
Restaurant: Lemongrass Restaurant Run by local chef, Minh Bui and offers the freshest local ingredients meticulously prepared and presented with his distinctive contemporary French/Vietnamese influences.
Bar: 5pm-2am
Business Facilities: Assistantce available
Conference Rooms: 8,350
Sports Facilities: Complimentary Health Club
Spa Services: Spa services are available in room or in the privacy of our exclusive spa room located on the second floor of the hotel.
Location: Downtown

HOTEL PROVINCIAL

Nestled in the heart of the French Quarter, the Hotel Provincial is within walking distance to all New Orleans has to offer.

The Provincial is situated in four beautifully restored buildings, with some situated on the National Historic Register. Enjoy 93 rooms and suites decorated with antiques and period reproductions and some are situated on picturesque courtyards.

Wake up and enjoy New Orlean's famous Beignets from Cafe Beignet and enjoy an evening of fine dining at Stella, one of New Orleans's best new restaurants.

We invite you to enjoy Unique 19th century charm blending seamlessly with modern convenience at the Hotel Provincial—New Orleans best kept secret!

Address: 1024 Chartres St, New Orleans 70116.

Phone: 504-581-4995 800-784-6948

Fax: 504-581-1018

Email: info@hotelprovincial.com

Web site: http://www.hotelprovincial.com

Room Rates: 79–249

Suite Rates: 149–355

No. of Rooms: 93

No. of Suites: 12

Credit Cards: Most Credit Cards accepted

Attractions: Located in the heart of the French Quarter, near all dining and entertainment hot-spots. Bourbon Street, Jackson Square, Mississippi River, Historic French Market, and the Aquarium are all at your finger- tips.

Services & Amenities: Valet service, On-site valet parking, Laundry, Cable TV, Telephone, Radio, Hair dryer, Iron and board, Voicemail, dataports, Coffee service in the lobby, Safe deposit boxes, Individual climate controls

Restrictions: No pets allowed, Children 17 and under free with parents, 3 rooms handicap equipped

Concierge: Front Desk 24 hours

Room Service: 7 a.m.- 4 p.m., 6–9:30 p.m.

Restaurant: Cafe Beignet–open 7 days a week from 7am-4pm. Our new restaurant, Stella, is open for fine dining from 6pm-10pm. Closed on Tuesday.

Bar: Honfleur Bar

Business Facilities: Normandie Room, perfect for special events and meetings

Conference Rooms: 1 room, capacity 50 theater style or banquet style

Sports Facilities: Outdoor swimming pool

Location: In the heart of the French Quarter

PONTCHARTRAIN HOTEL

The Pontchartrain Hotel, centrally located in the Garden District, was built in 1927 by the Aschaffenburg family and is now managed by Expotel. The magnificent draped entrance opens into a grand lobby with vaulted ceiling and gleaming chandeliers.

Each spacious guest room is individually decorated, no two alike. The suites in this hotel are truly extraordinary. For example, the Richard Burton suite is decorated on a "Camelot" theme in honor of the late, great actor; and the magnificent new Imperial suite has Napoleonic decor in the Malmaison tradition.

The Bayou Bar was inspired by the natural beauty of Louisiana scenic backwaters, again reflected in a Reinike wall mural. Piano music adds to your enjoyment of house specialties such as the mint julep and the Bayou Bomb.

The Pontchartrain Hotel offers conscientious quality service that is unrivaled anywhere.

Address: 2031 St. Charles Ave, New Orleans 70140
Phone: 504-524-0581
800-777-6193
Fax: 504-524-7828
Email:
sales@pontchartrainhotel.com
Web site: http://
www.pontchartrainhotel.com
Room Rates: 109–289
Suite Rates: 159–499
No. of Rooms 119
No. of Suites: 18
Attractions: Mississippi River cruises, French Quarter, Garden District, antique shopping, Audubon Zoo, IMAX Theatre, Aquarium of the Americas, Swamp Tours, Plantation Tours
Services & Amenities: Valet service, Laundry, Baby-sitting service, Garage and parking, Complimentary newspaper, Cable TV, Shampoo and conditioners, Hair dryers, Radio
Restrictions: No pets allowed, Some rooms handicap equipped
Room Service: 24 hours
Restaurant: Cafe Pontchartrain 7 a.m.–2:30 p.m., 5:30–9 p.m. Dress code: casual
Bar: Bayou Bar, Sun –Thurs 4 p.m. – midnight, Fri – Sat 11 a.m.–2 a.m.
Business Facilities: Audio-visual rental , fax
Conference Rooms: 7 rooms, capacity 500
Sports Facilities: Access to full-scale spa across from hotel
Location: Garden District

BAR HARBOR HOTEL - BLUENOSE INN

Set atop a granite-terraced hillside with spectacular views of sparkling Frenchman Bay and within close proximity to Acadia National Park, the Bluenose Inn is one of the most beautiful spots on the Atlantic.

Attention to detail and gracious service make the Bluenose Inn Oceanview resort Bar Harbor, Maine's premier AAA Four-Diamond hotel and restaurant.

In the beautifully appointed Queen-Anne style rooms, amenities include air-conditioning, cable TV with HBO movies, telephones and mini-refrigerator. Guests in the spacious Mizzentop suites, beautifully detailed in mauve, burgundy and green Waverly fabrics, may relax in fluffy robes to view breathtaking sunrises over Frenchman Bay. A king bed, love seat, easy chairs and crystal chandeliers provide comfort and grace. Walls are adorned with distinctive artwork. Many rooms and suites also have fireplaces.

Winner of *Wine Spectator* magazine's 2003 Award of Excellence; the Rose Garden features Four-Diamond dining, contemporary American regional cuisine and outstanding service. Try the Maine crab cakes and a decadent dessert of flourless chocolate cake while perusing the expertly prepared Wine List. Enjoy a selection of ports and single malt whiskies here, or in the Great Room with its plush and inviting furnishings, magnificent fireplace and handcrafted cherry-wood bar, offering nightly entertainment in-season.

Exercise facilities include a whirlpool, fitness center, outdoor heated pool with ocean views, and, undoubtedly, New England's most beautiful indoor pool.

The Bluenose Inn is a leisurely stroll from Bar Harbor with its many activities and historic sites, and is only 600 yards to the dock where the ferry makes its daily trip to and from Nova Scotia. Bicycling, kayaking, harbor cruises and whale watching are among the favorite ways to enjoy Bar Harbor and Acadia National Park.

Address: 90 Eden St, Route 3, Bar Harbor 4609.
Phone: 207-288-3348 800-445-4077
Fax: 207-288-2183
Email: reservations@bluenoseinn.com
Web site: http://www.bluenoseinn.com
Room Rates: 135–365
Suite Rates: 399–439
No. of Rooms: 97
No. of Suites: 30
Credit Cards: Visa
Attractions: Acadia National Park, Shops and Restaurants, Ferry to Nova Scotia, Whale Watching Excursions
Services & Amenities: Gift shop, Balconies/decks, Laundry service, TV, Hairdryers, Irons and Boards, Telephones with Voice Mail, Radio, Air conditioning, Handicap rooms available, Robes, Complimentary toiletries and newspaper
Restrictions: Non-smoking property. No pets.
Room Service: Breakfast & Dinner (dining hrs)
Restaurant: The Rose Garden, Breakfast 7-10:30 a.m., Dinner 5:30-9:30 p.m., Dressy/Casual
Bar: The Great Room, 5 p.m.-closing
Business Facilities: Copiers, Fax
Conference Rooms: 1 room, capacity 50
Sports Facilities: Indoor & Outdoor Pools, Whirlpool, Fitness Center, Nearby massage, sailing, tennis, hiking, and biki
Location: Eden Street, Route 3

THE LEDGELAWN INN

Built in 1904, this Colonial-style mansion is just a pleasant three-minute walk to downtown shopping, many fine restaurants and the waterfront. Bar Harbor's Historic Corridor is near other lodging, yet residential in nature, with lots of trees and gardens to enjoy. Both the Inn and the Carriage House are splendid examples of turn-of-the-century architecture, unique in features and design.

All rooms have private bath, antiques, TV and telephone. Others have four-poster beds, porches, working fireplaces, sauna and steambath plus whirlpool tubs. A typical room at the Ledgelawn has a fireplace, a couch, sitting area, wall-to-wall carpets, brass bed, flowered wallpaper, plants, reproduction furniture and oil paintings. Some rooms were renovated in 1998.

A complimentary, full European, buffet breakfast is served every morning on the Veranda and in the fireplace lounge area. Tea is served in the afternoon.

Nearby Acadia National Park & Carriage Paths and the oceanfront offer myriad outdoor activities.

Address: 66 Mount Desert St, Bar Harbor 4609.
Phone: 207-288-4596 800-274-5334
Fax: 207-288-9968
Email: desk@ledgelawninn.com
Web site: http://www.ledgelawninn.com
Room Rates: 70–250
Suite Rates: 155–275
No. of Rooms: 32
No. of Suites: 1
Attractions: Acadia National Park & Carriage Paths, Ocean activities such as whalewatching, cruises, beaches and birdwatching. Hiking, biking, kyacking, sightseeing.
Services & Amenities: Complimentary breakfast and afternoon tea, Parking, Baby-sitting service, 10 fireplaces, 12 balconies, Compimentary toiletries, Cable TV, Some rooms available for pets
Concierge: 9am–9pm
Restaurant: Breakfast only, 8 am.–10 am.
Bar: Ledgelawn Pub, 4 p.m.–11 p.m.
Business Facilities: Message center
Sports Facilities: Outdoor swimming pool, Aerobics, Weight training, Golf (18 holes) nearby, Sailing, Riding and tennis
Location: Historic District

BALANCE ROCK INN ON THE OCEAN

This beautifully restored oceanfront mansion has spectacular views that can be seen from most of the 19 guestrooms. Built in 1903 in the Colonial Revival style, the Balance Rock is located on 3 acres of oceanfront land.

The foyer uses rose and gray colors along with oriental rugs, polished hardwood floors and ornate painted woodwork. The sunny living room has a fireplace, grand piano, overstuffed furniture and oil paintings throughout.

A typical guestroom is large and sunny with a king-size canopy bed, writing desk, sitting area with fireplace, reproduction antique furniture, print wallpaper and wall-to-wall carpeting. Fresh flowers and plants add to the cozy atmosphere.

Breakfast is served in the lovely dining area with plush navy blue carpeting, floral wallpaper, and cushioned Queen Anne chairs. Wedgwood china and Oneida silver are used for the service. The Balance Rock is famous for its crepes! Afternoon tea is also available from 3-5 p.m.

There are many ocean activities if you so choose … whale watching, cruises, sailing, kayaking, island explorations and of course beaches for lounging and swimming. Nearby Acadia National Park is known for beautiful hiking, biking and views from mountains and shore.

The Balance Rock is the only restored oceanfront mansion with modern amenities in the area.

Address: 21 Albert Meadow, Bar Harbor 4609.
Phone: 207-288-2610 800-753-0494
Fax: 207-288-5534
Email: barhbrinns@aol.com
Web site: http://www.barharborvacations.com/welcomebri.htm
Room Rates: 125–495
Suite Rates: 395–625
No. of Rooms: 19
No. of Suites: 2
Attractions: Acadia National Park & Carriage Paths, Whale watching cruises, Beaches, Birdwatching, Views of Frenchman's Bay, shopping, sunset cruises
Services & Amenities: Most rooms have fireplaces, balconies, whirlpools, sauna. All have Cable TV/VCR, Telephone, Air-conditioning, Gilcrest & Somes toiletries, Complimentary newspaper, breakfast & afternoon tea. Select Comfort Mattresses, feather beds, 310 Chrisma Sheets
Restrictions: Well behaved children over 6 welcome, Well behaved pets welcome in some rooms
Concierge: 8 a.m.-11 p.m.
Room Service: 8 a.m.-10 a.m.
Restaurant: Breakfast only, 8 a.m.-10 a.m. Many excellent resturants within walking distance.
Bar: Popular patio and cigar bar
Business Facilities: Message center, Copiers
Sports Facilities: Exercise room, Heated swimming pool overlooking the ocean
Location: Oceanfront and Historic Shorepath

INN BY THE SEA

Located within Crescent Beach State Park, one of Maine's finest sand beaches, is the Inn by the Sea. The award-winning architecture of the Inn is reminiscent of the Cottage Shingled design of the 1890s. Surrounded by lush green lawns and ever- blooming perennials, the main house offers 25 one-bedroom suites and the adjacent cottages offer 18 two-bedroom suites—each with full kitchen, living/dining areas and patio or porch overlooking the Atlantic Ocean. Each suite is has three telephone, two televisions, a VCR, complimentary high speed Internet access, voice-mail.

Guestrooms in the main house are furnished with Chippendale cherry, while the cottages are furnished with simple white pine pieces; all are accented with original art. A unique collection of hand colored engravings by John J. Audubon are on display throughout the dining room and lobby area.

Indulge your senses and enjoy a gourmet dining experience in the romantic and intimate atmosphere of the Audubon Room. The menu offers new American regional cuisine with contemporary French overtones. There is always a variety of menu selections, offering only the freshest and finest of Maine's local gardens, fields and orchards. Native hand-picked seafood specialties provide the perfect compliment to the most impressive wine selections. Breakfast and dinner are served daily. During the summer, lunch and poolside service are available. The outdoor terrace is also open during the warmer months for evening cocktails and hors d'oeuvres.

A private boardwalk, leading through a beautiful natural estuary to the white sandy shore of Crescent Beach, is one of the highlights of the Inn. Amenities such as tennis, outdoor pool and shuffleboard are also offered. Sailing and excursion tours are available at the nearby Portland waterfront, as is an eclectic array of shops and restaurants in the Old Port district.

Address: 40 Bowery Beach Rd, Rt#77, Cape Elizabeth 4107.
Phone: 207-799-3134 800-888-4287
Fax: 207-799-4779
Email: info@innbythesea.com
Web site: http://www.innbythesea.com
Suite Rates: 169–639
No. of Suites: 43
Credit Cards: Visa
Attractions: Walk the "Old Port" with specialty shops, Cobblestone streets and Brownstone buildings, 30 minutes to LL Bean, Portland Headlight just 7 minutes away. Enjoy a tour of the Inns lavish garden with Head Gardner every Thursday June–October.
Services & Amenities: Valet laundry service, Free Parking, Baby and pet-sitting services available, Balconies, Cable TV's, VCR, Radio, 3 telephones per suite, Individual heat controls, Robes, Complimentary toiletries, Voicemail, Complimentary high speed Internet access.
Restrictions: No smoking; Pets & Children Welcome with Advance Notice
Room Service: 7 a.m.-9 p.m.
Restaurant: The Audubon Room—7 a.m.–9 p.m.
Business Facilities: Full-scale conference facilities
Conference Rooms: 2 rooms, capacity 60
Sports Facilities: Outdoor swimming pool, Croquet, Volleyball, Shuffleboard, Bicycles, Walking/jogging trails, Golf and
Spa Services: Massgae Therapist can be scheduled to come to the Inn and your suite.
Location: Quiet, non-commercial location, Seaside setting, Nearest airport–Portland

HARRASEEKET INN

The Harraseeket Inn is situated in the center of Freeport Village just two blocks from L.L. Bean. Upon entering the Harraseeket, the elegant mahogany paneling and cozy fireplaces exude the welcoming feel of an English country house.

In the guestrooms, the Colonial Revival theme is apparent from decorate touches of upholstered reproduction Colonial and Federal furniture and draperies. Many of the guestrooms and suites have working fireplaces.

The Harraseeket Inn's kitchen relies for its inspiration on locally raised ingredients—the justly famous seafood of the Gulf of Maine, produce from area gardens, and meats and poultry from farms just down the coast. The Inn is home to two restaurants. The Maine Dining Room is known as one of New England's best restaurants, and serves exciting interpretations of New England regional cuisine. The Broad Arrow Tavern offers traditional Down East cooking in an open kitchen with a wood-fired oven and grill with all the antique charm of an upcountry Maine hunting lodge. Al fresco dining on the terrace of the Inn's formal gardens makes for a perfect summertime repast. In keeping with the Inn's commitment to fresh, local, organically raised foods, the menus change with the seasons. The Inn's award-winning wine list is one of the best in the Northeast.

Complimentary tea is served daily in the Drawing Room. Full breakfast buffet is also included in the room rates. Cocktails are served in the Tavern.

The Harraseeket Inn is perfectly located for day-trips up the rocky coastline to Boothbay Harbor or explore Freeport's Wolfe Neck State Park and Mast Landing Audubon Society Center. Golf, skiing,fishing and antique hunting are within easy reach. L.L. Bean's Discovery School has fabulous courses and Portland, with its recreational, business, and cultural attractions, as well as its exciting nightlife, is only half an hour away. Harraseeket Inn is the proud winner of Condé Nast Traveler's Top 100 in the World Readers' Choice Award in November 2004 and Condé Nast Traveler's Gold List for 2005, (The Worlds' 700 Best Places to Stay). AAA four diamond.

The Inn's conference and banquet facilities and attention to the details of old-fashioned Maine hospitality are making it a destination of choice for business meetings, receptions, and unique weddings.

Address: 162 Main St, Freeport 4032.
Phone: 207-865-9377 800-342-6423
Fax: 207-865-1684
Email: harraseeke@aol.com
Web site: http://www.stayfreeport.com
Room Rates: 155–285
Suite Rates: 245–295
No. of Rooms: 84
No. of Suites: 6
Attractions: L.L.Bean Discovery school (learn to kayak, fly fish, skeet shoot, photograph), 150 Outlet stores, Wolfe Neck Park, Visit Maine Maritime Museum, Robert E. Perry Summer Island home, Shakers Museum.Explore Beaches, Fishing, Sailing, golf, great birding
Services & Amenities: Two restaurants,indoor pool,exercise room Library, Game area, Gift shop, a non smoking hotel, 18 in-room fireplaces, Cable TV, Radio, Robes, Whirlpool bath, free WIFI. Sewing kit, Complimentary breakfast and afternoon tea, Children welcome, pets welcome
Concierge: Yes
Room Service: 7 a.m.-10:30 p.m.
Restaurant: Maine Dining Room,full complimentary buffet breakfast, Fine Dining at night. Broad Arrow Tavern, Open kitchen, woodfired oven & grill. We serve Maine grown foods, natural or organic meats,chicken,etc
Bar: Broad Arrow Tavern, 11:30 a.m.-Midnight
Business Facilities: Full conference facilities, Message center, Copiers, Audio-Visual, Fax
Conference Rooms: 7 rooms, capacity 350
Sports Facilities: Croquet, Fitness center, Indoor pool
Location: Center of Freeport Village, Nearest airport is Portland International

CAPTAIN LORD MANSION

Enjoy an unforgettable romantic experience at the Captain Lord Mansion, where your personal comfort and romantic intimacy are assured by large, beautifully appointed and detail-filled guestrooms. The guestrooms are furnished with rich fabrics, fine linens, European paintings and seating areas with comfortably upholstered furniture. Also, each room has modern comforts such as a king or queen-size bed with posturepedic mattress, a telephone, individual A/C and a gas fireplace. All rooms have a private bath with European-style make-up mirror and hair dryer. Seven deluxe suites offer double Jacuzzi tubs, four baths include body-jet showers and there is one large bath with a steam shower. Six deluxe rooms overlook the expansive village green and the Kennebunk River.

The inn is situated in a quiet residential neighborhood of historic homes. The Mansion sits at the head of a sloping green, overlooking the Kennebunk River. The inn affords a picturesque, quiet, yet convenient location from which to explore the charming village of Kennebunkport. The Mansion also offers close proximity to extensive water-based activities such as whale watching, kayaking, canoeing, fishing, sailing, as well as easy access to bicycling, golf, tennis, art galleries, antique shopping and fine dining.

The inn has been designated an AAA 4-Diamond property for 23 consecutive years. The inn has also been given a "STAR" designation by Fromers and Fodors. Warm hospitality, delicious breakfasts, and incredible guestrooms, combined with meticulous attention to cleanliness and decorating details, make the inn an engaging and memorable vacation spot.

Address: PO Box 800, Kennebunkport 4046.
Phone: 207-967-3141 800-522-3141
Fax: 207-967-3172
Email: innkeeper@captainlord.com
Web site: http://www.captainlord.com
Room Rates: 125–399
Suite Rates: 289–449
No. of Rooms: 20
No. of Suites: 1
Credit Cards: Most Credit Cards accepted
Attractions: Whale watching, kayaking, canoeing, fishing, sailing, bicycling, golf, tennis, art galleries, antique shopping and fine dining.
Services & Amenities: Airport pick up, Gift shop, Card or game area, Complimentary newspaper, Fireplaces, Telephones, Radio, CD player, Non-alcoholic mini-bar, 4 baths with body jet showers, 1 bath with steam shower, Individual climate controls, Robes, Complimentary breakfast
Restrictions: No pets allowed, Not appropriate for children, No rooms handicap equipped
Concierge: 8 a.m.-10 p.m.
Business Facilities: Message center, Admin. assistance, E-mail, Copiers, Audio-visual, Teleconferencing, Fax, Modems
Conference Rooms: 3 rooms, capacity 16
Location: Lower village

KENNEBUNKPORT INN

The Kennebunkport Inn is a gracious late Victorian mansion built for a sea captain in the 1890s. The ideal blend of sophisticated small hotel and country inn, it has an intimate, personalized approach to service, yet is large enough to offer a wide array of services and amenities. Additional guest accommodations are located in the adjacent 1930s River House.

Each guestroom is individually decorated with period antiques, reproductions, and selected wallpapers and fabrics. Many include poster beds and comfortable sitting areas, and some rooms have views of the salt-water river and waterfront.

The Port Tavern Grille has two gracious dining rooms, elegantly appointed with two working fireplaces, wainscotting, chandeliers, and deep carpeting. Under the direction of Chef Robert Smith, the steaks and seafood items are innovative and exciting. In addition, the summer terrace Artemesia provides an inviting warm-weather dining alternative. It overlooks Dock Square, with umbrella-topped tables, potted plants, and pleasant salt breezes. Guests enjoy nightly piano music in the Port Tavern Pub, which features a lively ambiance.

Perfectly located in the center of the charming village at Dock Square, the Inn is within walking distance to wonderful shops and galleries. The waterfront and the Historic District, a neighborhood of white-clapboard sea captains' homes, tree-shaded gardens and white picket fences are also just steps away.

The Kennebunkport Inn is a sophisticated small hotel with the authentic atmosphere of an elegant sea captain's mansion.

Address: PO Box 111, One Dock Square, Kennebunkport 4046.
Phone: 207-967-2621 800-248-2621
Fax: 207-967-3705
Email: kportinn@adelphia.net
Web site: http://www.kennebunkportinn.com
Room Rates: 95–299
Suite Rates: 205–339
No. of Rooms: 46
No. of Suites: 4
Credit Cards: Visa
Attractions: Walking distance to shops, Historic District and harbor, Day sailing, Sightseeing, Deep-sea fishing excursions, Boat charters, 1 mile to beach. Antique shops, art galleries.5 golf courses are within minutes of the inn.
Services & Amenities: Parking, Cable TV, Telephones, Private bath, Complimentary toiletries, Views of village and river, Kitchen and fireplaces available. Pool on premise. Wireless Internet, Spa Services, Massage Showerheads, CD Players, resturant, piano bar
Restrictions: No pets allowed, Children welcome
Concierge: On premise
Restaurant: Port Tavern Grille serves grilled steaks & seafood. Country breakfast served and seasonal Artemesia's outdoor patio dining.
Bar: Port Tavern Pub, 5 p.m.-Midnight
Business Facilities: Fax, Copier, Wireless Internet
Conference Rooms: Two meeting rooms
Sports Facilities: Nearby five 9-and 18-hole golf courses, Tennis, Outdoor swimming pool
Spa Services: The Kennebunkport Inn is pleased to offer spa services available for our guests. We offer a wide selection of services and packages including Thereapeutic Massage and Spa Body Treatments.
Location: Center of Kennebunkport, 1½ hours–Boston, 25 miles–Portland Jetport

POMEGRANATE INN

Small and sophisticated, the Pomegranate Inn is located in the quiet, historic Western Promenade District. Within walking distance of the mid-town arts district and Old Port, this 1884 Italianate mansion boasts a fine and extensive collection of contemporary art and antique furnishings.

Classic room accommodations are complemented by hand-painted walls, custom and antique furnishings, and fine antique linens. Each room has its own private bathroom. Many of the rooms feature large porcelain tubs—most with showers—and pedestal sinks finish the exceptional interior design.

Guests are welcomed to the Pomegranate with tea and wine upon arrival (4pm-6pm).

A full breakfast is served to guests in the sunny, art and antique filled Dining Room. In winter, guests can enjoy breakfast by the fire and in summer French doors are opened onto the garden. Coffee, fresh fruit and juice, and morning entrees such as poached eggs with salmon and capers or flan-like French Toast with chicken and apple sausages are among the offerings.

Whether your sojourn is for business or pleasure, a stay at the Pomegranate Inn will add a sense of peace and privilege to your visit to this beautiful small city by the sea.

Address: 49 Neal St, Portland 4102.
Phone: 207-772-1006 800-356-0408
Fax: 207-773-4426
Web site: http://
www.pomegranateinn.com
Room Rates: 95–275
Suite Rates: 155–275
No. of Rooms: 8
No. of Suites: 1
Credit Cards: Most Credit Cards accepted
Attractions: Great restaurants, Museums, Galleries and Shopping abound. Easy access to Casco Bay Cruises and the Islands. 20 minutes to beaches.
Services & Amenities: Cable TV, Telephone, Air conditioning, Some fireplaces, Complimentary toiletries, Breakfast included in room rate
Restrictions: Minimum stay in season, no pets allowed, children over 16 welcome, 1 room handicap equipped
Concierge: 4-6 p.m.
Room Service: No
Restaurant: A full served breakfast from 8–9:30 a.m., Complimentary tea and wine upon arrival (4pm-6pm)
Bar: No
Business Facilities: Fax, Modems
Conference Rooms: No
Sports Facilities: No
Location: Western Promenade

THE CLAREMONT HOTEL

The Claremont hotel has provided a classic Maine vacation to visitors of Mount Desert Island, each summer since 1884. Our six acre ocean front resort accommodations include the historic hotel building with 24 rooms and the Phillips House with six rooms. Lodging is offered on the Modified American Plan, featuring fresh Maine lobster or Bed and Breakfast meal plans. Our 14 housekeeping cottages with fireplaces, decks and kitchenettes are ideal for family vacations, or romantic weekend getaways. On site facilities include, fine dining, dock, moorings, boat house, rowboats, tennis court and croquet courts. A private location for destination wedding weekends, family reunions and signature vacations in the Maine Coast tradition.

Acadia National Park, one of the East Coasts most popular family vacation destinations, offers the naturalist opportunities for hiking, mountain biking, kayaking, sailing and swimming. Other area activities include sailing, fishing, whale watching and three area golf courses. We are located twenty minutes from Bar Harbor with all its shops, activities and resources.

Address: Claremont Rd, Box 137, Southwest Harbor 4679
Phone: 800-244-5036
Fax: 207-244-3512
Email: clmhotel@adelphia.net
Web site: http://www.theclaremonthotel.com
No. of Rooms: 65
Attractions: Near by are: golf courses, fresh water swimming, boat tours, kayak and boat rentals, summer theater, the restaurants and shops of Southwest Harbor and all the resources of Acadia National Park.
Restaurant: The new hotel bar, which features an atrium skylight and detailed woodwork promises to be a popular setting for pre dinner cocktails.
Sports Facilities: Facilities include: clay tennis court, six and nine wicket croquet courts, bicycles, dock, rowboat

HARBOR COURT HOTEL

Harbor Court Hotel, located on Baltimore's picturesque Inner Harbor, offers European-style service with a distinctly American influence. From the grand staircase that greets guests to the original art and antiques that adorn the hotel, each detail was carefully crafted for its aesthetic beauty and style and offers a wide variety of services and amenities including Maryland's only Les Clefs d'Or Hotel concierge. Harbor Court has received numerous prestigious awards, including Five-Star Diamond Awards from the American Academy of Hospitality, 4-Diamond Awards from the American Automobile Association and 4-Star Awards from the *Mobil Travel Guide*.

Each Guestroom is lavishly decorated with traditional mahogany furniture, comfortable reading chairs, writing desks, armoires, and fine linens. The specialty suites offer four-poster beds, over-sized marble bathrooms, six-foot bathtubs, three telephones and overlook the Inner Harbor.

To sample Baltimore's finest cuisine, guests need not leave the hotel. Hampton's, Baltimore's only five-star diamond award-winning restaurant, from the American Academy of Hospitality Sciences, is a feast for the eyes as well as the palate. From the chef's seasonal American cuisine and the Maitre'd's expertly trained staff to the lavishly decorated dining room and breathtaking view of the harbor, it's not hard to understand why *Condé Nast* named Hampton's one of the top two restaurants in the nation. Brightons Restaurant with its lemon silk moiré walls and botanical theme offers more casual dining for breakfast, lunch and dinner as well as traditional afternoon tea. For classic cocktails, fine cigars and a sumptuous array of hors d'oeuvres and light fare, try Explorer's Lounge. Inspired by safari legends and adventure lore, the lounge offers live jazz every night of the week.

Harbor Court has a state-of-the-art fitness center with a swimming pool, aerobics or yoga. If you don't want to lift a finger, they offer sauna, whirlpool, massage and tanning.

Whether traveling for business or leisure, Harbor Court Hotel will always be a pleasure.

Address: 550 Light St, Baltimore 21202.
Phone: 410-234-0550 800-824-0076
Fax: 410-659-5925
Email: reservations@harborcourt.com
Web site: http://www.harborcourt.com
Room Rates: 225–325
Suite Rates: 375–3500
No. of Rooms: 171
No. of Suites: 25
Attractions: The National Aquarium, Oriole Park at Camden Yards, Mechanic Theater, Discovery Children's Museum, Maryland Science Center, Inner Harbor shopping and restaurants
Services & Amenities: Laundry, Valet, Parking, Full service beauty salon, Library, Car rental, Gift shop, House doctor, Baby-sitting service, Complimentary shoeshine, newspaper and toiletries, Children free in same room with parents
Restrictions: No pets allowed; 4 rooms handicap equipped
Concierge: 7:30 a.m.-10:30 p.m.
Room Service: 24 hours
Restaurant: Hampton's, 5-11 p.m., dress code, Brightons, 7 a.m.-10 p.m.
Bar: Explorer's Lounge 11 a.m.-2 a.m.
Business Facilities: Full-service Executive Business Center w/ admin support, Executive Office Suite, Audio-visual
Conference Rooms: 11 rooms, capacity 10-220, 8,000 sq.ft. of meeting space
Sports Facilities: Complete Fitness Center, Aerobics, Yoga, Racquetball, Tennis, Heated indoor pool, Sauna, Whirlpool,
Location: Baltimore Inner Harbor

MILLENNIUM BOSTONIAN HOTEL

Set in the heart of Boston across from famous Faneuil Hall Marketplace stands the Millennium Bostonian Hotel. The Hotel is located on the Freedom Trail in a stately red brick building that spans centuries. On display in the hotel's inviting lobby are some of Boston's earliest colonial artifacts which were discovered during the construction of the building.

The Millennium Bostonian Hotel is considered one of the best addresses to stay while visiting or conducting business in Boston. Winner of the Condé Nast Gold List for "one of the world's Best Places to Stay," the Millennium Bostonian Hotel offers guests superior accommodations, service and amenities. Guestrooms feature king or queen size beds, oversized bathtubs and French doors that open onto private balconies with flower boxes. Accented with light colored English country wallpaper are lovely Gracia Dayton watercolors. The hotel also boasts a number of specialty rooms complete with working fireplaces, exposed beams and European balconies overlooking Quincy Market. The Botolph Wing has floor to ceiling windows on the penthouse level that has spectacular views of Boston, Faneuil Hall and the skyline.

Seasons, the hotel's rooftop restaurant has won numerous awards for its food, décor and service, and most recently won the Award of Excellence as having "one of the most outstanding restaurant wine lists in the world" by *Wine Spectator* magazine. Seasons culinary team creates seasonally unique cuisine, which includes such delicacies as Butter Brushed Lobster, Mint Marinated Lamb Chops and New England Seafood Stew. Menus change four times annually to offer the best cuisine of each season.

The hotel staff takes great pride in this "one-of-a-kind" hotel and strives to give their most personal attention to guests' every wish.

Address: 26 North Street, Boston 2109.
Phone: 617-523-3600 800-343-0922
Fax: 617-523-2454
Email: bostonian@mhrmail.com
Web site: http://www.millenniumhotels.com
Room Rates: 169–299
Suite Rates: 450–750
No. of Rooms: 201
No. of Suites: 14
Attractions: Across from historic Faneuil Hall Marketplace and on the Freedom Trail Walking Tour, Financial District, Boutique shopping, Harbor cruises and Historic landmarks close by
Services & Amenities: Valet service, Garage nearby, Valet parking, Currency exchange, Complimentary shoeshine, House doctor, Baby-sitting service, Laundry, Turndown service, Cable TV, Radio, 11 fireplaces, 128 balconies, Wet bar, Robes, Phone in bathroom, Whirlpool, Internet
Restrictions: No pets allowed, 12 rooms handicap equipped
Room Service: 24 hours
Restaurant: Seasons–Monday-Friday 6:30 a.m.–10 a.m., Noon–2 p.m., Tuesday–Saturday 6 p.m.–9 p.m. last seating, Saturday and Sunday 7 a.m.–Noon
Bar: The Atrium Lounge, 2 p.m.-12:45 a.m.
Business Facilities: Business Center, audio-visual
Conference Rooms: 4 rooms, capacity 20-90
Sports Facilities: In-house fitness suite
Spa Services: Salon & Day Spa
Location: Downtown Boston, Nearest airport is Logan International

THE LENOX HOTEL

Built at the turn of the century as a gathering place for proper Bostonians, The Lenox stands proudly in its original Back Bay location, providing eloquent testimony to its distinguished heritage. Recent, award-winning renovations combine the gracious elegance of the past with the modern conveniences of today in this 212-room four-diamond hotel.

Spacious guestrooms and suites are designed with comfort in mind, featuring such luxurious necessities as plush terry bathrobes and walk-in closets. Modern amenities such as a fax machine, dual-line speakerphone with modem port, wireless Internet service, and personal voice mail are also provided. A crackling fire in one of the hotel's select fireplace rooms or the complimentary newspaper waiting at your door each morning may satisfy more rustic needs.

The Lenox is home to Azure, Robert Fathman's nationally acclaimed restaurant. Hotel guests can enjoy Calderone's exceptional Mediterranean-inspired cuisine either in Azure's dramatic dining room or in the privacy of their guestroom through the hotel's In-Room Dining service.

Guests searching for a taste of Boston's patriotic past will find it at the Solas Irish Pub. This popular local gathering place serves twelve distinct styles of freshly tapped Samuel Adams beer and pub-style food.

The Lenox can accommodate a wide variety of social and business events. The elegant Dome Room, with its gilded central dome and superb acoustics, has been the proud setting of many grand functions in the course of Boston's social history. The Board Room, with its oak paneling, antique furniture, and ornamental fireplace, brings a note of dignified refinement to small meetings and private luncheons.

Ideally located in the heart of Boston, The Lenox provides its guests with the perfect blend of old world charm and modern extravagance.

Address: 61 Exeter Street at Boylston, Boston 2116.
Phone: 617-536-5300 800-225-7676
Fax: 617-236-0351
Email: scullen@lenoxhotel.com
Web site: http://www.lenoxhotel.com
Room Rates: 225–428
Suite Rates: 695
No. of Rooms: 212
Attractions: Walking distance to Newbury Street, Shopping at Prudential Center and Copley Place, Trolley and Duck Tours, Hynes Convention Center, Boston Common and Public Gardens, Faneuil Hall Marketplace
Services & Amenities: Valet Service, Garage & Valet Parking, Car Hire, Currency Exchange, House Doctor, Laundry Service, Baby-Sitting Service, Cable TV, Phone in Bathroom, Radio, Robes, Hair Dryers, Iron & Ironing Board, Complimentary Aveda Toiletries, Newspaper & Umbrellas
Restrictions: No pets allowed, 4 rooms handicap equipped
Concierge: 24 hours
Room Service: 6:30 a.m.-midnight
Restaurant: Azure: Critically acclaimed restaurant of Robert Fathman, breakfast and dinner daily, Sunday brunch (reservations recommended). Solas: Authentic Irish Pub, lunch and dinner daily.
Bar: City Bar: 11:30 a.m.–1:30 a.m. daily
Business Facilities: Message center, Audio-visual, Fax, Modem ports, Full-scale conference facilities
Conference Rooms: 6 rooms
Sports Facilities: Exercise room with cardiovascular machines and weights
Location: Downtown Back Bay at Copley Square

CHARLES STREET INN

A spectacular **360 Degree Tour** of all nine rooms is available on our website.

Centrally located in the heart of Boston's historic Beacon Hill neighborhood, The Charles Street Inn is just a short walk away from the Boston Common & Public Gardens, the Freedom Trail, Newbury Street and the Back Bay, the Esplanade, Chinatown, the Theatre District and Faneuil Hall. Lined with gaslamps, red brick sidewalks and antique shops, Beacon Hill is Boston's most charming neighborhood.

Our nine Victorian suites are decorated and furnished in exquisite Second Empire Victoria style. Each room features the original working marble fireplace, authentic period art and antiques, original plaster cornices and ceiling medallions. The rooms are named after luminaries from Boston's Victorian era (e.g. Ralph Waldo Emerson, Louisa May Alcott, Oliver Wendell Holmes, etc.) and decorated to reflect the their personality.

Queen rooms enjoy roof top views, king rooms have garden views, and all rooms have luxury cherry wood and while Italian tile bathrooms that include large Ultra Thermo-Masseur whirlpools and Kohler showers, kitchenettes with sub-zero refrigerator/ freezers, high quality coffee makers, Frette linens including robes and slippers, and Crabtree & Evelyn toiletries. Modern amenities include DSL & wireless Internet, two phone lines with fax, Bose Wave AM/FM radio with CD player, cable Sony stereo television with DVD/VCR, free use of videos, in-room safes, CD and book library. With elevator access to all rooms, it is not necessary to climb stairs at the Charles Street Inn (one room is fully handicapped).

Owners Sally Deane and Louise Venden provide warm and attentive service, a deluxe continental breakfast served in your room, and helpful advice regarding local sites, shopping, tours and events.

Address: 94 Charles Street, Boston 2114.

Phone: 617-314-8900 877-772-8900 Fax: 617-371-0009

Email: info@charlesstreetinn.com

Web site: http:// www.charlesstreetinn.com

Room Rates: 225–375

No. of Rooms: 9

Credit Cards: Most Credit Cards accepted

Attractions: Historic Beacon Hill and Charles Street shopping, tours and restaurants. A short walk from the Freedom Trail, the Esplanade, the Boston Public Garden, Newbury Street, Mass. General Hospital, the State Capital and the Theater District.

Services & Amenities: Elevator, Cable TV/DVD/VHS, in-room HVAC controls, Phones w/Voicemail & private numbers, DSL & wireless Internet, BOSE radio/CD player, Frette linens, Ultra Thera Spa Whirlpools, 1860 Working Marble Fireplaces, Breakfast included, Parking, Baby-sitting

Restrictions: No smoking, Children free w/parents on 2 n/min., 2 n/min. weekends/holidays, 1 room handicap equipped

Concierge: 7 a.m.-9 p.m.

Room Service: 7am-9pm-24 hr on-site manager

Restaurant: Deluxe European style Breakfast is delivered to your room in the morning–fresh organic fruit, warm scones & croissants, yogurt, cereals, juice and choice of newspaper. Served 7:30 a.m.–10 a.m.

Business Facilities: FAX, DSL & wireless Internet, laptop available

Sports Facilities: Passes available for Health Clubs at Charles River Park ($15/day) & Sports Club LA.

Spa Services: Salon professionals providing spa services at other first-class Boston hotels now offer Swedish or Shiatsu Massage and Brown Sugar or Sea Salt Body Polish treatments at The Charles Street Inn.

HAWTHORNE INN

Beside the old road that has witnessed the courage of Minute Men, marching to first challenge the King's troops and fire "The shot heard round the world," Hawthorne Inn was raised (c.1870) on fertile earth that was once owned by Ralph Waldo Emerson, Louisa May Alcott and family, Nathaniel Hawthorne and surveyed by the famed naturalist, Henry David Thoreau.

Under the shade of ancient trees, you will find the Hawthorne Inn to be an intimate refuge that is filled with much to share: poetry and literature to entertain and to enlighten you, artworks and archaic artifacts that are a wonder to behold, weavings and coverlets to snuggle on a crisp autumn eve and burnished antique furnishings that speak of home and security.

The seven vibrant guestrooms offer gracious appointments that are inspired by a refreshing sense of tradition melded with an artist's whimsy and the unexpected. Highlighting the rooms are artworks and antique furnishings with a backdrop of wonderful colors that rests the soul and warms the heart. Each guest accommodation possesses ensuite bath replete with abundant amenities. Displayed throughout the Inn are fascinating collections of Japanese Ukiyo-e prints, Pre-Colombian artifacts, modern paintings and sculptures and a varied library that will satisfy all sensibilities. Guests enjoy an extensive continental breakfast served each morning on hand-painted Dedham pottery, around a convivial common table.

You may choose to pass your time basking near the whispering fire with a book in hand, be led by the resident cat to a seat in the bountiful floral gardens for a spot of tea or enjoy the day ambling pathways and exploring the many treasures of Concord's layered history. The Hawthorne Inn invites you to listen to the whispers of Concord's Muse and to take a moment to be refreshed in body, mind and spirit.

Address: 462 Lexington Rd, Concord 1742.
Phone: 978-369-5610
Fax: 978-287-4949
Email: inn@concordmass.com
Web site: http://www.concordmass.com
Room Rates: 125–305
No. of Rooms: 7
Credit Cards: Most Credit Cards accepted
Attractions: Walk to homes of authors [Hawthorne, Alcott (Little Women), Emerson] and explore the pathways about Walden Pond to visit Thoreau's cabin site. Near Old North Bridge, "Shot Heard Round the World," Concord Museum and Great Meadows National Wildlife Refuge.
Services & Amenities: Off-street parking, Common Room with books and fireplace, Air-Conditioning, Village setting with gardens and view of Nathaniel Hawthorne's home, fine toiletries, Complimentary Check-in goodies basket.
Restrictions: Smoke-free facility, No pets allowed, Minimum stay on holidays
Concierge: 9 a.m.-9 p.m.
Restaurant: Breakfast served to over-night guests at a convivial common table set with hand-painted Dedham pottery.
Business Facilities: Telephone w/ modem jack, early breakfast, Fax service
Sports Facilities: Walden Pond and 3 rivers for swimming and canoeing, 5 mile walkingtrail in Minute Man National Park
Location: American Mile Historic Village, 19 miles to Boston

CHARLOTTE INN

In stately Edgartown, on the island of Martha's Vineyard, stands The Charlotte Inn. A spirited revival of Edwardian-era elegance, this 1864 home has been a haven for generations of discriminating travelers during all four of the island's distinct seasons. Nestled on South Summer Street, shaded by magnificent linden and chestnut trees, The Inn is both secluded and accessible. The vibrant and historic town center is a leisurely stroll from the peace and tranquility found here. And beyond, the storied island of Martha's Vineyard awaits exploration.

The inn's accommodations bespeak a commitment to the finer things in life. Each room is unique, from its dimensions to its design. Original artwork, leather-bound books, and fine woods create an ambiance of warmth and conviviality. Rooms are appointed with sterling silver dresser sets, antique chests, brass and crystal lamps, goose down pillows and comforters, hand-cut crystal, fresh cut flowers, and hand-made European draperies of silk and linen.

An extensive collection of nineteenth-century art complements the Inn's Edwardian architecture and design. The respect for material treasures extends to the care and comfort of inn guests. Superior service is de regeur, unobtrusive yet attentive, discreet but personalized. Individual guest preferences are accommodated with pleasure.

The inn's gardens provide a unifying counterpoint to the diverse architectural elements. From every window guests can enjoy the marriage of nature's benevolence and the dedication of the inn's team of gardeners. Immaculate lawns, English ivy, and manicured hedges underscore the distinguished air of the inn's lush gardens. The Charlotte Inn is a member of Relais & Chateaux.

Some of New England's most acclaimed cuisine is found in The Charlotte Inn's restaurant, L'etoile. The menu celebrates French cooking traditions and native ingredients—complex and subtle sauces showcase ingredients from New England fields, streams and seas, and the bounty of local herb gardens. Sumptuous meals are presented amidst stunning surroundings.

"A little jewel of a place." *The Boston Sunday Globe.*

Address: P.O. Box 1056, Edgartown 2539.
Phone: 508-627-4751
Fax: 508-627-4652
Room Rates: 295–550
Suite Rates: 695–895
No. of Rooms: 23
No. of Suites: 2
Credit Cards: Visa
Attractions: Shopping ½ block away, Restaurants, Golf, Tennis and Beautiful beaches
Services & Amenities: Continental breakfast included in room rate, Full breakfast available, Parking, Radios, Complimentary newspaper, Cable TV, Telephones, Gardens, Air conditioning, Robes, Complimentary toiletries, Afternoon tea during summer months
Restrictions: No pets allowed, children over 14 welcome
Concierge: front desk 8am-11pm
Restaurant: L'etoile, evenings daily during season and weekends during off-season, dress code–jackets requested
Sports Facilities: Off site facilities within walking or driving distance: Sauna, Aerobics, Sailing, Golf, Riding, Tennis
Location: Downtown, half block off Main Street

CRANWELL RESORT, SPA & GOLF CLUB

This luxurious four-season resort and 100-year-old historic Gilded Age mansion in the Berkshire Hills accommodates leisure travelers, business and executive groups, weddings and special events with equal flair and attention to detail. Here where Henry Ward Beecher claimed, "One could see the very hills of heaven," guests can step outside their rooms to enjoy an 18-hole championship golf course, a new world-class 35,000 sq ft. spa, tennis, hiking, swimming, and, in winter, groomed cross-country ski and snowshoe trails.

Rooms in the Cranwell Mansion are individually designed in a gracious style, many with decorative fireplaces and four-poster beds. Rooms and suites are also available in the nearby Resort Buildings, many of which have glass enclosed links to the Spa and Fitness Center. Marble floors, Tudor wood paneling and ceilings, leaded windows, an imposing staircase, and spacious terraces are just a few of the architectural details of the lobby and meeting rooms in the Mansion.

Guests may relax with cocktails next to a roaring fire in the lobby or enjoy an elegant meal such as Thai Barbequed Australian Rack of Lamb lamb and the signature Cranwell Apple tart at the resort's Wyndhurst and Music Room restaurants. A prix fixe Grille Menu is also offered in the Mansion restaurants and lighter fare in a more casual setting can be found at Sloane's Tavern next to the the golf course.

Cranwell Resort is renowned for exceptional banquet and event services. Cranwell's Certified Professional Meeting Planners will attend to the details of conferences of up to 200.

Additional local attractions include downhill skiing, antique shopping, art galleries, numerous seasonal cultural events and tours of the lovely and historic Berkshire Hills.

Address: 55 Lee Road, Lenox 1240.
Phone: 413-637-1364 800-272-6935
Fax: 413-637-4364
Email: info@cranwell.com
Web site: http://www.cranwell.com
Room Rates: 165–345
Suite Rates: 265–495
No. of Rooms: 107
Credit Cards: Most Credit Cards accepted
Attractions: Tanglewood, Jacob's Pillow, Norman Rockwell Museum, art centers, Museums and historic sites, Theatre and musical productions, Ski areas.
Services & Amenities: Rooms are equipped with coffee-makers, hair dryers, ironing boards make-up mirrors and data ports.
Restrictions: Smoking rooms available, Children under 12 free in parent's room,
Concierge: Yes
Room Service: Yes
Restaurant: Three acclaimed restaurants: Wyndhurst—elegant dining, Music Room—Breakfast and dinner, and Sloane's Tavern—casual lunch & dinner. The Spa Cafe is also open daily.
Bar: Music Room Lounge & Sloane's Tavern
Business Facilities: Message Center, copiers, Audio-Visual & fax. Full-scale conference facility.
Conference Rooms: 12: Capacity 10-200
Sports Facilities: Spa, Fitness Center, indoor pool, 18-hole golf course, X-C ski trails
Spa Services: The Spa at Cranwell: heated indoor pool, whirlpools, saunas, steamrooms, Fitness Center, Spa Shop, Spa Cafe,16 treatment rooms, over 35 professional services available, reservations recommended.
Location: Berkshires County

THE PORCHES INN

Six 1890's row houses, once the homes of mill workers during North Adams industrial heyday, are given new life as the Porches Inn. As the first hotel to open near the upstart Massachusetts Museum of Contemporary Art, the completely renovated buildings, which are linked by two long front porches, have been cleverly redesigned to accommodate 50 distinctive guestrooms and suites.

Each of the six buildings has been painted a different vivid color. Behind the main reception house, a separate "ping pong" building houses a game room and sauna. Inside the Inn, the public rooms feature a living room with fireplace, den, a breakfast room, small gift shop and meeting room accommodating 20 people.

Four color schemes are featured in the guestrooms and suites. Beadboard walls are painted terra cotta, pale blueberry, celery green and sage green to complement wooden floors that have been painted olive green, red, pumpkin and buttercup respectively. Wool area rugs further highlight the floors. An extensive collection of lamps from the 1940s and 1950s, etched glass mirrors and vintage vinyl upholstered furniture in bright colors are mixed with an eclectic assortment of vintage furniture. The large bathrooms feature either Jacuzzi-style tubs or clawfoot bathtubs with separate showers. All bathrooms boast slate floors and distinctive mirror frames.

The Porches Inn offers a complimentary European style buffet breakfast featuring a house coffeecake. Guests who prefer to eat in their rooms may have breakfast delivered in a galvanized metal lunch box, modeled after those used by the workers who originally lived on the property.

A Historic Hotels of America member, the Porches Inn is an eye-opening synthesis of contemporary and retro design.

Address: 231 River St, North Adams 1247.
Phone: 413-664-0400
Fax: 413-664-0401
Email: info@porches.com
Web site: http://www.porches.com
Room Rates: 135–285
Suite Rates: 185–425
No. of Rooms: 52
No. of Suites: 21
Attractions: Close to MASS MoCA, Williamstown Theatre Festival, the Sterling & Francine Clark Art Institute, Mt. Greylock and the surrounding Berkshire Hills
Services & Amenities: Parking, Gift shop, Baby-sitting service, CableTV/DVD, Complimentary newspaper, Telephones, Radio, Honor bar, Individual climate controls, Robes, Complimentary toiletries, Complimentary breakfast
Restrictions: No pets allowed, Children all ages welcome, 2 rooms handicap equipped
Concierge: Available
Room Service: Available for breakfast only
Restaurant: Porches guests have check-signing privileges at several area restaurants, including "eleven at MASS MoCA."
Bar: 3 p.m. and on
Business Facilities: Copiers, Audio-visual, Teleconferencing, Fax, Modems
Conference Rooms: 2 rooms, capacity 30
Sports Facilities: Fitness Room, Year-round outdoor swimming pool, Hottub, Sauna, Massage
Spa Services: Massage available by appointment
Location: Across the street from MASS MoCA

YANKEE CLIPPER INN

Located on the rocky shoreline of Rockport, Massachusetts, The Yankee Clipper Inn consists of an oceanfront, 1929 Art Deco mansion and magnificent contemporary cape with panoramic ocean views. Rolling lawns and gardens frame colorful vistas to the ocean. In season take timeout to relax under the umbrellas on the terrace for a quiet read. Take laps in the salt waterpool. The Yankee Clipper was voted "Best Nearby Escape" by *Boston Magazine*, "Best Seaside View" and "One of the 25 Best Inns in the Country" by *Arringtons Journal*, and has been featured on *The Great Country Inns* Television Program and in *Country Living Magazine*.

The inn offers several choices for accommodations. Three of the rooms offer ocean side sun rooms, which provide a perfect place to relax and read a book or to make plans for your day. Fifteen rooms provide magnificent ocean views. Two of the rooms offer access to the oceanfront grounds directly from their private entrances.

The Inn is the perfect location for an unforgettable wedding or business meeting. The Special Occasion Room or Rose Garden can be the perfect location. Many international and American celebrities have been guests over the years, and the inn has served as a location for TV and movies.

The Yankee Clipper Inn offers the opportunity to relax, while enjoying the scenic beauty of a spectacular location.

Address: 127 Granite St, Rockport 1960.

Phone: 978-546-3407 800-545-3699

Fax: 978-546-9730

Email: info@yankeeclipperinn.com

Web site: http://www.yankeeclipperinn.com

Room Rates: 129–379

Suite Rates: 199–355

No. of Rooms: 16

No. of Suites: 3

Credit Cards: Most Credit Cards accepted

Attractions: Boutiques and shops on Bearskin Neck which overlooks Rockport Harbor, Beaches, Hiking, Whale watching only minutes away.

Services & Amenities: Complimentary breakfast included in room rates, Cable TV, Private bath, Telephone. Several rooms have jet tubs and DVD players. Two have marble baths. 15 of the 16 offer spectacular ocean views

Restrictions: No pets allowed, Children welcome, Completely non-smoking facility

Concierge: Yes

Room Service: No

Restaurant: The oceanfront Sapphire Dining Room is open for traditional afternoon tea, with tea sandwiches, scones, and sweets. Reservations are recommended. Sapphire will be open for dinner in Spring 2005!

Bar: no

Business Facilities: Multiuse oceanfront meeting room

Conference Rooms: Multiuse oceanfront meeting room

Sports Facilities: Outdoor swimming pool

Location: Quiet residential neighborhood of Pigeon Cove

THE DANIEL WEBSTER INN & SPA

This award-winning, boutique Inn, set in the heart of Sandwich Village, offers guests the romance of the past with today's conveniences. Located on the site of a tavern built before the American Revolution, the inn is named for its most famous 19th-century habitue.

All guest chambers and suites are elegantly appointed with exquisite period furnishings and canopy or four-poster beds. Luxurious fireplace suites feature oversized whirlpools, heated tile floors and the exclusive Suite Dreams Experience with choice of pillow, memory foam mattress, air purification system, plush bathrobe and more. The Fessenden House, a restored Sea Captain's home, offers private two-room suites. The Dan'l Webster Suite, set atop the main inn, features a king-size master bedroom with balcony overlooking the Great Marsh, a marble bathroom and whirlpool for two with skylight.

Surround yourself in the refined ambiance of one of The Dan'l Webster's five distinctive dining rooms including the magnificent glass-walled Conservatory.

Named among the top 1% of restaurants in the country by DiRona, savor delicious, creative cuisine and innovative chef's specials including Veal Napoleon and Lobster and Scallop Fontina using fresh, local seafood. The Dan'l Webster features excellent service as well as one of the most acclaimed wine cellars in the region. State of the art technology allows the Dan'l Webster to offer over 20 different wines by the glass to complement any entree. For casual fare, relax in the Tavern at the Inn and sample one of their famous wood-grilled pizzas, light entrees or hearty sandwiches.

The new Spa at The Dan'l Webster offers the ultimate in luxury for Men and Women—from completely organic Body Treatments and relaxing Massages to soothing Facials and more, we will pamper your mind, body and soul!

Address: 149 Main St, Sandwich 2563.
Phone: 508-888-3622 800-444-3566
Fax: 508-888-5156
Email: info@danlwebsterinn.com
Web site: http://www.danlwebsterinn.com
Room Rates: 119–399
No. of Rooms: 53
No. of Suites: 16
Credit Cards: Most Credit Cards accepted
Attractions: Historic attractions, Museums, Heritage Plantation, Sandwich Glass Museum, Thornton Burgess Museum, Hoxie House, Factory Outlet Mall, Antique Shops, Cape Cod Canal, Ocean & Beaches
Services & Amenities: Full-service Spa, wireless Internet access, Parking, Gift shop, Gathering room for guests, Lounge, Equipment for physically impaired, Nightly turndown service, Cable TV, Individual climate control, Robe, Hair dryer, Elegant toiletries
Restrictions: No pets, 2-night minimum stay on weekends and some holidays, Children under 12 free with parents
Concierge: Daily
Room Service: 8 a.m.-8 p.m.
Restaurant: Named "Best Fine Dining" restaurant by *Cape Cod Life* since 1992, recipient of the DiRona–Distinguished Restaurants of North America–placing it in the top 1% of restaurants in the country.
Bar: Tavern, 11:30 a.m. to midnight
Business Facilities: Audio-Visual equipment, Copiers, Message
Conference Rooms: 6 rooms, capacity 10–150
Sports Facilities: Spa, Outdoor swimming pool, Golf/tennis nearby
Spa Services: Full service spa featuring 100% organic products created especially for The Dan'l Webster by an Apothocary in Vermont.

RED LION INN

"The new hotel is a graceful structure in the colonial style, simple yet elegant and appointed after the luxurious fashion of a gentleman's country house." So reported The Berkshire Courier in an April 1897 article about The Red Lion's reconstruction following a devastating fire that burned the original structure to the ground. Built in c.1773 as a stop between Boston and Albany, the Inn was a meeting place for dissident colonists and later hosted at least five presidents of the United States.

The white Victorian clapboard structures magnificent porch full of white wicker is the perfect spot for watching the comings and goings of this lovely Berkshire Hills town, which its late resident Norman Rockwell loved to sketch. To step inside is to enter a world of memorabilia, much of which was saved from the original inn. Public areas feature displays of antiques, beautiful flowers, colonial pewter, Canton china, and photographs of Old Stockbridge. The guestrooms are comfortably furnished with period pieces and cozy comforters. Each has a unique color scheme, delicate wallpapers, and Oriental rugs.

As the recipient of the 2003 Wine Spectator Award, the Inn has a remarkable selection of fine wines to be enjoyed with the delicious contemporary New England cuisine served in the elegant main dining room. More casual fare can be had at Widow Bingham's Tavern. Within walking distance of the Inn are the Norman Rockwell Museum, antique shops, boutiques, and Mission House, a museum of early colonial life.

Whether you visit this picturesque village as spring unfolds, in summer to enjoy the Tanglewood Music Center, in colorful fall when foliage beckons, or to ski at a nearby mountain in winter, you'll enjoy one of New England's best-loved hostelries.

Address: 30 Main Street, Stockbridge 1262.
Phone: 413-298-5545
Fax: 413-298-5130
Email: reservations@redlioninn.com
Web site: http://www.redlioninn.com
Room Rates: 110–225
Suite Rates: 185–435
No. of Rooms: 108
No. of Suites: 25
Credit Cards: Visa
Attractions: Close to Tanglewood concerts, Jacob's Pillow (oldest dance festival in US), Berkshire Theatre Festival, Berkshire Garden Center, Mission House, Wildlife Sanctuaries, Lenox, Williamstown, Norman Rockwell Museum, Chesterwood & Naumkeag.
Services & Amenities: Parking, baby-sitting service, gift shop, library, special packages, Cable TV, vintage clawfoot bathtubs, eyelet shower curtains, shaving mirrors, complimentary robes and country inn toiletries.
Restrictions: Pets allowed, inquire with reservations for details.
Room Service: Restaurant hours
Restaurant: Breakfast 7:30-10 am in The Main Dining Room. Lunch noon-2:30 pm, dinner 5:30-9 pm and 5-10 pm in season, Sunday lunch 12-4 pm, in the Dining Rooma and The Widow Bingham's Tavern.
Bar: Lion's Den Pub, 4 p.m.- 1 a.m., Lunch, weekends, in season
Business Facilities: Yes
Conference Rooms: 5 rooms, capacity 2-100
Sports Facilities: Outdoor swimming pool, Massage, Tennis, Golf, Riding, Sailing and skiing nearby
Location: Center of village, 40 miles to Albany Airport

CEDAR GROVE INN

This fine Antebellum Estate is one of the largest and most elegant bed and breakfasts in the South. Capture "Gone With the Wind" elegance and romance in exquisite guestrooms/suites in the Mansion Inn or in one of the restored historic bed and breakfast cottages, the Carriage House Suites or Pool side Garden Cottages all nestled in five acres of gardens. Enjoy a gourmet, romantic candlelight dinner in our elegant "Andre's," voted Best Restaurant in Vicksburg, Mississippi.

Our restaurant is named in honor of our original Chef, Andre Flowers, who passed away in December 2001. Today, Chef Shunta Burks, carries on many of Chef Andre's traditions, such as his famous brandy bread pudding, while adding his own personal flair to many of our other dishes such as the Creole Catfish with wild pecan rice. Shunta has worked for Andre's nine years and strives to make each customer's dining experience exceptional. Let our warm, friendly staff provide you with gracious southern hospitality in a cozy, romantic atmosphere and you will feel all your cares just float away.

Address: 2200 Oak St, Vicksburg 39180.
Phone: 601-636-1000 800-862-1300
Fax: 601 619 6862
Email: marlene@cedargroveinn.com
Web site: http:// www.cedargroveinn.com
Room Rates: 120–185
Suite Rates: 160–240
No. of Rooms: 10
No. of Suites: 23
Credit Cards: Most Credit Cards accepted
Attractions: Vicksburg National Military Park–2.5 miles The Old Court House Museum–1.5 miles Southern Cultural Heritage Complex–1 mile Biedenharn Museum of Coca-Cola Memorabilia–1 mile Yesterday's Children Antique And Toy Museum–1 mile Gray & Blue
Services & Amenities: We offer our guest complimentary sherry and chocolate turndown service, an elegant two course breakfast and a tour of the mansion. If you are celebrating a birthday or anniversary flowers and/or champagne can be put in your room for an additional charge
Room Service: Yes
Restaurant: Andre's Restaurant at the Cedar Grove Mansion Inn is open seven nights a week. Cocktails are available in the mansion bar at 5 pm and dinner reservations begin at 6 pm.
Bar: Yes, open at 5pm
Business Facilities: Yes
Conference Rooms: Yes
Sports Facilities: Tennis Court, Croquet, Swimming Pool
Spa Services: The 3rd floor Spa is one mile from Cedar Grove and offers a variety of spa services from manicures to body wraps and facials. Let front desk know of your interest and we'll schedule it for you!
Location: 1 mile from downtown Vicksburg

THE RAPHAEL

For travelers who appreciate what makes a city unique, the Country Club Plaza is the place to see and The Raphael is the place to stay. Originally constructed in the 1920's, the restored hotel is one of Kansas City's enduring architecturally significant buildings. Its landmark features include hand-made wrought iron gates and twin canopies adorning the hotel entrance. The intimate lobby, with its mahogany-paneled ceiling, ornate woodwork, intricately detailed chandeliers, fine art and richly textured fabrics, is reminiscent of a small European hotel.

Guest accommodations are generously sized rooms and suites. Amenities include many of the modern comforts today's traveler expects, including communications system with voice mail and complimentary high-speed Internet access, plus French terry robes, personal refrigerator with refreshment center and coffee maker. Same day laundry service is available if needed, as is 24-hour room service.

The Raphael Restaurant, with its quaint French bistro décor and cozy bar area, is noted as one of the city's most romantic restaurants. The menu features contemporary American cuisine with international influences. The dinner menu changes weekly and features a prix fixe meal with a wine pairing option. The restaurant features noted regional chefs for special dinners and presents a wine and food appreciation session the second Saturday of each month.

Address: 325 Ward Parkway, Kansas City 64112.
Phone: 816-756-3800 800-821-5343
Fax: 816-802-2131
Email: information@raphaelkc.com
Web site: http://www.raphaelkc.com
Room Rates: 150–200
No. of Rooms: 123
No. of Suites: 88
Credit Cards: Most Credit Cards accepted
Attractions: Within walking distance of Nelson Atkins Museum, shopping, dining and entertainment.
Services & Amenities: Telephones with voicemail and high-speed Internet access, Iron and board, Coffee maker, Refrigerator, Hair dryer, In-room pay for view movies, Plush cotton robes, Radio alarm clock, Individual climate controls, VCR and CD player rental
Restrictions: Not pets allowed, Children under 18 free with parents, Non-smoking rooms
Concierge: 24 hours
Room Service: 24 hours
Restaurant: Raphael Restaurant– Breakfast 6:30 a.nm.–10 a.m. Lunch 11 a.m.–3 p.m., Dinner 5 p.m.–10 p.m., Dress code, Closed Sunday.
Bar: Raphael Bar–11 a.m.– midnight. Live piano music Friday and Saturday
Business Facilities: Audio-visual equipment, Copiers, Message center, Catering for breakfasts and dinners
Conference Rooms: 18 suites, capacity 12 each
Sports Facilities: Guest privileges at Universal Fitness Express, Jogging trails and Tennis courts nearby
Location: Ideally situated on a tree-lined neighborhood boulevard

TRIPLE CREEK RANCH - RELAIS & CHATEAUX

Triple Creek Ranch is a wondrous place of serenity, beauty and comfort nestled in a secluded, unspoiled mountain wilderness. The resort offers luxurious accommodations, world class cuisine, outstanding service, exhilarating activities and spectacular scenery with abundant wildlife.

The main lodge, which houses a dining room, a rooftop lounge and a library, is a Western style three story log and cedar structure tiered with balconies providing a panoramic view of the mountain landscape. The lodge is the focal point for the social activity on the ranch.

Nineteen individual custom designed log cabins take luxury to a new height. They are truly magnificent and are the perfect romantic destination. Sapphire is the newest cabin nestled in a pine forest above a flowing creek, featuring 2 fireplaces, a spacious living room with wooded view, dining area and kitchen, two bedrooms with massive King size log post beds. The tri-level deck offers the ultimate in privacy for the outdoor hot tub.

The Triple Creek Ranch Restaurant with fireplace and vaulted, wood-beamed ceiling offers intimate candlelit dining. Fine linens, fresh flowers and soothing background music create elegance in the heart of the wilderness.

The endless array of activities, at any time of year, will satisfy any taste from horseback riding, hiking and fishing to downhill and cross-country skiing. There is golf nearby as well as art galleries and specialty shopping.

Triple Creek is the perfect hideaway for couples seeking romance and sublime tranquility.

Address: 5551 West Fork Rd, Darby 59829.
Phone: 406-821-4600 800-654-2943
Fax: 406-821-4666
Email: tcr@bitterroot.net
Web site: http://www.triplecreekranch.com
Room Rates: 510–995 all
Suite Rates: 650–995 all
No. of Rooms: 19
No. of Suites: 4
Attractions: 30 mi to ski resort, Lewis & Clark Trail, Bitterroot River, Salmon River, Trapper Peak (highest peak in SW Montana), Art galleries, Specialty shops, Lost Trail Powder Mtn, Chief Joseph Pass, Big Hole Battlefield National Monument, Whitewater rafting, Skii
Services & Amenities: Airport pick up, Parking, Gift shop, Library, Laundry, Game area, Fireplace, Deck, Telephones w/dataports, Satellite TV with DVD/VCR, Radio, Iron & ironing board, Wet bar, CD player, Climate controls, Robes, Toiletries, Hair dryer
Restrictions: Pets 20 pounds and under, Children 16 and over welcome
Concierge: 8 a.m.-9 p.m.
Room Service: 7 a.m.–9 p.m.
Restaurant: Triple Creek Ranch Restaurant, 8 a.m.–8:30 p.m., All meals included in room rate
Bar: Rooftop Lounge, Open bar/bartender in evenings
Business Facilities: Message center, Small scale conference facility, E-mail, Copiers, Fax, Modems
Conference Rooms: 1 room, capacity 20
Sports Facilities: Outdoor heated pool, Massage, Fitness ctr, Riding, Putting green, Tennis, Hiking, Fishing
Location: West Fork of the Bitterroot River

THE INNS & SPA AT MILL FALLS

Nestled among the foothills and overlooking the clear waters of Lake Winnipesaukee, stands the Inns & Spa at Mill Falls and the Mill Falls Marketplace. Once a linen mill, the entire area has been exquisitely transformed.

Within the historic setting of an old mill, a covered bridge, and tumbling waterfall, the Inns & Spa at Mill Falls create an atmosphere of warmth, comfort and easy relaxation. Combining Old World charm—crackling fireplaces, cozy nooks with spacious guestrooms and suites—the Inns give new meaning to the traditions of a country inn. The Inn at Bay Point offers the ultimate in lakeside accommodations. Bay Point's rooms are designed with private lakeside balconies, cozy fireplaces and personal whirlpools. They also offer spectacular views and unrivaled quality and charm. The Chase House is decorated with rich textures and warm colors to create a calming, soothing atmosphere. The rooms all have panoramic lake views, fireplaces and romantic sitting areas. Church Landing offers 58 designer decorated rooms and suites, all with a fireplace and a spectacular view of the Lake. In addition, Cascade Spa offers a full line of spa treatments, a deluxe fitness room, and an indoor/outdoor pool. To top it all off, there are 2 swimming areas, docking for up to 20, and function facilities for up to 350!

Dining at the Inns is a varied and exceptional experience. The Waterfall Cafe, with it's unique setting at the top of the waterfall, offers sumptuous breakfasts, light lunch and salads to go. A short walk across the courtyard is Mame's. Built in 1825, it is uniquely New England and offers lunch, dinner, brunch or cocktails. Lago Costa Cucina at Bay Point offers an authentic old world dining experience combined with lakeside dining. Camp at the Chase House is a nostalgic lakeside restaurant featuring wonderful food and spirits served around a fieldstone fireplace. Giuseppe's Ristorante is a full service Italian bistro located in the cozy warmth of the old mill building. The Lakehouse Grille, located at Church Landing offers the flair of an open kitchen while you sit lakeside and enjoy the view!

Address: 312 DW Hwy #28, Meredith 3253.
Phone: 603-279-7006 800-622-MILL
Fax: 603-677-8695
Email: info@millfalls.com
Web site: http://www.millfalls.com
Room Rates: 99–359
Suite Rates: 209–359
No. of Rooms: 159
No. of Suites: 10
Attractions: New Hampshire's Lakes Region–Four Season Playground, Lake Swimming, Boating, Fishing, Water skiing, Golf, Cruise Aboard the M/S Mt. Washington, Alpine and Cross-Country Skiing,Ice Skating, Shopping, Antiquing
Services & Amenities: Two Indoor Pools and One Outdoor pool, Dry Sauna, Meeting Facilities, Complimentary Toiletries, Two Swimming Areas, In-Room Fireplaces and Whirlpool Tubs, Seven Dining Experiences.
Restrictions: 6 rooms handicap equipped, No pets allowed, Children 12 and under free in parent's room
Room Service: 6:30 am-2 pm, 5-9 pm limited
Restaurant: Lago Costa Cucina, Camp, Mame's, Waterfall Cafe, Giuseppe's Pizzeria and Ristorante,Town Docks, & The Lakehouse Grille.
Bar: 6 bars
Business Facilities: Copiers, Audio-visual, Fax, Modems
Conference Rooms: 14 rooms, capacity 300
Sports Facilities: Indoor Swimming Pool, Whirlpool, Sauna, Spa, & Deluxe Fitness Room
Spa Services: Cascade Spa offers total relaxation in a nurturing, serene environment. Soothe mind, body and soul as you indulge in our exclusive treatments.

QUEEN'S HOTEL

The Queen's Hotel is an elegant, victorian hotel in the center of Victorian Cape May, one block from the Atlantic ocean. Rooms feature modern comforts such as private bath, television, and telephone along with antique furnishings. The central location is within minutes' walk from some of the State's best restaurants and shops and numerous tours of the historic district. Several rooms have a private balcony with an ocean view framed by some of the town's spectacular Victorian architecture.

The Queen's Hotel and the renowned Queen Victoria Bed and Breakfast offer the same quality of lodging and restoration that made the bed and breakfast so famous.

Rates at the hotel include a wonderful Europeon Breakfast Buffet served in the elegant lobby under a soaring ceiling featuring custom-screened Bradbury and Bradbury wall coverings. Attractive Butler's trays are provided for guests to enjoy their morning meal on the porch, on their private balcony, or in the privacy of their room.

Enjoy the complimentary bicycles to tour this charming seaside National Historic Landmark town. Beach chairs and towels are provided during the warmer seasons.

Address: 601 Columbia Ave, Cape May 8204.
Phone: 609-884-1613
Email: reservations@queenvictoria.com
Web site: http:// www.queenshotel.com
Room Rates: 80–275
No. of Rooms: 10
No. of Suites: 1
Credit Cards: VisaMasterCard
Attractions: 2 blocks to Washington Street Pedestrian Mall, antiques, boutiques, specialty shops, 1 block from the ocean. World famous bird observatory, 3 wineries, Cape May Zoo, Cape May lighthouse nearby.
Services & Amenities: Pantry w/ice & sodas. Rooms feature individual climate control, in-room coffee makers, refrigerators, phones, cable TV, marble baths, heated towel bars, hair dryers, whirlpool tubs in 3 rooms, iron/ironing board, wireless high speed Internet, toiletries.
Restrictions: No pets allowed. Smoking permitted on porches and outdoors only.
Concierge: 8 a.m.–9 p.m
Restaurant: Walking distance to a variety of restaurants.
Sports Facilities: 1 block to beach. Complimentary bicycles
Spa Services: In room massage available. Spa packages available.
Location: Downtown Cape May historic district.

VIRGINIA HOTEL

In 1879 Alfred and Ellen Ebbitt established a tradition of hospitality as the innkeepers of the small and elegant Virginia Hotel. Today this famous hostelry offers accommodations and a level of service that appeal to today's most discriminating traveler.

The public areas are furnished to provide an atmosphere that is intimate and refined. Guests are invited to enjoy the unique art and periodical collection. Or, gather around a crackling fireplace to listen to the baby grand piano.

The 24 well-appointed guestrooms are designed to cater to your comfort and feature exquisite custom furnishings, down comforters, and all the expected amenities of a modern hotel including evening turn-down service and complimentary continental breakfast complete with morning newspaper.

Dining at the Virginia Hotel is a pure delight. Named in honor of the original owners, the Ebbitt Room is a romantic and intimate atmosphere. Start with the Tagliatelle and Duck Confit with spinach, goat cheese and wild mushroom sauce appetizer. For an entree, try the Spice Roasted Monkfish and Maine Lobster with Porcini Mushrooms, Melted Leeks, Roasted Squash and Banyuls Jus. And for dessert, the Sticky Toffee Pudding, with toffee sauce and vanilla ice cream is the perfect end to an excellent meal.

From the remarkable renovation of the exterior to the most intricate detail of each guestroom, The Virginia Hotel sets a new standard for hospitality in Cape May's Historic District.

Address: 25 Jackson St, PO Box 557, Cape May 8204.
Phone: 609-884-5700 800-732-4236
Fax: 609-884-1236
Email: virginia@virginiahotel.com
Web site: http://www.virginiahotel.com
Room Rates: 85–425
No. of Rooms: 24
Attractions: Historic Jackson Street, ½ block from beach, Washington Street Mall, Historic District
Services & Amenities: Parking, Valet service, Complimentary newspaper, Cable TV w/VCR & HBO, Telephone, Radio, CD player, Individual climate controls, Robes, Exclusive Bulgari amenities, In-room dataport, Down comforters, 2 rooms have whirlpool tubs, 4 rooms oversized shower
Restrictions: No handicap equipped rooms, Assistance dogs only, Children welcome, under 5 free with parents
Concierge: 7 a.m.-11 p.m.
Room Service: 8-10 a.m., 6-9 pm
Restaurant: The Ebbitt Room, open for dinner nightly, dressy casual attire, jackets and ties not required
Bar: Ebbitt Lounge, 5:30 p.m.- 12 midnight
Business Facilities: Message Center, Copiers, Audio-visual, Fax, Modems, Conference facilities
Conference Rooms: 2 rooms, capacity 18 & 35
Sports Facilities: Beach resort, Massage
Location: In the center of downtown Cape May

CONGRESS HALL

Set amidst a sweeping lawn overlooking the Atlantic Ocean, Congress Hall offers a vibrant atmosphere and modern-day comforts within the grand serenity of this lovingly renovated nineteenth-century hostelry.

Congress Hall's public areas have been designed with this same sense of simple, relaxed luxury. The entrance lobby retains the hotel's original black and white marble floor, 12-foot tall doors and black wicker furniture. This is set against the restored yellow plaster walls and crisp white woodwork. While the fixtures are historic, the lobby's mirrors, palms, fans, and ocean breezes ensure that it is also airy and comfortable. It's a wonderful place to sit and watch the hustle and bustle of the hotel, to have a drink or to wait for a friend.

In the guestrooms, which range from doubles to luxurious suites, you'll find state of the art amenities in an environment of timeless calm. Congress Hall's L-shaped design, a tradition among Cape May hotels, affords many guestrooms uninterrupted views of the broad sweep of the Atlantic beach. Designed by Colleen Bohuny, the rooms blend both antiques original to the building with custom furnishings created specifically for Congress Hall. Fragments of the original 1920s rag rug have been used to inspire a fun reinterpretation of that carpet for the guestrooms, providing a playful, fresh pallet of color on the floor.

Hotel guests and the general public are welcome daily for breakfast, lunch or dinner in the two distinctive dining rooms of the Blue Pig Tavern. Its name derives from a gambling parlor sited in Congress Hall in the mid-1800s. Each of the two dining rooms in the Blue Pig provides a different mood. One has an open, airy garden feel, with a large skylight providing dramatic views of the colonnade and Congress Hall's historic façades. The second room is reminiscent of a cozy tavern, with dark green paneled walls, a large fireplace, natural wood floors, and comfortable banquettes. Both dining rooms serve the Congress Hall restaurant's signature American fare—nostalgic, simple and fresh—utilizing local seafood and produce in creative, accessible ways.

Surround yourself with the classic relaxed elegance that made Congress Hall famous.

Address: 251 Beach Ave, PO Box 150, Cape May 8204.
Phone: 609-884-8421 888-944-1816
Fax: 609-884-6094
Email: congress@congresshall.com
Web site: http://www.congresshall.com
Room Rates: 100–385
Suite Rates: 280–up
No. of Rooms: 106
No. of Suites: 5
Attractions: The hotel is located directly across the street from one of the Cape's finest beaches in the heart of the Victorian district, a few minutes' walk from Cape May's wealth of stores.
Services & Amenities: Parking, Valet parking, Night club, Fitness room, 16 retail shops, Hairdryer, Aveda toiletries, Climate controls, Color TV w/remote, DVD player, Telephones with dataports, Twice daily maid service, Iron and board
Concierge: On duty
Room Service: Available 7:30am-9pm
Restaurant: Blue Pig Tavern–Breakfast, Lunch, and Dinner
Bar: The Brown Room, The Boiler Room
Business Facilities: Executive conferencing with state-of-the-art A/V equipment
Conference Rooms: Multiple meeting rooms and The Grand Ballroom
Sports Facilities: Fitness room, two 18 hole golf courses & tennis within 10 minutes
Spa Services: The Cape May Spa at Congress Hall is a full-service spa offering state-of-the-art spa services in a relaxing, tranquil, richly appointed ambiance of total comfort.
Location: Four acres of fun overlooking the Atlantic in cool Cape May, NJ

CHATEAU INN & SUITES

Located in Spring Lake, one of New Jersey's most unspoiled sea-side resorts, The Chateau Inn is a jewel of a Victorian inn. Built in 1888, it was most recently refurbished in 2003. One enters the lobby through oak and beveled-glass doors. A Victorian desk, fresh flowers, ceiling fans, and stained glass windows usher you into yesteryear.

All rooms and suites feature individual heat and air-conditioning, color cable TVs and VCRs, Casablanca paddle fans, in-room safes, refrigerators, two telephones and private marble bathrooms. Luxury suites and parlors feature marble baths with double soaking tubs for two, wet bars, sofa-furnished sitting areas, marble-clad wood-burning fireplaces and private balconies overlooking Spring Lake Park and Lake.

The Chateau Inn is located at the foot of Spring Lake, for which the town was named. It overlooks two parks with ancient shade trees and footbridges, and Constitution Gazebo. A newly inaugurated 800-square-foot Conference Room is now available, and a new breakfast room serves an optional Continental Breakfast Buffet to guests.

The staff can advise you on dining, shopping, and other activities. The Chateau Inn provides complimentary beach and tennis passes. The Atlantic Club, a private full-service fitness center, offers complimentary access to Chateau guests. Bicycles can be rented from the Inn.

Open year-round, the Chateau offers a lovely respite just one hour from New York, Philadelphia, and Atlantic City.

Address: 500 Warren @ 5th Ave, Spring Lake 7762.
Phone: 732-974-2000 877-974-LAKE
Fax: 732-974-0007
Email: info@chateauinn.com
Web site: http://www.chateauinn.com
Room Rates: 79–299
Suite Rates: 125–299
No. of Rooms: 37
No. of Suites: 4
Credit Cards: Most Credit Cards accepted
Attractions: The beachfront community of Spring Lake, Six Flags Great Adventure, Allaire State Park, Garden State Arts Center, Monmouth Park Race Track and Freehold Raceway, Jenkinson Aquarium
Services & Amenities: Baby-sitting service, Laundry service, Cable TV, VCR, Radio, Refrigerator, In-room safe, 2 telephones per room, Complimentary toiletries, Casablanca ceiling fans, High speed Internet access, Personal voice mail
Restrictions: No pets allowed, 1 room handicap equipped, Non-smoking rooms available
Room Service: 8-10:30 a.m.
Business Facilities: Message center, Copiers, Audio-Visual, Fax, Data ports.
Conference Rooms: 1 room, capacity 25
Sports Facilities: The Atlantic Club available to Chateau guests.
Location: Historic Spring Lake, 1 hour from New York, Atlantic City, and Philadelphia

1770 House, *East Hampton, NY* PAGE 124

Villa Montana Resort, *Isabela, PR* PAGE 147

SEA CREST BY THE SEA

"It doesn't get any better than this", per Pamela Lanier during a recent stay at Sea Crest by the Sea.

From the moment you enter our luxury inn in the picturesque seaside village of Spring Lake, New Jersey, you know you are in the midst of something extraordinary. Soft jazz plays in the background, tea is set in the parlor and our professional staff assists you in leaving the day-to-day routine behind.

The sound of the surf lulls you to sleep and the only decision required is whether to drink in the cool breeze from the porch or cozy up by the fireplace in your private suite. Sea Crest by the Sea is a very adult and utterly romantic inn—the epitome of warmth, elegance, privacy and good taste.

Your room is a sanctuary where yesterday's elegance marries today's comfort. DUX beds, steam showers and private decks with ocean views. Fresh flowers, an exceptionally comfortable DUX bed dressed in fine linens, a spacious Jacuzzi for two and cozy fireplace await you. Arrange for an in-room massage, pop in a CD, order a moonlit champagne picnic and the escape is complete.

Should you decide to leave your suite, a candlelit gourmet breakfast begins at the civilized hour of 9 a.m. The antique French sideboards are laden with fresh fruit, yogurt and granola, warm from the oven buttermilk scones, a hearty entrée, home-baked breads, fresh-squeezed orange juice, award-winning coffee and a decadent dessert.

Once fortified, explore the charming town of Spring Lake. A few steps from our front porch you will find quiet beaches and the longest non-commercial boardwalk at the Jersey Shore. Venture beyond the beach to discover excellent restaurants, galleries and shops worthy of a big city—and only one hour from NYC & Philadelphia.

Looking for more active pursuits? We provide our guests with their choice from a stable of bikes, beach badges, and passes to the exclusive Atlantic Club, which includes fitness center, spa, tennis and more. The Spring Lake area also boasts nearby golf courses, nature preserves and river cruises. Cruise Spring Lake, too. Our Sea Crest rowboat awaits you.

Make your reservation for a weekend getaway or an extended retreat. You'll leave relaxed, rejuvenated and eagerly awaiting your return to Sea Crest By The Sea Bed and Breakfast.

Address: 19 Tuttle Ave, Spring Lake 7762.
Phone: 732-449-9031 800-803-9031
Fax: 732-974-0403
Email: capt@seacrestbythesea.com
Web site: http://www.seacrestbythesea.com
Room Rates: 300–350
Suite Rates: 350–475
No. of Rooms: 3
No. of Suites: 5
Credit Cards: Visa
Attractions: Pristine beach. Quiet non-commercial boardwalk. Bike to antique shops, boutiques. Paddle the Sea Crest rowboat around Spring Lake. Bird watching, golf, tennis, fishing, boating, thoroughbred racing nearby. Daytrip to Atlantic City, NYC, NJ lighthouses.
Services & Amenities: Spa tubs for two. Fireplaces. DUX beds. Stocked fridges. Welcome wine & Godiva chocolates. Frette bed linens. Luxury robes. Wireless Internet. Private decks. Ocean views. Full breakfast, afternoon tea. Bikes, beach badges & health club privileges.
Concierge: Yes
Room Service: No
Bar: No
Business Facilities: Yes
Conference Rooms: Yes
Sports Facilities: Atlantic Club, beach
Spa Services: In-room massage services available. Privileges at award-winning spa & fitness club.
Location: Seaside

INN OF THE ANASAZI

Newly built in 1991, The Inn of the Anasazi is adjacent to the Palace of the Governors, the oldest building in Santa Fe, and ½ block from Santa Fe's Historic Plaza.

Typical southwestern architectural style is reflected throughout the hotel. Each guestroom and suite has a gas-lit kiva fireplace, four-poster beds and beamed ceilings. Earthtone colors are used extensively in throw rugs and wall hangings, many of the latter being exhibited by local artists. Furnishings are hand hewn, and all these element combines to create an aura of comfort.

Guestrooms are equipped with luxurious cotton bed linens, robes, bath sheets, organic bath oils, shampoos and soaps. Amenities include stereos, TVs, VCRs, a mini-bar and private security safes. There are also coffee makers and custom-blend coffee beans.

The award-winning Anasazi Restaurant features Comtemporary Southwestern cuisine. Among the appetizers is Hudson Valley Foie Gras on Peppered Salmon with Golden Raisin-Brandy Sauce. Entrees include Cinnamon-Chile Rubbed Beef Medallions with White Cheddar Mashed Potatoes and Mango Salsa.

Adjacent to the bar is a stairway leading to the private wine cellar. There is also a private library for guests who are interested in the history, myths and legends of Santa Fe's cultures. This room can also function as a boardroom for small corporate meetings. Guides escort guests to the ancient Anasazi ruins of Bandelier National Park or the eight northern pueblos, as well as other historic sites. Fishing, golf, skiing, horseback riding and many other activities are nearby. Museums, galleries, world-class shopping, gourmet dining, historic sites are all within walking distance of the Inn.

Address: 113 Washington Ave, Santa Fe 87501
Phone: 505-988-3030
800-688-8100
Fax: 505-988-3277
Email:
reservations@innoftheanasazi.com
Web site: http://
www.innoftheanasazi.com
Room Rates: 205–475
No. of Rooms 57
No. of Suites: 0
Credit Cards: Most Credit Cards accepted
Attractions: Galleries, Museums, excursions to Anasazi Ruins , special private sightseeing can be arranged. Great shopping close to the Inn. Outdoor activities include golf, fishing, skiing, horseback riding, whitewater rafting, mountain biking, hiking, etc.
Services & Amenities: Valet service, Garage and parking, Car hire, Laundry, Babysitting service, Library, Fireplaces, Complimentary newspaper, Cable TV w/VCR, Honor bar, CD players in suites, Telephone, Robes, Complimentary toiletries
Restrictions: 1 room handicap equipped, Children under 12 free
Concierge: 8:30 a.m.-6:30 p.m.
Room Service: 6:30 a.m.-11 p.m.
Restaurant: The Anasazi Restaurant is one of Santa Fe's finest. Chef Tom Kerpon serves Contemporary Southwestern Cuisine in a sophisticated, romantic setting. Restaurant hours: 7 a.m. – 10 p.m.
Bar: The Anasazi, 11 a.m. – 2 a.m.
Business Facilities: Copiers, Computer access, Audio visual
Conference Rooms: 2 room, Wine Cellar (capacity 14) & Library (capacity 40)
Sports Facilities: Horseback riding, Hiking, Skiing, Rafting close by
Spa Services: In-room massage arranged by concierge.
Location: Historic Plaza District

LA POSADA DE SANTA FE

La Posada is synonymous with Santa Fe style. This pueblo revival village is situated on six beautifully landscaped acres just steps away from the historic plaza. The readers of *Travel & Leisure* and *Condé Nast Traveler* have voted La Posada among their favorite hotels.

The hotel has deep historic roots and incorporates some of Santa Fe's most celebrated landmarks. The 19th century Staab House stands at the core of the lobby and restaurant complex, a testament to the fashionable Santa Fe in the 1880s. Some say that the lady of the house, Julia Staab, loved this home so much that she has yet to leave.

There are 157 newly refurbished rooms and suites characteristic of the early adobe art colony that originally occupied the site. The extensive La Posada art program showcases sculpture, paintings and photographs throughout the grounds and public spaces. Four suites are appointed with original works of art from some of Santa Fe's most prestigious art galleries. Featured in *Architectural Digest*, the unique rooms reflect the colors and charm of the Southwest with traditional viga and latilla ceilings, many with Kiva fireplaces and shady patios. Amenities include plush robes, nightly turndown service, complimentary newspaper, neighborhood shuttle service,cable television,luxury amenities, valet parking and concierge.

There are several dining options including breakfast, lunch and dinner in our AAA Four-Diamond restaurant, Fuego, and on the patio during the warmer weather. Tapas and lighter fare are available in the Staab House along with jazz three nights a week. The Avanyu Poolside Grill offers a backyard cookout menu and drinks during the summer. Full menu room service is also available.

In the center of the resort is the Avanyu™ Spa. The extensive menu offers specialized signature body treatments, many that feature indigenous ingredients. Facilities include the Fitness Center, heated outdoor pool, whirlpool, private steam rooms and locker rooms.

Address: 330 E Palace Ave, Santa Fe 87501.
Phone: 505-986-0000 800-727-5276
Fax: 505-982-6850
Email: kristenm@lpdsf.com
Web site: http://www.laposadadesantafe.com
Room Rates: 199–396
Suite Rates: 429–539
No. of Rooms: 115
No. of Suites: 42
Credit Cards: Most Credit Cards accepted
Attractions: Artists fill the city for the annual Spanish and Indian markets. Opera and performing arts are dazzling. Many ways to enjoy the outdoors include hiking, biking, rafting, skiing and golf. Indian pueblos and historic villages are just a drive away.
Services & Amenities: Plush robes, nightly turndown service, luxury amenities, complimentary newspaper, neighborhood shuttle service, valet parking, concierge, dry cleaning and laundry service, cultural resort activiites.
Concierge: 9 am–9 pm
Room Service: Full Menu
Restaurant: In Santa Fe dining has been raised to a fine art and Fuego has become the local masterpiece. Fuego is a feast for all the senses with the finest foods, steeped in tradition, beautifully presented.
Bar: Staab House, 11:30–11:30 pm
Business Facilities: Business Center, high speed Internet access, fax and copying
Conference Rooms: 4,500 sq feet of meeting space
Sports Facilities: Hiking, skiing, golf and horseback riding nearby.
Spa Services: The Avanyu™ Spa is an oasis for the senses in the heart of La Posada with regionally inspired signature treatments. Complete with Fitness Center, heated pool and outdoor whirlpool.
Location: Downtown Santa Fe, two blocks from the historic plaza

INN ON THE ALAMEDA

Relax and feel far from the world, though you're just moments from all that Santa Fe offers. Nestled between the historic Plaza and the galleries of Canyon Road, the Inn on the Alameda offers guests the privacy, comfort and charm of a garden courtyard tucked within adobe walls.

Situated downtown in the heart of Santa Fe's beautiful residential neighborhoods, the Inn is just around the corner from the Canyon Road arts district, brimming with galleries and shops that showcase the many talented artisans of the City Different. The Plaza, fine dining, museums and unique shopping are just a stroll away, and a short drive takes you to Native American Pueblos, skiing, hiking, white-water rafting, golf and fishing.

The Inn's 69 rooms and suites are all furnished in distinctive Southwestern style, with singular bath amenities, triple-sheeted beds with duvet coverings and 300-count linens, and plush robes. Romantic kiva fireplaces, patios, balconies and unstocked refrigerators are available in select rooms and suites. A fully-equipped exercise room, two open-air whirlpools, and on-call massage ensure a relaxing and refreshing experience. Parking, local and toll-free calls are complimentary, and a guest e-mail center is open from daily from 9 a.m. to 9 p.m. A friendly, knowledgeable and attentive staff is always available to help create lasting memories of the Land of Enchantment.

A sumptuous complimentary continental "Breakfast of Enchantment" features homemade breads, muffins and pastries, low-fat selections, seasonal fruits, a variety of granolas and hot and cold cereals, fresh-squeezed juices, and locally-roasted coffee, all served daily in the Inn's delightful country kitchen. Each afternoon, a Welcome Reception is held in the Inn's Agoyo Room, offering guests the chance to savor complimentary wines and cheeses.

A variety of imaginative meeting styles can be created for the executive guest, with windowed spaces and kiva fireplaces providing a warm, comfortable and inspiring setting for retreats, board meetings and incentive excursions. Gourmet catering services and an on-site coordinator ensure a productive and successful gathering.

Address: 303 E Alameda, Santa Fe 87501.
Phone: 505-984-2121 888-335-3408
Fax: 505-986-8325
Email: info@inn-alameda.com
Web site: http://www.innonthealameda.com
Room Rates: 129–209
Suite Rates: 210–350
No. of Rooms: 59
No. of Suites: 10
Attractions: Closest hotel to the Canyon Road Arts District. Restaurants, Concerts, Theatre, Opera, Nightclubs, Craft Fairs, Indian and Spanish Markets, Art Galleries, Museums, Shops and Historic Plaza all nearby. Regional Airport is Santa Fe Municipal.
Services & Amenities: Free Parking, Free local & 800# calls, Guest Laundry, Same-day Dry Cleaning, Baby-sitting, Library, Exercise Room, 2 Outdoor Whirlpools, Massage, Cable TV/HBO, Guest E-mail Center, Lavish Comp. Continental Breakfast, Comp Afternoon Wine & Cheese Reception
Restrictions: One pet (under 30#) accepted—nightly fee, Handicapped access 3 rooms, Children under 16 stay free
Concierge: Available
Room Service: 7 a.m.-11 a.m.
Bar: 4 p.m.-10 p.m.
Business Facilities: Meeting Rooms, Audio-Visual Equipment, Guestroom Dataport, Gourmet Catering, Fax & Copying Available
Conference Rooms: Conference Room & Board Room, Maximum Capacity 40
Sports Facilities: White-water Rafting, Bicycling, Hiking, Skiing, Tennis, Golf, Fishing, all nearby
Location: Downtown Santa Fe, Nearest international airport Albuquerque Sunport

PLAZA REAL

The Hotel Plaza Real, located in the heart of old Santa Fe and steps away from the historic Plaza, is a picturesque boutique hotel offering 56 deluxe suites and guestrooms—most featuring wood-burning fireplaces and private balconies. All feature hand-crafted furnishings, art and Santa Fe's most luxurious bed. Experience the ultimate in world-class art, shopping, and dining at this charming Santa Fe style hotel.

Just steps from the historic Plaza and blocks from the Capitol, Hotel Plaza Real is perfect for your next small meeting, reception or retreat.

With the highest standards of excellence and impeccable service, let our staff help you plan your next meeting and oversee the details to make your meeting and unqualified success.

SANTA CLARA ROOM 18' x 22.5'

Located on the second floor this room is perfect for luncheons, dinners, receptions, and meetings. Offering views of the Sangre de Cristo Mountains, the Santa Clara is used in conjunction with the Library and second floor patio, offering flexible seating capacities.

Address: 125 Washington Ave, Santa Fe 87501
Phone: 505-988-4900
877-901-7666
Fax: 505-983-9322
Email: hotelplazareal@buynm.com
Web site: http://santafehotelplazareal.com
No. of Rooms: 56
No. of Suites: 45
Credit Cards: Most Credit Cards accepted
Attractions: Historic Santa Fe Plaza, World-renowned Santa Fe Opera, galleries, shopping, dining, museums, snow skiing, river rafting, golf, wineries.
Bar: Jesse's
Conference Rooms: Meeting rooms
Location: steps away from the historic Santa Fe Plaza

LA FONDA

An historic landmark on the Plaza, La Fonda is known for its award-winning pueblo style Spanish architecture and décor, including thick wooden beams, carved corbels and a myriad of other details created by local artisans. The lobby, hallways and meeting rooms are filled with colorful artwork and memorabilia.

Fonda is Spanish for "inn" and there has been a fonda on the Plaza since the town was founded in 1607. Today's La Fonda was built in 1922 and is part of the National Trust for Historic Preservation, Historic Hotels of America.

Each of its 167 colorful rooms and suites is uniquely decorated with hand-painted wooden furniture and other distinctive touches created by the hotel's staff artist. Although it is historic, La Fonda has thoroughly modern amenities—including a brand new spa, opened in spring 2002. Each guestroom offers individual climate control, a safe, a hair dryer, iron and ironing board, dataport telephone lines, high speed Internet access and cable television. Room service and valet laundry are available. There is covered parking and a heated outdoor swimming pool. The interesting and busy lobby features part of La Fonda's eclectic art collection as well as a newsstand, several interesting shops and galleries and a highly professional concierge desk.

A special attraction is the La Terraza rooftop garden featuring 14 private and secluded luxury rooms and suites that offer special amenities including concierge services, an outdoor hot tub and a pool house with exercise equipment.

At the heart of La Fonda is La Plazuela, a beautiful enclosed courtyard restaurant featuring an award-winning culinary team and interesting, contemporary Nuevo Latino cuisine as well as New Mexican favorites. Executive Chef Lane Warner, C.E.C., participated in preparing a special gourmet dinner at the prestigious James Beard House in New York in the summer of 2002.

La Fiesta Lounge, next to the restaurant, features light fare, a special lunch buffet and live entertainment nightly. The hotel's Bell Tower Bar is open from late spring through early fall for cocktails and the best sunset views in town.

La Fonda has always been Santa Fe's gathering place, and the tradition continues today with more than 15,000 sq. ft. of charming meeting space available for conferences, banquets, parties and weddings. Each meeting room is full of unique architectural and decorative details, making La Fonda the ideal spot for groups to savor the essence of Santa Fe.

Address: 100 E San Francisco St, Santa Fe 87501.
Phone: 505-982-5511 800-523-5002
Fax: 505-988-2952
Email: reservations@lafondasantafe.com
Web site: http://www.lafondasantafe.com
Room Rates: 219–389
Suite Rates: 349–529
No. of Rooms: 167
No. of Suites: 36
Attractions: Only hotel on the historic Plaza, Galleries, Shopping, Historic churches, Museums, Restaurants
Services & Amenities: Covered parking, Newsstand, Shops, Lounge, Laundry service, Fireplaces, Balconies, Cable TV, Clock radio, Individual heat & air-conditioning control, Hair dryers, Irons & ironing boards, Dataport phones, High Speed Wireless Internet access
Restrictions: 5 rooms with handicapped access, No pets allowed, Children under 12 no extra charge in room
Concierge: 9 a.m.-6 p.m
Room Service: 7 a.m.-10 p.m.
Restaurant: La Plazuela–7a.m.-10 p.m.
Bar: La Fiesta Lounge, 11 a.m.-Midnight, Live entertainment
Business Facilities: Copiers, Fax, High Speed Internet access
Conference Rooms: 8 rooms, capacity from 6 to 600
Sports Facilities: Outdoor swimming pool, Whirlpool, Massage, Exercise Room, Skiing nearby
Location: Downtown Historic Plaza

RIVEREDGE RESORT HOTEL

Located in the heart of the beautiful 1000 Islands, the Riveredge Resort Hotel is as spectacular as its surroundings. Rising four floors above the majestic St. Lawrence River and overlooking magnificent Boldt Castle, the resort offers an elegant yet comfortable atmosphere complemented by superior service and hospitality.

With 129 deluxe accommodations, most with a river view, the entire facility has earned the coveted AAA Four-Diamond award as has its fine dining room, the Jacques Cartier Room, for fourteen consecutive years. The French Provincial furnishings and soft color schemes lend an air of elegance and comfort to the well-equipped rooms. The wide array of services and the activities at hand create a haven for business meetings and for unforgettable, intimate weddings.

Windows on the Bay, the Hotel's main dining room, offers casual dining for breakfast, lunch and dinner on the main floor overlooking the magnificent St. Lawrence River. The Jacques Cartier Room is located on the fourth floor and provides a spectacular panoramic view of the 1000 Islands while offering fine dining in an elegant atmosphere. The Jacques Cartier Room features creative American cuisine prepared before your eyes in its display kitchen, extensive wine list rated Excellent by *Wine Spectator* magazine, live dinner music and tableside preparations of Caesar Salad and gourmet coffees. The RiverWatch Lounge offers the best in beverage service in a relaxed environment with live entertainment.

Guests may relax on their guestroom balcony and enjoy the sights and sounds of the beautiful St. Lawrence River and the bustling Alexandria Bay harbor. In the spring, summer and fall the river is alive with pleasure boats and ocean-going freighters from all over the world. Within walking distance is the village of Alexandria Bay with its shops, boutiques, nightclubs and restaurants, and where sightseeing vessels depart regularly for guided cruises through the islands. A stop at Boldt Castle, a 122-room replica of a Rhineland castle, is a must.

The Riveredge Hotel Resort is easily accessible from Highway 401 in the province of Ontario as well as from Route 81 in New York State.

Address: 17 Holland St, Alexandria Bay 13607.
Phone: 315-482-9917
800-ENJOY-US
Fax: 315-482-5010
Email: enjoyus@riveredge.com
Web site: http://www.riveredge.com
Room Rates: 99–318
Suite Rates: 141–338
No. of Rooms: 129
No. of Suites: 41
Credit Cards: Most Credit Cards accepted
Attractions: Antique Boat Museum, Clayton, NY. Frederic Remington Art Museum, Ogdensburg. Old Fort Henry, Kingston, Ontario. Sightseeing cruises with stop at Boldt Castle. Hiking and x-country ski trails. Golf, fishing with professional river guides, Aqua Zoo and more
Services & Amenities: Valet Parking, Gift shop, Lobby Boutiques, Lounge, Babysitting service, Wet bar, Radio, Cable TV, Pay-per-view movies/Video games, 2 phones w/data ports & voice mail, hairdryer, Iron/board, In-room coffee, Laundry Service, Indoor/Outdoor pools, Tikki Bar
Restrictions: Pets are allowed, 6 rooms equipped for handicap
Concierge: 8 a.m.-8 p.m.
Room Service: 6:30 a.m.-10 p.m.
Restaurant: Casual dining for breakfast lunch & dinner in the Windows on the Bay Restaurant and fine dining in the elegant Jacques Cartier Room rated Four Diamonds by AAA
Bar: 11 a.m.-1 a.m.
Business Facilities: Message center, Admin. assistance, Copiers, Audio-Visual, Fax
Conference Rooms: 8 rooms, capacity 10-250
Sports Facilities: Indoor pool & Jacuzzi, Fitness room, 2,000 feet of dock space with power, water & cable TV hook-ups,
Location: Walk to Alexandria Bay. Hancock airport 99 miles

DE BRUCE COUNTRY INN ON THE WILLOWEMOC

Located within the Catskill Forest Park, the De Bruce Country Inn on the Willowemoc is a secluded and elegant setting for enjoying wooded trails, wildlife and game, trout-fishing streams, and lake and mountain views within the Inn's own private preserve. Guests receive unpretentious, heartfelt hospitality, the offerings of a gifted and award-winning chef, and the charm of a lovingly and authentically restored turn-of-the-century country hostelry.

On the ground floor of this Federal-style building is the formal dining room with long-leaf yellow pine floors and coffered ceiling, and the comfortable parlor/library with its fieldstone fireplace. The guestrooms, all with private baths, have brass beds with Posturepedic mattresses, homemade bedspreads, Indian or Oriental rugs, Victorian hurricane lamps, and ceiling fans. Original art work and decorative craft items provide a unique accent throughout the Inn, and the art gallery has exhibits of contemporary arts and crafts in small formats.

After a day of fly-fishing, taking in fall foliage or just lounging on the porch or by the pool, you can enjoy Apple Toddies at the Dry Fly Lounge, followed by fresh Willowemoc trout at Ianine's Restaurant. The summer dining terrace allows full enjoyment of the fresh air and views of the valley and mountains beyond.

Address: 982 De Bruce Rd, De Bruce 12758.
Phone: 845-439-3900
Web site: http://www.debrucecountryinn.com
Room Rates: 200 and up
Suite Rates: 230 and up
No. of Rooms: 12
No. of Suites: 2
Attractions: Antiques, Herb gardens, Covered bridges, Fly-fishing Museum, Music festivals, Rafting on nearby Delaware River, Outlet malls, State Park with boating, swimming and trails.
Services & Amenities: Parking, Gift shop, TV lounge, Library, Two meals included, Complimentary toiletries.
Restrictions: Children & pets at owner's discretion, No rooms are handicap accessible
Restaurant: Award-winning Ianine's, Call for hours.
Bar: The Dry Fly Lounge, Call fo hours.
Business Facilities: Fax, Copier
Conference Rooms: 1 room, capacity 15
Sports Facilities: Whirlpool bath, Sauna, Swimming pool, Hiking, Walking, Nearby golf, Skiing, Boating, Riding, Tennis,
Location: Willowemoc Wild Forest in the Catskill Forest Preserve

BAKER HOUSE 1650

The magnificently refurbished Baker House 1650 (formerly the J. Harper Poor Cottage) in East Hampton has been recognized as one of the finest luxury inns in the United States. It was named "Inn of the Month" by *Travel and Leisure* magazine, and *Town and Country* said the cottage "offers the kind of plush accommodations that you'd expect to find in an area famous for its residential real estate". *Time Out New York* said "the most distinctive B&B on the East End is so mind-bogglingly gorgeous that it's hard to believe anyone is actually allowed to sleep here."

The Baker House, one of the oldest continuously occupied structures in the United States, dates back to the earliest settlers of the Village of East Hampton. The house, first constructed in 1648 by a sea captain, Daniel Howe, was sold to Thomas Baker in 1650, one the Town's original founders, who turned it into Baker's Tavern. It served many other functions in the newly settled area, including town meeting hall, community center, and as the first location of religious services.

Joseph Greenleaf Thorp, a prominent turn-of-the-century architect with ties to the English Arts and Crafts Movement, was employed to dramatically expand the house in the Elizabethan style that was his signature, and the renovation concluded in 1917, when the shingled house was wrapped in stucco, completing the transformation of an American Colonial house with hand-hewn beams into an expansive English manor of many rooms and refinements.

Each bedroom is beautifully decorated, with individually controlled central air conditioning and heat, Bartech minibar, in-room security safe, televisions with full cable services and DVD, top-of-the-line Bose radios and CD players, multiple telephone lines, and wireless Internet access. Most of the rooms have wood-burning fireplaces, whirlpools and flat screen televisions. Bathrooms are lavish, with amenities by L'Occitane and bathrobes by Mascioni.

Each morning begins with a sumptuous breakfast (using local organic produce and farm products) served in the garden-side breakfast room, in the garden itself during spring, summer and fall, or before a wood burning fire in the winter, from 8.30am to 10.30am. You can also opt for continental breakfast in your own room, delivered with your choice of morning paper.

Address: 181 Main St, East Hampton 11937.
Phone: 631-324-4081
Fax: 631-329-5931
Email: info@bakerhouse1650.com
Web site: http://www.bakerhouse1650.com
Room Rates: 200–695
No. of Rooms: 5
Credit Cards: Most Credit Cards accepted
Attractions: Spectacular ocean and bay beaches, nature walks, historic tours, horseback riding, bicycling, boating, fishing, tennis, golf, Boutiques, antique stores, art galleries, museums, farmer's markets, craft and antique fairs, outlet stores, & superb restaurants
Restrictions: No pets allowed, Smoking outside only, Children over 12 welcome.
Concierge: Yes
Room Service: 8 a.m.-10 p.m.
Bar: Noon-11 p.m.
Business Facilities: Wireless Internet, Buisness Computer, Fax
Conference Rooms: Yes
Sports Facilities: State of the art Spa
Spa Services: The opportunity for guests to reserve the state-of-the-art spa (lap pool, spa tub, sauna, steam shower) privately for massage and purification, provides unparalleled luxury for an hotel this size.
Location: Main Street in East Hampton Village

1770 HOUSE

The 1770 House, built over 200 years ago as a private residence, is now an inn of exceeding comforts and a restaurant of elegance and distinction.

Air-conditioned rooms with flat screen TV's, luxurious beds and the finest linens might even tempt you to skip the complimentary breakfast. The inn also offers a separate carriage house that sleeps four.

At dinner, Chef Kevin Penner starts with local ingredients: the lobster, duck, skate and striped bass, sweet corn and tomatoes of Eastern Long Island; but unlike his 18th-century counterparts, he'll offer you Dover sole, Colorado lamb, Hudson Valley foie gras-a distinctively American menu that has earned glowing reviews from *The New York Times*. The wine list is astounding-15 champagnes, 100 whites, 200 reds, from all over the world, including several hard to find gems. Finally, when you've savored the last morsel of your banana financier you can contentedly sip a single-malt scotch, a cognac or armagnac, or any of the 10 different vintages of Chateau D'Yquem.

Whether you join us for an evening or a weekend, your time at The 1770 House will have you feeling completely relaxed and refreshed.

The 1770 House is nestled on Main Street in the heart of East Hampton Village. A short bike ride will take you to some of the best beaches in the United States. Sun-drenched, majestic elm trees will line your path to the ocean shore. Our staff can provide you a parking pass for the village beaches should driving be your preference.

Beyond beaches, East Hampton offers the finest retail shops on the East End. Since everything is nearby, you can take in an art opening and see a performance at Guild Hall. Visit the home of Jackson Pollack and Lee Krasner and take part in the Hamptons Film Festival on Main Street.

Address: 143 Main St, East Hampton 11937.
Phone: 631-324-1770
Fax: 631-324-3504
Email: innkeeper@1770house.com
Web site: http://www.1770house.com
Room Rates: 100–525
No. of Rooms: 8
Credit Cards: Visa
Attractions: Village beaches, Retail shops on the East End, Art galleries, Theater at Guild Hall, Home of Jackson Pollack and Lee Krasner, The Hamptons Film Festival.
Services & Amenities: Library, Complimentary newspaper, Cable Plasma TV, Telephone, CD Player, Fresh fruit, Fresh flowers, Bottled water, Hair dryers, Makeup mirrors, Frette towels, sheets and robes, Air conditioning, Complimentary breakfast
Restrictions: No pets allowed, Children over 12 welcome, Non-smoking, Minimum stays required during some seasons
Restaurant: Dining Room: Sunday Brunch, Dinner daily
Bar: Full bar/Tavern
Sports Facilities: Shuttle to tennis, pool & ocean beach
Location: East Hampton Village

INN AT GREAT NECK

Located in the heart of the Village of Great Neck Plaza, on picturesque Long Island, minutes from Manhattan, surrounded by 300 shops, restaurants and entertainment spots, the Inn at Great Neck offers 85 luxurious guestrooms and suites.

Every guestroom is furnished and appointed in an Art Deco style reminiscent of the golden era of the 1920's. All rooms have separate reading and work areas and feature multi-phase lighting, two line speaker phones with facsimile and personal computer capabilities, video players, minibars and marble bathrooms with oversized bathtubs or Jacuzzis. In addition, a complimentary high speed Internet connection is available in all guestrooms.

The luxurious restaurant, serving breakfast, lunch, dinner and Sunday brunch, features the best in American Continental Cuisine. The Giraffe Room, offers an exquisite ambiance suitable to a romantic dinner for two, a group celebration or a gathering of friends and business associates.

The Inn at Great Neck offers four private meeting and banquet rooms, the Empire, the Gotham, the Manhattan and the Boardroom, facilitating groups of 10 to 350 and providing unequaled catering for reception and corporate meeting events. When the banquet rooms are combined, a ballroom emerges offering an elegant setting for weddings and social gatherings. The Inn at Great Neck is Long Island's premier banquet and meeting destination specializing in innovative cuisine and complete event and menu planning.

Minutes from Manhattan and moments from Long Island's famed North Shore, The Inn at Great Neck offers the perfect location for the business or leisure traveler visiting New York City and points east on Long Island. The Inn provides the perfect atmosphere for a relaxing escape.

Address: 30 Cutter Mill Road, Great Neck 11021.
Phone: 516-773-2000
Fax: 516-773-2020
Email: innatgreatneck1@aol.com
Web site: http:// www.innatgreatneck.com
Room Rates: 219–259
Suite Rates: 319–359
No. of Rooms: 85
No. of Suites: 6
Attractions: Village of Great Neck Plaza, over 300 shops, restaurants, and entertainment spots. Downtown Manhattan, Shea Stadium, Belmont Race Track, National Tennis Center (Site of US Open).
Services & Amenities: Valet, Twice daily maid service, spacious vanities, multi-phase lighting, marble bathrooms w/oversized bathtubs/Jacuzzis, mini-bars, cable TV & VCR, Complimentary video rentals, 2 line speaker phones, data port & complimentary high speed Internet access
Concierge: Front Desk
Room Service: 7 a.m.–11 p.m.
Restaurant: The Giraffe Room, open daily 7 a.m.–11 p.m.
Bar: Lounge: 12 noon–1 a.m.
Business Facilities: Catering and conference facilities
Conference Rooms: 4 rooms, capacity 350
Sports Facilities: Exercise Room
Location: 16 miles from JFK, 20 minutes from Manhattan

THE ANDREW

Centered in the heart of the Village of Great Neck, The Andrew is the first designer boutique hotel in Long Island. Its modern design sensibility and unique approach to luxurious minimalism and restrained elegance makes it a must for business or vacation getaways.

Some highlights are custom-designed cherry and limed oak furniture and decadent fabrics such as ostrich skin, mohair and raw silk in the guestrooms; a lobby featuring rosewood wall panels, limestone floors and a front desk surrounded by purple glass; and a fresh white stucco and gray limestone exterior.

There is more to The Andrew than exquisite design. Unprecedented service and high attention to detail is second nature to the staff. Quietly and inconspicuously they provide for your needs.

Nestled among 300 restaurants and designer retailers, and close to baseball, tennis, golf and the seashore, the location is a perfect fit almost anyone.

And, if business brings you to Great Neck, a complete conference and business center can provide anything from a small boardroom meeting, access business equipment and supplies, to full catering services. In addition, each room features technological amenities such as High speed Internet ports, DVD player, and cordless phones.

Since The Andrew is a mere 25 minutes from New York City, it's for people who might want a little break from the hustle and bustle while still getting "that hip energy."

Address: 75 North Station Plaza, Great Neck 11021.
Phone: 516-482-2900
Fax: 516-482-4643
Email: ngafni@andrewhotel.com
Web site: www.andrewhotel.com
Room Rates: 165–295
Suite Rates: 330
No. of Rooms: 62
No. of Suites: 5
Attractions: Miracle Mile shopping, Shea Stadium, Arthur Ashe Tennis Stadium, Jones Beach, US Golf Open. Tennis and golf are two miles away. North Shore University Hospital, US Merchant Marine Academy, State Park.
Services & Amenities: Airport pick up, Garage/parking, Valet parking, Comp. shoeshine, Baby-sitting, Car hire, Laundry, Comp. newspaper, Cable TV/VCR, CD player, Telephone, Radio, Wet bar, Climate controls, Robe, Molten Brown of London toiletries, Deluxe continental breakfast
Restrictions: Pets welcome with $150 deposit, Children welcome and free with parents, 1 room handicap equipped
Concierge: 24 hours
Room Service: 12 p.m.–11 p.m.
Restaurant: Colbeh Restaurant, open daily, Glatt Kosher & has favorable reviews in the *New York Times* and *Newsday*; famous for delectable food, enormous portions, reasonable prices, & Persian authenticity.
Business Facilities: Complete Business Ctr: Message ctr, E-mail, Copiers, A/V, Teleconferencing, Fax, Modems, Translators
Conference Rooms: Full-scale conference facilities: 1 room, capacity 12
Sports Facilities: Indoor swimming pool, Massage, Aerobics, Weight traiing, Privileges at NY Sports Club
Location: Village Center, 25 minutes from NYC, Long Island Railroad 1 block away

THE BENJAMIN

Built in 1927, The Benjamin has been restored to its classic elegance and European style, bringing a new level of comfort to travelers in a sophisticated, boutique-style manner.

The dramatic two-story lobby of marble and carved silk damask features a domed ceiling and sweeping staircase leading to The Benjamin Lounge. The lobby is warm and inviting, exuding Old World charm and elegance. The Benjamin's guestrooms and suites are luxuriously appointed with all the amenities travelers desire. Fabrics such as chenille, mohair, and linen in warm shades of cream and taupe are used together with mahogany-finished furniture to decorate each room. Custom-designed beds and 11-choice pillow menu—enhanced by their renowned expert Sleep Concierge—ensure a perfect night's sleep.

Guests wishing for a stress-relieving retreat can visit the hotel's Affinia Wellness Spa. The Spa offers a complete menu of spa and fitness services, including massage and aromatherapy treatments. Located in Midtown, The Benjamin is near the Rockefeller Center, United Nations, Bloomingdale's, and an endless variety of fine restaurants.

When you choose The Benjamin, you choose the best. Guests will experience a luxurious spa and unforgettable service, all within an historic building of neoclassic detail and unmistakable grandeur.

Address: 125 East 50th Street, New York 10022.
Phone: 212-320-8002 888-4-BENJAMIN
Fax: 212-465-3697
Email: info@affinia.com
Web site: http://www.affinia.com
Room Rates: 629–2,200
No. of Rooms: 209
No. of Suites: 97
Attractions: Rockefeller Center, United Nations, Saks Fifth Avenue, Bloomingdales, Restaurants, Central Park, Grand Central Station
Services & Amenities: Cable TV/In-room movies, CD player, Laundry & valet service, Shoeshine, Fully equipped galley, Honor bar, Aromatherapy bath amenities, Hairdryer, Robe, Iron & board, Executive desk/ergonomic chair, High-speed Internet, WebTV, Direct dial phone/fax lines
Concierge: 24 hour
Room Service: 24 hour
Restaurant: Breakfast, lunch and dinner
Bar: 5 p.m.-Midnight (Mon-Sat), 12 p.m.-1 a.m. (Tues-Fri), 4 -11 p.m. Sunday
Business Facilities: Voice mail, Dual-line speakerphones, In-room fax/printer/copier, Dataports, Audio-visual equipment
Conference Rooms: 2 rooms, capacity 150
Sports Facilities: 24-hour Fitness Center, Full-service spa
Location: Midtown Manhattan

BEEKMAN TOWER HOTEL

Near exclusive Sutton Place and the United Nations, the Beekman Tower is ideally situated only a few steps from the corporate headquarters of Midtown. Personal service and attention, combined with the quiet neighborhood setting, create a welcome "home in New York" feeling.

Built in 1928, The Beekman has long been a distinctive sight on the New York skyline. This landmark building, whose elaborate tower is an outstanding example of Art Deco style, successfully combines elegance and period architecture. The hotel offers 174 handsomely furnished studios, as well as one- and two-bedroom suites, all with complete kitchens. Suites are decorated in soft shades of moss, rose and gold. French prints adorn the walls creating an elegant sophistication. A typical deluxe one-bedroom suite features an oversized living room, dining room with queen-size pullout sofa, 27" TV/VCR, spacious bedroom with king-size bed, one and a half baths, and fully equipped kitchen. These spacious suites give guests all the room they need to spread out their work, hold a meeting, entertain friends or even bring along the family.

For spectacular views of Manhattan, visit Top of the Tower, a sophisticated cocktail lounge on the 26th floor. Dramatic décor and glass wraparound terraces in an elegant setting make this one of the most romantic and memorable spots in the city. Live piano entertainment is featured on the weekends.

For those travelers who love Art Deco settings and are concerned with personal service and attention to detail, the Beekman Tower will fulfill all your needs.

Address: 3 Mitchell Place at 49th and First Avenue, New York 10017.
Phone: 212-320-8018 800-637-8483
Fax: 212-465-3697
Email: info@affinia.com
Web site: http://www.affinia.com/6_2_bee_overview.cfm
Suite Rates: 349-749
No. of Suites: 174
Attractions: Restaurants & shops nearby, Sutton Place, United Nations, adjacent gardens
Services & Amenities: Valet and parking service, Laundry service, Kitchen facilities, Individual heating and air conditioning, Cable TV/VCR, Radio, High-speed Internet
Restrictions: Children under 12 free, No charge for baby crib, 2 rooms handicap access
Concierge: 11 a.m.-7 p.m.
Room Service: 7 a.m.-1 a.m.
Restaurant: Breakfast daily: 7–10:30 a.m.
Bar: Daily 5 p.m.-1 a.m.
Business Facilities: Voice mail, Dual-line telephones, Copiers, Audio-visual, Fax in one-bedroom suites, Dataports
Conference Rooms: 4 rooms, capacity 150
Sports Facilities: Fitness center with saunas
Location: Midtown East, Turtle Bay

THE LOWELL

Ever-so-elegant, The Lowell, the jewel in the crown for those who like their hotels discreet and intimate, defines what makes a small hotel grand. It's the only hotel where you can have your own private terrace as well as a cozy romantic evening in front of a wood-burning fireplace. Its prestigious Upper East Side address, East 63rd Street between Madison and Park Avenues, is just steps away from world-famous boutiques and fabulous restaurants on Madison Avenue as well as Museum Mile. A member of The Leading Small Hotels of the World, The Lowell was voted among *Travel & Leisure*'s Greatest Hotels in the World, January 2003.

Individually appointed deluxe guestrooms and suites reflect The Lowell's immaculate attention to detail. From Scandinavian down comforters to Chinese porcelain, the decor of the rooms embodies an Old-World charm. Each has a marble bath with aromatic BVLGARI toiletries. All accommodations are outfitted with mini bars including gourmet foods from Fauchon and Dean & Deluca, fully equipped kitchens, Large-screen TV with VCR, DVD and CD players, multi-line telephones with voicemail, fax machines and complimentary wireless high-speed Internet access. 33 Suites also feature wood-burning fireplaces and 11 have private terraces. Newly renovated Deluxe Double rooms, Junior Suites and Deluxe One-Bedroom suites feature creamy Italian marble bathrooms with seperate shower and bathtub, flat-screen television at foot of tub and mood lighting.

The Post House, an award-winning restaurant, is reminiscent of a distinguished Gentleman's dinner club, with its spacious dining room and long, polished bar flanked by glass wine cases. A collection of American artifacts, treasured paintings, and handsome leather armchairs decorate this venerable New York establishment. Befitting one of the finest steak and seafood restaurants in America, a library of rare Cabernet, Bordeaux and Burgundy wines as well as an extensive list of California wines are available for connoisseurs to relish.

Located on the second floor and overlooking East 63rd Street is the fully equipped fitness center with Cybex equipment, free weights and an extensive range of cardiovascular equipment. Personal trainers are available by request.

Address: 28 E 63rd St, New York 10021
Phone: 212-838-1400
800-221-4444
Fax: 212-319-4230
Email: reservations@lowellhotel.com
Web site: http://www.lhw.com
Room Rates: 465–575
Suite Rates: 775–5,000
No. of Rooms 23
No. of Suites: 47
Attractions: Shopping on Madison and Fifth Avenues, Metropolitan Museum of Art, The Guggenheim Museum, The Frick Museum, The Whitney Museum, Central Park, Rockefeller Center and Broadway Theatres.
Services & Amenities: Suites w/ wood-burning fireplaces, 11 with private terrace, 24 hour room service, TV/VCR/DVD/CD, complimentary wireless high-speed Internet fax, BVLGARI toiletries, complimentary beverage on arrival and complimentary FIJI water w/ turndown service.
Restrictions: Limited handicapped access
Concierge: 24 hours
Room Service: 24 hours
Restaurant: The Post House, noon to 10:30 p.m., weekends 5:30 p.m.-10:30 p.m., The Pembroke Room, breakfast, afternoon tea, weekend brunch, special holiday dinners, social affairs.
Bar: The Post House, noon to 10:30 p.m.
Business Facilities: Complimentary in-room wireless high speed Internet access
Conference Rooms: 2 rooms, capacity 12 & 75, Also specialty suites available
Sports Facilities: Fully-equipped fitness center on second floor – 6:30 a.m. – 10 p.m.
Location: Upper East Side, 30 minutes from La Guardia, 1 hour from JFK Airport

THE MICHELANGELO

As you enter the Italian marble lobby of the Michelangelo, you will wonder whether you are in New York or Rome. The classic decor, light woods, peach marble and chandeliers are reminiscent of a magnificent Italian residence. Fresh flowers and potpourri are among the elegant touches everywhere.

The 178 guestrooms range in decor from Art Deco to Country French. The oversized marble bathrooms feature deep soaking tubs, mini-televisions and European amenities.

Located in the heart of Manhattan's business center, theater, shopping and cultural districts are all nearby, The Michelangelo is an oasis of calm in the heart of the most exciting city in the world. It offers personalized service in an elegant yet relaxed atmosphere with Italian style.

Address: 152 W 51st St, New York 10019
Phone: 212-765-1900 800-237-0990
Fax: 212-541-6604
Email: reservations@ michelangelohotel.com
Web site: http:// www.michelangelohotel.com
Room Rates: 435–595
Suite Rates: 655–1350
No. of Rooms: 178
No. of Suites: 55
Credit Cards: Most Credit Cards accepted
Attractions: Fifth Avenue shopping, Theatre district, unlimited restaurant options, Rockefeller Center, Radio City Music Hall,Times Square, MOMA, St. Patrick's, American Girl Place, close to major transportation hubs and all the excitement of New York City.
Services & Amenities: High speed internet, Valet service, Garage & parking, Laundry, Complimentary shoeshine, Toiletries & Newspaper, House doctor & baby-sitting on call, Cable TV/VCR, Bose CD/Radio, Individual heat & air-conditioning control, Robes, TV & phone in bathroom
Restrictions: No pets allowed, call for handicapped availability. Children under 16 free
Concierge: 24 hours
Room Service: 24 hours, Comp. toiletries
Restaurant: Complimentary Italian Style "Buondi" breakfast consisting of coffee, tea, espresso, cappucino, and assorted pastries served in the lobby lounge each morning. 7am-9am M-F, 8am-10am Sat.& Sunday.
Bar: Lobby Lounge, 11am–1am
Business Facilities: Fax, Printer, Message center, Admin. assistance, Copiers, Audio-Visual, Teleconferencing, Translator
Conference Rooms: 3 rooms, Full scale conference facilities
Sports Facilities: Complimentary 24-hour fitness center on property. Nearby indoor swimming pool, whirlpool and massage.

HOTEL PLAZA ATHENEE

Nestled among the residences of the Upper East Side of Manhattan on a lovely tree-lined street, this charming, boutique hotel is just a short stroll away from Central Park, Madison Avenue shopping, museums, galleries and the midtown business area. This elegant, European-style hotel offers 115 guestrooms and 35 suites emphasizing the ultimate in personalized service and award-winning dining. Voted "One of the Top Hotels in the World," by *Condé Nast Traveler* Gold List, 2004, and "One of the Top 75 Hotels in the World" by *Institutional Investor*, 2003. This hotel is home to Arabelle restaurant, voted "25" for Excellence in Food, Service and décor in the Zagat Hotel Survey, 2004.

The ambiance of the guestrooms are reminiscent of fine homes, thoughtfully furnished, with rich European fabrics. Guestrooms features include CD players, high speed Internet access, in room movies, two-lined speaker phone, large writing desk, deluxe toiletries, Belgian linens, plush bathrobes and hairdryers. Complimentary services include 24-hour concierge, 24-hour room service, twice daily maid service, choice of newspapers, shoe-shine, and access to fitness center.

Among the newly refurbished suites, some feature spectacular indoor atriums and outdoor balconies with a stunning skyline view of Manhattan. Spacious and residential in décor, these suites are decorated in soothing pale yellow walls and blue or maroon fabrics and fine European furnishings.

Their award-winning Zagat-rated restaurant is home to some of the most innovative cuisine in New York City, and is also known as having the Best Sunday Brunch in the City. The Bar Seine features New York City's only leather-floored lounge.

Address: 37 E 64th St at Madison Ave, New York 10021.
Phone: 212-734-9100 800-447-8800
Fax: 212-772-0958
Email: res@plaza-athenee.com
Web site: http://www.plaza-athenee.com
Room Rates: 515–685
Suite Rates: 1,200–3,600
No. of Rooms: 115
No. of Suites: 35
Credit Cards: Most Credit Cards accepted
Attractions: Steps away is Madison Avenue offering some of the best shopping in New York City with designer boutiques and department stores. Museums and a wide selection of casual to chic restaurants surround the hotel. 1 block to Central Park.
Services & Amenities: CD players, high speed Internet access, in room movies, two-lined speaker phone, large writing desks, Belgian linens, deluxe toiletries, plush bathrobes and hairdryers.
Restrictions: Small pets allowed, Some rooms handicap equipped
Concierge: "Clef d'Or," 24 hours
Room Service: 24 hours
Restaurant: Arabelle and the Bar Seine Lounge.
Bar: Bar Seine lounge w/ leather floors, animal prints, and plush velvets
Business Facilities: Via concierge desk, Meeting room and private dining room available
Conference Rooms: 2 elegant rooms for meetings and banquets from 20 to 150
Sports Facilities: Complimentary access to Fitness Center. Central Park.
Spa Services: In room massage available.
Location: Upper East Side

THE SURREY HOTEL

If it's the Upper East Side you want, and you'd like to find something reasonable in price, look no further! The Surrey, with studios and one-and two-bedroom suites, offers terrific value and comfort in an appealing neighborhood of stately brownstones, Madison Avenue's dramatic boutiques, and the Metropolitan Museum of Art (without a doubt one of the best art museums this side of the Louvre). You'll be right on the corner of Madison and 76th Street, a block from Central Park, and within walking distance of the Metropolitan.

Step into a large lobby, where antique reproductions stand out against highly polished marble floors and walls. Crystal chandeliers, fresh flowers, and an outgoing concierge complete the picture of a special environment. The fully furnished suites feature executive-size desks, two-line telephones with voice mail, dataports, 25" TVs with VCRs and well equipped kitchens or kitchenettes. Our favorite suite has an Oriental rug on the gleaming hardwood foyer floor, a large living room with mahogany bookcases, beveled mirrors, fireplace, terrace, and a striking marble bathroom.

Daniel Boulud's Cafe Boulud at the Surrey Hotel is an artful addition to the Upper East Side's museum mile. With a relaxed atmosphere and sleek décor, Cafe Boulud combines the best of classic French cooking, regional specialties and world cuisine. This highly rated restaurant has earned praise from *The New York Times* and some of the most respected food critics in the country. The ambiance is sophisticated yet warm, the service attentive, and the food in harmony with the seasons. The à la carte menu is complemented with creative tasting menus and an extensive wine list. During summer months patrons may enjoy cocktails on the charming sidewalk terrace. Cafe Boulud also provides room service for the hotel guests.

Address: 20 East 76th Street, New York 10021.
Phone: 212-320-8027 800-637-8483
Fax: 212-465-3697
Email: info@affinia.com
Web site: http://www.affinia.com/6_10_sur_overview.cfm
Suite Rates: 399-1699
No. of Suites: 131
Attractions: Metropolitan Museum of Art, Guggenheim Museum, Whitney Museum, Yorkville and Gracie Mansion, Shopping at Menage a Trois, Bloomingdale's, Armani, Sonia Rykiel, Ungaro, Gucci and Kenzo
Services & Amenities: Valet parking, Fully equipped kitchens or kitchenettes, Honor bar, Grocery shopping service, Cable TV and VCR, Climate controls, Laundry, Radio, Hair dryer, Iron & ironing board, Plush robe, TV web browser, Wireless keyboard, High-speed Internet
Concierge: 10 a.m.-6 p.m.
Room Service: 7 a.m.-10:30 p.m.
Restaurant: Cafe Boulud, Dinner, Monday through Sunday, Lunch, Tuesday through Saturday
Bar: Noon-2:30 p.m., 5:30-11 p.m.
Business Facilities: Voice mail, Copiers, Fax, Dataport for in-room fax and computer hookups, Dual-line speaker phones
Sports Facilities: Fitness center in hotel, Horseback riding, Jogging paths nearby in Central Park
Location: Upper East Side Manhattan, Near Central Park, Airports–JFK & LaGuardia

THE PENINSULA NEW YORK

The Peninsula New York, which opened in 1905 as the Gotham Hotel, has been fully restored to its original beaux-arts elegance and designated for landmark preservation. Entering the lobby is like stepping into the grandeur of the Belle Époque. Rich marble abounds and a multifaceted crystal chandelier highlights the Renaissance details of the original Gotham ceiling. In 1998 the hotel had an extensive renovation and now offers a premier level of amenities, comfort, and 21st Century technology to a clientele that seeks excellence.

Guestrooms were given top priority and 14 new suites were added. Spacious guestrooms are decorated in a Classic Contemporary style, most with king-size beds, writing desks, and seating areas. Oversized marble bathrooms feature luxurious six-foot tubs. State-of-the-art technology centers allow guests to regulate temperature, lighting, telephones and audio/visual systems with a fingertip.

Two restaurants provide a variety of dining delights. The Adrienne, with its color palette of rich crème and antique silver, features modern French cuisine. Bistro's lunch and dinner menu offers lighter fare and has piano music nightly. In the Gotham Lounge, high tea can be enjoyed in the afternoon. The Pen-Top Bar and Terrace provides dramatic views of Manhattan.

The crowning feature of this hotel is the Peninsula Spa, a rooftop tri-level glass-enclosed health club offering the most extensive facilities of any hotel in New York. It includes an indoor swimming pool and whirlpool, massage, aerobics, weights, fully equipped exercise rooms, and steam and saunas in the dressing rooms.

For those seeking European elegance, proximity to Manhattan's cultural, entertainment and shopping opportunities, and all the facilities and technologies to renew oneself after a long day, The Peninsula New York is the place.

Address: 700 Fifth Ave, New York 10019.
Phone: 212-956-2888 800-262-9467
Fax: 212-903-3949
Email: pny@peninsula.com
Web site: http://www.peninsula.com
Room Rates: 550–690
Suite Rates: 750–8,500
No. of Rooms: 186
No. of Suites: 55
Credit Cards: Most Credit Cards accepted
Attractions: In the heart of Manhattan's cultural, entertainment, and shopping district
Services & Amenities: Valet service, Garage/valet parking, Comp. Theater limo service, 9 non-smoking floors, Laundry service, Baby-sitting service, Cable TV, Radio, Refrigerators, Phone in bath, Robes, Comp. toiletries, NY *Times* & shoeshine, Water Bar, In-room safe, Hairdryers
Restrictions: Children welcome, Non-smoking rooms available, Fully ADA compliant
Concierge: 24 hours
Room Service: 24 hours
Restaurant: Adrienne, fine dining, 7 a.m.-10:30 p.m.; Bistro, casual dining for lunch and dinner
Bar: The Gotham Lounge 11-1 am; Pen-Top Bar & Terrace 5pm-midnight Tue-Sat.
Business Facilities: Message center, Copiers, Audio-Visual, Teleconferencing, In-room fax & High speed T1 Internet access
Conference Rooms: 6 rooms, Full-scale conference facilities
Sports Facilities: Full health spa, Pool, Whirlpool, Sauna, Massage, Aerobics, Weight training
Location: Fifth Avenue & 55th Street, Downtown/theater district

THE KIMBERLY HOTEL

Offering European-style elegance and service, this 185-room hotel is conveniently located in the heart of midtown Manhattan's fashionable east side, steps away from the world-renowned shops on Madison, Fifth, and Park Avenues, and from Rockefeller Center.

The Kimberly guests enjoy the luxury of over-sized one- and two-bedroom suites, which feature a separate living room with dining area, marble bathrooms, a fully equipped kitchen, and private balcony.

Complimentary access to the New York Health & Racquet Club provides guests of the hotel with the most extensive network of sports facilities available in Manhattan, inclusive of swimming pools, squash, racquetball, indoor golf, strength training and cardiovascular equipment. Sunset cruises during the spring and summer weekends allow hotel guests to luxuriate on a 75-foot yacht during the evening.

The hotel has two excellent dining options: George O'Neills's brings classic steakhouse cuisine and exceptional service to life in a sophisticated yet cozy setting. Enjoy breakfast, lunch, dinner or late night supper at George O'Neills's. Vue is the 21st century's version of a supper club. It provides a visually stunning and ultra hip venue, which seamlessly blends uptown elegance with downtown chic. Open for dinner only, the restaurant serves an American eclectic fare. At 10 PM the atmosphere transforms itself into a disco.

A wraparound veranda that offers panoramic views of Manhattan's Upper East Side surrounds the Penthouse Suite. It extends the entire length of the hotel's 31st floor, making an opulent backdrop for festive receptions, intimate weddings and executive board meetings.

Address: 145 E 50th St, New York 10022.
Phone: 212-755-0400 800-683-0400
Fax: 212-486-6915
Email: info@kimberlyhotel.com
Web site: http://www.kimberlyhotel.com
Room Rates: 259–349
Suite Rates: 299–1,000
No. of Rooms: 26
No. of Suites: 159
Attractions: Park Avenue, Madison Avenue, Fifth Avenue shops, Rockefeller Center, UN Headquarters, Radio City Music Hall, Museum of Modern Art, New York Public Library and St. Patrick's Cathedral
Services & Amenities: Same-day valet, Turndown service (upon request), In-room safe (large enough for laptops), In-room two line telephones w/dataport, Complimentary health club access, Bath robes, Honor bars, Daily newspaper, Seasonal sunset cruises on 75' yacht.
Concierge: 8 a.m.-11 p.m.
Room Service: 6 a.m.-11 p.m.
Restaurant: George O'Neills's, open for breakfast, lunch and dinner. Vue open for dinner only, dancing after 10 p.m.
Bar: George O'Neills's, 5 pm-2 am, Mon-Sat. Vue Bar, Tues. 6pm-2am, Wed-Sat 6pm-4am
Business Facilities: In-room fax/printer, comp. business center, voice mail, High speed Internet access
Conference Rooms: 1 executive meeting room, cap. 30 conference style, receptions, cap. 50
Sports Facilities: Complimentary off-site squash, Racquetball, Indoor golf, Swimming pools, Strength training & cardiov
Location: Midtown Manhattan's fashionable East Side, 30 min.–La Guardia, 1 hr. JFK

THE WALDORF TOWERS

Peerless elegance, exceptional privacy, and highly personalized service are all hallmarks of The Waldorf Towers, New York's premier boutique hotel. For business or pleasure, the hotel's spacious guestrooms and suites, surrounded by residential ambiance, offer an enclave of luxury at a preeminent midtown Manhattan address. Through this private entrance, just steps off Park Avenue, the gifted art of service quietly fulfills its enchanting promise.

Encompassing the 28th–42nd floors of the world famous Waldorf-Astoria, The Waldorf Towers affords hotel guests convenient access to all the restaurants, shops and services of the adjoining landmark hotel. However, The Waldorf Towers maintains its own dedicated entrance, concierge desk, reception, private elevators and a hotel staff trained to gracefully accommodate every wish of some of the world's most demanding guests. It is indeed the preferred New York residence of heads-of-state, royalty, celebrities and corporate moguls.

The Waldorf Towers offers a distinctive array of splendidly oversized accommodations, all of which are individually decorated with antiques and museum-quality reproduction pieces. In themes ranging from French Provincial to Old English with Oriental accents, each suite has its own signature look. Crystal chandeliers hang from 15-foot ceilings, while Oriental rugs, oil paintings and prints complete the opulent decor.

Distinguishing our services are twice-daily maid service, twenty-four hour room service, and complimentary in-room premium movie channels. All guests of The Waldorf Towers are also afforded exclusive access to the Astoria Lounge, featuring complimentary continental breakfast and evening canapés, and complimentary use of the Plus One Fitness Center. In addition, guests of The Waldorf Towers have the luxury of New York's most diverse dining destination being housed under their roof. Without leaving the building they can avail themselves of the hotel's acclaimed restaurants, bars and lounges, including Bull and Bear steakhouse, and Oscar's Brasserie.

Since its 1931 opening The Waldorf Towers has been the setting for great historical moments and home to some of the world's most outstanding citizens. We have hosted kings, queens and six decades of US presidents. Now we invite you to experience The Waldorf Towers.

Address: 100 East 50th Street, New York 10022
Phone: 212-355-3100
800-WATOWER
Fax: 212-872-4799
Email: waldorf_towers@hilton.com
Web site: http://www.symbolicepc.com/waldorf/towers/
Room Rates: 369–799
Suite Rates: 499 and up
No. of Rooms 180
No. of Suites: 101
Credit Cards: Most Credit Cards accepted
Services & Amenities: Fitness center, Florist, Valet sevice, Gift shop, Parking, Beauty salon, Dry cleaning
Restrictions: No pets over 35 pounds
Concierge: 24 Hours, 7 Days
Room Service: 24 Hours, 7 Days
Restaurant: Bull and Bear Restaurant, chef Eric Kaplan, Prime grade certified Angus Beef, Hours 12 p.m.-11:30 p.m.
Bar: Sir Harry's 1p.m – 2:30 a.m.
Business Facilities: Complete Business Service Center
Conference Rooms: 40 Conference Rooms, Copiers, Audio-visual, Fax, Modems, Mes
Sports Facilities: Gym, Weight Training, Sauna, Massage
Spa Services: Unique healing massage therapies, expert facials, and therapeutic body treatments

BEEKMAN ARMS - DELAMATER INN

Since the Revolutionary War, the Beekman Arms has served as the center of graciousness and hospitality in the Hudson Valley. Ten buildings now comprise this Inn, which has been in continuous operation longer than any other hotel in the United States. The Main Inn was completely remodeled and refurbished in 1995.

Each of the 67 rooms and suites is uniquely decorated and all offer modern private baths, televisions, and air-conditioning. Rooms in the Beekman Arms continue the colonial theme. The Delamater Inn is located just a few doors away from the original building. This property is a combination of old and new buildings including the Delamater House, an historic Victorian Gothic Home. Many of the rooms feature wood-burning or gas fireplaces.

Wide plank floors, overhead beams and huge stone hearth beckon guests as they enter the lobby of the "Beek" recalling a simpler and gentler way of life.

Colonial styling, antiques and a well-kept greenhouse in the new Traphagen Restaurant add to the ambiance. American country fare such as Camembert Crisp with Apple

Chutney, Crabmeat stuffed Brook Trout with Goat Cheese Polenta, and Creme Brulee has earned a rating of "excellent" by the New York Times.

This is a Village Inn set in a walking village with a variety of boutiques, antique shops and nearby places to visit including the FDR Home and Library, the Culinary Institute of America and many Hudson River estates such as Montgomery Place, Olana, and the Vanderbilt Mansion.

Address: 6387 Mill Street, Rhinebeck 12572.
Phone: 845-876-7077
Fax: 845-876-7077
Email: beekmanarm@aol.com
Web site: http://www.beekmandelamaterinn.com
Room Rates: 100–250
Suite Rates: 175–250
No. of Rooms: 67
No. of Suites: 2
Attractions: FDR Library, Vanderbilt Mansion, World-known Culinary Institute of America in Hyde Park (8 miles away), World War I Aerodrome.
Services & Amenities: Parking, Library, Card area, Sundries shop, Baby-sitting service, Fireplaces, Cable TV, Telephones, Wet bars, Complimentary toiletries.
Restrictions: Pets restricted, 4 rooms handicap equipped, 2 night minimum stay on seasonal weekends.
Restaurant: Traphagen Restaurant, 11:30 a.m.-10 p.m.
Bar: Tap Room, 11:30 a.m.-1 a.m.
Business Facilities: New conference center at Delamater, capacity 32
Conference Rooms: 1 room, capacity 32
Location: Center of Village, 37 miles to airport at Newburgh, 90 miles from New York.

THE ADELPHI HOTEL

It was called the Queen of the Spas, and no wonder. The legendary Adelphi Hotel was built in the high Victorian style that prevailed just before the turn of the century, with 12-foot ceilings and window treatments to match. Today it remains replete with classic Victorian furnishings, and reflects all of the opulence of that era. The hotel has added a beautifully landscaped outdoor swimming pool as part of its major renovation. The lodgings have also been updated to provide guests with full baths, air conditioning, and other modern conveniences. Still, the original facade of ornamental brickwork and three-story Victorian columns with elaborate fretwork at the top remain, retaining the aura of the era.

Guestrooms are unusually large, and each is uniquely decorated with a variety of wall coverings and color schemes. Suites are furnished in a variety of styles including English Country, French Provencal, Adirondack, and High Victorian.

The hotel's Cafe Adelphi consists of several rooms, one featuring a wrap-around mural, and another, an enclosed patio overlooking the flower-laden courtyard. The Cafe offers specially blended drinks, unique wines, desserts, espresso, and cappucinos. It is a popular gathering place after the track, a ballet, or orchestral performance at the performing arts center.

Saratoga Springs is a charming town in which to stroll, and guests of the hotel find interesting antique shops and restaurants. Also of interest are the Saratoga Performing Arts Center, the Saratoga Raceway, and several large and small museums.

Address: 365 Broadway, Saratoga Springs 12866.
Phone: 518-587-4688
Fax: 518-587-0851
Web site: http://www.adelphihotel.com
Room Rates: 115–285
Suite Rates: 150–470
No. of Rooms: 39
No. of Suites: 16
Credit Cards: Visa
Attractions: Near Saratoga Performing Arts Center, Saratoga Raceway, Museums, Antique Shops, Restaurants
Services & Amenities: Cable TV, Air-conditioning, Telephone, Complimentary toiletries, Complimentary breakfast
Restrictions: No pets allowed, Children welcome
Restaurant: Cafe Adelphi–serves specially blended drinks, unique wines, espresso, cappucino, cocktails, desserts
Bar: Cafe Adelphi, 5 p.m.-midnight
Sports Facilities: Outdoor swimming pool
Location: Broadway, Nearest airport is Albany

THE VILLAGE LATCH INN

This famous Country House Hotel, situated on a lovely 5-acre estate, is perfectly located within walking distance to Southampton village's most fashionable shopping streets and beautiful ocean beaches. Sophisticated, romantic and intimate with an international flavor, the furnishings and décor are truly unique.

Created and run by artists, the décor is a study in diversity. Puppets from Burma, masks from New Guinea, artifacts from Africa, rugs from Tibet, furniture from Bali to England. There are antique filled or modern units all decorated with warmth and a gracious ambiance. Each room is different, and this is the unique charm of the hotel. Besides its eclectic ambiance, all rooms have modern conveniences: private baths, AC, cable TV's, phones and hairdryers. Imagine mansion buildings to spacious suites to wicker filled sitting rooms, some with fireplaces, balconies, and decks. There are even large studios, 2 and 3 room suites and duplexes. One of the fireplace suites has English pine furniture, an antique sleigh bed, Laura Ashley print curtains and wallpaper, and dusty rose wall-to-wall carpeting.

Despite its lavishness, the inn is cozy—the sort of place where guests can help themselves to coffee or a cold drink any time of day, even if the sign says "Kitchen Closed."

There is a Continental breakfast on weekends which might include bagels, cream cheese, yogurt, fresh fruit, homemade breads and muffins. Breakfast is served in the dining room with its lush green Italian chairs.

Exclusive private villas are available for such events as family reunions, weddings, corporate outings and photo-shoots. The villas include a magnificent living room, country kitchen and from 5 to 16 bedrooms depending upon the group's needs—all have modern conveniences. There are additional rooms available in the main buildings.

An outdoor pool with privacy hedges, health club privileges close-by, a tennis court and a former conservatory complete with a tranquil fish pond are located at various points around the lawn that connect the assorted buildings of this boutique Hotel. It has been the #1 choice in over 50 Inn books from *Frommer's* to *Fodor's* as the best place to stay in the Hamptons. Also a member of "LUXE Premiere Boutique Hotels."

Since 1901 it has been the legendary Great Gatsby Hotel of the rich and famous . . . it still remains so.

Address: 101 Hill St, PO Box 3000, Southampton 11969.
Phone: 631-283-2160 800-54-LATCH
Fax: 631-283-3236
Email: mail@villagelatch.com
Web site: http://www.villagelatch.com
Room Rates: 140–395
Suite Rates: 295–595
No. of Rooms: 67
No. of Suites: 8
Credit Cards: Most Credit Cards accepted
Attractions: Art galleries, Boutiques, Wineries, Theatre, Boating, Golf, Cultural events. Miles of world famous unspoiled beaches. Walking distance to all shops, boutiques, museums, premier restaurants in historic Southampton village.
Services & Amenities: Free parking. Some rooms with fireplaces, many with balconies or decks; all with cable TV, individual heat and air-conditioning control. Heated pool and tennis court. Baby-sitting service.
Restrictions: Some pets by prior arrangements. Some rooms available for children. Minimum stay on peak weekends.
Concierge: On premises
Business Facilities: Message center with fax and copier. Private villas available for private affairs, weddings, etc.
Conference Rooms: Several informal meeting rooms and 2 larger rooms–Up to 50
Sports Facilities: Outdoor heated pool, tennis court, bicycle rentals, special health club privileges.
Spa Services: Walking distance to Spa. In-room massages arranged.
Location: Walking distance to the village of Southampton, NY

THE SANDERLING

This intimate retreat features 88 luxury guest rooms and suites in three inns and four Station Bay villas containing three and four bedroom accommodations.

For your dining pleasure there are lots of choices. The 1899 Lifesaving Station Restaurant and The Left Bank, our fine dining restaurant, The Pine Island Diner (located down the road in Corolla), and a bar and lounge in the Lifesaving Station Restaurant.

Whether for business or pleasure, a full-service spa and fitness center, and an IACC-certified conference center are available to meet your needs.

The wide, tranquil waters of Currituck Sound are a serene backdrop to your own quest for calm, contentment and renewal at the Sanderling Spa. Here, at this luxurious North Carolina spa, you'll find yourself immersed in surroundings designed to introduce a feeling of complete comfort and relaxation even before your treatment begins. Our hospitable staff of licensed spa technicians, trained in the most advanced American and European spa philosophies and techniques, will welcome you and guide you through your preparations for a deeply satisfying experience during your North Carolina vacation.

The Sanderling Spa's menu of service presents a delightful selection of massage, body, skin or nail care treatments - many of them created uniquely for The Spa and utilizing sea mud and minerals of local provenance . Enter the spa at the water's edge and rediscover the you that nature intended.

The Sanderling Spa is open from 8:00am–8:00pm Monday through Saturday and 9:00am–6:00pm on Sundays.

The Sanderling's luxurious accommodations and amenities are designed to appeal to adults.

The Sanderling now offers air service direct from Norfolk to Pine Island 3 miles north of The Sanderling. Please visit Sea Air's website at www.seaair.com for rates and schedules

Address: 1461 Duck Rd, Duck 27949
Phone: 252-261-4111
800-701-4111
Fax: 252-261-1638
Email:
comments@thesanderling.com
Web site: http://
www.thesanderling.com
Room Rates: 132–402
Suite Rates: 193–593
No. of Rooms: 88
No. of Suites: 12
Credit Cards: Most Credit Cards accepted
Attractions: Pine Island Audubon Sanctuary, Jockey's Ridge State Park, North Carolina Aquarium, Currituck Lighthouse, Wright Brother's Memorial, Elizabethan Gardens, Lost Colony, Roanoke Island Festival Park, Bodie Island Lighthouse, Ocracoke Island Lighthouse
Services & Amenities: Spa, Off-Site Fitness Center, Pool, Gift Shops, Shuttle Bus, Limo, Parking, Laundry, Balconies/Decks, Cable TV/VCR, Radio, Coffeemaker, Refrigerator, Robes, Beach Towels, Afternoon Tea & Cookies & Morning Bakery Baskets delivered to your room.
Restrictions: 2 guests per room, $50 extra person charge – per person, per night, Pets are not allowed.
Concierge: 9:00am – 5:00pm
Room Service: 7:30am – 9:00pm
Restaurant: The Lifesaving Station Restaurant – Breakfast, Lunch & Dinner. The Left Bank – Dinner Only – Blazers optional. The Pine Island Diner – Breakfast, Lunch and Dinner (located down the road in Corolla).
Bar: Swan Bar and Lounge, 12:00pm – 9:00pm
Business Facilities: Copiers, AV, Fax, Message service, Full scale conference facilities
Conference Rooms: Board Room, Swan & Heron rms, Executive Suite, capacity 100
Sports Facilities: Indoor swimming pool, Tennis & outdoor pool nearby, Golf & Racquet Club nearby

THE CAMPBELL HOUSE

The Campbell House Inn is a Queen Anne shingle-style Victorian Estate, nestled in beautifully landscaped grounds adjacent to hiking trails and bicycle paths in the East Skinner Butte Downtown Historic District of Eugene. Originally built in 1892 by gold miner and timber owner John Cogswell, completely renovated and opened up as a city inn in 1993.

Elegant, light guestrooms, beautifully appointed and sporting designer fabrics and wallpapers, luxury bedding, and all the modern amenities you would expect in a fine European Hotel: desk, telephone, TV with VCR or DVD player, wireless high speed Internet, CD players, just to name a few. Our luxury suites feature: fireplace, Jacuzzi tub and four-poster bed.

The Campbell House Dining Room is open for breakfast, dinner and room service. Breakfast starts with scones and locally fresh roasted coffee, we always have our mini-Belgium waffles, oatmeal, Inn-made granola and feature a Breakfast special each day. Our dinners are simple and exclusive to our guests and their guests. Offering only a couple of specials each evening prepared with locally grown produce, the freshest cuts of meats, poultry or fish; beautifully orchestrated together by our Chef. All are served with fresh vegetables and sprigs of herbs and edible flowers, many grown in the Inn's own gardens.

The Campbell House is also ideal for a meeting, retreat, reunion or wedding. The Inns beautiful gardens in adjacent to the parlor, library & dining rooms (that can also be combined into one room) make an ideal setting for an elegant event.

The Inn beckons you to relax in front of a crackling fireplace with a glass of wine, walk the gardens, hike the adjacent butte, stroll to boutique shops, sample the delicacies of world class restaurants, rent a bike and tryout over 10 miles of riverside bicycle paths, 8 golf courses within 30 minutes, hire a river guide, visit the breathtaking Oregon Coast only one hour away, or whatever your desire is—it is all within your reach at The Campbell House, A City Inn.

Address: 252 Pearl St, Eugene 97401.
Phone: 541-343-1119 800-264-2519
Fax: 541-343-2258
Email: campbellhouse@ campbellhouse.com
Web site: http:// www.campbellhouse.com
Room Rates: 92–345
Suite Rates: 175–345
No. of Rooms: 19
No. of Suites: 8
Credit Cards: Most Credit Cards accepted
Attractions: Adjacent to the Butte for hiking, 2 blocks to the River, 10 miles of Bicycle & running paths. Walking distance to Autzen Stadium, restaurants, boutique & antique shops, and the Hult Center for Performing Arts. Fishing, Rafting, Golfing just minutes away.
Services & Amenities: Other amenities not mentioned: Parking, laundry, gift shop, library, exclusive Athletic Club passes, comp. newspaper, individual heat control, air-conditioning, in-room refrigerator with refreshments, robes & toiletries.
Restrictions: Minimum stay some weekends, 1 room handicap equipped
Concierge: 8:30 a.m.–10 p.
Room Service: 7 a.m.–10 p.m.
Restaurant: Breakfast & Dinner are available in your room, the dining room or the outside courtyard. Breakfast 7 a.m.–10 a.m. everyday. Dinner 6 p.m.–9:30 p.m., Wednesday through Saturday nights.
Bar: Cocktail & Wine Bar from 5 p.m.–10 p.m.
Business Facilities: Copier, Audio-visual, Teleconferencing, Dataport for computer and fax, Full catering menu available
Conference Rooms: 3 rooms, capacity 20 each room, Banquet size up 60 inside
Sports Facilities: Guest passes to Downtown Athletic Club, 2 golf courses, Riverside bicycle paths, Whitewater rafting

O'DYSIUS HOTEL

The O'dysius Hotel welcomes you warmly to a visit filled with romance and elegance. Overlooking the beautiful Pacific Ocean, the property features turn of the century European architecture and antiques. We offer all of the charm and friendliness of a bed and breakfast with the privacy and attention to detail of a small luxury hotel. At the O'dysius, we are committed to ensuring that your stay is unparalleled in quality and excellence.

Featured in independent publications such as *Frommer's Oregon Guide*, *Best Places to Stay in the Pacific Northwest*, and *Best Places in the Northwest*, our dedication and attention to our guests has earned us the prestigious AAA four-diamond rating—making us Lincoln City's only four-diamond hotel.

Join us for your next get-away. Feel lavished by in-room breakfast services, spectacular ocean views, fireplaces and Jacuzzi tubs. Congregate with friends and family in the evening for soft piano jazz and a tasting of wines from Oregon's premiere vineyards. Your enjoyment is our sole focus and we look forward to serving you and welcoming you again and again, as one of our ever-growing family of guests.

Address: 120 NW Inlet Court, Lincoln City 97367.
Phone: 541-994-4121 800-869-8069
Fax: 541-994-8160
Email: odysius@harborside.com
Web site: http://www.odysius.com
Room Rates: 149–189
Suite Rates: 219–299
No. of Rooms: 30
No. of Suites: 8
Credit Cards: Visa
Attractions: 7 mi.of sandy beaches,one of 10 Best Places to Antique in U.S., Art Galleries, Casino w/headline entertainment, Fine Dining, 2 Movie Theaters, Newport Aquarium, Local Museum, Hatfield Marine Science Center, Glass blowers, Outlet Stores, Live Theater
Services & Amenities: Some covered parking, Gift shop, Library, Card/game area, Fireplaces, Some Balconies/decks, Complimentary newspaper, Cable TV/VCR, Telephones, Radio, Honor bar, Robes, Whirlpool tubs, Complimentary toiletries, Complimentary breakfast, evening wine.
Restrictions: Small pets 20# Max. welcome, select rooms. Children over 12 welcome, 2 rooms handicap equipped
Concierge: 8 a.m.-10 p.m.
Room Service: 8 a.m.-10 p.m.
Restaurant: Kyllos Seafood Restaurant (next door), 11 a.m.–10 p.m.(closing). Many other fine restaurants are conveniently located.
Bar: Next door at Kyllo's Restaurant
Business Facilities: Message center, E-mail, Copiers, Audio-visual, Fax, Modems, small conference facilities
Conference Rooms: 1 room, capacity 25
Sports Facilities: Whirlpool, Massage, Aerobics, nearby Golf courses, racquet club
Spa Services: None
Location: Wayside Park at the "D" River in the center of town

GOLDEN PLOUGH INN

Set in scenic central Bucks County countryside, The Golden Plough Inn is part of Peddler's Village, an 18th-century style shopping, dining, lodging and family entertainment attraction. The property features over 75 unique specialty shops and restaurants, family entertainment center with a beautifully restored antique carousel, year-round events, waterwheel, fish pond, and gazebo, all set amidst 42 acres of award-winning landscaped grounds and winding brick pathways. The buildings are reproduction Bucks County stone-and-wood architecture. The 70 rooms of the inn are subtly scattered throughout the entire property, with many located atop the shops.

Each room is individually appointed and spacious. Color schemes range from colonial blues and maroons to deeper hued greens and pinks, to summer pastels. Most are 18th-century American Country, plus some newer English-Country style. All rooms include a work area and queen or king beds, and some have firm, double-sized wall beds. Many rooms offer gas-lit fireplaces and double-sized jetted tubs. Designer fabric treatments on windows, bedding and crown canopies help create a warm, elegant ambiance.

The Golden Plough excels at pampering. Upon arrival, guests will find a complimentary split of champagne, snacks and beverages. Complimentary toiletries are presented in attractive baskets. The Inn is an ideal location for business meetings, reunions and wedding that require overnight accommodations. Golf, tennis, exercise facilities, wineries, antiques and New Hope are nearby.

Seasonal festivals, Murder Mystery Dinner Theater, and a Piano Bar are just some of the enticements found at this location. An overnight stay at the Inn includes a hearty continental breakfast at the Spotted Hog Restaurant, which also serves lunch, dinner and late-night snacks. Additional restaurants on-site serve lunch and dinner. Jenny's Bistro, for both casual and special occasion dining, focuses on fresh seasonal fare with a creative touch in a setting that combines Victorian elegance and country French.

Address: Rt 202 & Street Rd, Lahaska 18931.
Phone: 215-794-4004
Fax: 215-794-4008
Email: lodging@peddlersvillage.com
Web site: http://www.goldenploughinn.com
Room Rates: 125–245
Suite Rates: 270–375
No. of Rooms: 66
No. of Suites: 4
Attractions: Giggleberry Fair Family Entertainment Center, Shopping village on-site, Nearby outlets, Wineries, Antiques, Museums, Historic sites, Covered bridges, Hiking, New Hope. Convenient to Princeton, NY, Philadelphia, Lehigh Valley and Atlantic City.
Services & Amenities: Gift shop, Library, Cable TV, Phone, Radio, Individual climate controls, In-room coffee/tea service, Hair dryer, Iron, Complimentary champagne, snacks, soft drinks, toiletries, Contintental plus breakfast included in room rate, Special packages available.
Restrictions: No pets allowed, Children welcome, under 2 free with parents, 3 rooms handicap equipped
Concierge: Front desk
Restaurant: Jenny's Bistro–lunch, Sunday brunch and dinner, Cock 'n Bull–lunch, Sunday brunch and dinner, Spotted Hog–breakfast, lunch and dinner.
Bar: The Spotted Hog, Jenny's Bistro, Hart's Tavern
Business Facilities: Message center, Admin. assistance, Copiers, Audio-visual, Fax, Full scale conference facilities
Conference Rooms: 8 rooms, capacity 250
Sports Facilities: Extended privileges to nearby gym and golf course
Location: Peddler's Village

LEOLA VILLAGE INN & SUITES

If you enjoy surrounding yourself in warm comfort and rich history, Leola Village Inn and Suites offers you just that. Located in historic Lancaster County and surrounded by lush farmland, you'll find each room and suite uniquely and beautifully decorated with down comforters, genuine Amish quilts and antique reproduction furniture.

It is our attention to detail that has helped to distinguish us from other inns and hotels. See for yourself what Leola Village has acheived.

Johansens Condé Nast recommends Leola Village for its "impressive hospitality" in the 2004 and 2005 guide to North American Hotels, Inns and Resorts.

Leola Village was inducted as a member in the Trust for Historic Preservation by Historic Hotels of America for preserving and maintaining the historic integrity, architecture and ambiance of our property.

We feature two bridal suites, extended stay executive suites with living quarters, and even a Wine Cellar suite which was formerly a fruit cellar with original stone walls and an arched storage room to hold bottles of wine.

We have restored an old tobacco barn built in 1875 into a beautiful lobby. You can enjoy our complimentary European continental breakfast in our Lancaster House Community Parlor, and we also serve afternoon teas for any scheduled occasion.

Design Interiors has designed and decorated all of our rooms to give you the feeling of homey comfort right down to the cozy terry cloth robes provided for your use. You can visit Design Interiors located conveniently at 134 W. Main St. in Leola or shop from inside the hotel for home decorating and personal needs.

Our 4 Diamond property currently has 57 guestrooms and suites available for lodging. We have our fitness room for your workout needs. It contains a treadmill, recumbent bicycle, spinner bicycle, elliptical machine, multi gym and sauna.

Address: 38 Deborah Drive, Leola 17540.
Phone: 717-656-7002 800-678-8946
Fax: 717-656-7648
Email: sleeptight@leolavillage.com
Web site: http://www.leolavillage.com
Room Rates: 150
Suite Rates: 190–240
No. of Rooms: 57
No. of Suites: 30
Attractions: Beautiful Lush Farmland, Amish Attractions, Lancaster Quilt & Textile Museum, Kitchen Kettle Village, PA Railroad Museum, Historic Strasburg, Sight & Sound Theatre, Outlet Shopping, Historic Covered Bridges, Minor League Baseball, Hershey attractions
Services & Amenities: Leola Village offers: Complimentary European Continental Breakfast, Terry bathrobes, Down Comforters, Cable TV/DVD Players, movie rentals, valet service, gift shop, complimentary shoeshine, guest laundry facility, mini-fridge/microwaves/coffee maker
Restrictions: No Pets
Concierge: 24 hours
Room Service: Mazzi's Restaurant
Restaurant: Mazzi Designed Dining Monday-Saturday 11:30 AM-10 PM, Sunday 5 PM-9 PM
Bar: Ralph's Wine Bar
Business Facilities: Yes
Conference Rooms: Yes
Sports Facilities: Fitness Center, Sauna, Billards Room
Spa Services: On-site Hair/Nail/Tanning Salon, Therapeutic Massage Therapist
Location: Historic Lancaster County

THOMAS BOND HOUSE

Thomas Bond was a doctor best known, along with Benjamin Franklin and Dr. Benjamin Rush, for helping to found the first public hospital in the United States. His house, built in 1769, is an important example of the classic revival Georgian style architecture. Today it stands as a carefully restored townhouse with an ambiance of quiet luxury, and is listed on the National Register of Historic Places.

The recently refurbished guestrooms and suites have private baths and are exquisitely furnished with period furniture and authentic accessories. In keeping with the custom of the Federal Period, the most luxurious accommodations are those closest to the first floor. The charming parlor serves as a gathering place where guests relax and enjoy a game of chess or bridge and start their evening with complimentary wine and cheese. Evening time has freshly baked cookies. During the week guests are served a continental breakfast featuring freshly squeezed orange juice and freshly baked muffins, and, on weekends, a sumptuous full breakfast is served.

In the heart of Philadelphia's Old City with easy access to downtown, The Bond House is walking distance to many historic sites, including Independence Hall. It is on the doorstep of fine restaurants, theaters, museums, world-class shopping and the internationally acclaimed Academy of Music and Philadelphia Orchestra.

Thomas Bond House has been selected as one of the 25 best Historic Inns and has been rated by AAA and Mobil. It is the only inn located in Independence National Historical Park and is owned by the National Park Service.

Address: 129 S Second St, Philadelphia 19106.
Phone: 215-923-8523 800-845-2663
Fax: 215-923-8504
Email: ctheall@dddcompany.com
Web site: http://www.winston-salem-inn.com/philadelphia
Room Rates: 95–145
Suite Rates: 175
No. of Rooms: 12
No. of Suites: 2
Credit Cards: Visa
Attractions: University of Pennsylvania, Barnes Art Collection, All sites in Philadelphia, Independence National Historical Park
Services & Amenities: Parking, Car hire, Game room, Library, Cable TV, Telephone, Radio, In-room climate control, Hair dryer, Desk, Some fireplaces & whirlpool tubs, Complimentary wine/cheese in evening, Complimentary toiletries & free local calls
Restrictions: Children welcome under supervision, No pets, 2 rooms smoking allowed, No smoking in public areas
Concierge: Innkeeper
Restaurant: Complimentary continental breakfast on weekdays, Full breakfast on weekends, Also nearby restaurants for dining
Bar: Walk to City Tavern, noon–10 p.m.
Business Facilities: Copiers, Fax, Modem ports
Conference Rooms: 1 room, capactiy 25
Sports Facilities: Sheraton Health Club privileges at a modest fee.
Location: Old City Area

THE PRIORY

The only European-style hotel in the city of Pittsburgh, The Priory's 24 guestrooms have been carefully restored to Victorian elegance, while nevertheless maintaining the modern amenities of a larger establishment.

Guests can sip wine by the fire in the sitting room in the winter, relax in the lush courtyard in the summer, and enjoy a book in the library any time of year.

The Priory offers a hearty continental breakfast including meats, cheeses and hard-cooked eggs every morning in its cheerful dining room.

The Priory is within walking distance of downtown Pittsburgh, with its galleries, theaters, and restaurants, as well as many North Side attractions, such as the Warhol Museum, PNC Park, Heinz Field, the Children's Museum, the National Aviary, the Carnegie Science Center, the Mattress Factory, and the Photo Antiquities Museum.

The Priory has a well-equipped fitness room; parking is free.

Address: 614 Pressley St, Pittsburgh 15212.

Phone: 412-231-3338

Fax: 412-231-4838

Email: info@thepriory.com

Web site: http://www.thepriory.com

Room Rates: 119–125

Suite Rates: 134–195

No. of Rooms: 24

No. of Suites: 3

Attractions: Galleries, theaters, and restaurants, as well as many North Side attractions, such as the Warhol Museum, PNC Park, Heinz Field, the Children's Museum, the National Aviary, the Carnegie Science Center, the Mattress Factory, the Photo Antiquities Museum.

Services & Amenities: Shuttle to downtown Pittsburgh on weekdays, Parking, Library, Car hire, Game area, Cable TV, Complimentary newspaper, Telephone, Radio, Internet access, Individual climate control, Complimentary toiletries, Complimentary continental breakfast

Restrictions: No pets allowed, Children under 13 free with parents, 2 rooms handicap equipped

Room Service: Limited Room Service

Restaurant: While The Priory does not have a restaurant, many fine restaurants are within close walking distance.

Bar: Honor Bar in Library

Business Facilities: Complete Business Service Center w/access to fax, DSL line, Copier, Workspace

Conference Rooms: 2 rooms, capacity 30–350

Sports Facilities: Full fitness center

Spa Services: Massage services

Location: North Shore

SKYTOP LODGE

Up 'here you get the feeling that you're on top of the world. For over 75 years, the Lodge has been refining the traditions, service and amenities you'll enjoy at Skytop.

Accommodations include standard rooms, mini-suites, cottages or exclusive lodging at the inn at Skytop with three meals daily included in the rate. The cuisine is world-class with American and Continental influences. You will find added value in our Golf Package, Family Fun Package, Honeymoon/Romantic Getaway Package, and Conference Packages for business groups.

In Spring and Summer, our 5,500 acres blossom with nature's bounty. Nature walks are led by our staff naturalist. Activities abound throughout the estate including golf, tennis, hiking, trout fishing, kayaks, canoes, boats, biking, sporting clays and lawn bowling.

Enjoy Winter activities such as downhill and cross-country skiing, sledding, ice skating and snow-shoeing—all on-site. Indoors there are spa services, an indoor pool, exercise room, game room and lounge.

A member of National Trust Historic Hotels of America, Skytop has been welcoming guests since 1928.

Address: One Skytop, Skytop 18357.
Phone: 570-595-7401 800-345-7759
Fax: 570-595-9618
Email: skytop2@ptd.net
Web site: http://www.skytop.com
Room Rates: 350–490
Suite Rates: 550–720
No. of Rooms: 193
No. of Suites: 3
Attractions: Skiing–downhill and cross country (on site), Ice skating, Snow shoeing, Trout fishing, kayaking, boating, canoeing, Biking and hiking, Sporting Clays
Services & Amenities: Shuttle service, Airport pick up, Valet service, Gift shop, Library, Parking, Baby-sitting, Laundry, Game room, Cable TV & VCR, Telephone, Radio, Some rooms with fireplace and/or balconies, Individual climate controls, Robes, 3 meals included in room rate
Restrictions: No pets allowed, Children free in same room as parents, 4 rooms handicap equipped
Room Service: During meal hours
Restaurant: Windsor Dining Room–7:30–9 a.m., 12 noon–1 p.m., 6:30–8 p.m., dress code for dinner (Jackets for men); Afternoon tea with piano music in Pine Room
Bar: The Tap Room, Noon–Midnight, with Jazz music nightly
Business Facilities: Full scale conference facility with 10,000 sq ft meeting spaces & business service center
Conference Rooms: 17 rooms, capacity 250
Sports Facilities: Indoor and outdoor swimming pool, Whirlpool, Massage, Aerobics, Weights, Croquet, 18 holes golf, Ski
Spa Services: We offer Swedish, Deep Tissue, Neuromuscular and Sports Massages, a variety of European facials, French Thalassotherapy Marine Treatment bodywraps for energy balancing, detoxifying, firming and toning
Location: Pocono Mountains

VILLA MONTANA RESORT

Villa Montana Beach Resort is an exclusive, private resort nestled between the lush tropical vegetation of a high cliff and pristine sandy beaches that are protected by an offshore reef.

This full service resort offers optimum personal attention to guests, the property and the environment. The villas have been ideally situated on this twenty-six acre property to insure privacy and serenity. The abundance of green areas, overflowing with blossoming tropical plants, accentuates the sense of harmony with nature that permeates throughout. Within the ground, there are two swimming pools, two synthetic grass tennis courts with lights for night play and a rock climbing wall. Villa Montana Beach Resort also has sea kayaks, snorkeling equipment, mountain bicycles and horseback riding at the stables adjacent to the hotel.

The resort's thirty five villas offer a total of fifty-five units comprised of eighteen hotel rooms, twenty-one—one bedroom villas and sixteen two-bedroom villas. The unique design of our villas allows us to offer three-bedroom villas by easily connecting our one- and two-bedroom villas.

The villas have wooden beamed cathedral-style ceilings with fans and are equipped with individual climate control air conditioners, telephones, CD players and digital cable television with over 100 channels. The hotel rooms have either king or queen beds, full bath and patio terrace.

Superb yet informal dining at the beachfront Eclipse Restaurant and Bar, serving an everchanging eclectic menu of Caribbean/Asian fusion cuisine highlighting local seafood. Special Request? Not a problem. Our Executive Chef will be pleased to create a menu tailored for your enjoyment. We only request 48 hours notice to insure that we obtain the freshest ingredients.

Small conferences, executive retreats and private events for up to 100 persons are welcome, with audio visual equipment and personalized catered menus available. We provide the highest degree of customized planning and execution to take care of every detail for you.

Whether for families on vacation or select corporate clients, Villa Montana Beach Resort combines the privacy of an intimate beachside resort with the full resources and services of a sophisticated, yet casual retreat.

Address: PO Box 530, Isabela 662.
Phone: 787-872-9554 888-780-9195
Fax: 787-872-9553
Email: sales@villamontana.com
Web site: http://www.villamontana.com
Room Rates: 250
Suite Rates: Villas: 315–1
No. of Rooms: 18
No. of Suites: 37
Attractions: Scuba diving in the Blue Holes, surfing, windsurfing, or sea kayaking. Horseback riding trip through unspoiled nature trails. Rock climbing lesson on our own "rock." Tennis on our synthetic grass tennis courts. Mountain bike trail ride.
Services & Amenities: Airport pick up, Valet, Library, Car hire, Parking, Baby-sitting, Laundry, Fans, Individual climate control air conditioners, Telephones, CD players, Hairdryers, Digital cable television with over 100 channels. Some have Jacuzzis and roofless showers.
Restrictions: Children welcome, No pets allowed, 1 room handicap equipped
Concierge: 7 a.m.-9 p.m.
Restaurant: Eclipse Restaurant and Bar offers an everchanging menu of tropical favorites
Bar: 10 am -11 pm
Business Facilities: Small conferences, executive retreats, private events for up to 100 people
Sports Facilities: 2 swimming pools, Tennis courts, Rock climbing wall, Sea kayaks, Snorkeling equipment, Mountain bike
Spa Services: Massage service is offered in the privacy of your villa or overlooking the sea
Location: At the tip of Puerto Rico's pristine northwest coast

1760 FRANCIS MALBONE HOUSE INN

Step back in time to enjoy 18th century charm with 20th century amenities at The Francis Malbone House Inn. The elegant inn is located on Newport's Historic Harborfront on Thames Street. From the outside you can hardly imagine what pleasures are to come, but once inside you are welcomed with four guest parlors with luxurious furniture, a grand foyer, and a secret garden in the center of the inn.

The beautiful bedrooms are individually decorated with antiques and period reproduction Queen Anne furniture. Walls are painted authentic colonial colors and decorated with antique paintings and prints. Rooms feature king and queen size beds and wing back chairs. All of the suites and eight courtyard rooms offer Jacuzzi tubs and all have plush cotton robes and large bath towels, complimentary toiletries and hair dryers.

The Counting House Suite is the most popular room. The king size canopy bed, large sitting room, dining area with chandelier, and bath with double Jacuzzi make this room perfect for honeymoons, anniversaries and romantic getaways. To further enhance the suite and to heighten the romance, there is also a gas fireplace, Bose stereo and private entrance from the courtyard and from Thames Street.

The sunny fireplaced dining room complements the colonial mansion in spectacular fashion. A gourmet breakfast is served each morning as guests gaze through the glassed enclosed colonnade that looks out into the manicured courtyard. One of the parlors, The Blue Room offers menus for guests to preview from all of Newport's top restaurants and the innkeepers are happy to recommend their favorites and make reservations for dinner.

The innkeepers have over 25 years of combined experience. They know when a guest needs attention or desires anonymity. The results are a relaxful stay and healthy way to see the wonderful sites of the city-by-the-sea.

Address: 392 Thames Street, Newport 2840.
Phone: 401-846-0392 800-846-0392
Fax: 401-848-5956
Email: innkeeper@malbone.com
Web site: http://www.malbone.com
Room Rates: 99–365
Suite Rates: 200–510
No. of Rooms: 20
No. of Suites: 3
Credit Cards: Visa
Attractions: One of the top vacation destinations in the country–Newport Cottages, 10 mansions, Newport Harbor, Cliff Walk, 3 local beaches, Tennis Hall of Fame, Touro Synagogue, Redwood Library, Ocean Drive, Specialty shops, Antique stores, Wonderful restaurants
Services & Amenities: Parking, Library, Cable TV/VCR, Telephone, Radio, CD player, Almost all rooms have fireplace, Some rooms have semi-private gardens, wet bars, Individual climate controls, Robes, Complimentary toiletries, 12 rooms have Jacuzzi tubs
Restrictions: 1 room handicap equipped, No pets or smoking allowed, Children over 12 welcome.
Concierge: 7 a.m.-11 p.m.
Restaurant: A gourmet breakfast is served in our Dining Room from 8:30–10. Breakfast consists of two entree choices, homemade pastries and fresh fruit. Afternoon Tea is served daily from 3-5 p.m.
Business Facilities: Message center, Admin. assistance, Copiers, Audio-visual, Teleconferencing, Fax, Modems
Conference Rooms: 6 rooms, capacity 20–Small conferences a specialty
Location: Downtown Harborfront

CLIFFSIDE INN

The celebrated Cliffside Inn, home of former legendary Newport, Rhode Island artist Beatrice Turner, has earned a worldwide reputation as one of America's favorite boutique luxury Inns.

Seamlessly blending today's most luxurious amenities—whirlpools, steam baths, fireplaces, grand beds, fine linens, LCD TVs—with exquisite design and decoration, antiques, Turner artwork, Victorian elegance, warm hospitality and attentive service. Our manor house is a one-of-a-kind place, in a unique setting near Newport's acclaimed Cliff Walk, beaches and mansions.

Come discover why Cliffside has been named Frommer's and Zagat's top Rhode Island Luxury Inn; "One of America's Most Elegant B&Bs," by *Getaways for Gourmets*; Top Coastal Honeymoon destination by *Bride's Magazine*; One of the Great Tea Rooms of America; and AAA Four Diamond.

Address: 2 Seaview Ave, Newport 2840.

Phone: 401-847-1811 800-845-1811

Fax: 401-848-5850

Email: innkeeper@ legendaryinnsofnewport.com

Web site: http:// www.cliffsideinn.com

Room Rates: 245–400

Suite Rates: 375–625

No. of Rooms: 8

No. of Suites: 8

Credit Cards: Visa

Attractions: Historic Cliff Walk, Bellevue Avenue gilded age mansions, Antique shops along the harborfront, Tennis Hall of Fame, Newport Art Museum, Beach access, Southern New England Vineyards and Wineries

Services & Amenities: Multi-course Breakfast, Afternoon English High Tea (named one of America's 20 Best), Twice Daily Maid Service, Turndown, Handcrafted Artisan Chocolates, Flat Screen LCD TVs, DVD, CD, VCR, Movie Library, Complimentary high-speed wireless Internet access

Restrictions: Children over 14 welcome, No pets allowed

Concierge: 7 a.m.-9 p.m.

Restaurant: Named one of America's 20 Great Tea Rooms, our acclaimed afternoon high tea is served daily at 4:30 in the Victorian Parlor. This elegant tea service is only available to guests.

Bar: In-Room Wine Service

Location: Seaside

PLANTERS INN

Charleston's historic district, the 18th-Century city market area, abounds with antique shops, restaurants, flower vendors and boutiques. The district's inns have traditionally played an important role in visitors' enjoyment of this venerable Old South seaport. The Planters Inn, a Relais & Chateaux member, sets a whole new standard in elegant charm with courteous, professional service. Designed in the manner of Charleston's fine Antebellum homes, the lobby features detailed crown molding and fireplace mantle, antique furnishings and fine art.

The 62 oversized rooms and suites feature high ceilings, four-poster beds, large closets, and beautifully oversized bathrooms done in travertine marble and equipped with telephone, TV, and toiletries. Many rooms open out to a wrap-around veranda overlooking the Garden Courtyard. Guests are pampered with nightly turndown service and and breakfast at Peninsula Grill.

Planters Inn is home to the nationally award-winning Peninsula Grill. Chef Robert Carter puts his Southern influence on classic metropolitan fare in the city's most sophisticated dining room, a tasteful blending of traditional Charleston style with contemporary accents. The walls are covered with rich velvet, antique cypress woodwork, 19th century oil paintings and contemporary artists' renderings of vignettes of local plantation life and coastal marshlands. These elements combine with views of its lush gardens outside to create an elegant yet comfortably relaxed setting for exquisitely prepared and presented award-winning local cuisine. Steaks and chops, fish and oysters, Champagne and lobster.

The Planters Inn (circa 1844) is the only historic inn overlooking Charleston's famous City Market.

Address: 112 N. Market St, Charleston 29401.
Phone: 843-722-2345 800-845-7082
Fax: 843-577-2125
Email: reservations@plantersinn.com
Web site: http://www.plantersinn.com
Room Rates: 179–375
Suite Rates: 395–675
No. of Rooms: 56
No. of Suites: 6
Attractions: Surrounded by Charleston\xd5 s finest dining, Shopping, and Entertainment, Annual Spoleto Festival (May 27-June 12)
Services & Amenities: Valet parking, Laundry, Gift shop, Baby-sitting service, Remote control cable TV, Radio, CD player, Phone, Individual climate control, Complimentary newspaper, European turndown service, In-room safes
Restrictions: No pets allowed, Children stay free with adults
Concierge: 24 hours
Room Service: limited
Restaurant: Peninsula Grill, Monday–Thursday 5:30–10 p.m., Friday and Saturday 5:30–11 p.m.
Bar: Peninsula Grill, 5:30 p.m.-midnight
Business Facilities: Message center, Admin. assistance, Copiers, Audio-visual, Translators
Conference Rooms: 2 rooms, capacity 120
Sports Facilities: Massage, Nearby golf, Sailing and riding, Access to nearby Health Club and Day Spa
Location: Historic district, 10 miles to Charleston airport

VENDUE INN

The luxurious Vendue Inn is located in the heart of the Historic District at the beautiful Waterfront Park on Charleston Harbor. This in-town gem, famous for comfort, excellent staff service and convenience, was lovingly restored from c. 1860 French Quarter warehouses. Walk to historic homes and churches, art galleries, antique shops, the old City Market, or stroll through parks and along the Battery.

The accommodations at the Vendue Inn reflect the history of Charleston, from indulgent suites with fireplaces and whirlpool tubs to charming historic quarters in the inn's original style. Here exquisite comfort and attentive service are a way of life.

All 66 rooms and suites, many with poster, canopy or sleigh beds, are individually decorated with 18th century style English or French period furnishings, and antiques. Fireplaces and marble bathrooms with Jacuzzis and separate showers are available in Junior and Deluxe Suites. Soft bathrobes, Egytian Cotton linens, and other fine amenities add to the comfort.

Mornings begin with a delicious complimentary Southern breakfast buffet or continental breakfast served in your room while you read the morning paper. Wine and cheese are served each afternoon in the Music Room. Cordials are offered each evening. When returning to your room, you will find your bed turned down and imported chocolates on your pillow.

Don't miss the Roof Top Bar & Restaurant, a favorite spot to savor the colorful sunsets over the picturesque steeples and rooftops of historic Charleston.

The Library, an intimate restaurant, exemplifies the Inn's standards of excellence, offering progressive American cuisine prepared with a uniquely Charleston flare.

You'll agree you've found a very special place at Charleston's Vendue Inn where comfort, cobblestone streets and Southern hospitality await.

Address: 19 Vendue Range, Charleston 29401.
Phone: 843-577-7970 800-845-7900
Fax: 843-577-2913
Email: info@vendueinn.com
Web site: http://www.vendueinn.com
Room Rates: 135–245
Suite Rates: 215–355
No. of Rooms: 66
No. of Suites: 22
Credit Cards: Visa
Attractions: Heart of Historic Distric walk to Restaurants, Antique Shops, Boutiques, Art Galleries, Museums, City Market and Aquarium. Plantations, Garden and Historic Forts are all nearby. Numerous golf courses are a short distance. Walking tours & carriage rides.
Services & Amenities: Full Souther Breakfast Buffet, Valet Parking, Afternoon Guest Reception, Evening Cordials, cookies and Milk, Turndown Sservice
Restrictions: Non-smoking, ADA Handicap Room, Pets by special permission
Concierge: 24 hours
Room Service: Limited, 7 am -9:30 pm
Restaurant: The Roof Top Bar & Restaurant, voted Charleston's best rooftop bar. Outstanding views of & live entertainment. The Library, serves an evening small plates menu in a casual intimate setting.
Bar: Roof Top Bar & Restaurant, Live Entertainment
Business Facilities: Computer, Fax, Copier
Conference Rooms: Elegant Parlors for 5-50 people
Sports Facilities: Complimentary Bicycles, Sailing, Tennis, Beaches, Golf Nearby
Location: Historic District at Waterfront Park

GOVERNOR'S HOUSE INN

A National Historic Landmark, the Governor's House Inn reflects the civility and romance of Charleston. The former governor's mansion is considered one of the South's most romantic inns and a favorite destination for all special occasions.

The Governor's House Inn (circa 1760) is ideally situated in the heart of the country's first and largest preservation area. The Inn is surrounded by tree-lined streets and the Antebellum homes in Charleston's most prestigious neighborhood.

The grounds of the Inn reflect the majesty and elegance of what Southern Living called "a flawless urban hideaway." For many guests, the favorite part of the mansion is its extraordinary double verandah, where breakfast and afternoon tea are served (weather permitting) year round.

The spacious living areas are elegantly furnished with period antiques and reproductions, accented by original fireplaces, 14' ceilings, hardwood floors, crystal chandeliers, triple hung windows and striking hand-painted wall paper. The focal point of the Inn's immense foyer is the grand Victorian mahogany staircase, added during post-Civil Ware renovations in 1880.

All of the Inn's 11 guestrooms are totally unique and though all are traditional in style, each room has an individual personality. Guests have either a king or queen 4-poster bed, most with canopies. Five rooms have whirlpool tubs and standing Italian marble showers. Five rooms have wet bars. Seven rooms have porches or balconies. All are elegantly decorated with sitting areas.

Address: 117 Broad St, Charleston 29401.
Phone: 843-720-2070 800-720-9812
Email: staff@governorshouse.com
Web site: http://www.governorshouse.com
Room Rates: 179–345
Suite Rates: 345–395
No. of Rooms: 11
No. of Suites: 2
Attractions: Near the Old Market, Battery, beaches, antique shopping, fine dining, house and garden tours, Spoleto Arts Festival, golf.
Services & Amenities: Parking, gift shop, Afternoon Tea, evening sherry, complimentary newspaper, cable TV, telephone, radio, individual climate controls, robe, complimentary toiletries. Some rooms have fireplace, balconies, wet bars and whirlpool baths.
Restrictions: No pets allowed, Minimum stay on weekends and special events
Concierge: 8 a.m.-11 p.m.
Room Service: 8 a.m.-9:30 a.m.
Restaurant: Breakfast included in room rate.
Business Facilities: Fax and modems
Sports Facilities: Massage available
Location: In the heart of Charleston's famous Historic District

KING'S COURTYARD INN

Here at the King's Courtyard Inn you inhabit a slice of Charleston's history. The 3-story Greek Revival building was erected in 1853 and features unusual Egyptian detail. The adjoining building dates to the 1830s and still has the original heart pine floors and plaster ceilings.

The Inn has served a variety of functions over the years, and now offers a selection of rooms around two inner courtyards and a rear garden. Extreme care has been taken to ensure the necessary architectural and historic accuracy, for which Charleston is famous, maintaining the residential atmosphere of lower King Street. Rooms are furnished in 18th-century reproduction furniture, with large windows, high ceilings, and oriental rugs over hardwood floors. In one suite the original 1830s living room maintains the ornate plaster ceiling moldings and the original fireplace.

The Inn is within easy walking distance of Charleston's historic homes, gardens, churches, and the City Market area. Explore one interesting shop after another, barter for the unusual in the open market, or enjoy a delicious meal at one of the many delightful restaurants. King Street is a center for the antique trade, and the Inn is literally surrounded by shops filled with fine collectibles.

From the moment of your arrival, you realize that courteous and impeccable service to guests is the primary goal of the staff at the King's Courtyard, who seem to desire nothing so much as your comfort and satisfaction. This factor, coupled with the gracious surroundings, make for a pleasant respite in the courtyard. Business travelers can take advantage of the services at the Inn, including an elegantly restored room with an original tin ceiling available for small meetings or receptions.

This is an elegant, time-stopping retreat in old Charleston.

Address: 198 King St, Charleston 29401.
Phone: 843-723-7000 800-845-6119
Fax: 843-720-2608
Email: dwilson@charminginns.com
Web site: http://www.kingscourtyardinn.com/kings-index.asp
Room Rates: 130–235
Suite Rates: 200–270
No. of Rooms: 37
No. of Suites: 4
Credit Cards: Most Credit Cards accepted
Attractions: Walking distance to historic houses, High Battery, Waterfront park, Antique shop district, City Market, Over 40 restaurants
Services & Amenities: Free Wireless Internet Special packages, Parking, Baby-sitting service, Outdoor Jacuzzi, Fireplaces, Balconies, Cable TV, Telephones, Radio, Individual climate control, Complimentary toiletries, Complimentary wine/sherry and continental breakfast
Restrictions: No pets allowed, Children welcome, 2 rooms handicap equipped
Concierge: 24 hours/day
Room Service: 7 a.m.-11 a.m.
Restaurant: Circa 1886
Bar: cocktails available at request
Business Facilities: Admin. assistance, Copiers, Audio-visual, meeting facilities
Conference Rooms: 2 rooms, capacity 20-50
Sports Facilities: Sailing nearby, Golf 5 to 25 miles away, Public tennis courts nearby, 3 blocks to full-equipped "Y"
Spa Services: Spa at Wentworth
Location: Center of Historic District surrounded by antique shops, 12 mi. to airport

JOHN RUTLEDGE HOUSE INN

John Rutledge was one of 55 men who signed the Constitution of the United States. His home, which he built in 1763 as a wedding gift to his wife, is one of only 15 belonging to those signatories that have survived, and the only one that is now a boutique hotel accommodating lodging guests.

The Inn is a complex of three buildings—the main house and two carriage houses—that enclose a courtyard garden of plants indigenous to coastal South Carolina. There are tables in the courtyard for guests who wish to eat their breakfast outdoors.

All rooms have parquet floors, Italian marble fireplaces, 14-foot ceilings with equally tall classic window treatments, and crystal chandeliers. The second-floor ballroom is a public area where the Colonial experience is recreated for the edification of guests. Wine and sherry are offered.

Guestrooms are decorated with accurate period reproduction furniture and some antiques, individual climate control, remote-control color TV and refrigerators. Suites feature parlors, fireplaces in the bedrooms, and have double whirlpools and a separate shower.

There is no full service restaurant at the Inn, but afternoon tea and refreshments are served daily.

The Inn specializes in small, upscale meetings and offers a full range of meeting and catering services. Wild Dunes and Kiawah, two nearby golf resorts, extend privileges to our guests.

The Inn is located in the heart of Charleston's historical district, directly across from the famous antebellum mansions. Fine restaurants, theaters, shopping, Charleston Place and the Market are within a few minutes' walking distance.

Address: 116 Broad St, Charleston 29414.
Phone: 843-723-7999 800-476-9741
Fax: 843-720-2615
Email: kleslie@charminginns.com
Web site: http://www.johnrutledgehouseinn.com/jrh-index.asp
Room Rates: 185–325
Suite Rates: 290–375
No. of Rooms: 16
No. of Suites: 3
Attractions: Convenient to tours, Shopping, Dining, Battery and Market areas
Services & Amenities: Parking, Free Wireless Internet, Laundry, Baby-sitting service, Library, Some rooms with fireplaces and/or whirlpool baths, Individual climate controls, Telephone, Radio, Cable TV, Robes, Complimentary paper, toiletries, wine, sherry, tea & snacks
Restrictions: No pets allowed, 2 rooms handicap equipped
Concierge: 24 hours
Room Service: 7 a.m.-10 a.m.
Business Facilities: Message center, Admin. assistance, Copiers, Audio-visual, Complete business service center
Conference Rooms: 1 room, capacity 20
Sports Facilities: Golf resorts nearby, Sailing nearby, tennis courts nearby
Spa Services: Recommends Spa at Wentworth
Location: Historic District, downtown Charleston, 12 miles to Charleston Airport

1843 BATTERY CARRIAGE HOUSE INN

The Battery Carriage House Inn is "No. 20 on the Battery," built in 1843, and the childhood summer home of the owner's grandmother. Beyond the wrought iron gates of No. 20 lies beautiful White Point Gardens in Charleston's Historic Residential District at the quiet end of the Battery overlooking Charleston Harbor.

Eight guestrooms are located in the old carriage house in the garden of the antebellum mansion, and another three rooms are on the ground floor in what was once the kitchen area of the mansion. Each room has a private entrance and each is individually decorated. The atmosphere is European, garden-centered, history-laden, romantic and intimate. Of course, all conveniences are provided, including private steam bath shower units in some rooms, whirlpool tubs in others, staff to assist you with reservations and tours, and a private phone line with answering machine in each room.

The most unusual room is a small suite, which was the old cistern of the house! This extremely private lodging has its own sitting area under the porch.

Guests begin their day with the deluxe continental breakfast served with the morning newspaper, either in-room or under the Lady Bankshire rose arbor. For dinner, it's just a 10- to 15-minute walk up High Battery to Charleston's celebrated selection of fine restaurants.

This is definitely the right spot for a gracious, relaxing, European-style getaway south of the Mason-Dixon Line.

Address: 20 South Battery, Charleston 29401.
Phone: 843-727-3100 800-775-5575
Fax: 843-727-3130
Email: info@batterycarriagehouse.com
Web site: http://www.batterycarriagehouse.com
Room Rates: 99–299
No. of Rooms: 11
No. of Suites: 1
Attractions: Historic Charleston, Fort Sumter, Plantations and House museums
Services & Amenities: Continental breakfast included, Checks accepted, Card/game room, Cable TV, Telephone, Radio, Whirlpools, Robes, Complimentary newspaper
Restrictions: No pets allowed, No smoking, 2 night minimum stay on weekends
Concierge: 9 a.m.-10 p.m.
Sports Facilities: Golf nearby
Location: Quiet historic waterfront residential district, 10 miles to airport

MARKET PAVILION HOTEL

A member of the exclusive Leading Small Hotels of the World, the Market Pavilion Hotel in Charleston pairs old-world charm, service and ambiance with modern comforts in a a luxurious setting. Located in the heart of the America's largest living historic district, this charming boutique hotel is located at the corner of Charleston's most famous intersection, Market and East Bay, just steps from the City Market, waterfront, historic landmarks, shopping and antebellum homes. Designed in the fashion of the Era of the Grand Hotels of the 1880s to 1920s, Market Pavilion Hotel offers opulent guestrooms and suites featuring crown molding, mahogany poster beds, luxurious residential appointments, broadband Internet access, CD players, multi-line voicemail telephones with personal direct-dial telephone numbers, in-room temperature control, lavish European marble baths. Suites are uniquely furnished reflecting the grand colorful style of colonial Charleston. Select suites offer private terraces, grand pianos, drawing rooms and panoramic city and harbor views.

The hotel is home to Grill 225 and the Pavilion Bar & Cafe, two of Charleston's best dining venues. At the open-air Pavilion Bar, atop the hotel, guests receive gracious service while enjoying the commanding views of the city and harbor.

At Grill 225, Charleston's only USDA prime steakhouse, Executive Chef Demetre Castanas presents a selection of steaks, chops and seafood, served with the service dedication only found in the world's great city restaurants. Grill 225 boasts the AAA 4 diamond mark and is awarded the distinction of DiRona, Distinguished Restaurantas of North America.

A visit to the Market Pavilion Hotel is a trip back to a time when guest service was not a buzz-phrase, but a passion. Please join us here in Charleston, and experience "the art of Southern hospitality".

Address: 225 East Bay Street, Charleston 0.
Phone: 843-723-0500 877-440-2250
Fax: 843-723-4320
Email: sales@palashospitality.com
Web site: http:// www.marketpavilion.com/
Room Rates: 425–495
Suite Rates: 550–3000
No. of Rooms: 70
No. of Suites: 9
Credit Cards: Most Credit Cards accepted
Attractions: Charleston has received praise as one of America's top destination cities. Guests of the hotel are a short walk from dozens of historic museum homes, harbor tours, galleries, fine restaurants and the South Carolina waterfront Aquarium.
Services & Amenities: Pavilion Level rooftop with panoramic views of city and harbor accommodates up to 250 guests for private events. Jasmine Ballroom seats 100. Constantine Boardroom has plasma flat screen and accommodates 12.
Concierge: 8 a.m. until 8
Room Service: 7 a.m. until 11 p.m.
Restaurant: Grill 225, annually ranked as one of the premier restaurants of Charleston, is renowned for generous cuts of USDA prime beef, exceptional seafood, a world-class wine menu and glamorous ambiance.
Bar: Grill 225 Bar on the lobby level and Pavilion Bar atop the hotel
Business Facilities: Complimentary broadband Internet access in all guestrooms. Fax, copy, secretarial services 24 hrs.
Conference Rooms: Constantine Boardroom and Jasmine Ballroom with breakout roo
Sports Facilities: Rooftop Cascading pool, cardio fitness center, spa services, bicycle rentals.
Spa Services: Our concierge is pleased to arrange in-room massages and facials, or schedule a wide range of treatments at one of the nearby full-service spas.

WENTWORTH MANSION

Charleston's only AAA five diamond hotel. Set proudly in the heart of historic Charleston, the Wentworth Mansion is one of the world's finest and most unique inns. Built in 1886 and designed not as a lodging house, but as an opulent private residence, the Wentworth Mansion is a place of hand-carved marble fireplaces, intricate woodwork, Tiffany stained glass windows and never-ending detail. The Mansion offers wine and hors d'oeuvres and exquisite buffet breakfasts served on the sun porch. For some, the highlight of their stay is the breathtaking view of Charleston, accessible via the spiral staircase that leads to the Mansion's towering cupola. Guests may stroll through immaculate surroundings, unchanged since the days of the original owner, and sleep soundly in accommodations over a century old.

Each of the twenty-one guestrooms and suites have been historically restored and furnished with antiques. All of the most up-to-date conveniences and comforts have been discreetly added. All rooms have king beds and oversized whirlpools, most with a separate, spacious shower and working gas fireplace. Several rooms have day beds or sofa beds for additional guests.

The restaurant, Circa 1886, is located in the carriage house adjacent to the Mansion. The décor is paneled walls and ceilings, crisp white linens, polished crystal and silver, large windows and, in the winter, a romantic fireplace. Enjoy top-shelf spirits, exceptional wines by the glass, or a selection from our wine list.

The world-class Wentworth Mansion promises guests an experience that will remain forever one of their fondest memories and bring them back year after year.

Address: 149 Wentworth St, Charleston 29401.
Phone: 843-853-1886 888-INN-1886
Fax: 843-720-5290
Email: bseidler@charminginns.com
Web site: http://www.wentworthmansion.com
Room Rates: 225–415
Suite Rates: 375–695
No. of Rooms: 14
No. of Suites: 7
Attractions: Historic Charleston, Fort Sumter, Plantations, High Battery , Waterfront Park, City Market, Shopping, Antiquing and Dining
Services & Amenities: On-site parking, Library, Complimentary breakfast buffet, Wine and hors d'oeuvres, Turndown service, Cable TV, Individual climate control, Whirlpool bath, Complimentary newspaper, Fireplaces
Restrictions: pets allowed, Children welcome
Concierge: 24 hours
Restaurant: Circa 1886 5 p.m.-11 p.m. Monday-Saturday, Bar Circa 1886 5pm-11pm Monday-Saturday, Last seating at 9:30 p.m.
Bar: The Circa 1886, 5 p.m.-11 p.m.
Business Facilities: Free wireless Internet
Conference Rooms: Yes
Spa Services: On-site spa available
Location: Historic downtown

LITCHFIELD PLANTATION

Along the banks of the Waccamaw River in coastal South Carolina stands the Litchfield Plantation. Known for its beauty and magnificent natural setting at the end of a quarter-mile avenue of 250-year-old live oaks, the stately Plantation House, c1750, overlooks former rice fields and offers four historic and elegant suites. The Guest House is an 8,250-sq.-ft. brick and stucco residential mansion surrounded by courtyards, landscaped patio, covered walkways, and a natural pond.

In addition to the numerous suites available in the Plantation House, guests may also choose to stay in a private cottage. The cottages complement the Plantation by providing elegantly furnished country inn-style accommodations with modern touches. The Tuckers Woods Cottages, for example, are situated around a quiet pond in a tranquil wooded setting. These spacious homes include two and three bedrooms, private bathrooms, modern kitchen and dining room, telephones, cable television, and washer/dryer. The master bedrooms may feature a canopy bed, a whirlpool tub, or a private veranda overlooking a lake.

The handsome Carriage House Club, emulating a fine country home, provides the perfect setting for a romantic dinner for two, an intimate dinner party, or an elegant reception for 300 or more. The prestigious on-site dining facility gives guests the flexibility to enjoy a quiet night out while feeling pampered by an attentive staff. Guests can indulge in such culinary delights as House Grouper, Russian Blinis with Caviar, and Bourbon Pecan Pie. Other specialties include Chicken Mango, Grilled Salmon with Creamy Dill Cucumber Sauce, Honey Glazed Scallops, and Lemon Chess Pie.

The Plantation's extensive conference and recreational facilities complement a guest's stay. Guests may choose from numerous conference rooms, an outdoor pool with cabana, an on-site marina, tennis, and nearby golf, fishing, boating, and horseback riding. The in-house concierge is always available to assist guests in their planning needs. Nearby attractions include historic Charleston and Georgetown, Brookgreen Gardens (the world's largest outdoor sculpture garden), Myrtle Beach, and live entertainment.

Address: PO Box 290, Kings River Road, Pawleys Island 29585.
Phone: 843-237-9121 800-869-1410
Fax: 843-237-1041
Email:
vacation@litchfieldplantation.com
Web site: http://
www.litchfieldplantation.com
Room Rates: 148–172
Suite Rates: 192–620
No. of Rooms: 16
No. of Suites: 22
Attractions: 600 acre estate with small lakes & streams on property, 375 acres of ancient rice fields & canals, Brookgreen Gardens, historic Charleston, riverwalk in nearby Georgetown and a variety of entertainment in Myrtle Beach nearby.
Services & Amenities: Complimentary full breakfast, ample Parking, Library, Kitchen facilities, Fireplaces, Balconies, Cable TV, Radio, Wet bar, Individual heat & air-conditioning, Whirlpool bath, Complimentary toiletries, Turndown service, Newspaper.
Restrictions: 1 room with handicapped access, No pets allowed, Children over 12 welcome
Concierge: 8:30 a.m.-8 p.m.
Restaurant: Carriage House Club–Breakfast 7-10 a.m., Dinner 6:30 p.m.-8:30 p.m.
Bar: 5 p.m.-11 p.m.
Business Facilities: Message center, Admin. assistance center, E-mail, Copiers, Fax
Conference Rooms: 6 rooms, capacity 50
Sports Facilities: Outdoor swimming pool, Jacuzzi, Tennis courts; Nearby horseback riding, boating, golf and beach club
Spa Services: Nearby spa offers full range of spa services.
Location: 2 miles to downtown, 22 miles south of airport

GENERAL MORGAN INN & CONFERENCE CENTER

Nestled in the Appalachian foothills of Northeast Tennessee, the historic General Morgan Inn is located in downtown Greeneville, 12 scenic miles from Interstate 81 between Knoxville and the Tri-Cities area. Constructed in 1884, the General Morgan Inn offers elegantly appointed guestrooms, many with original fireplace mantles and views of the historic district. Several historic sites, along with antiques and gift shops, are within easy walking distance of the Inn.

This landmark facility boasts a comfortable, relaxed atmosphere. Brumley's, the Inn's full service restaurant and lounge, is perfect for lunch and dinner. With small-town service and attention to detail in its repertoire of features, the General Morgan Inn offers spacious meeting and banquet facilities.

The General Morgan Inn is only minutes away from the President Andrew Johnson National Historic site, the Dickson-Williams Mansion, and David Crockett's Birthplace. Guests can enjoy the gift and antiques shops of downtown Greeneville as well as numerous outdoor activities. So, while you are visiting beautiful Northeast Tennessee, come stay at a place that is out of the ordinary not out of the way!

Address: 111 N. Main Street, Greeneville 37743.
Phone: 423-787-1000 800-223-2679
Fax: 423-787-1001
Email: frontdeskmgr@generalmorganinn.com
Web site: http://www.generalmorganinn.com
Room Rates: 89–104
Suite Rate: 235
No. of Rooms: 52
No. of Suites: 1
Credit Cards: Most Credit Cards accepted
Attractions: Visit the Dickson-Williams Mansion (1828 mansion where General Morgan spent his last night); Andrew Johnson National Historic Site (17th President); or the Nathanael Greene Museum (Revolutionary War hero); all conveniently located within walking distance.
Services & Amenities: Architecturally unique guestrooms & suite, ADA & non-smoking rooms, elegant furnishings, deluxe linens, Bath & Body Works toiletries, marble vanities, in-room coffee, iron & ironing board, wireless accessible, Business Services, guest passes to local gym
Restrictions: Restrictions on pets–call first.
Room Service: Available all hours the restaurant is open
Restaurant: Brumley's is a full service restaurant, serving B/L/D Monday–Saturday, and a Sunday brunch that is the BEST DEAL in East Tennessee! For the current menu check www.generalmorganinn.com
Bar: Beautifully furnished bar with the original 1930's hand etched mirror
Business Facilities: Small or Large meetings can be accomodated & most business services available at the front desk

COOPER GUEST LODGE

When you drive through the gates of The Cooper Aerobics Center, you enter a 30-acre oasis in the middle of the city.

Wellness is in the air at the famed complex developed by Dr. Kenneth Cooper, and everything about the intimate Cooper Guest Lodge hotel's setting—from the beautifully manicured lawns and towering trees to the winding walking trails to the gracious Southern Colonial architecture—evokes feelings of relaxation and seclusion.

Cooper Guest Lodge caters to discerning individuals and corporate groups, offering comfortable, luxurious accommodations, 8,000 square feet of International Association of Conference Centers accredited meeting facilities, and access to the world-rated Cooper Fitness Center.

Guestrooms are elegantly appointed and spacious, with entry foyers and French doors opening onto private balconies overlooking the grounds. High-speed wireless Internet access in guestrooms, meeting rooms, and pool and lobby areas makes leisure-time browsing or business communication easy.

With an overnight stay, guests receive a complimentary expanded continental breakfast and full use of the 40,000-square-foot Fitness Center. This amenity inspired *Men's Health* magazine to name Cooper Guest Lodge "best place to stay fit on the road."

You can enjoy a wide array of resort activities. Jog on the one-mile cushioned outdoor trail, swim in a climate-controlled pool, play tennis, work out on state-of-the-art equipment, attend a yoga, Pilates or other exercise class, or bring your staff for a teambuilding day. You can also get a treatment at the day spa or arrange for a stress reducing in-room massage by one of The Spa's licensed therapists.

The Colonnade Restaurant is the main dining room. Light and airy, with white linens and rose-colored cushioned chairs, the restaurant features delicious cuisine prepared by The Colonnade's skilled executive chef. For something light and quick, guests can choose the deli-style restaurant, Tyler's.

Guest Lodge Getaway hotel/spa packages make the planning easy—including hotel stay, spa treatments, fitness services, and more. And by joining our Executive Reward Club program, you can earn points redeemable for airline miles, hotel stays, and merchandise.

Address: 12230 Preston Rd, Dallas 75230.

Phone: 972-386-0306 800-444-5187

Fax: 972-386-5415

Email: dlittle@theguestlodge.com

Web site: www.theguestlodge.com

Room Rates: 165–195

Suite Rates: 270–450

No. of Rooms: 62

No. of Suites: 12

Attractions: North Park and Galleria shopping malls. Near to Addison entertainment and dining district. Downtown, Preston Center, and Richardson business districts within short drive.

Services & Amenities: Concierge service. Courtesy transportation within a 3-mile radius. Free continental breakfast. Terry cloth robes. Wireless Internet. Free use of 40,000-sq-ft gym with group exercise classes, cardio and weight equipment, tennis courts, heated pools, & more.

Restrictions: No pets allowed. Non smoking.

Concierge: 24 hours

Room Service: 11am-2pm, 5-10pm M-F; 6-8pm Sat-Sun

Restaurant: The Colonnade Restaurant–lunch and dinner. Open 11 a.m.-2 p.m. Mon-Fri and 6-8 p.m. Sat-Sun. Tyler's–counter-service deli-style sandwiches, hot entree of the day, soups, salads, and smoothies.

Business Facilities: Secretarial services, copiers, audiovisual, fax, wireless Internet, teambuilding, wellness speakers.

Conference Rooms: Int'l Ass. of Conference Centers property; 8 meeting rooms.

Sports Facilities: 40,000 sq ft gym, personal trainers, cardio, weights, 2 heated pools, whirlpools, saunas.

Spa Services: Full-service day spa on property. In-room massage available.

Location: On 30 acres of beautiful grounds amidst residential area in North Dallas

HOTEL ST. GERMAIN

The AAA 4 Diamond Award winning boutique Hotel St. Germain offers seven luxury suites, two parlors, two dining rooms and a New Orleans-style courtyard. The Hotel and Restaurant are both winners of the prestigious Zagat Award.

All of the suites are decorated with turn-of-the-century antiques from France and New Orleans and each has a working fireplace. Feather beds are canopied with luxurious fabrics from fourteen-foot ceilings. Amenities include cable television, VCR and CD/cassette players plus Jacuzzis or soaking tubs, European toiletries and signature terrycloth robes.

The convenience of a 24-hour concierge, a butler, room service, valet parking and business services are available. The Hotel specializes in catering, banquets, weddings and special events.

At Hotel St. Germain, guests dine by candlelight in the dramatic Old-World ambiance of the romantic grand Dining Room overlooking the ivy-covered garden courtyard. Wines from the extensive cellar are served in imported cut crystal and meals are presented on the proprietor's collection of antique Limoges china. The sumptuous seven-course, gourmet dinner changes monthly. Dinner is prix fixe and is available Tuesday through Saturday evenings by advance reservation.

Address: 2516 Maple Ave, Dallas 75201.

Phone: 214-871-2516 800-683-2516
Fax: 214-871-0740
Email: genmgrstgermain@aol.com
Web site: http://
www.hotelstgermain.com

Suite Rates: 290–650

No. of Suites: 7

Attractions: Boutique shopping across the street, 30 restaurants, 25 art galleries, 20 antique shops

Services & Amenities: Valet, Beauty/Barber shop/full spa service across street, Laundry service, Lounges, Shoeshine, Fireplaces, Balconies, Cable TV/VCR, Radio, CD/ Cassette players, Mini-bar, Robes, Whirlpools, Toiletries & newspaper, Deluxe European breakfast included

Restrictions: 7 day cancellation policy, small pets (under 20 lbs) $50 per night

Concierge: 24 hours

Room Service: 24 hours

Restaurant: Hotel St. Germain Restaurant, Dinner Tues-Sat, advance reservation. Restaurant AAA 4-Diamond Award

Bar: Parisian Style Champagne Bar: Extensive Champagne List, Caviar,Foie Gras,Canapes

Business Facilities: Message center, Admin. assistance through concierge, Staff speaks several languages

Conference Rooms: 3 rooms, capacity 175

Sports Facilities: Massage by appointment through concierge, Nearby full health facility for small fee

Location: Oak Lawn, Near downtown, Nearest airports: Love Field & Dallas Fort Worth

HOTEL ZAZA

Hotel ZaZa is unlike any other downtown Dallas luxury hotel you have ever experienced. Its soul lies in a rich combination of sensual hotel design, unmatched luxury, impeccable attention to detail and, above all, a "can-do" staff whose mission is to exceed your expectations.

Hotel ZaZa is a unique luxury hotel that rests in the heart of Uptown Dallas, just north of downtown Dallas, among many of the city's best restaurants, shops and museums. The hotel's "South of France" design exudes a magical luxury and warm welcome to every downtown Dallas luxury hotel guest.

Discover the magic that infuses our exclusive downtown Dallas luxury hotel. Immerse yourself in worldly culture and enjoy our stimulating surroundings. We strive to make your satisfaction our number one priority.

Address: 2332 Leonard Street, Dallas 75201.
Phone: (241) 468-8399
Fax: (214) 468-8397
Email: info@hotelzaza.com
Web site: http://www.hotelzaza.com/
Room Rates: 189–350
Suite Rates: 450–1695
No. of Rooms: 153
No. of Suites: 21
Credit Cards: Most Credit Cards accepted
Attractions: Just outside ZaZa's doors are the fine art galleries, shops and restaurants of Uptown Dallas. Five minutes away, Downtown Dallas offers the shops and restaurants of the West End District, to the museums and performance centers of the Dallas Arts District.
Concierge: Services Available
Room Service: Available 24 Hours
Restaurant: Created in collaboration with award-winning Chef Stephan Pyles and led by Executive Chef Scott Blackerby, Dragonfly is much more than a restaurant or lounge—it engages every sense, every time.
Bar: Urban Oasis
Business Facilities: Complimentary high-speed Internet access
Conference Rooms: Unique facilities to accommodate from 10 to 300
Sports Facilities: Swimming on site, Fitness room, Yoga classes at hotel
Spa Services: Whether your goal is invigoration or relaxation, the Za Spa's steam baths, massage services, skin care, nail treatments, hydrotherapy bath sessions will refresh and renew your mind, body and spirit.
Location: Hotel ZaZa is located in the heart of Uptown Dallas.

THE MANSION ON TURTLE CREEK

The first Rosewood hotel and flagship of the collection, The Mansion on Turtle Creek, retains the intimate ambiance and charm of the private 1920s estate it once was. This Five-Star, Five-Diamond hotel boasts meticulously restored interiors, hand-carved fireplaces, and marble floors impart a sense of grandeur.

Elegantly furnished rooms with luxurious baths, private balconies, and thoughtful amenities ensure the absolute comfort of every guest.

The Mansion Restaurant's Southwestern cuisine is widely thought to be one of the finest dining experiences in America. Under the leadership of Chef Dean Fearing, The Restaurant has been awarded many accolades including Best Restaurant and Best Food in the World by publications such as *Conde Nast Traveler, Travel & Leisure, Gourmet* and *Wine Spectator*.

Five private salons and a spacious ballroom offer an array of private entertainment choices, accommodating up to 300 people. The cozy alcove of the Wine Cellar is an ideal choice for small gatherings or intimate dinners.

The Mansion was recently awarded the "World's Best Service" by *Travel & Leisure*, a first for a North American hotel.

Address: 2821 Turtle Creek Blvd, Dallas 75219
Phone: 214-559-2100
800-527-5432
Fax: 214-528-4187
Email:
themansion@rosewoodhotels.com
Web site: http://
www.mansiononturtlecreek.com/
Room Rates: 400–500
Suite Rates: 675–2,400
No. of Rooms: 127
No. of Suites: 16
Attractions: Near Highland Park Shopping Center, Art galleries, Boutiques, Central business district
Services & Amenities: Valet, Car hire, Complimentary limousine service within 5 mile radius, Beauty salon, Currency exchange, Baby-sitting, Laundry, House doctor, Cable TV, Radio, Bath phone, Robes, All-natural toiletries, Complimentary shoeshine & newspaper, Two line phones
Restrictions: Small pets (deposit required), Handicap equipped rooms available
Concierge: 24 hours
Room Service: 24 hours
Restaurant: The Mansion on Turtle Creek Restaurant, Dress Code except Sat.-Sun. before 5:00 p.m.
Bar: The Mansion Bar, 11:30 a.m.-1:00 a.m.
Business Facilities: Fax machines, Business & message center, Admin. assistance, Copiers, High speed Internet access
Conference Rooms: 7 rooms, capacity 15-200
Sports Facilities: Heated swimming pool, Fitness studio
Location: 18 miles from Dallas/Ft. Worth Airport

GOLDENER HIRSCH INN

Located mid-mountain at Deer Valley, this intimate, elegant, yet friendly Austrian-style chalet is situated in an idyllic mountain setting with four-season beauty. The Hirsch's location offers ski-in, ski-out access in the winter and immediate access to mountain-biking in the summer. All other winter and summer sports, as well as Park City's shopping, theater, museums, restaurants, and galleries are minutes from the inn.

Executive Chef Jean Louis Montecot oversees the Goldener Hirsch Restaurant, which features superb Continental and American cuisine in an elegant, yet relaxed Austrian setting. The menu features Austrian specialties and nouveau American cuisine with French influences. In the winter, the lounge features an apres ski menu and live entertainment, and the restaurant is open daily for breakfast, lunch, and dinner. In the summer, we offer dinner Wednesday through Sunday.

The 20 guestrooms are uniquely decorated with hand-carved, hand-painted Austrian furniture. Inviting country prints grace the sofas, chairs, and draperies. All rooms feature king-sized beds with lush down comforters. Three suites have romantic king-size canopy beds. All rooms and suites are spacious, and most have private balconies and wood-burning fireplaces. All public and private rooms at the Hirsch were recarpeted in 2001, and all guestrooms received new draperies and mattresses.

The Hirsch was featured in the November 2001 edition of Andrew Harper's *Hideaway Report* as "a delightful gem for those seeking an intimate and warmly personalized European atmosphere." The January 2002 issue of *Ski* magazine rated the Hirsch as one of "The 10 Best Small Hotels" for weekend escapes.

Willkommen!

Address: PO Box 859, 7570 Royal St E, Park City 84060.
Phone: 435-649-7770 800-252-3373
Fax: 435-649-7901
Email: ghi@goldenerhirschinn.com
Web site: http://www.goldenerhirschinn.com
Room Rates: 100–490
Suite Rates: 150–975
No. of Rooms: 3
No. of Suites: 17
Attractions: Shopping, theater, museums, art galleries, restaurants, August art festival, January Sundance Film Festival, open-air concerts, skiing, snowmobiling, cross-country skiing, snow-boarding, hot-air ballooning, mountain biking, golf, fly-fishing, hiking
Services & Amenities: Concierge, valet service, underground parking, gift shop, TV lounge, complimentary newspapers, cable TV, robes, indoor and outdoor hottubs, sauna, 2 exercise machines, complimentary breakfast, complimentary local shuttle service.
Restrictions: Children welcome, No pets allowed, One room handicap-equipped, all rooms non-smoking
Concierge: 7 a.m.-11 p.m.
Room Service: 7 a.m.-10 p.m.
Restaurant: Superb Continental and American cuisine. Ski season: breakfast, lunch, apres ski, and dinner daily (entertainment 3–5 p.m.). Summer: dinner Wed.–Sun.
Bar: 11 a.m.-1 a.m.
Business Facilities: Copiers, Audiovisual, Full conference facilities
Conference Rooms: 1 room, capacity 25
Sports Facilities: Skiing, Mountain Biking, Hiking, Horseback riding, Ballooning, Fly Fishing, Golf
Spa Services: In-room massage available at guest request.
Location: Silver Lake Village, Deer Valley

GREEN VALLEY SPA

The marvelous accommodations at Green Valley Spa have received raves from guests and travel critics. The 2005 Travel Guide from the AAA rated it "4 Diamonds" for exceptional hospitality, service and attention to detail. The readers of *Condé Nast Traveler* rated it the 11th best resort spa in all of North America, Hawaii & the Caribbean. *Virtuoso* named Green Valley as "The Best of the Best."

Each room is meticulously detailed with large whirlpool baths, fireplace, four poster bed, goose down comforters & pillows and freshly ground Starbucks coffee. This intimate resort (only 45 rooms) should be on the list of every discriminating traveler.

Green Valley offers hikes for all fitness levels; Trails include Zion National Park, Bryce Canyon, and the Red rock trails of Snow Canyon State Park. The Vic Braden Tennis College offers year round Tennis Camps. The world famous Spa offers 70 different treatments. Guests can choose from All-Inclusive packages which include, four diamond accommodations, meals, spa treatments & guided hikes or the option of reserving a room only and selecting from the Ala-Carte menu the activities & spa treatments of your choice.

Address: 1871 W Canyon View Dr, Saint George 84770.
Phone: 435-628-8060 800-237-1068
Fax: 435-673-4084
Email: webmaster@greenvalleyspa.com
Web site: http://www.greenvalleyspa.com
Suite Rates: 99 pp/dbl
No. of Suites: 45
Credit Cards: Most Credit Cards accepted
Attractions: Daily hiking in Red rock canyons, Grand Canyon, Zion National Park, Bryce Canyon, 1½ hours from Las Vegas
Services & Amenities: Guests also enjoy 20,000 sq ft spa center, Serene Yoga Room, State of the Art Fitness Studio, Rose Gardens, Hi-Speed wireless Internet, conference and lecture room, meditation room, 2 gift shops (the clubhouse and the spa shop), dining room, and much more
Restrictions: Pets allowed
Concierge: 7 a.m.-7 p.m.
Room Service: Meals can be served in room
Restaurant: Casual dining in an elegant atmosphere. Our two chefs have a combined experience of 39 years in the culinary arts. They create exciting and inventive dishes.
Business Facilities: Full scale conference facility for up to 60 people, 10 foot screen and projector
Sports Facilities: 15 outdoor, 4 indoor tennis courts, 2 racquetball courts, 6 swimming pools, Golf/tennis camps, Indoo
Spa Services: Green Valley's award winning spa treatments were created to both refresh your spirit and calm your mind. Try the steaming stones massage.
Location: In Southern Utah, 90 minutes from Las Vegas, NV

ARLINGTON'S WEST MOUNTAIN INN

Arlington's West Mountain Inn is a charming 1850's Colonial-style farmhouse with white clapboard, green shutters and seven gables. Furnished with country antiques, a wood-stove and high beamed ceilings, the Inn offers a warm, hospitable environment. Enjoy fabulous views of the Battenkill Valley, the Green and Red Mountains, and miles and miles of lush country meadows. Located close to the historic village of Arlington, guests can enjoy outlet shopping, historic Hildene, and other outdoor adventures.

All of the rooms are individually decorated with antiques, comfortable reading chairs, canopy beds and fireplaces. The Rockwell Kent Suite has a wood-paneled cathedral ceiling, a king-sized canopy bed, a large living area with wood-burning fireplace, and a view of a beautiful llama pasture with the majestic Red Mountains looming in the distance. Each bathroom is individually decorated and contains a full bath with tub and shower.

After an afternoon of exploring 150 acres of gardens, lawns, hiking trails and meadows, relax with a snack of homemade cookies or muffins while sipping the Inn's special hot spiced cider with spiced rum. For those special occasions, there is a country barn which seats 125 people. It has a dance floor where guests can dance the night away while celebrating that special occasion. After a fun-filled day, luxuriate in a hot bath using the complimentary toiletries.

Dine by candlelight in the wood-paneled dining room adorned with fresh-cut flowers and wood-burning fireplace. Maybe start with baked brie in filo dough with walnuts, followed by Black Angus filet mignon with wild mushroom jus. To top of the delicious meal, how about maple-pecan pie ala mode.

At the Arlington West Mountain Inn, take pleasure in a fabulous setting, wonderful views, and a warm, friendly staff.

Address: PO Box 40, Arlington 5250.
Phone: 802-375-6516
Fax: 802-375-6553
Email: info@westmountaininn.com
Web site: http://www.westmountaininn.com
Room Rates: 155–221
Suite Rates: 155–269
No. of Rooms: 18
No. of Suites: 7
Attractions: Historic village and shopping within walking distance, 8 miles south of Manchester for Outlet shopping, Historic Hildene, Golf, etc., 20 minutes from Bromely for skiing.
Services & Amenities: Gift shop, TV lounge, Game area, Library, Babysitting upon request, Mid-week packages, Some kitchen facilities, fireplaces & balconies, Some rooms w/ cable TV and/or telephones, Complimentary toiletries, Individual climate controls, snacks all day
Restrictions: 2 rooms handicap equipped, no pets allowed
Concierge: 7:30 a.m.-10:30 p.m.
Restaurant: West Mountain Inn Restaurant, 8-10 a.m., 6-9 p.m., evening casual dress code
Bar: Noon–11 p.m., Hors d'oeuvres served 6-7 p.m.
Business Facilities: Copiers, Fax, Modem ports
Conference Rooms: 2 rooms, capacity 35
Sports Facilities: Massage upon request, 20 minutes to skiing, Canoeing, River tubing and swimming, Mountain biking, Hiking
Location: In the Country

THREE MOUNTAIN INN

The Three Mountain Inn, located in the small, unspoiled village of Jamaica, Vermont is a perfect choice to spend a few days of rest and relaxation. The Inn, conveniently located on Vermont's scenic Route 30, between the towns of Brattleboro and historic Manchester Center, dates from the 1790's and remains a cornerstone of the small town.

Peacefully set among Vermont's Green Mountains, the Inn overlooks the woodlands and trails of Jamaica State National Park and is just minutes away from the famed Stratton, Bromley and Magic Mountain Ski areas.

With its wide-planked walls and multiple fireplaces, the Three Mountain Inn has an abundance of history and a sense of luxury. Whether you enjoy a romantic dinner in one of two intimate dining rooms, relax by one of the many fireplaces, or explore the various outdoor possibilities, the Three Mountain Inn will revive your senses.

Jennifer and Ed invite you to enjoy a warm and comfortable atmosphere, with exceptional food and the finest personal service. Come and experience the best Vermont has to offer. The Three Mountain Inn is the ideal setting to create perfect memories.

Address: P.O. Box 180, Jamaica 05343.
Phone: 802-874-4140 800-532-9399
Fax: 802-874-4745
Email: stay@threemtn.com
Web site: http://www.threemountaininn.com
Room Rates: 165–345
Suite Rates: 295–345
No. of Rooms: 15
No. of Suites: 3
Attractions: So. Vermont Art Center, 120 outlet stores, 10 minutes to ski lifts, Snowmobile tours, Snowshoeing, Golf, Horseback riding, Off-roading, Hiking, Antiques, Art Galleries, Relaxation
Services & Amenities: Parking, TV Lounge, Library, Newspaper, Cable TV/VCR, in-room phones, Individual A/C, Robes, Jacuzzi tubs, Video Library
Concierge: 7:30 AM–10 PM
Restaurant: This historic 1790 culinary landmark, showcases contemporary Vermont Fresh Cuisine. Recognized with the AAA Four Diamond Award, and Wine Spectator's Award of Excellence.
Bar: On Site
Business Facilities: Room Phones, Wireless Internet in Common Areas
Conference Rooms: On Site
Sports Facilities: Outdoor Hiking and Pool
Spa Services: In Room Massages Availible by Appointment
Location: Southern Vermont Green Mountains

THE CHARLES ORVIS INN AT THE EQUINOX

This elegant 19th-century residence on historic Main Street has been completely restored. Located in Manchester Village, it was once home to Charles Orvis, the fly-fishing entrepreneur and founder of the Orvis Company, and has been operating as an inn since 1883. Victorian in design with Tudor-style windows, the Inn has nine luxurious one- and two-bedroom suites. Nestled in the village, it is surrounded by the Green Mountains and Battenkill River. The Inn offers special package rates including golf, skiing, spa, honeymoon, and anniversary stays.

Offering the highest level of service, this exclusive country retreat is ideal for both business and leisure travelers. The lobby sets an elegant tone with coffered ceilings, oak floorings, and richly textured fabrics. The Tying and Billiard Rooms are beautifully appointed in timeless club ambiance. The stately Board Room, with recessed audio/visual equipment, accommodates fifteen people. An experienced staff oversees the banquet facilities.

Complimentary breakfast is presented to guests daily, and afternoon tea is also served. Fine dining is available at the distinguished Colonnade Room at The Equinox, the Charles Orvis Inn's sister hotel next door.

The Equinox also shares with the Charles Orvis Inn its newly redesigned 18-hole Rees Jones golf course facilities, a fitness spa featuring an indoor pool, steamroom, sauna, cardio-vascular equipment, Nautilus, pro shop, mountain bikes, year round tennis, snowmobiling, iceskating, and snowshoeing. Adjacent to the fitness spa is a large outdoor pool.

The newest feature of The Equinox is the opening of The Land Rover Driving School, the first permanent manufacturer-supported 4x4 driving school of the U.S., and the British School of Falconry.

Address: P.O. Box 46, Manchester Village 5254.
Phone: 802-362-4700 800-362-4747
Fax: 802-362-0013
Email: reservations@equinoxresort.com
Web site: http://www.equinoxresort.com
Room Rates: 399
Suite Rates: 679–899
No. of Rooms: 15
No. of Suites: 9
Attractions: Dorset Playhouse, So. Vermont Art Center, Norman Rockwell Museum, Hildene (Robert Todd Lincoln's home), 120 outlet stores, 10 miles to ski lift, Snowmobile tours, Snowshoeing, Volleyball, Horseback riding, Off-roading
Services & Amenities: Parking, Airport transfers, Valet laundry service, TV Lounge, International currency exchange, Library, Complimentary shoeshine and newspaper, Cable TV/VCR, 2 in-room phones, Wet bar, Individual A/C, Robes, Jacuzzi tub
Restrictions: No pets allowed
Concierge: 8 a.m.-9 p.m.
Room Service: 7 a.m.-10 p.m.
Restaurant: The Colonnade, Sun. Brunch 11:30 am-2:30 pm, Wed.-Sun. Summer, 6-9:30 pm, Marsh Tavern, 7 am-9:30 pm, Dormy Grill 11:30 am–4pm Lunch summer/fall; Evening Lobsterfest
Bar: Marsh Tavern, noon–closing
Business Facilities: Message center, Copier, Audio-Visual, Teleconferencing, Fax
Conference Rooms: 1 room, capacity 15
Sports Facilities: Indoor & Outdoor Pools, Croquet, Sauna, Massage, Aerobics, Weights, Tennis, Golf, X-country skiing,
Location: 61 miles to Albany County Airport in NY

WILBURTON INN

Welcome to the Wilburton Inn, Manchester Vermont's 20 acre grand Victorian estate specializing in holiday vacations, romantic getaways, sport vacations, executive retreats and elegant country weddings. Our web site www.wilburton.com is just an introduction. We look forward to greeting you at the Wilburton Inn and sharing with you all its romance, adventure, history and beauty.

High on the crest of a hill overlooking the Battenkill Valley and Vermont's Green Mountains, the Wilburton Inn was once the largest private estate in Manchester Village. Everything about it is superlative: fabulous location, ambiance and architecture. Since 1902, when the mansion was completed, there have been five owners of the property, each holding fast to a standard of excellence.

Driving past stone-walled estates on River Road, you sense that you are returning to an era of gracious living, undisturbed by the pressures of contemporary life. The day at the Wilburton begins with a full country breakfast served in the terrace dining room, including, of course, blueberry pancakes and genuine Vermont maple syrup. From the wide windows, admire breathtaking panoramic views of the mountains and the valley. This is one of the most exceptional views in all of Vermont.

After breakfast, take a pleasant stroll through the extensive grounds and the sculpture gardens. During the day, explore the shopping, recreational and cultural activities in town just one mile away. Hike the Green Mountains, or try sports at nearby ski, spa and golf centers. Enjoy a game of tennis at the Inn or relax by the pool. Read a newspaper or a book from the deck off your room.

Afternoon tea is served on the terrace or in the living room. Have a cocktail or glass of wine by the living room fireplace before dinner. Dining at the Wilburton is a wonderful experience. The handsome dining room has a massive fireplace. The menus feature fresh premium ingredients with herbs and salads cut from the garden. The pastry chef creates delicious desserts and artisan breads in the Wilburton kitchen. The wine captain will help select the perfect wine to pair with your dinner.

Address: River Road, Manchester Village 5254.
Phone: 802-362-2500 800-648-4944
Fax: 802-362-1107
Email: wilbuinn@sover.net
Web site: http://www.wilburton.com
Room Rates: 155–315
Suite Rates: 200–350
No. of Rooms: 35
No. of Suites: 7
Credit Cards: Visa
Attractions: In winter, ski, snow shoe & cross country ski. In spring, go fishing. In summer, hike our mountains, play tennis, swim, golf, canoe, enjoy concerts and theater. In fall, enjoy the colors of Vermont folliage. Year round shopping, antiqueing and dining.
Services & Amenities: The Wilburton Inn's spectacular setting is romantic, soothing and inspirational with sculpture gardens and a gazebo for contemplation. Our front desk has information on area activities and makes reservations. We offer guests a shopping discount booklet.
Restrictions: no pets please.
Room Service: Yes
Restaurant: Dinner is served by the massive fireplace in the handsome Billiard Room. Our gourmet menu reflects American, European and Asian influences. Our wine list is extensive.
Bar: Dining Room, Terrace and Living Room
Business Facilities: Some AV, Computer, Copy, Fax
Conference Rooms: Small Conference Rooms Available
Sports Facilities: Pool, Tennis Courts, Walking Trails
Spa Services: We can make reservations for spa services at nearby spas and exercise centers. We can also arrange for in room services.

THE MOUNTAIN ROAD RESORT AT STOWE

Guests will find The Mountain Road Resort at Stowe on seven acres of beautifully landscaped grounds situated in the heart of the scenic resort town of Stowe. The Resort reflects the innkeepers experiences in their travels around the world, with superlative style in accommodations and facilities.

A massive stone fireplace is the centerpiece of the comfortably furnished living room. The cozy atmosphere is created with shades of green and burgundy.

The Mountain Road Resort offers luxury guestrooms, studios and condo-suites. These unique retreats have world-class amenities such as fireplaces, dining areas, lofts, kitchens, and tiled baths with whirlpools. These luxury accommodations will bring that additional sense of extravagance that you vacation deserves.

Guests have exclusive use of all of the Resort facilities that includes a complimentary breakfast in the New Main Lodge, afternoon refreshment, and vintage wines from Billy's Wine Bar. You will enjoy the beautifully landscaped outdoor swiming pool and MoonSpa surrounded by lovely flowering gardens. There is also the "AquaCentre" with an indoor pool, grand Jacuzzi, alpine sauna and mini-gym.

At The Mountain Road Resort, the staff knows what guests really want: excellence in service, hospitality and accommodations. And, kindness too!

Address: PO Box 8, 1007 Mountain Road, Stowe 5672.
Phone: 802-253-4566 800-367-6873
Fax: 802-253-7397
Email: stowevt@aol.com
Web site: http://
www.stowevtusa.com
Room Rates: 120–225
Suite Rates: 225–585
No. of Rooms: 30
No. of Suites: 6
Attractions: Downhill and cross-country skiing, Winter Carnival, sleigh rides and snow-shoeing, Colorful boutiques, 40 restaurants, Summer antique car show, Nearby Ben & Jerry's Ice Cream plant, Green Mountains
Services & Amenities: Valet service, Laundry, Library, Baby-sitting service, Card/game area, Some fireplaces, wet bars, balconies, Comp newspaper, Cable TV w/VCR, Multiple telephones, Radio, CD player, Audio cassette player in suites, Robes, Climate controls, Rooms non-smoking
Restrictions: 2 rooms handicap equipped, Children welcome, One pet welcome per room
Room Service: 7:30 a.m.-10 a.m. breakfast
Restaurant: French Country breakfast buffet in "The Library"
Bar: The Library, Wine Bar, 12 noon–10 p.m.
Business Facilities: E-mail, Copying, Fax, Some rooms and suites have cable high speed Internet
Conference Rooms: 1 room, capacity 30
Sports Facilities: Indoor and Outdoor swimming pools, Croquet, Indoor and outdoor whirlpools, Sauna, Mini-gym, Tennis,
Location: In the world famous resort town of Stowe, Vermont

Planters Inn, *Charelston, SC* PAGE 150

Hotel Bellwether, *Bellingham, WA* PAGE 176

Hotel Du Palais, *Paris France* PAGE 204

WOODSTOCK INN & RESORT

Truly valued traditions endure the test of time—and so it is with the Woodstock welcome. For over 200 years there has been an Inn on Woodstock's village green. Although it was built in 1969, the present Woodstock Inn & Resort is the latest in a line of hostelries that dates back to 1793. Their amenities have expanded greatly through the years, yet their philosophy has not: provide guests with an experience that will be fondly remembered long into the future.

The colonial architecture of this celebrated Inn conceals a modern hotel with the finest facilities. 142 large guestrooms and suites offer fine accommodations typified by the hand-sewn quilts that grace the beds.

This year-round resort offers a wealth of activities including an 18-hole Robert Trent Jones, Sr. golf course. Other activities include hiking riding, six clay and four all-weather tennis courts, their own Suicide Six downhill Ski Area with great terrain for all ability levels and 60 km of groomed trails at their Ski Touring Center.

The indoor Health & Fitness Center is another outstanding facility with its pool, sauna, whirlpool, two indoor tennis courts, squash, racquetball, an extensive exercise room, massage and croquet.

A short distance from the Inn is the Billings Farm and museum, one of the country's premier agricultural museums, keeping alive the spirit and values of Vermont's rural heritage.

Dining is an experience not to be missed. From the Eagle Cafe and the Dining Room to the Clubhouse at our Country Club. The emphasis is on quality. Quality of the food, quality in its preparation, service, presentation and selection.

The readers of *Condé Nast Traveler* magazine have rated Woodstock Inn & Resort one of the best places to stay in the world. Come see for yourself.

Address: 14 The Green, Woodstock 5091.
Phone: 802-457-1100 800-448-7900
Fax: 802-457-6699
Email: email@woodstockinn.com
Web site: http://www.woodstockinn.com/
Room Rates: 139–409
Suite Rates: 360–654
No. of Rooms: 142
No. of Suites: 7
Credit Cards: Visa
Attractions: The Woodstock area offers something for everyone. The Marsh-Billings-Rockefeller National Historic Park, The Billings Farm and Museum, Golfing, Downhill and X-country skiing, Sleigh rides, biking, canoeing, fishing, glass blowing, swimming, Museums,
Services & Amenities: Valet Service, On-property shuttle; Admissions to the Billing Farm & Museum; Gift shop; Babysitting Service; Afternoon tea & cookies; Cable TV; Turndown Services; Some rooms with fireplaces; Concierge; Ski Area; Golf Course; Health & Fitness Center
Restrictions: No pets; No smoking; Families are welcomed
Concierge: 9am to 5pm
Room Service: 7am to 9pm
Restaurant: The Main Dining serves dinner dinner & Sunday brunch The Eagle Cafe is casual dining and serves breakfast, lunch and dinner. Richardson's Tavern serves a light dinner.
Bar: 5pm to 11pm or later
Business Facilities: Business Center; copier; fax; Internet
Conference Rooms: 9 room; capacity 2–330
Sports Facilities: Year around tennis; golf; downhill & x-country ski; racquet sports; hiking; biking; canoe; I/O pools
Spa Services: Our Health & Fitness Center offers spa service as well as the indoor pool, sauna, whirlpool & excerise area. Massages, manicure, facials and pedicures are offered as well as personal training session

HIBISCUS BEACH HOTEL

The best of the Caribbean lifestyle is yours at the oceanfront Hibiscus Beach Resort.

When daydreaming about the Caribbean, do visions of lush, green foliage, crystal blue waters, sugar sand beaches, quaint ice-cream colored shops, exotic rain forests, exquisite sun-drenched days, romantic starlit nights, dramatic sunsets, fascinating museums and intriguing historic ruins come to mind?

That is what you get on St. Croix.

Now add to that a resort that understands your need to be here—to relax, be pampered, eat well and have a "real vacation."

That is what the Hibiscus Beach Resort and H_2O bistro is all about.

The Hibiscus Beach Resort consists of 38 individual rooms located on four acres of the most prestigious beachfront property, with white sandy beaches that stretch more than a third of a mile. Each of our rooms is a retreat in itself, with a private veranda overlooking the Caribbean Sea.

Take a dip in our freshwater pool by the ocean or step out onto one of the finest white sand beaches on the island. Calm your senses beachside in one of our lounge chairs or let one of our friendly attendants outfit you with complimentary snorkeling gear so you can indulge in the crystal clear turquoise sea.

While enjoying your visit to St. Croix, Hibiscus will provide you with impeccable service. Enjoy breakfast, lunch, dinner, Sunday brunch, and the only late night menu on the island at our open-air bistro, H_2O or see what is happening at the hottest new bar in town, The Star Bar.

Besides our gorgeous sandy beach and fabulous restaurant, the Hibiscus Beach Resort offers a freshwater pool, meeting facilities, and nearby golf and tennis. We are located 10 minutes from historic Christiansted, noted for shopping, dining and entertainment. We are a short 15 minute ride from the airport, and car rental agencies will deliver your rental car to the hotel for your convenience!

The Hibiscus Beach Resort offers special dive, honeymoon, and golf packages. For rates and packages, please see our website at www.hibiscusbeachresort.com

Address: 4131 La Grande Princesse, Christiansted, St. Croix 820.
Phone: 340-773-4042 800-442-0121
Fax: 340-773-7668
Email: hibiscus@viaccess.net
Web site: http://www.hibiscusbeachresort.com
Room Rates: 130–280 US$
No. of Rooms: 38
Attractions: The best part of a St. Croix vacation is the choices you have: do nothing but lounge on the beach or fill your days with hiking, sailing, snorkeling, scuba diving, fishing, horseback riding or kite surfing, and you'll have the vacation of your dreams!
Services & Amenities: At Hibiscus, we want to make sure you experience the ultimate Caribbean vacation, whether it is to explore exotic tropical surroundings, romance the one you love, dive deep in our waters, or golf your day away.
Concierge: 7am to 11pm
Room Service: Available 11:30am to midnight
Restaurant: Enjoy breakfast, lunch, dinner, Sunday brunch, and the only late night menu on the island at our open-air bistro, H_2O or see what is happening at the hottest new bar in town, The Star Bar.
Bar: Open 11:30am to midnight
Business Facilities: Accommodates 400
Conference Rooms: Seating available for 200
Location: Best beach on St. Croix

SECRET HARBOR BEACH RESORT

Secret Harbour Beach Resort is the Caribbean's most intimate beachfront resort, famous for its casual elegance and generous island hospitality. With its seaside location, ceiling fans, tile floors, and tropical plants, this is a perfect escape to tranquility and tropical splendor. On the quiet sun-kissed beach or poolside, lounge barefoot and revel in the soft ocean breeze. Here, unwind and bask in the sheer indulgence and breathtaking view. Magnificent sunsets close each day.

Secluded and romantic, Secret Harbour Beach Resort features studio, one- and two-bedroom suites with private decks or patios. Each suite contains a full kitchen, king or two twin beds, a double sofa bed, Cable TV, Caribbean views, ceiling fans, and private tanning balcony or patio.

Guests can immerse themselves in fun, sun and relaxation. Swim, sail, windsurf and snorkel or scuba dive in the refreshing, crystal clear protected water. Explore the calm and peaceful bay, which has been declared a Marine Sanctuary, or investigate exotic underwater reefs on your own or with the on-site PADI 5-star dive watersport center. Play a game of tennis on one of the all-weather courts, enjoy golf at Mahogany Run or duty-free shopping in Charlotte Amalie. St. Thomas' culture and nightlife can be explored with visits to popular island attractions and historic sites.

Enjoy breakfast or lunch, or feast on island delicacies each evening at the Blue Moon Café, a true seaside restaurant. As the sun slips down over the bay, celebrate a magnificent sunset and feel the romance of another island night unfolding. At the "Barefoot Beach Bar" sample the house specialty drinks.

Play and relax in an enchanting Caribbean paradise where the faces are friendly, service is gracious—and the feeling will bring you back again—and again.

Address: 6280 Estate Nazareth, St. Thomas 802.
Phone: 340-775-6550 800-524-2250
Fax: 340-775-1501
Email: info@secretharbourvi.com
Web site: http://www.secretharbourvi.com
Room Rates: 179–300
Suite Rates: 149–589
No. of Rooms: 4
No. of Suites: 60
Credit Cards: Visa
Attractions: Close to St. John Ferry, Shopping at Red Hook, Short drive to downtown Charlotte Amalie for tax and duty free shopping, Close to Mahogany Run Golf Course, Many restaurants within 2 miles, Exceptional calm beach on a Marine Wildlife Preserve
Services & Amenities: Parking, Airport pick up, Car hire, Balconies/patios, Cable TV, Telephone, Radio, Ceiling fans, Fully equipped kitchens, Air conditioning, Comp. toiletries, Special packages
Restrictions: No pets allowed, 4 rooms equipped for physically challenged, Children under 13 stay free
Restaurant: Blue Moon—An All American Cafe, 8 a.m.-10 p.m. serving breakfast, lunch and dinner in a seaside setting.
Bar: Barefoot Beach Bar, 8 a.m.-10 p.m. Welcome Managers Party on Tuesdays
Business Facilities: Copiers, Fax, HSI
Conference Rooms: 1 room, capacity 70
Sports Facilities: Outdoor pool, Massage, Tennis courts, Aqua Action Dive/Watersport center, Fitness Center
Location: Secret Harbour, Nazareth Bay, East End of Island

THE BERKELEY HOTEL

The Berkeley Hotel stands at the crossroads of Richmond's business district and Historic Shockoe Slip. First opened in 1988, The Berkeley Hotel's ambiance exudes serenity and warmth that convinces many first-time guests that it's been around for ages.

Dark wood paneling in the boutique lobby and its adjacent Dining Room boasts a European flair where dramatic windows push to the ceiling, offering diners a view of the Slip's cobblestone and lamp lights. The Dining Room serves many fine products from Virginia including bison, venison, lamb, veal, fish and shellfish, as well as fresh vegetables and fruits.

Fifty-five elegantly appointed guestrooms are well appointed with solid cherry furnishings and traditional high-quality fabrics with lovely botanical watercolors adoring the walls. The Berkeley Hotel offers uncompromising AAA Four-Diamond service including in-room amenities such as a coffee maker, shower massage, iron, ironing boards, hair dryers, and voice-mail. The Governor's Suite features two full baths, a luxurious king bed, large private terrace and an elegant peaked-ceiling living room with a panoramic view of Historic Shockoe Slip.

The Berkeley Hotel itself is reminiscent of that time, more than one hundred years ago, when Shockoe Slip was the center of commerce and politics. The hotel's appointments, the graciousness of its classic restaurant and the tasteful furnishings of its guestrooms take you back to an era when inn-keeping was an art.

Address: 1200 East Cary St, Richmond 23219.
Phone: 804-780-1300 888-780-4422
Fax: 804-343-1885
Email: jmoore@berkeleyhotel.com
Web site: http://www.berkeleyhotel.com
Room Rates: 185–250
Suite Rate: 675
No. of Rooms: 55
No. of Suites: 1
Credit Cards: Most Credit Cards accepted
Attractions: Historic Shockoe Slip, Boutique shopping, Restaurants. Nearby: Canal Walk, Carytown, Historic Plantations, Museums.
Services & Amenities: Valet parking ($12 per night, per auto), Comp. Health-Club Privileges, Cable TV/HBO, In-room Coffee-Makers, Nightly turndown service, Complimentary weekday newspaper, In-room Voice Mail, Same day laundry service and dry cleaning (Monday-Friday)
Restrictions: No pets allowed, Children (under 18 years old) complimentary with parent(s)
Concierge: 24 hours
Room Service: 7 a.m.-10 p.m.
Restaurant: The Dining Room at The Berkeley Hotel, 7 a.m.-10 p.m., Reservations Suggested
Bar: Nightingales, 5:30 p.m.-11 p.m.
Business Facilities: Copier, Audio-Visual, Fax
Conference Rooms: 3 rooms, total capacity 150
Sports Facilities: Nearby massage, aerobics, weight training
Location: Historic Shockoe Slip, Nearest airport is Richmond International

INN AT GRISTMILL SQUARE

This colorful Virginia historic landmark conveys the romance and tradition of the Allegheny Mountains. The Inn at Gristmill Square, a whole complex of restored buildings around a small square, is a 19th-century country village with the modern convenience of private baths with bathrobes, hair dryers and toiletries, and cable TV. You'll enjoy the special touches, such as fresh flowers, classic linens and a welcoming fruit and cheese platter.

Guestrooms are located throughout four of the five original turn-of-the-century buildings, previously a mill, blacksmith shop, hardware store and two private residences. The 17 rooms and suites are individually furnished in traditional décor with the feel of a country home. Many rooms have their own fireplace. A complimentary continental breakfast featuring fresh fruit and specialty breads still warm from the oven is served to each room.

Guests may enjoy fresh local trout at The Waterwheel restaurant, located in the restored gristmill. The ambiance here is rustic country, with fine prints and fresh wildflowers in season. Before dinner, patrons choose their own bottle from the wine cellar next to the millstream.

For summer recreation, guests can utilize the outdoor pool, sauna and 3 tennis courts. The mineral-rich Warm Springs thermal pools are a mile away. Fishing, hiking and horseback riding are available at nearby George Washington National Forest. Also nearby are championship golf courses and an annual chamber music festival.

Address: PO Box 359, Warm Springs 24484.
Phone: 540-839-2231
Fax: 540-839-5770
Email: grist@tds.net
Web site: http://www.gristmillsquare.com/
Room Rates: 90–125
Suite Rates: 95–150
No. of Rooms: 17
No. of Suites: 5
Credit Cards: Visa
Attractions: Warm Springs thermal pools, 200 miles of hiking trails, Fly fishing, Driving tours of the Allegheny Mountains
Services & Amenities: Gift shop, Baby-sitting service, Cable TV, Telephones, Robes, Complimentary newspaper and toiletries, Complimentary breakfast
Restrictions: No pets allowed, Children welcome
Room Service: 7 a.m.-11 p.m.
Restaurant: The Waterwheel, 6 p.m.-10 p.m.
Bar: Simon Kenton Pub, 6 p.m.-10 p.m.
Business Facilities: Fax
Conference Rooms: 1 room, capacity 40
Sports Facilities: Outdoor swimming pool, Sauna, Tennis, Nearby golf, Skiing, Riding
Location: Mountain-spa country

HOTEL BELLWETHER

In the intimate and tranquil setting of Bellingham Bay, lies the Hotel Bellwether, the Pacific Northwest's brightest waterfront jewel.

Each of The Hotel Bellwether's 66 guestrooms and suites are meticulously appointed with imported Italian furnishings, original artwork, Hungarian down comforters and pillows, and Austrian linens. Indulge yourself in the thermomasseur bathtub for two designed with shutters allowing you to relax while enjoying spectacular views.

Pour yourself a glass of wine from your fully stocked bar and watch the sunset from your private balcony or drift away in front of a roaring fire, pampering yourself with an in-room massage. While each of our signature suites have a unique personality of their own, they each boast breathtaking views of the San Juan Islands.

For the ultimate in romance, stay in the 3-story lighthouse, complete with 360° obeservation deck overlooking Mt. Baker and the San Juan Islands.

Watch the boats drift by from the Harborside Bistro and Sunset Lounge. The Sunset Lounge offers the perfect waterfront haven for lighter fare, spirits, and our award-winning wine list.

Hotel Bellwether pampers you in the luxury of European tradition.

Address: One Bellwether Way, Bellingham 98225.
Phone: 360-392-3100 877-411-1200
Fax: 360-392-3101
Email: info@hotelbellwether.com
Web site: http://www.hotelbellwether.com
Room Rates: 139–239
Suite Rates: up to 699
No. of Rooms: 66
No. of Suites: 15
Attractions: San Juan Islands and Mt. Baker views. 220 ft. private dock for guest moorage. Fleet of boats for charter. Float plane accessible.
Services & Amenities:
Underground parking, Valet service, Gift shop, Fireplaces, Balconies, Newspaper, Cable TV, 2 Telephones, Radio, CD player, In-room safe, Full mini bar
Restrictions: Pets welcome w/$65 non-refundable charge, Children under 12 free w/parents, Handicap accessible
Concierge: Front Desk 24 hours
Room Service: 6 a.m.–11 p.m.
Restaurant: Harborside Bistro–11 a.m.–11 p.m.
Bar: Sunset Lounge–11 a.m.–11 p.m.
Business Facilities: Complete business service center and full-scale meeting facility
Conference Rooms: 6 rooms, capacity 700
Sports Facilities: Fitness center, Sailing, Boating, Kayaking, Bike rentals, Jogging trails
Spa Services: In-room massage/Adjacent to Hotel is a full service Spa/Salon.
Location: On Bellingham Bay's waterfront

ALEXIS HOTEL

In the historic Waterfront Place district midway between Pike Street Market and Pioneer Square, this 1901 hotel listed on the National Register of Historic Places is a centerpiece of Seattle's fascinating downtown restoration. The outer shell has been preserved, while the interior has been redone in sophisticated European style.

Each guest is treated to special personalized services upon arrival, use of the hotel's steam room (guaranteeing a restful night's sleep), nightly turndown service, complimentary shoeshine and choice of morning newspapers. In addition, there is an evening wine reception where guests can paint postcards, as well as morning coffee service in the lobby featuring Torrefazione coffee.

Each of the 109 guestrooms, almost half of them suites, is beautifully decorated with antique tables, overstuffed chairs, brass reading lamps and cable TV concealed in an armoire. Some of the dramatic baths feature black tile, marble counters, luxurious linens and robes, telephones and abundant Aveda toiletries. Several suites have woodburning fireplaces and large whirlpool baths.

The Library Bistro restaurant features contemporary American cuisine in a cozy, neighborhood setting. The Bookstore Bar, one of Seattle's best gathering spots for locals and tourists alike, is well-known as a great little cigar bar.

For a small fee, guests can enjoy privileges to the Seattle Club and Pure Fitness athletic centers. A scenic jogging route along the Seattle waterfront starts at The Alexis' front door.

Address: 1007 First Ave at Madison, Seattle 98104.
Phone: 206-624-4844 800-426-7033
Fax: 206-621-9009
Email: sales@alexishotel.com
Web site: http://www.alexishotel.com
Room Rates: 299–319
Suite Rates: 419–599
No. of Rooms: 109
Attractions: In the heart of Seattle's historic district, Alexis is two blocks from the waterfront;five blocks from Pioneer Square;four blocks from world famous Pike Place Market and shopping is *everywhere* . . . as well as the excellent restaurants Seattle has to offer!
Services & Amenities: Alexis offers packages for the senses: Art Lovers, Art of the Perfect Weekend and a glorious Art of Romance Package. Alexis works with Seattle Art Museum and the Seattle Symphony to promote the arts in Seattle.
Concierge: 10a.m.-7p.m.
Room Service: 24 hour
Restaurant: The Library Bistro– Breakfast Mon-Fri 7–10 a.m., Brunch Sat-Sun 8 a.m.–2 p.m., Lunch Mon-Fri 11:30 a.m.–2 p.m.
Bar: Bookstore Bar 11:30–12 a.m. daily
Business Facilities: Some
Conference Rooms: 3 rooms, max. capacity 120 reception style
Sports Facilities: Fitness Center
Spa Services: Guests can relax in our private steam room and take advantage of the wonderful spa treatments offered at the on-site Aveda Spa.
Location: Downtown Seattle-Historic District

PIONEER SQUARE HOTEL

This elegant, thoroughly restored turn-of-the-century hotel, is conveniently located in heart of downtown Seattle's Pioneer Square Historic District, just one block from the waterfront, takes guests back to a bygone era of style, grace and comfort.

The 75 romantic rooms and suites come in a variety of classic decors updated to the needs and comforts of today's guests. All rooms have individual heating and air-conditioning; direct-dial, fax/modem; data port telephones; color cable TV with remote control; and beautifully appointed individual bathrooms with corian counters, hairdryers and Neutrogena products and amenities. For an excellent night's sleep, Serta Perfect Sleeper mattresses and soundproof double-pane wood windows are standard. Some rooms have wrought iron, New Orleans-style balconies and French doors overlooking Yesler Way, while others have a view of the Puget Sound. Room rates include evening turndown service and a complimentary deluxe continental breakfast.

Fitness facilities are available nearby at the Pure Fitness Health Club. Al Boccalino's, located next door, is rated as the Best Italian restaurant in Seattle, providing room service for lunch and dinner. The Pioneer Square Hotel is the perfect location for wedding parties, receptions, meetings, and family reunions or simply for that romantic weekend get-away.

The many nearby attractions include Seattle's historic Pioneer Square, Safeco Field "Home of the Seattle Mariners," the Stadium Exhibition Center, the new Seahawks Football Stadium, the world famous Pike Place Market, Bell Harbor Cruise Terminal, the Washington State Ferry system and Aquarium, shopping and art galleries, and Seattle's famous restaurants and night life.

Address: 77 Yesler Way, Seattle 98104.
Phone: 206.340.1234 800.800.5514
Fax: 206.467.0707
Email: info@pioneersquare.com
Web site: http://pioneersquare.com
Room Rates: 99–199
Suite Rates: 179–279
No. of Rooms: 72 guestrooms
Attractions: Safeco Field, Seahawks Stadium, Stadium Exhibition Ctr, Fed./County Courthouse, Historic Pioneer Square, Underground, Klondike Gold Rush Museum, Waterfront, Smith Tower, WA State Ferry System, Cruiseship Terminals, Aquarium, Amtrak & Pike Place Market
Services & Amenities: Romance & Honeymoon Packages, Garage/Parking, Car hire, Valet Service, Laundry, Baby-sitting service, Library, Fireplace, Balconies, Individual bathrooms w/hairdryers, In-room climate control, Cable TV, Radio, Comp. continental breakfast, Turndown
Restrictions: Service animals only, 3 Rooms handicap-equipped, Smoking and non-smoking upon request
Concierge: Bellstaff/Front desk
Room Service: Lunch and dinner
Restaurant: Al Boccalino, located just next door, voted as Seattle's Best Italian Restaurant. Room Service is available for Lunch and Dinner. Reservations are suggested.
Bar: Located next door, Pioneer Square Saloon, Noon–2 a.m.
Business Facilities: Boardroom Facilities with DSL Internet, Copiers, Fax, Fax Modems, Voicemail, Dataports, Fed Ex & UPS
Conference Rooms: Executive boardroom w/comp. breakfast and / or beverages
Sports Facilities: Whirlpool, Sauna, Massage, Aerobics, Weight training, Priviledges at Pure Fitness Health Club located two blocks from Hotel
Location: In Historic Downtown Seattle Waterfront, Closest Hotel to Seattle Mariners

MONTVALE HOTEL

Built in 1899 and abandoned in 1974, the 36-room Montvale re-opened in January 2005 as both Spokane's "oldest" and "newest" hotel.

This landmark hotel combines turn of the century architecture with unique furnishings and excellent service—providing guests a comfortable stay while honoring its colorful past. The long forgotten two-story atrium and balcony have been turned into an "urban lodge-like" space. Hotel rooms, lobby and atrium all have free high-speed wireless and network connectivity. Two state-of-the-art conference rooms are available with drop down screens and projectors. Many of the Montvale's suites include flat panel LCD televisions, jetted tubs and fireplaces. In addition to the hotel's European artwork and antiques, Spokane-area artists display their work in the hotel's lobby and two-story atrium.

Located in downtown Spokane's emerging First Avenue arts district, the Montvale Hotel anchors the most popular entertainment area in the city. Rooms offer some of Spokane's best urban vistas overlooking landmarks such as the Fox Theater, the Steam Plant and the Big Easy Concert Hall. The Montvale is surrounded by many nightclubs, restaurants and music venues, including Centerstage, Ella's Supper Club, The Met, and Marilyn's on Monroe.

Deep in the cellar of the hotel, the Catacombs Pub, a European-style restaurant, offers room and catering service for the hotel. Along with Far West Billiards and the Twilight Room, Catacombs offers guests a fun and eventful experience.

Address: 1005 West First Avenue, Spokane 99201.
Phone: 509-747-1919 1-86-MONTVALE
Fax: 509-789-8345
Email: info@montvalehotel.com
Web site: http://www.montvalehotel.com
Room Rates: 145–175
Suite Rates: 275–400
No. of Rooms: 36
No. of Suites: 4
Attractions: The Montvale Hotel is located across the street from the Fox Theatre (Spokane Symphony) and the Met Theater, near Riverfront Park and Riverpark Square (Shopping Area), Financial Buildings, Arts and Entertainment District, Restaurants and Shopping
Services & Amenities: Airport Pickup and Shuttle Service, Valet parking, Complimentary Town car service within the Downtown corridor, Complimentary wireless Internet, Cable TV, Telephone, CD player with radio, Climate Controls, Complimentary Newspapers and Toiletries
Restrictions: No Smoking, No pets, Children welcome, 2 rooms handicap equipped
Concierge: Ask Front Desk
Room Service: 11 a.m.- 11 p.m.
Restaurant: Catacombs Pub features a brick fireplace and historic European flare. Catacombs offers the best in European cuisine with stone-fired thin-crust pizzas, traditional goulash and chicken paprikash.
Bar: Catacombs Pub, 11a.m.–12 a.m.
Business Facilities: E-mail, Copier, Audio-Visual, Fax
Conference Rooms: 2 rooms, capacity 30-40
Sports Facilities: Nearby Fitness Center, Skiing, Sailing, Horseback Riding, Tennis
Location: Downtown–City Center

MARCUS WHITMAN HOTEL & CONFERENCE CENTER

Nestled in the heart of Washington wine country, the Marcus Whitman Hotel & Conference Center provides luxury and tradition in downtown Walla Walla. Within walking distance, guests will find a variety of wine tasting rooms, eclectic shops and sidewalk art.

Opening in 1928, the hotel was completely renovated and restored to its original elegance before reopening in 2001. From the quaint Georgian Room complete with fireplace to the Grand Lobby, guests will enjoy the rich décor and comfortable atmosphere.

Each guestroom is richly appointed in the Renaissance style featuring handcrafted Italian furnishings. Guests may choose between standard rooms in the newer West Wing or luxury suites in the historic Tower.

The Marc Restaurant, located just off the hotel's main lobby, specializes in regional, seasonal fun with Pacific Northwest Cuisine. The Executive Chef and his staff use only the finest quality ingredients to craft show-stopping, taste-tempting meals. Certified Angus Beef, Seasonal Wild Pacific Seafood, Foraged Morels, Artisan Cheeses and the finest products offered by the Walla Walla Valley are incorporated to create an unforgettable dining experience. Guests may choose from an extensive local and regional wine list, both in The Marc and in the adjoining Vineyard Lounge. For a truly unique experience, guests may also schedule a Chef's Table Dinner, where up to eight people can enjoy a meal prepared to their specifications.

With more than 10,000 square feet of event space, the ballrooms of The Marcus Whitman Hotel & Conference Center are the largest and most technologically advanced in Eastern Washington. Guests will find free Wi-Fi access is available throughout all the hotel's public areas including conference rooms, the business center, the restaurant, lounge and Grand Lobby.

Address: Six West Rose, Walla Walla 99362.
Phone: 509-525-2200 866-826-9422
Fax: 509-525-9282
Email: info@marcuswhitmanhotel.com
Web site: http://www.marcuswhitmanhotel.com
Room Rates: 89–134
Suite Rates: 179–254
No. of Rooms: 91
No. of Suites: 16
Attractions: Walla Walla offers a variety of activities including the oldest continuous symphony west of the Mississippi. Visitors will discover quaint art galleries, historic sites and homes, museums, eclectic shops and more than 60 wineries and tastings rooms.
Services & Amenities: Free Wi-Fi access in all public areas, free high-speed Internet access, a business center, fitness room and airport transporation are among the services and amenities offered. A deluxe continental breakfast is available every morning.
Restaurant: The Marc Restaurant offers Angus Filet, white truffle cream & wild mushroom Ragu. Chef Bear Ullman and staff create culinary magic with the freshest products available. Lunch and Dinner.
Bar: Vineyard Lounge–open Monday through Saturday at 5 p.m.
Business Facilities: Business center with free Wi-Fi access, laptop hookups, PCs, copy and fax capabilities.
Conference Rooms: More than 10,000 square feet of conference space.
Sports Facilities: Three 18-hole golf courses nearby.
Location: Downtown

SUN MOUNTAIN LODGE

Tucked high on the eastern slope of Washington's North Cascades, the Methow Valley today comprises one of the largest Nordic ski centers in North America. Sun Mountain Lodge sits smack in the middle of the ski trail system, with its 175 kilometers of groomed trails.

The lodge itself consists of three sections: The main lodge, and the Gardner building and the Mt. Robinson buildings just next door. All of these buildings feature huge log beams similar to what is found in a classical national park lodge. All of the logs and woodwork have been sandblasted and polished to a light, sunny looking tint. The Mt. Robinson guestrooms feature gas fireplaces, private decks, jetted tubs, stocked refreshment centers and spectacular views.

The rooms feature Northwest cane furniture, using alder and willow canes bent into the shapes of headboards, chairs and couches.

The dining room is one of only four restaurants in Washington to get a four-diamond rating from AAA. Meals are now by Executive Chef Kevin Kennedy, and feature local and regional specialties such as Coriander Crusted Chinook Salmon and Broiled Tenderloin of Washington State Beef. Children's menus available.

The Northwest's oldest and largest cross-country ski resort, Sun Mountain offers scenic and exhilarating skiing. The pro staff gives individual or group lessons for all levels of skate skiing, track and telemark techniques. Rental equipment and retail gear are available.

Address: 604 Patterson Lake Road, PO Box 1000, Winthrop 98862.
Phone: 509-996-2211 800-572-0493
Fax: 509-996-3133
Email: sunmtn@methow.com
Web site: http://www.sunmountainlodge.com
Room Rates: 170–350
Suite Rates: 325–650
No. of Rooms: 91
No. of Suites: 6
Credit Cards: Most Credit Cards accepted
Attractions: Downtown Winthrop "Old West" theme town, North Cascades National Park
Services & Amenities: Gift shop, TV lounge, Baby-sitting service, Card/game area, Library, Fireplaces, Balconies in some units, Individual climate controls, Air conditioning, Complimentary toiletries
Restrictions: 2 night minimum stay on weekends, Children welcome and under 12 free with parents, No pets allowed
Concierge: 8 a.m.-8 p.m.
Room Service: 7 a.m.-10 p.m.
Restaurant: Sun Mountain Lodge Dining Room, 7:30 a.m.-9 p.m., Wolf Creek Bar & Grill, deck featuring outdoor dining
Bar: Wolf Creek Bar & Grill, 2–11 p.m.
Business Facilities: Copiers, Audio-visual
Conference Rooms: 6 rooms, capacity 150
Sports Facilities: Swimming pool, Whirlpool, Weight training, Riding, x-country ski, Biking, Fishing, Golf, River rafti
Spa Services: New day spa & wellness center with massages, reflexology, facials, manicures, pedicures, haircare
Location: Sun Mountain

BLENNERHASSETT HOTEL

From the elegant rooms and fine dining to unprecedented hospitality and state-of-the-art technology, The Blennerhassett provides business and leisure travelers an excellent choice of accommodations and facilities. Every detail has been meticulously set in place to provide our guests with an experience that can only be found at The Blennerhassett.

With a variety of classically designed European-style rooms and suites, The Blennerhassett offers something for both business and leisure travelers. Every detail has been attended to in anticipation of your stay with us. A daily newspaper and ice delivered to your room are standard fare, with our courteous staff attending to guests with an elevated standard of service rarely found in today's fast-paced world. The spectacular rooms feature rich, jewel-toned fabrics, while the bedding is triple-sheeted, along with a choice of down or synthetic pillows to meet your preference. The Blennerhassett is the perfect blend of old-world charm and modern convenience with high-speed, truly wireless, broadband Internet access throughout the hotel, and state-of-the-art motion sensors that control the heating and air conditioning when you enter the room and turn closets lights on and off.

Address: Fourth & Market St, Parkersburg 26101.
Phone: 304-422-3131 800-678-8946
Fax: 304-485-0267
Email: kswisher@theblennerhassett.com
Web site: http://www.theblennerhassett.com
Room Rates: 75–250
Suite Rates: 99–250
No. of Rooms: 91
No. of Suites: 14
Credit Cards: Most Credit Cards accepted
Attractions: Blennerhassett Island Historical State Park, Blennerhassett Museum, Oil & Gas Museum, Smoot Theater, Actors' Guild, TransAllegheny Books Historic District Walking Tour, Shopping, Fenton Glass, Lee Middleton Doll Factory, Holl's Swiss Chocolatier
Concierge: Ms. Rachel Laver
Room Service: Yes
Bar: Full-Service Bar
Conference Rooms: 5
Location: Downtown

THE WASHINGTON HOUSE INN

The Washington House Inn was Cedarburg's first inn, built in 1846 on this site. In 1886, the present Victorian cream-city brick building replaced the original structure. The Washington House existed as a hotel until the 1920s when it was converted into offices and apartments. In 1983 its ownership changed hands and work began to restore the Washington House to its original use as an inn. The building is now listed on the National Register of Historic Places.

The romance of country Victorian style is captivating as one enters the Washington House Inn, the ultimate in bed and breakfast accommodations. A lovely collection of antique Victorian furniture and a marble-trimmed fireplace offer a warm reception. Tastefully appointed, the comfortable, elegant guestrooms feature antiques, cozy down quilts, whirlpools, fireplaces and fresh-cut flowers.

Each evening guests may join one another for a complimentary wine and cheese social hour, and relax in front of a cheery fire prior to dining at one of the excellent Cedarburg restaurants. The innkeeper will make dinner reservations at a restaurant of your choice.

A delicious continental breakfast is served each morning in the warm gathering room. Homemade muffins, cakes and breads are baked in the Inn's kitchen using recipes from an authentic turn-of-the-century Cedarburg cookbook. Fresh fruit, cereal, freshly squeezed juices, and a fine selection of tea and coffee are also offered.

The staff is friendly and helpful, with attention to detail their foremost concern.

Address: W62 N573 Washington Ave, Cedarburg 53012.
Phone: 262-375-3550 800-554-4717
Fax: 262-375-9422
Email: whinn@execpc.com
Web site: http:// www.washingtonhouseinn.com
Room Rates: 95–235
Suite Rates: 165–235
No. of Rooms: 34
No. of Suites: 11
Credit Cards: Visa
Attractions: Unique shops, Many historic buildings, Cedar Creek Settlement, Cedar Creek Winery, Cedar Creek Park
Services & Amenities: Gathering room, Complimentary wine & cheese social hour each evening, In-room cable TV/VCR, Telephones, Radios, Individual heat & A/C control, Some rooms with whirlpool baths & fireplaces, Complimentary toiletries & newspaper, Gift Certificates available
Restrictions: No pets allowed, Handicapped facilities & elevator available
Concierge: Innkeeper
Restaurant: Walking distance to restaurants
Business Facilities: Copier, Audio-Visual, Fax
Conference Rooms: 1 room
Sports Facilities: Whirlpool, Sauna, Nearby golf, skiing and horseback riding
Location: Downtown Cedarburg, 20 miles north of Milwaukee, Nearest airport–Mitchell

THE GENEVA INN

There's more to The Geneva than a breathtaking view of Geneva Lake. Its charming European elegance is inviting and comfortable. Maybe it's the presence of fine craftsmanship in every architectural detail. Or the personal touches that make you feel extraordinary: thick fluffy bathrobes, chocolates at turndown, your own private in-room bar, oversized vintage or whirlpool baths, and private balconies. All this and more await the discerning traveler.

The Geneva Inn is the only property located directly on the shores of Geneva Lake—a premier recreation area in Wisconsin. Guests will find seclusion and uncommon comfort in the peaceful atmosphere of this traditional English Inn fashioned after the grand old country-house hotels. Common areas of the Inn include a three-story atrium with raised hearth fireplace, piano lounge, landscaped terrace and patio. Boat owners can tie up at the Inn's private marina.

Guestrooms and suites are tastefully decorated in country manor-style, interspersed with antiques. Most rooms include a whirlpool or vintage bath and private balcony, many with outstanding lake views. Beds range from luxurious four-post kings to queens and doubles. Amenities include televisions with video players (complimentary classical videos), cable, fully stocked private bar refrigerators, early morning coffee on each floor, and exclusive use of the Inn's exercise facility. Guests are treated to a complimentary, continental buffet breakfast, including fresh fruit and bakery items, delicious meats and cheeses, rich coffee and fragrant teas.

No matter how you spend your day, return to The Geneva Inn's renowned Grandview Restaurant for a romantic, candlelight dinner featuring distinctive American Contemporary cuisine. Every table offers a scenic vista of Geneva Lake through large panoramic windows. Guests enjoy spectacular sunsets with quiet, unobtrusive service and softly played piano classics.

The Geneva Inn is a getaway unlike any other. Guests will find the beautiful surroundings mesmerizing and relaxing. Service and complete attention to detail stand out, which creates an atmosphere that caters to guests' needs.

Address: N2009 S. Lake Shore Dr, Lake Geneva 53147.
Phone: 262-248-5680 800-441-5881
Fax: 262-248-5685
Email: luxury@genevainn.com
Web site: http://www.genevainn.com
Room Rates: 155–275
Suite Rates: 375
No. of Rooms: 33
No. of Suites: 4
Credit Cards: Visa
Attractions: Inland lake resort area, Boat excursions on lake, Quaint shops in downtown, Antiques
Services & Amenities: Valet service, Parking, Gift shop, Laundry, Baby-sitting service, Cable TV/VCR, Radio, Private in-room bar, Individual heat & air conditioning control, Robes, Whirlpool, Complimentary toiletries, Weekday newspaper (M-F) & Continental buffet breakfast
Restrictions: No pets allowed, 4 rooms with handicap access
Concierge: 24 hours
Restaurant: The Grandview Restaurant. Serving Lunch, Early Dinner and Dinner daily. Weekend Champagne Brunch served Saturday & Sunday.
Bar: The Grandview Lounge
Business Facilities: Full-scale conference facilities, Copiers, Audio-visual
Conference Rooms: 2 rooms, capacity 40-80
Sports Facilities: Exercise Room, Individual whirlpools, Golf, Skiing, Riding, Tennis nearby
Location: Linn Township–residential

THE BROWNSTONE INN

Experience the elegance of yesterday in this 1907 Brownstone Inn. The architecture of this Inn with its stain glass, marble, hand carved fireplaces, mahogany panelling, arched ceilings with sculptured or hand painted design, grand staircase and original brass light fixtures will capture your imagination of years gone by. The grandeur of the ballroom with stage or the mystique of the billiard room with stone fireplace will take you off to a Cinderella dance or bring out the competitiveness in you. Your warmth and comfort are embraced with sumptuous four poster beds, double whirlpool baths, soothing showers and heated tile floors. Curl up in front of one of the many fireplaces or sit out on several of the airing porches with a fine book. The gardens await your leisurely afternoon strolls or awake the morning with a fresh cup of coffee while enjoying the beauty of the wonderful continental breakfast which may be brought to your room upon request. Lake Michigan with its never ending sand beaches, array of shops, fine restaurants, theater, hiking, sport fishing, kayaking and world class golf are just a short thought away. Home to the 2004 PGA Championship the Pete Dye courses of Whistling Straits, Irish, River and Meadows will keep you coming back for more or enjoy the forever challenging Jack Nicklaus Signature Course called the "Bull" for a unforgettable experience. Corporate gatherings, cocktail parties, weddings and special events are all welcome here at the Inn. Enjoy a day at our affiliated spa with many packages to choose from. Come and experience yesteryear here at the Brownstone Inn.

Address: 1227 North 7th Street, Sheboygan 53081.
Phone: 1-920-451-0644 1-877-279-6786
Fax: 1-920-457-3426
Email: brwnstninn@aol.com
Web site: http://www.brownstoneinn.com
Room Rates: 150–300
Suite Rate: 200
No. of Rooms: 6
No. of Suites: 1
Credit Cards: Visa
Attractions: World Class Golf of Whistling Straits, Irish, River or Meadows, The Bull; Sport Fishing, Fine Restaurants, shops of all kinds, hiking, biking, kayaking, Kohler Art Museum, Sailing, Kettle Morain and Terry Andrea Parks, Road America
Services & Amenities: Double Whirlpool baths, showers with body sprayers, four poster and sleigh beds, porches, fireplaces, billiards, ballroom, baby grand player piano, gardens, breakfast, high speed Internet, refreshments, TV, Telephone, Ballroom, conference rooms
Restrictions: Inappropriate for Children under 16, No Smoking, No Pets
Concierge: Yes
Room Service: Yes
Restaurant: Many award-winning restaurants throughout the area
Bar: No, free wine & beer
Business Facilities: Yes, telephones, high-speed Internet
Conference Rooms: Big and small, audio visual
Sports Facilities: No
Spa Services: Several packages for our affiliated spa
Location: 1227 North 7th St., Sheboygan, WI 53081

AMANGANI

Amangani, near Jackson Hole, Wyoming, means "peaceful home." The 40-suite, three-story resort is set on the cliff-edge of a butte in an all-but-seamless melding with the land and the mountains that ring it. Its hipped roof, crafted of cedar shakes and sod, flows like a natural outcropping. Amangani makes extensive use of Oklahoma sandstone, Pacific redwood, and Douglas fir and cedar also lend shape and style to the resort.

Amanresort's accommodations include 29 superior suites, six deluxe suites and four Amangani Suites and one Grand Teton Suite. All suites are air-conditioned and include a bedroom/living room and a spacious bedroom/dressing room. The living area consists of a king-size, platform bed and a rock-and-patined-metal fireplace. There's also a mini-bar, CD player, TV/VCR and two-line phone with high speed Internet connection. A deep soaking tub with a window view highlights the large bathroom/dressing area.

Amangani's Health Center emphasizes the individual guest experience in its two exercise studios, four treatment rooms and separate steam rooms for men and women. A variety of one-on-one programs are offered in the exercise salon, including aerobics, restorative yoga and meditation.

Amangani's year-round outdoor swimming/lap pool is finished in frost-colored quartzite tiles and linked to a whirlpool. There are also tennis courts, an equestrian center and Nordic center nearby. Amangani is located at the southern end of the Greater Yellowstone Ecosystem, a huge expanse of mountain and meadow, sage flats and river bottoms, national forests, wildlife refuges and two National Parks—Grand Teton and Yellowstone. Within this rich and varied ecosystem, activities are all but unlimited.

The Grill is open for breakfast, lunch and dinner and specializes in steaks, chops, seafood and regional produced organic foods. The Zinc Bar is defined by rugged sandstone columns and an intimate, window-side setting.

The Amangani, luxury and comfort situated in a wild and beautiful landscape.

Address: 1535 N East Butte Rd, Jackson Hole 83001
Phone: 307-734-7333
877-734-7333
Fax: 307-734-7332
Email: amangani@amanresorts.com
Web site: http://www.amanresorts.com/gani_m.html
Suite Rates: 700–1,200++
No. of Suites: 40
Attractions: Mountain biking, Hiking, Hot air ballooning, Excursions, National Elk Refuge, Yellowstone National Park, The Grand Tetons, The Gros Ventre Range, Flat Creek, Blacktail Butte, Jackson Hole, Snake River Range, Grand Teton National Park, The Gallery
Services & Amenities: Private airport transfer, Parking, Barber/Beauty shop, Gift shop, House doctor, A/C, Library, Balconies/terraces, Fireplace, Minibar, CD player, TV/VCR, Two-line phone, High-speed Internet, Mountain & valley views, Twin vanities, Full-length mirror
Restrictions: 2 rooms handicap equipped, Children welcome, No pets allowed
Concierge: 24 hours
Room Service: 6 a.m.–10 p.m.
Restaurant: The Grill—6 a.m.–10 p.m.
Bar: Zinc Bar, open daily until 12 a.m.
Business Facilities: Special Occasion Room, E-mail, Copiers, Fax, Modems
Sports Facilities: Swimming pool, Health center, Tennis & skiing, Aerobics, Yoga, Meditation classes, Massage, Spring C
Location: Twenty minutes from Jackson Hole Airport

LOST CREEK RANCH

Lost Creek Ranch & Spa is a beautiful, privately owned guest ranch centrally located in Jackson Hole, Wyoming, bordered by the Grand Teton National Park and the Bridger-Teton National Forest. This unique piece of property boasts one of the best locations in Jackson Hole, surrounded by over 4 million acres of public lands and situated at the base of the majestic Teton Mountain Range. The Ranch offers an ideal setting for outdoor adventure with miles of horseback riding and hiking trails leading out from the ranch. The days are warm, the nights are cool, and the air is clear and invigorating.

The lodge and cabins, for which the Ranch is famous, reflect quality and comfort with distinctive furnishings and décor. Impressive features of the 6,000 square foot rustic lodge are the spectacular living room and the spacious dining room, both with breathtaking views of the Grand Teton. The cabins are designed to meet the highest accommodation standards with a western flair and to ensure a warm welcome for each guest.

Guests choose from a variety of small group activities while at the ranch. Wranglers lead horseback trips into wilderness areas of unbelievable solitude and beauty, and an expert guide takes the guests floating on the meandering Snake River where wildlife is abundant. Sightseeing trips into Yellowstone National Park are led by knowledgeable guides. Guided fly-fishing trips and golf can be arranged for an additional charge.

For relaxation, the lodge deck is the perfect place to absorb the ever-changing panorama of the Grand Teton and the Jackson Hole valley. For those guests wanting to be further pampered after enjoying the great outdoors, the Spa provides relaxing body and skin treatments to nourish the mind and body for an additional charge. The steam, sauna, aerobics and weight rooms are open to all guests. Cardio machines are located on the covered deck overlooking the Tetons and daily yoga and pilates classes are available to all guests.

Not many places boast incredible scenery, indigenous wildlife, real cowboys and cowgirls and luxurious accommodations all in one location. One that does is the world-class resort, Lost Creek Ranch and Spa.

Address: PO Box 95RGH, Moose 83012.
Phone: 307-733-3435
Fax: 307-733-1954
Email: ranch@lostcreek.com
Web site: http://www.lostcreek.com
Suite Rates: 5,840–13,710/wk
No. of Suites: 10
Credit Cards: Most Credit Cards accepted
Attractions: Grand Teton and Yellowstone National Parks, Jackson Hole Galleries and Shopping, Jackson Hole Rodeo, National Elk Refuge, National Museum of Wildlife Art, Snake River, Wildlife, Scenery.
Services & Amenities: Airport pick-up, Fireplaces, Complimentary newspaper, Decks, Radio, Individual Heat Control, Full service spa, Gift shop, Beauty salon, Laundry, Parking, Game area, Billiards room, Limited babysitting, Complimentary toiletries, In-room coffee service.
Restrictions: No pets
Restaurant: Lost Creek Ranch 7:30-9 a.m., 12:30-1:30 p.m., 7 p.m
Bar: Mixers & Set-ups–beer & wine at dinner
Business Facilities: Message center, E-mail, Fax, High-speed and wireless Internet
Sports Facilities: Horseback riding, Hiking, Scenic float trips, Skeet range, Tennis, Full Service Spa, Fitness & Pool
Spa Services: Wyoming-sized hot tub, Sauna, Spa Treatments, Aerobics, Weight training, Yoga, Pilates, Personal Training, Youth Programs, Nearby Guided Fly-Fishing and Golf
Location: At the base of the Grand Tetons in Jackson Hole, WY

HOTEL HERITAGE

Once built as a private mansion in 1869, and later in the hands of bankers, this magnificent 19th century Classical building has been renovated and converted into a fine 4 star luxury hotel.

The Hotel Heritage offers its guests elegant, stylish rooms, all characterized by individual decoration, nice soft furnishings, and well appointed bathrooms with all the modern amenities. The Hotel has 4 suites with marble bathrooms with Jacuzzi and seperate shower, the rooms overlooking the unique city skyline of Bruges.

The Hotel offers a pleasant welcoming lounge with bar. And, although the Hotel has no restaurant, a splendid buffet breakfast is served in the charming 1869 room, which reflects the glorious past of the house.

This four-star hotel has many attractive features, such as a health center with sauna, Turkish steambath, relaxation area and solarium, and a fitness room installed in a marvellous 14th Century cellar. All guests get a personal welcome and a first class personal service. In the attractive lounge, with open fire and decorated with Italian fabrics, guests can relax for afternoon tea or coffee, or get their pre-dinner drinks.

Address: Niklaas Desparsstraat 11, Brugge 8000
Phone: 32-(0)50-444-444
Fax: 32-(0)50-444-440
Email: info@hotel-heritage.com
Web site: http://www.hotel-heritage.com
Room Rates: € 140–227
Suite Rates: € 322–385
No. of Rooms: 20.
No. of Suites: 4.
Credit Cards: Visa
Attractions: Cozy restaurants, Interesting museums, Elegant shops, Romantic carriage rides, Boat rides on Brugge's famous canals, Chocolate tasting
Services & Amenities: Private baths, Hairdryer, Cosmetic mirror, Television, Minibar, 2 direct dial telephones, Safe, Trouser press and ironing facilities, PC and modem line, Air conditioning, Buffet breakfast, Wireless-Internet access (Wi-Fi), DVD-&CD player in all rooms
Restrictions: Sorry, no pets allowed, no handicap-equipped rooms, Adults only
Concierge: 7 am – 11 pm
Room Service: 24 hours
Restaurant: The Hotel has no restaurant, but there is a large choice of fine restaurants in the near vicinity of the hotel (walking distance).
Bar: Lounge with bar – 7 a.m. – 1 a.m.
Business Facilities: Seminar and business meeting facilities
Sports Facilities: Health center (small charge) with sauna and Turkish steambath and Sunbed. Fitness center free.
Spa Facilities: The Hotel is also equipped with a superb health center with sauna and hammam (turkish steambath). You can also get a nice tan on the sunbed. Get in shape in the superbly equipped fitness room.
Location: In the heart of medieval Bruges.

WICKANINNISH INN & POINTE RESTAURANT

Located on Vancouver Island's magnificently rugged West Coast, the Wickaninnish Inn is minutes from the picturesque township of Tofino. At the gateway to Pacific Rim National Park Reserve and the renowned beauty of Clayoquot Sound, the Inn is situated on a rocky promontory at the western most point of Chesterman Beach.

The first thing guests notice as they enter every one of the 75 spacious guestrooms and suites is the awe-inspiring ocean and beach to ocean views, revealed by floor to ceiling picture windows. In keeping with the Inn's commitment to the environment, the furniture has been fashioned from recycled old growth fir, western red cedar and driftwood. The textures found in nature are reflected in the wool sisal carpet, natural stone tile and rough hewn cedar mantelpieces. Custom-made armoires and desks, while rustic in appearance, are finished with top quality hand forged hardware. Completing the collection, each room features a handmade driftwood chair, individually numbered by the artist, Maxwell Newhouse.

As guests explore their rooms, they'll discover that every need has been anticipated—from the interesting book collection, binoculars, private bar, CD clock radio, writing desk, microwave, coffee maker, to the large screen television in the armoire, and a down duvet on the king or queen-sized bed. Enjoy a hot bath in the oversized soaker tub enhanced by aromatherapy bath salts. Relax, in comfortable armchairs, by the fireplace in terry bathrobes to read a good book or simply watch nature unfold outside the window.

Tofino is an intriguing mix of wide sandy beaches and old growth forests, fishing boats and whale-watching zodiacs, loggers and surfers, casual eateries and eclectic fine dining.

The award-winning Pointe Restaurant and Chef Andrew Springett showcase fresh coastal foods and farm-fresh ingredients. Savor the Foie Gras & Portobello Mushroom Stuffed Pheasant Breast with a Yam & Sun-dried Cherry Ratatouille. And for dessert, splurge with the White Chocolate & Basil Pyramid with Mandarin Caramel Sauce. Delicious!

For those seeking paradise, look no further than the Wickaninnish Inn.

Address: P.O. Box 250, Tofino, BC V0R 2ZO
Phone: 250 725-3100
800 333-4604
Fax: 250 725-3110
Email: info@wickinn.com
Web site: http://www.wickinn.com
Room Rates: 155–365 US $
Suite Rates: 225–1,050 US $
No. of Rooms: 75
No. of Suites: 12
Attractions: Walk Chesterman Beach (1½ miles), Winter storm watching, Beachcombing, Whale watching, Hot Springs Cove, Rain Forest walks, Kayaking, Bird watching, Hike in the National Park, Fly fishing, Salmon fishing, Hot Springs, Surfing.
Services & Amenities: Ancient Cedars Spa, Ocean views, Fireplaces, Private balconies, Down duvets, Oversize soaker tubs, Terry robes, Aromatherapy bath products, Private bar, Microwave, Coffee maker, CD clock radio, Beach, Guided Nature Walks, Library,
Restrictions: Limited number of pet allowed rooms available, Minimum stay required on weekends and holidays
Concierge: 9 a.m.-5 p.m.
Room Service: Breakfast only
Restaurant: Renowned for award winning Cuisine The Pointe Restaurant is open for breakfast 8 – 11 a.m., lunch 11:30 a.m.-2 p.m., dinner 5 – 9 p.m.
Bar: On the Rocks Bar and Lounge – 11 a.m.-11 p.m., lounge menu 2 -9 p.m.
Business Facilities: 2-line access in guestrooms, Copier, Currency exchange, Audio-visual, VCR & monitor, built-in screen
Conference Rooms: 720' meeting/banquet room – cap. 80; 450' boardroom – cap 10

WEDGEWOOD HOTEL

The Wedgewood Hotel & Spa, in the heart of downtown Vancouver's fashionable Robson Square, owes its European elegance to Greek-born owner Eleni Skalbania.

Skalbania's attention to detail is one of the reasons this four diamond property is so popular. And *Condé Nast Traveler* agreed and rated the Wedgewood on the Gold List of Hotels for 2004, not to mention the recently awarded "Best Hotel in Vancouver" by *Travel & Leisure* magazine 2004, as well as Best Value Hotel "No.1 in Canada" & "5th in the World" The public areas exude warmth from the personal collections of antiques and works of art that Skalbania brought from her home. To complement her private collections, she commissioned craftsmen to build custom-designed furniture. From the elegant lobby, to the award-winning restaurant Bacchus, to the Garden Terrace, it's impossible not to feel at ease, and at home, at the Wedgewood. But home was never like this.

Guestrooms overlook either the Robson Square gardens or mountain or city views. Whether visitors are on their honeymoon, a romantic getaway, or a business trip, they can choose accommodations ranging from Executive rooms to One Bedroom, Wedgewood, and Penthouse Suites. While all rooms include balconies, top quality bedding with fluffy duvets, luxurious terry bath-robes, turndown service with homemade cookies and bottled water, 24-hour room service, a box of Belgian truffles, in-room safes, and air conditioning, the suites go above and beyond even these outstanding amenities. Including his & hers bathrooms complete with Jacuzzi tub and Roman Marble Stand up Shower.

Guests shouldn't expect to spend all their time in the comfort of their rooms, though. Not with the Four Diamond Award-winning Bacchus Restaurant at the Wedgewood ready to satisfy their every culinary need. Relax, refresh and renew your mind, body and spirit at the new Spa and Fitness Centre at the Wedgewood Hotel. A wonderful array of rejuvenating body and soul treatments await guests and visitors in this luxuriously serene setting.

Address: 845 Hornby St, Vancouver, BC V6Z 1V1
Phone: 604-689-7777
800-663-0666
Fax: 604-608-5348
Email: reservations@wedgewoodhotel.com
Web site: http://www.wedgewoodhotel.com
Room Rates: 151–261 US $
Suite Rates: 317–468 US $
No. of Rooms: 83
No. of Suites: 42
Credit Cards: Most Credit Cards accepted
Attractions: Elegant shops at Robson Street, Pacific Centre, Granville Island, Stanley Park, Robson Square, Vancouver Art Gallery, Orpheum hosts Vancouver Symphony Orchestra (VSO), Theaters
Services & Amenities: Airport limo service, Garage, Valet, Currency exchange, Baby-sitting service, Laundry, Cable TV, Internet, Radio, Iron, Some fireplaces/wet bars, Indv. climate control, Comp. shoeshine, paper, robe, coffee/tea, Belgian truffles, Portable phones, Balconies
Restrictions: No pets allowed, Smoke-free environment, 1 room handicap equipped
Concierge: Available
Room Service: 24 hours
Restaurant: The Bacchus Restaurant – Modern French cuisine, exceptional Weekend Brunch, and Traditional Afternoon Tea. Live entertainment nightly.
Bar: The Bacchus Lounge, Live entertainment Nightly Monday-Saturday, Hours 6:30 a.m.
Business Facilities: 2 line phones w/dataports, Complete business center, Copiers, Audio-visual, Fax
Conference Rooms: capacity 80
Sports Facilities: Fitness Centre with Eucalyptus Steam Room
Spa Facilities: The Spa at the Wedgewood – New Spa and Fitness Centre.Italian marble steam room, pleasure, wellness and relaxation packages are available.

ABIGAIL'S HOTEL

Abigail's Hotel, built in the 1930's, has been lovingly restored as Victoria's finest Bed and Breakfast Inn. This boutique hotel offers the perfect blend of old world charm and modern conveniences. Abigail's is a downtown historic property located just three blocks from beautiful downtown Victoria and the lively Inner Harbour. Wood-burning fireplaces and jetted tubs are featured in many of the rooms. Aveda bath amenities, plush Turkish Cotton towels, luxurious robes, fresh flowers, you may never want to leave your room!

The open kitchen in the dining room allows guests to watch the chef create their three-course gourmet breakfast from the finest ingredients around the Pacific Northwest. This sumptuous breakfast is included with every stay. In the evening Social Hour is in the cozy fireside Library with complimentary refreshments before venturing out for dinner. The friendly staff has a multitude of suggestions for dining within minutes of the hotel.

It is a pleasant walk to many of the city's offerings, from the museums and galleries and shops to a variety of world-class restaurants. Abigail's Hotel offers a variety of getaway ideas such as their Spa packages or an all day adventure into the wine country of Vancouver Island for a Wine Tasting Getaway.

Victoria offers an eclectic mix of old world traditions and new world adventures. Try afternoon tea at one of many teahouses; visit the famous Butchart Gardens for a stroll through an astounding landscape of colour. Victoria also has great diversity in shopping with a fine collection of antique shops along 'Antique Row' on Fort Street. A romantic? Try taking a horse-drawn carriage for a tour of the city or the Dallas waterway. Victoria also features world-class golf. Open year round, some of the most beautiful scenery around can be enjoyed from several of Victoria's fine courses. For the more adventurous there is whale watching, sailing, kayaking or hiking. What ever your taste Victoria has plenty to offer.

Abigail's Hotel continues to receive accolades, awarded "Five Stars" by *Canada Select* for the sixth year in a row. *Frommer's 2004* has named Abigail's as "Victoria's Best Small Hotel." The third consecutive year for this honor! Victoria News Group readers' poll named this charming property "#1 B&B—Best of the City" from 2000–2004.

Address: 906 McClure St, Victoria, BC V8V 3E7
Phone: 250-388-5363
800-561-6565
Fax: 250-388-7787
Email: innkeeper@abigailshotel.com
Web site: http://www.abigailshotel.com
Room Rates: 115–310 US $
No. of Rooms: 23
No. of Suites: 0
Attractions: Victoria is host to a large variety of activities including: Butchart Gardens, Royal BC Museum, Royal London Wax Museum, Greater Victoria Art Gallery and Craigdarroch Castle, Whale Watching, Golfing, Kyaking, Fishing, Hiking, and Cycling.
Services & Amenities: Abigail's provides a 24 hour Front Desk and Concierge service, every evening guests are invited to the Library for refreshments, we stock complimentary bottled water in-room daily and Welcome Cookies await your arrival. Free parking is also available.
Restrictions: Adult oriented, no elevators and TV's only in some rooms
Concierge: Available 24 hours
Room Service: Limited
Restaurant: Abigail's Hotel provides a decadent three course gourmet breakfast included in the room rates. Abigail's has partnered with a few amazing local restaurants for packages or preferred service.
Spa Facilities: Abigail's has partnered with a local spa to provide packages or preferred services. Check out our Romantic Spa Package or the Couples Luxury Spa Retreat.
Location: Downtown, Inner Harbour

VICTORIA REGENT HOTEL

The Victoria Regent Hotel offers a choice of recently redecorated spacious rooms with king-size beds and a view of "Old Town" Victoria, or newly renovated large one- and two-bedroom luxury apartment-style suites overlooking Victoria's picturesque Inner Harbour. The suites have fully-equipped kitchens, dining areas, gracious living rooms, balcony and separate bedroom(s), each with its own ensuite bathroom.

Complimentary services include Continental Breakfast, high speed Internet in all rooms, in-room coffee, morning newspaper, secured underground parking, passes to a nearby fitness center, and movie and sports channels. Other services include coin-operated laundry facilities, business center, free Internet access and computer use in lobby and valet service. Whale-watching tours depart daily from the waterfront wharf, and float plane terminals with service to Vancouver are within walking distance. Discounted moorage rates are also available for Regent guests.

The Water's Edge Cafe offers complimentary continental breakfast buffet daily. Enjoy a bowl of fresh fruit, assorted homemade muffins and pastries, coffee and juice while enjoying the friendly service and Inner Harbour activities at the waterfront cafe.

The choice location allows guests to easily explore downtown Victoria. Shops, theatres, the world-renowned Royal British Columbia Museum, the conference center and the city's year-round attractions are all within walking distance.

Address: 1234 Wharf St, Victoria, BC V8W 3H9
Phone: 250-386-2211
800-663-7472
Fax: 250-386-2622
Email: info@victoriaregent.com
Web site: http://www.victoriaregent.com
Room Rates: 109–169 US $
Suite Rates: 169–329 US $
No. of Rooms: 10
No. of Suites: 36
Attractions: Victoria is home to the Royal BC Museum featuring "Tibet: Mountains and Valleys, Castles and Tents" and "Living Land, Living Sea" beginning March 2005. Don't miss the world famous Butchart Gardens – a horticultural dream world.
Services & Amenities: Valet service, Garage & parking, Laundry service, Baby-sitting service, Balconies, Cable TV, Telephones, Wet bar, Kitchen in suites, Some fireplaces & whirlpool baths, Sundries available at the front desk
Restrictions: No pets allowed, Children up to age sixteen free with parents, Two rooms equipped for handicapped
Concierge: 7 a.m.-11 p.m.
Room Service: 7 a.m.-11 a.m.
Restaurant: Water's Edge Cafe, 7 a.m.-11 a.m., Catered receptions for up to 40 people by prior arrangement Room Service also available at lunch and dinner from "Bravo on Wharf" restaurant.
Business Facilities: Business Center, Admin. assistance, Copiers, Audio-Visual, Fax, Internet
Conference Rooms: 2 rooms, capacity 40, Theatre
Sports Facilities: Guest priviledges at the Y.M.C.A.
Spa Facilities: We offer a variety of spa treatments in the comfort of your own suite.
Location: On Vancouver Island in the heart of Downtown Victoria, Overlooking harbour

ROSEWOOD VICTORIA INN

A charming Inn located only two blocks from Victoria's Inner Harbour and three blocks from the U. S. Ferry Terminals, the Rosewood Victoria Inn boasts the best location in Victoria. A short walk to the Royal British Columbia Museum, Beacon Hill Park, downtown shopping, shuttle bus to Butchart Gardens, the Empress Hotel, whale watching expeditions and a variety of tours.

The Inn is decorated in an English Country motif. Each room is unique with warm colors, rich wallpapers, antique furniture, luxurious goose down duvet's and luxury linens. All rooms have a sitting area, private bathroom, TV and telephone. Most rooms have a balcony or patio. Special occasion suites are available with fireplaces and double soaker tubs. Some rooms have four poster beds, either King or Queen size, and twins for those who prefer to have their own bed.

An English country Inn with your comfort in mind. Guests are encouraged to enjoy the living room library where they can select a book and read by the fire.

Rosewood Victoria Inn is renown for its breakfasts which are complimentary and are served each morning in the large plant-filled conservatory.

The Rosewood Victoria Inn is a unique small hotel where fine art and unparalled comfort are combined to create an atmosphere of casual elegance for their guests enjoyment.

Address: 595 Michigan St, Victoria, BC V8V 1S7
Phone: 250-384-6644
1-866-986-2222
Fax: 250-384-6117
Email: rvi@aviawest.com
Web site: http://www.rosewoodvictoria.com
Room Rates: 125–250 US $
No. of Rooms: 17
No. of Suites: 0
Credit Cards: Visa
Attractions: 2 blocks from Victoria Inner Harbour, Parliament Building and Royal B.C. Museum, Walking distance to U.S. Ferries, Major tourist attractions
Services & Amenities: Parking, Library, Fireplaces, Balconies, Cable TV, Telephones, Whirlpool bath, Complimentary: toiletries, breakfast in the conservatory amongst plants, Guest lounge with Internet access and games room.
Restrictions: One room equipped for handicapped, No pets allowed, Children over 10 years of age welcome
Location: 2 blocks from downtown, 20 kilometers from airport

LA PINSONNIERE

Set amidst Quebec's majestic Laurentian Mountains, La Pinson-niere is an oasis of calm and elegance with a European flair. Nestled among ancient cedars, high above the broad St. Lawrence River, the inn provides a sweeping view of the gorgeous Charlevoix region, a treasured UNESCO World Biosphere Reserve. The graceful lines of this French country manor only hint at the luxury guests will discover inside. From the moment you enter the refined reception lobby, as you sip a "kir maison" in the stylish bar or relax in front of the stone fireplace in the sophisti-cated warmth of the living room, you will be welcomed and pam-pered by discrete, impeccably trained staff.

Many of La Pinsonniere's spacious guestrooms feature queen- or king-sized beds, oversized whirlpool bathtubs, fireplaces and views of the St. Lawrence or the charming village of Cap-a-L'Aigle. Some of the grand deluxe rooms enjoy private access to the main terrace, while others boast a private sauna or turret. And then, there is Room 312! This premium deluxe suite has a king-sized bed, fireplace, sofa-bed, oversized whirlpool, sauna, multi-jet shower, a small private balcony and a stunning view of the water. All rooms include private bathrooms, hair dryer, luxurious terry-cloth robes, duvets, cable television, ceiling fans and air-condi-tioners.

Dining at La Pinsonniere is magical. Gleaming wood, crisp white linen, sparkling stemware and china, glowing candlelight and soft colors set the stage for the evening in the recently expanded and renovated dining room. The inn's award-winning chef creates gourmet cuisine for the most discriminating palates, using local ingredients and creative presentations. In addition to its sumptuous cuisine, La Pinsonniere boasts an amazing collec-tion of superb wines. Wine tastings are available upon request in the grotto wine cellar.

The inn's mini-spa provides a serene escape, with everything from a heavenly four-hand massage, to mineral mud hand or foot treatments, algae body wraps and facial care. There is also an indoor pool and an outdoor tennis court. From the tennis court, guests can meander down a steep staircase to a secluded rocky beach for a private picnic.

Address: 124 Saint Raphael, La Malbaie (Cap-a-L'Aigle), QC G5A 1X9
Phone: 418-665-4431
800-387-4431
Fax: 418-665-7156
Email:
pinsonniere@relaischateaux.com
Web site: http://www.lapinsonniere.com
Room Rates: 100–250 US $
Suite Rates: 230–375 US $
No. of Rooms: 19
No. of Suites: 6
Attractions: Nearby artist's town of Baie-Saint Paul galleries, Whale watching cruises (by boat or raft), Sea kayaking, Dog-sled outings
Services & Amenities: Valet service, Terry-cloth robe, Parking, Laundry, Gift shop, Baby-sitting service, Library, Spa
Concierge: 8 a.m.-10 p.m.
Room Service: 8 a.m.-8 p.m.
Restaurant: La Pinsonniere Dining Room, 6 p.m.-9 p.m.
Bar: La Pinsonniere Bar, Noon-midnight
Business Facilities: Message center, Copiers, Audio-visual
Conference Rooms: 1 rooms, capacity 60
Sports Facilities: Indoor swimming pool, Sauna, Massage, Tennis, Nearby golf, Skiing, Whale-watching cruises, Riding
Spa Facilities: Oil massages, aromatherapy, rain-bed massages, warm stones massages, chocolate massages, body sandings, sea water wraps, algea wraps, chocolate wraps, paraffin wax treatments, mineral mud treatments,
Location: 90 miles from Quebec City Airport

WATERLOO HOUSE

Named by *Travel & Leisure* magazine the "most sophisticated jewel of a small hotel in Bermuda." Waterloo House is an elegant manor house with surrounding cottages dating back to 1815. Just a stone's throw from the bustling capital rests this exquisite oasis of calm and tranquility.

Waterloo House is one of only two hotels on the Island to achieve the distinction of membership into the prestigious Relais & Chateaux chain of charming hotels. It nestles amidst four acres of manicured terraced gardens with stunning views over Hamilton Harbour. It is not only ideally located close to many historical and cultural sites on the Island, it also has the advantage of being within walking distance of the center of Hamilton, a colonial style town offering a large variety of shops, bars, clubs, bistros and fine restaurants. However, should you wish to spend the day resting on the beach, then in no more than 10 minutes you will be sinking your toes into the rejuvenating pink sand of one of their sister properties, the private Coral Beach & Tennis Club. Guests are also encouraged to enjoy all of the facilities of the other sister property, Horizons & Cottages.

Waterloo House is an oasis of charm and tranquility with its individually appointed rooms and cottages equipped with air-conditioning, safes, direct-dial telephones, fax and Internet access. All of the luxurious, blissful rooms and suites have been meticulously designed, using only the best French and Italian fabrics and furnishings, creating a level of comfort that you will never want to leave behind. Despite this, each of the rooms maintains its own individuality. Perhaps this is one of the reasons Waterloo House was named on the *Condé Nast Traveller's* Gold List for the past four years, the only hotel in Bermuda to achieve such a coveted title.

Waterloo House is known around the world as one of Bermuda's best restaurants. A winner of the AAA's five star diamond award for four years running, Waterloo House and its Executive Chef, Henry Guiasda, have won countless awards for the cuisine both in North America and Europe. The Poinciana Terrace, on the water's edge, is the place to be for al fresco luncheon or romantic candlelit dinners under the stars.

Address: 100 Pitts Bay Road, Hamilton, Bermuda HM 08
Phone: 441-295-4480
800-468-4100
Fax: 441-295-2585
Email: reservations@waterloohouse.bm
Web site: http://www.bermudasbest.com
Room Rates: 340–460 US $
Suite Rates: 440–780 US $
No. of Rooms: 20
No. of Suites: 10
Credit Cards: Most Credit Cards accepted
Attractions: Affiliation: Relais & Chateaux; Guests have privileges to use facilities at the exclusive Coral Beach & Tennis Club, where a European spa is also located.
Services & Amenities: Babysitting, Library, Games Room, Bellman, Night Bar, Gym, Cable TV, T1 and wireless Internet access.
Concierge: Available
Room Service: 24 hours
Restaurant: Poinciana Terrace (outdoor dining), Wellington Room, Exchange dining facilities with Horizons & Cottages and The Coral Beach & Tennis Club
Bar: Long Bar, Terrace Bar, Night Bar
Business Facilities: Conference facilities, In-room business service, Audio-visual equipment, Admin. assistance, Internet
Conference Rooms: Boardroom (conference table, cap. 24) or (theatre, cap. 50)
Sports Facilities: Swimming pool, Fitness center, Golf, Tennis at sister properties.
Spa Facilities: Spa available at the exclusive Coral Beach & Tennis Club.

HORIZONS & COTTAGES

Founded on an 18th Century Plantation, Horizons & Cottages is Bermuda's oldest and most exclusive Cottage Colony set on a hilltop amongst 25 acres of exotic gardens. It commands breathtaking views of the island's revered South Shore. The main house (9 rooms) and the cottages (39 rooms) are of pure Bermudian architecture and offer luxurious accommodations, tastefully appointed, equipped with air-conditioning, safes, direct-dial telephones and Internet access.

All the cottages and suites at Horizons & Cottages offer a supreme comfort with private gardens and ocean terraces that magnify the essence of Bermuda. Enjoy breakfast each morning either in your cottage prepared and served by your maid, or meet with fellow guests on the ocean Terrace to plan the day's activities. Begin the evening with an aperitif in the shade of the hibiscus, followed by a romantic dinner with superb food and wine out on the terrace gazing at the moon's reflection in the ocean below.

Horizons & Cottages is a member of the exclusive Relais & Chateaux collection of properties, one of only two in Bermuda (the other one being its sister property, Waterloo House). It serves as an ambassador for the French "art de vivre" and the highest culinary standards. Horizons & Cottages embodies the association's quality charter of the five "Cs"—Courtesy, Charm, Character, Calm and Cuisine.

While the resort specializes in laid back luxurious relaxation, guests are offered a full range of activities on land and in the water. The Horizon's management staff arrange a variety of activities every week such as the Monday night complimentary cocktail party where you can indulge in local drinks, meet the Manager, other guests and plan activities for your stay. Guests at Horizons & Cottages may enjoy privileges at the exclusive Coral Beach & Tennis Club with its spectacular private pink sand beach, restaurants, championship tennis courts, croquet, squash, fitness center and the newly opened European Spa with a variety of pampering treatments for face and body and half day beauty treatments.

Address: 33 South Road, Paget, Bermuda PG 04
Phone: 441-236-0048
800-468-0022
Fax: 441-236-1981
Email: reservations@horizons.bm
Web site: http://www.bermudasbest.com
Room Rates: 330–500 US $
Suite Rates: 460–610 US $
No. of Rooms: 45
No. of Suites: 3
Credit Cards: Most Credit Cards accepted
Attractions: Affiliation: Relais & Chateaux; Guests have privileges to use facilities of exclusive Coral Beach & Tennis Club; European Spa & Fitness Center at sister property, Horticulturist tours
Services & Amenities: Babysitting, Library, Bellman, Games Room, Cycle rental
Concierge: Available at Front D
Room Service: Available – Breakfast only
Restaurant: Ocean Terrace-formal outdoor dining, Barbeque Terrace-casual, Middleton Room-formal, Poolside terrace-casual; Full afternoon tea-main house/pool terrace;Exchange dining facilities w/ sister properties
Bar: The English Pub
Business Facilities: Conference facilities, In-room business services, Audio-visual equipment, Admin. assistance
Conference Rooms: Boardroom-Conference table, cap. 20 or theatre, cap. 40
Sports Facilities: Swimming pool, Mashie golf course, Tennis courts, Walks, Croquet lawn, Putting green, Private beach
Spa Facilities: Spa available at the excutive Coral beach & Tennis Club

CHARELA INN

The ultimate hideaway on the famous seven-mile Negril Beach, the Charela Inn is an oasis of peace and tranquility built around its lush inner tropical garden. Guests will be enraptured from the moment they enter the wood-paneled lounge with its marble tiles and tropical floral prints.

Charela is an intimate, friendly Inn with only 49 rooms, enabling the staff to cater to each guest's individual wishes. Three of these rooms are specially fitted for the comfort of physically challenged persons, with easy access to the entire property including the swimming pool and the beach. Decorated in vibrant greens with beige granite tiles, each room has two doubles, one queen, or one king-sized four-poster bed covered with cozy blankets and plush pillows. Telephone with direct dialing and digiport connections for PCs, CD players in the Deluxe and Seaview rooms and radio only in the Standard rooms. There is also a hairdryer, in room safe, cable TV, small refrigerator, air conditioning and ceiling fan in all our rooms.

All rooms have a patio or balcony offering either a breathtaking view of the Caribbean Sea (sea front rooms) or views of the lush tropical garden with its central round fresh water swimming pool.

Guests will enjoy a dip in the cool water encircled by lush green foliage! A stroll along the white sandy shore at sunset is a romantic experience not easily forgotten.

There is entertainment three nights a week: Reggae and other popular music on Thursday nights and Folkloric dance on Saturday nights.

The Inn's "Le Vendome Restaurant" delights diners with the flair of French cuisine combined with a blend of Jamaican spices. Open arches surround the festively decorated, cloth-covered tables, allowing the fresh breeze to waft over the guests. Tiffany cut-glass lamps, floral arrangements, and the fountain in the middle of the restaurant complement the building's beauty. Guests will enjoy menu items like Canard à l'Orange, seafood crepes, and heavenly eclairs for dessert; the gourmet pizzas are not to be missed. Many of the products served come from the owner's farm, ensuring guests that no additives or colorings are added to the food.

Guests return time and time again to the Charela Inn, where the ambiance is infused with relaxation and friendliness.

Address: Norman Manley Blvd., Westmoreland, Negril, Jamaica
Phone: 876-957-4648
Fax: 876-957-4414
Email: chareca@cwjamaica.com
Web site: http://www.charela.com
Room Rates: 108–210 US $
Suite Rates: 49
No. of Suites: 0
Credit Cards: Visa
Attractions: 5 miles from famous Rick's Cafe, 15 minutes by small plane and 54 miles by road to Montego Bay city, 2 hours drive to famous Y.S. Falls and Black River Safari
Services & Amenities: Parking, Laundry, TV lounge, International currency exchange, Terraces or balconies, Telephone, Radio, Hair dryer, Air conditioning, 5 sea view first floor deluxe rooms have whirlpool and Jacuzzi, Complimentary toiletries
Restrictions: No pets allowed, Children under 10 free with parents
Room Service: 10 a.m.–9 p.m.
Restaurant: Le Vendome, 7 a.m.–10 p.m.
Bar: 7 a.m.–10 p.m., Live Reggae and folkoric entertainment
Business Facilities: E-mail, Copiers, Fax
Sports Facilities: Outdoor swimming pool, Exercise gym, Sunfish sailing, Windsurfing, Kayaking, Hobie Cat sailing, Imme
Location: Beach resort on Negril Beach

THE TRYALL CLUB

The magnificent Tryall Great House, built in 1834, is the focus of the 2,200-acre Tryall Club overlooking the Caribbean on Jamaica's beautiful Sandy Bay. Established in 1960, it is constructed of natural gray stone blocks, presiding as the resort's Grande Dame as well as great house, charmingly updated without losing its original grandeur. Unblushingly regal in the Caribbean sunshine, the Great House and its secluded, elegant Estate villas overlook the azure ocean and immaculate grounds lush with native flora.

Experience Tryall's relaxing club-like lifestyle while playing on their internationally acclaimed par 72, 18-hole Championship golf course, which has hosted the Johnnie Walker World Championships among other well known golfing events. Tryall also has 9 all-weather tennis courts, of which several are lit for evening play. In addition, there is a Kids Club with arts and crafts, nature walks, scavenger hunts, and treks in the woods. And baby-sitting services are available.

Soft pastel hues harmonize with the fine mahogany furnishings in the Great House main lounge. The villas take maximum advantage of dramatic ocean, garden and pool views in their personal design and décor.

Experience fine food and personal service at your villa or at the Beach Cafe and Great House Restaurant, which offers international and Jamaican cuisine. A tempting selection of lobster entrees or other seafood specialties are just a small sample of the elaborate menu. The Jamaican Mixed Grill is another popular choice, topped off perhaps by the house dessert—Orange Rum Creme Brulee. Also indulge in the well-known tropical delights at the newly remodeled outdoor patio of the Great House cocktail bar while enjoying the breathtaking view of the Caribbean Sea and Montego Bay at night.

Relax and enjoy the beauty and elegance of The Tryall Club.

Address: P.O. Box 1206, Montego Bay, Jamaica
Phone: 876-956-5660-3
Fax: 876-956-5673
Email: administration@tryallclub.com
Web site: http://www.tryallclub.com
Suite Rates: 430–2,400 US $
No. of Rooms: 0
No. of Suites: 0
Credit Cards: Visa
Attractions: Hilton High day tour of Jamaican plantation, Negril Beach, Rocklands Feeding Station bird sanctuary, boutique shopping, horseback riding & Jeep safari, Mayfield waterfalls, aquasize, nature & river walks, Pool & beach volleyball, reggae & soca dancing
Services & Amenities: Massage Center, Gift Shop, Beauty Salon, Parking, Car hire, International currency exchange, Baby-sitting services available, Laundry, Cable TV, Afternoon tea, Group Package rates, Kids program, Fitness Room
Restrictions: No pets allowed
Restaurant: Great House Dining Room for breakfast, Terrace for dinner and Afternoon tea, Beach Cafe for lunch
Bar: Ninth Hole 8:30am-6pm high ssn, Beach Bars 10am-6:30pm, Great House 5pm-Midnight
Business Facilities: By prior arrangement-Admin. assistance, Translators, Audio-visual, Fax
Conference Rooms: One room available, 110 Theater style/100 Banquet/Classroom
Sports Facilities: Outdoor swimming pool, lighted tennis courts, championship golf course, non-motorized water sports,
Location: 2200-acre plantation overlooking the Caribbean, 12 miles from town

SEBASTIAN'S ON THE BEACH HOTEL

Sebastian's On the Beach Hotel & Restaurant is located on a luxurious, white sand beach in Little Apple Bay on Tortola's North Shore. The charming 26-room hotel offers the ultimate in breathtaking scenery and total relaxation. At this casual, intimate hideaway, guests will awaken to the sound of gently lapping waves and cool sea breezes.

Offering spectacular ocean views, the luxury junior suites feature private balconies, marble and mirror baths, and kitchens with refrigerators, toaster ovens and microwaves. All units are air conditioned with ceiling fans and have 12' glass sliding doors, TV/VCR with a film library, telephone, and Turkish rugs. Two deluxe units feature exotic teak, whirlpool baths, separate shower with extra large granite vanities, a mirrored make-up area, built-in dressers and large closets. Hairdryers and plug-in phones for Internet access are also included.

Tortola is an ideal location for all types of water sports and activities. Everything from sailing, snorkeling and diving, to surfing, tennis, horseback riding and hiking can be arranged through Sebastian's. They also assist with jeep and car rentals—though many guests prefer to lie on the beach with a rum punch and a good book. On weekends, dance under the stars to the live music of the islands' best fungi & steel bands at the beach bar.

Sebastian's award-winning seaside restaurant is one of the islands' favorite dining spots, offering both continental and Caribbean cuisine. The menu features fresh seafood, steaks and vegetarian dishes. Dine inside for a romantic candle lit atmosphere or outside on the comfortable palm-fringed terrace. Start with West Indian Fritters—crispy deep fried fritters served with remoulade sauce. As a main course, try chicken breast marinated in jerk seasonings and served with Jamaican jerk sauce. For dessert, don't miss the fresh brewed coffee with Sebastian's home blended rum, topped with whipped cream and a sprinkle of fresh grated nutmeg.

Sebastian's On the Beach Hotel & Restaurant is an ocean-lovers paradise.

Address: Box 441 Little Apple Bay, Road Town, Tortola BVI
Phone: 284-495-4212
800-336-4870
Fax: 284-495-4466
Email: info@sebastiansbvi.com
Web site: http://
www.sebastiansbvi.com
Room Rates: 85–230 US $
Suite Rates: Villas 150–300 US $
No. of Rooms: 26
No. of Suites: 9
Attractions: Horseback riding, Hiking, Jeep and car rentals for touring Tortola, sufing in winter,
Services & Amenities: Private bath, Refrigerator and Air conditioning in all rooms, coffeemaker, iron, ironing board, hairdryer in most rooms, juniour suites have kitchenettes, phone, TV, VCR, 2 units have teak whirlpool
Restrictions: Children welcome, pets welcome, not handicap accessible
Concierge: Yes
Restaurant: Seaside Grill- award winning restaurant – breakfast, lunch and dinner dining inside or on palm-fringed terrace
Bar: Beach bar with barbecue and live music
Business Facilities: Internet Desk in Reception
Sports Facilities: Dart board, surfing, snorkeling, -windsurfing, daysails, diving, tennis nearby
Spa Facilities: Spa services close by (1/2 mile)
Location: Located on Little Apple Bay on Tortola's North Shore

MAKANDA BY THE SEA

Located just off the main road between Quepos and Manuel Antonio National Park, Makanda By the Sea is 12 acres of sanctuary, 1000 feet above the ocean. All of Makanda's Villas and Studios have been carefully placed in the botanical rainforest gardens with spectacular views of the sixty mile coastline. It is truly a haven for the adventurist seeking relief from controlled environments of modern life.

The luxurious accommodations include a full breakfast served to your room each morning and a host of amenities in each room to guarantee your comfort and relaxation. Pamper yourself with incredible ocean views and a 4 to 1 guest ratio that ensures you first-class service not generally found in jungle environs. Our reception desk is available to help you plan the perfect honeymoon, anniversary, wedding or unforgettable romantic vacation with an extensive choice of tours, activities, and spa treatments. Our adults only policy helps to maintain the quiet ambiance you deserve during your stay at Makanda.

Sunspot Poolside Bar & Grill creates exciting dishes bring new flavor to Manuel Antonio. Using only the finest seafood, meats, poultry and vegetables. Most items are prepared on the grill and all dishes are accented with fresh herbs and spices from the area. One of only 8 restaurants in Costa Rica to win the coveted 5 spoons award from the Tico Times.

At Makanda By the Sea you will find a number of ways of keeping comfortable on even the hottest of tropical days. From our infinity pool, follow the passage of monkeys, sloths, pizotes and other jungle life as they wind their way through the surrounding rainforest down to our own secluded beach. Or unwind in the Jacuzzi while the wildlife watches you!

The theme here is "Romance in Nature" and we infuse that in all that we do!! Join us for an unforgettable vacation experience!!

Address: Apartado 29, Quepos, Costa Rica
Phone: 506-777-0442
1-888-MAKANDA
Fax: 506-777-1032
Email: makanda@racsa.co.cr
Web site: http://www.makanda.com
Room Rates: 175–400 US $
Suite Rates: 175–400 US $
Suite Rates: 11
No. of Rooms: 11
Credit Cards: Visa
Attractions: Canopy Tours, ATV Rentals, Jet Skis, Sailing, Mangrove Tours, River Rafting, Kayaking, Deep Sea Fishing, Horseback Riding, Dolphin Watch, National Park Tours, Secluded Beaches, Snorkeling, Surfing, Scuba Diving, Mountain Bikes, Spa Treatments, and more!
Services & Amenities: Full service concierge and tour desk. All rooms have cable tv, cd players, kitchens with fresh coffee, full mini-bar, tropical flower arrangement, robes for guests use, hairdryer, safe, and more. All rooms feature fabulous ocean views.
Restrictions: Regretfully we do not accept children under 16 years of age.
Concierge: Yes
Room Service: Yes
Restaurant: Sunspot Poolside Bar & Grill, open 11 a.m. until 10 p.m. daily, dinner reservations suggested. Room service available during restaurant hours. Happy Hour by the pool 4 to 6 each evening.
Bar: Yes
Business Facilities: Wedding receptions, and special events.
Conference Rooms: No
Sports Facilities: Outdoor infinity pool, Jacuzzi.
Spa Facilities: We offer in room spa services or a full array of spa treatments at the nearby luxurious Sea Glass Spa.
Location: between Quepos and Manuel Antonio National Park

THE BEAUFORT

Step back to a time when customer service really mattered at The Beaufort where the staff go that extra mile to ensure guests have a truly memorable stay.

Decorated in soft, calm colours and furnished throughout with bespoke maple pieces it is obvious that much thought and attention has been given to comfort and luxury - setting these accommodations apart from a standard hotel. Each guest bedroom offers air-conditioning, CD players, radio, state-of-the-art televisions with free Internet, email & movies, chocolates, biscuits, mineral water, fresh flowers and magazines plus twice daily maid service.

Almost as large as the bedrooms, the beautiful marble bathrooms have power-showers, bath tubs and of course plenty of fluffy towels.

Complimentary continental breakfast is delivered to you in bed by the hotel's discreet and friendly staff. Fine Wedgwood china and silver cutlery show off the warm croissants, delicious preserves, fresh fruit salad, orange & grapefruit juice and, of course, steaming hot pots of tea and coffee.

Other complimentary offerings include drinks from the Sitting Room bar and a truly scrumptious cream tea with homemade scones and clotted cream.

The Beaufort is home to a unique collection of original English watercolours, the largest in the world, with over 300 floral paintings complementing the colours of the rooms.

Everything is designed to make the guest feel as relaxed and spoilt as possible. The extraordinary worldwide reputation of this small hotel can be credited to the originality of its owners and warm personalities of the staff members.

Address: 33 Beaufort Gardens, Knightsbridge, London SW3 1PP
Phone: 44-207-584-5252
Fax: 44-207-589-2834
Email: reservations@thebeaufort.co.uk
Web site: http://www.thebeaufort.co.uk
Room Rates: 230–350 US $
Suite Rates: 550 US $
No. of Rooms: 29
No. of Suites: 7
Attractions: Just a short stroll to Harrods, the boutiques of Knightbridge & South Kensington, the world famous Victoria & Albert, Science & Natural History Museums & Hyde Park's 200 acres. And 10 minutes by taxi to the theatres and nightlife of the West End.
Services & Amenities: Complimentary continental breakfast, unlimited drinks from the Sitting Room bar, traditional cream tea with homemade scones and clotted cream
Restrictions: No pets allowed
Concierge: Available at Recepti
Room Service: Complimentary cream tea between 3 & 5pm
Restaurant: Peruse our restaurant guide for The Beaufort's own reviews and critics on an eclectic range of restaurants in London.
Bar: Complimentary – soft drinks 24 hours a day & alcohol from 3-11 p.m.
Business Facilities: Date Port in all guest bedroom, Wireless Internet access, Secretarial Services
Conference Rooms: Small meeting room for up to 10 people
Sports Facilities: Special rate for daily membership to a top London health club, just minutes to Hyde Park for jogging
Spa Facilities: Guests benefit from a preferential price a top London Health Club only 5 minutes from the hotel.
Location: Tucked away in a quiet cul-de-sac, next to Harrods in fashionable Knightsbr

THE CLAVERLEY

As previous winners of the Spencer Trophy, the premier award for the best Bed and Breakfast Hotel in Central and Greater London, the Claverley has proven that they meet the expectations of the most discerning traveler. This intimate, elegant and friendly designer hotel is located on a quiet tree-lined cul-de-sac in prestigious Knightsbridge, a two-minute stroll from Harrods.

From the moment guests walk through the door, they feel as though they are coming home. The hotel prides itself on the warmth of its service, its sumptuous full English breakfast and the quality of its well appointed, refurbished rooms, most featuring marble bathrooms with power showers. Each of the thirty-three guestrooms has been individually decorated to create its own distinct character and appeal. Some boast the luxury of a four-poster bed, and all have color television with satellite channels including CNN and direct dial telephones.

The leafy quiet of Hyde Park is within easy walking distance, as are the Royal Albert Hall, and the treasures of the Victoria and Albert Museum and the Science, Geological and Natural History Museums. Leicester Square, Oxford Street, Regent Street, the West End and the heart of London's nightlife are all within easy reach by bus, underground or taxi. From Knightsbridge Underground Station, guests are only forty minutes from Heathrow Airport, via the Piccadilly line.

Guests can start their day well fortified by enjoying a unique, full English breakfast, featuring traditional bacon, tomato, egg & Cumberland sausage, as well as homemade waffles with maple syrup and their own delicious specialty, fresh salmon kedgeree, cooked to order. Guests can count on being served by a warm and friendly staff in the hotel's breakfast room. Throughout the day, complimentary coffee, tea, hot chocolate and biscuits are available in the paneled reading room.

The Claverley ensures the ambience of a traditional town house in the heart of London.

Address: 13-14 Beaufort Gardens, Knightsbridge, London SW3 1PS
Phone: 44-(0)20-7589-8541
1800-747-0398
Fax: 44-(0)20-7584-3410
Email:
reservations@claverleyhotel.co.uk
Web site: http://www.claverleyhotel.co.uk
Room Rates: 143–270 US
Suite Rates: 360–396 US
Suite Rates: 30
No. of Suites: 7
Attractions: Hyde Park, Harrods, Sloane Street, V&A Museum, Natural History Museum, Buckingham Palace, Houses of Parliament, Oxford Street, Knightsbridge, Shopping, Madame Tussauds, Trafalgar Square, Major museums, Theatreland
Services & Amenities: Reading Room, Direct dial telephones, VAT, Color TV w/ satellite channels, Hair dryers, Porter service, Ironing facilities, Free coffee/tea/hot chocolate/biscuits 24 hrs., Safes, Same day laundry service, Full English Breakfast and all taxes included
Restrictions: No pets allowed, 20 non-smoking rooms
Concierge: Porter service
Restaurant: Full English breakfast
Bar: The Lounge with its complimentary tea, coffee, hot chocolate, biscuits and newsp
Business Facilities: Fax, Copier, Administrative assistance, wireless broadband Internet access
Location: 40 minutes from Heathrow Airport

LONDON ELIZABETH

The London Elizabeth, in a beautiful historic building, overlooks Hyde Park. Full of charm, character and originality, the hotel has a fascinating history including some notable and extraordinary residents. The atmosphere is warm, welcoming and relaxed, and is matched by attentive yet unobtrusive service.

Accommodations are comprised of just 49 guestrooms, including executive and deluxe bedrooms and six luxurious suites. All deluxe bedrooms and suites are non-smoking and fully air-conditioned. The London Elizabeth's Deluxe Bedrooms offer the highest level of luxury and elegance with an atmosphere reminiscent of a splendid country house rather than a hotel guestroom. Furnished with accessories and objects d'art, they offer striking features such as four-poster beds, antique fireplaces, furnished balconies or are split-level. The Suites offer some of London's most beautiful accommodations. From the enormous Hyde Park Suite, beautifully restored to its elegant Victorian origins, to the spectacularly panoramic views of the Conservatory Suite, The London Elizabeth never fails to impress its guests.

The hotel restaurant, The Rose Garden is temporarily closed for lunch and dinner. During this time The Rose Garden is fully open for breakfast service. The Bar service and Room and lounge service operate 24 hours daily. Furthermore, whilst lunch and dinner service is closed, the room and lounge service has menu choices which will provide a healthy comfort with a country flair for guests and served wherever in the hotel you wish (including the dining room). Whether you simply want a snack, a full meal or just a bite of dessert, our room service menu will suit you. The menus change seasonally and all items are freshly home cooked.

The London Elizabeth, a traditional Victorian hotel set between the calm of Hyde Park and the excitement and bustle of modern-day London.

Address: 4 Lancaster Terrace, Hyde Park, London 0.
Phone: 44-20-7402 6641
800-721 5566
Fax: 44-20-7224 8900
Email: reservations@ londonelizabethhotel.co.uk
Web site: http:// www.londonelizabethhotel.com
Room Rates: 150–200 US $
Suite Rates: 150–200 US $
Suite Rates: 49
No. of Suites: 6
Attractions: Based in the heart of London, enjoy London's history and sightseeing tours. West End theatres and entertainment. Museums, galleries and London culture easily accessible. Huge range on London restaurants. Hyde Park hosts concerts from pop to classical.
Services & Amenities: Private car parking, Air conditioning, Four-poster beds, Fireplaces, Galleried split-level, Furnished balconies
Restaurant: The Rose Garden serves Country Classic dishes
Business Facilities: Boardroom for small meetings
Sports Facilities: Yes
Spa Facilities: Yes

HOTEL DU PALAIS

The Hotel du Palais radiates charm. It is a hotel rich in memories, style and history. In faithful observance of the grand tradition of a long forgotten standard of living, this palatial hotel blends sumptuousness with the elegant restraint of an exquisite, prosperous era. The hotel was formerly a summer home known as "Villa Eugenie," commissioned in 1852 by Napoleon III and his new bride, Eugenie de Montijo. Modern-day guests now have the rare opportunity to luxuriate in breathtaking surroundings while enjoying the superb service and attention to detail that are the hallmarks of the hotel's experienced staff.

Located within a hundred meters of the city center and near the casino, the hotel overlooks the far-stretching beach of Biarritz. Victor Hugo was so enchanted by Biarritz in 1830 that he selfishly prayed that ". . . Biarritz would never become fashionable." While Monsieur Hugo's prayer was ignored, the unique beauty that once drew such legendary figures still thrives.

The Palais prides itself on tradition, elegant accommodations, excellent service and fine dining. The soul of the Palais is best revealed in its rooms and apartments, where vast spaces bear witness to the banquets of a bygone era. The carefully selected artwork and graceful intimacy create a pleasant, luxurious atmosphere of absolute serenity. With 134 air-conditioned rooms and 22 suites, guests will delight in the individual décor and charm of each room. In addition to elegant guestrooms, the Palais offers a heated seawater swimming pool with solarium, a fitness center, three fine dining establishments, state-of-the-art conference facilities and a multitude of organized outdoor activities.

The magnificent Hotel du Palais is a grand experience in the truest sense. Guests will find it hard not to return to this opulent location year after year.

Address: 1 Avenue De L'Imperatrice, Biarritz F-64200
Phone: +33-559-41-6400
Fax: +33-559-41-6799
Email: reception@hotel-du-palais.com
Web site: http://www.hotel-du-palais.com
Room Rates: € 350–500
Suite Rates: € 500–1,350
No. of Rooms: 132
No. of Suites: 22
Credit Cards: Visa
Attractions: 10 Golf courses nearby, International training center, Boutiques, Green hillsides, Beach of Biarritz, Casino, Museums, Tours and excursions, Prehistoric caves
Services & Amenities: Parking, Currency exchange, Hairdresser, Solarium, Special packages, Continental breakfast delivered to your room each morning (26 Euro per person/per day), Interactive TV (34 channels), Minibar, direct dial phone, Complimentary toiletries.
Restrictions: Pets welcome, Children up to 10 stay free in parent's room
Concierge: 24 hours
Room Service: 24 hours
Restaurant: L'Hippocampe, Informal lunch around pool; Rotonde, Lunch or Dinner with music ambiance, facing the sea; Villa Eugenie, Gastronomic restaurant
Bar: Bar on premises
Business Facilities: Business Center
Conference Rooms: 7 meeting & seminar rooms, capacity 15-250
Sports Facilities: Heated sea-water swimming pool with direct access to beach, Pitching green, Nearby tennis, squash, a
Location: Biarritz, a refined sea resort on the other South of France.

HOTEL MONT BLANC

A legendary hotel in the heart of Megeve, Le Mont Blanc has the advantage of a really exceptional situation. Next to the Chamois telepherique, it is opened to the Rochebrune and Mont d'Arbois Massif for walks or for skiing.

More than a style, a special atmosphere is prevalent for guests to rediscover the mountain once again. The antique wood's warmth and décor blend with harmony the styles of English, Austrian and Savoyard, giving Le Mont Blanc an uncommon style, where each object finds its natural place.

Its Spa with Jacuzzi and sauna invite you to relaxation and to fitness. In the lounges, you have the possibility to choose and taste the different home chocolates near the fireplace. In the summer, you will be able to enjoy the Patio and the outdoor swimming pool.

Some people will speak of "tour de force", others of magic. The magic of a cherished town, Megeve, that proudly shows off the elegance and luxury from ancient times and standing in the heart of it, the Mont-Blanc.

Address: 29 Place de l'Eglise, Megeve F-74120
Phone: 33-4-50-21-20-02
Fax: 33-4-50-21-45-28
Email: contact@hotelmontblanc.com
Web site: http://www.c-h-m.com
Room Rates: € 200–396
Suite Rates: € 374–638
No. of Rooms: 29
No. of Suites: 11
Attractions: Gardens on-site, hiking and lunch around a table d'hôte to Alpage de Pré Rosset, spa and beauty farm, three restaurants. Sister hotels: Lodge Park, Les Fermes de Marie, Au Coin du Feu. Properties to rent : Chatel et Hauteluce.
Services & Amenities: Cable TV, Telephone, Health and Beauty Center on site, Library with fireplace, Safe, Minibar, Antiques abound
Concierge: Available
Restaurant: In our sister hotels, Les Fermes de Marie, Lodge Park and Au Coin du Feu Restaurants
Sports Facilities: Full scale health spa, Outdoor swimming pool, Sauna, Nearby skiing, hiking, golf, horseback riding,
Location: In the center of the town of Megeve

LA BASTIDE DE MARIE

Ideally located in the heart of the regional natural park of Luberon, between Gordes and Bonnieux, La Bastide de Marie is one of the most splendid proprieties in the region. This 18th-century structure, surrounded by 15 hectares of vineyards, is a standing invitation to discover the subtle fragrances of Provence.

La Bastide de Marie embodies the discreet harmony of Impressionist lighting. Each of the 8 rooms and 6 suites are decorated with Provençal furniture discovered in the region's many antique shops. The warmth of the district's colors and shades continues to inspire artists, just as they did Picasso and Nicolas de Staël. Sunflower yellow, aster mauve, and wild anise create an atmosphere of inspiration that intensifies with each passing moment. Several of the rooms boast canopy beds and all have unique views of the magnificent countryside.

In addition, Grenache is a gorgeous renovated XVIIIth century Bastide with all the charm of a Provençal farm, set in the Luberon natural Park amongst the most beautiful scenic countryside of southern France. This beautiful domain is standing in 15 hectares of vineyards, overlooking lavender fields and cherry orchards. This splendid property shows a very elegant interior; on the ground floor are a dining room, a small lounge with a library equipped with DVD player, canal satellite, stereo; another living room with a fireplace and well-equipped kitchen. Upstairs there are five bedrooms, four bathrooms and one shower room. Most of them are equipped with TV, CD player and stereo.

There is plenty of recreation in the area including golf, cycling, hiking and ballooning. Notre-Dame-des-Graces chapel and the ancient abbey of St. Hilaire are historical landmarks, and there are several fascinating bories, ancient dry-stone huts, along the small roads and fields surrounding the village.

Each dish at the hotel's restaurant is a journey in taste. Fresh ingredients from various local markets are rich in the colors and fragrances of the region. Don't miss the Ripe Tomatoes with Fresh Basil and Goat Cheese or the Cold Summer Vegetable Soup with Courgettes and Grilled Pumpkin Seeds. As a perfect accompaniment, indulge in a white, red or rosé Domaine de Marie wine.

La Bastide de Marie opens its doors to a world where visitors will long to stay.

Address: Route de Bonnieux – Quartier de la Verrerie, Menerbes F-84560
Phone: 33-4-90-72-30-20
Fax: 33-4-90-72-54-20
Email: bastidemarie@c-h-m.com
Web site: http://www.c-h-m.com
Room Rates: € 415–515
Suite Rates: € 620–715
No. of Rooms: 8
No. of Suites: 6
Attractions: Scenery, Menerbes, Historical sites, Vineyards, Provence, Lacost Castle
Services & Amenities: Breakfast included, Dinner w/aperitif and house wine included, Garage & parking, Laundry service, Baby-sitting on request, TV, Telephone
Restrictions: Pets allowed
Restaurant: La Bastide de Marie, 12-2:30 p.m. and 7:30-9:30 p.m.
Sports Facilities: Outdoor swimming pool, Golf, riding, tennis and sailing nearby
Location: In the natural regional park of Luberon

BOURGOGNE & MONTANA

Just opposite the Palais Bourbon, two steps from Concorde, Invalides, Tuileries gardens, the Bourgogne & Montana Hotel**** is very well centrally located in this elegant and aristocratic district of the 7th arrondissement.

In this historic edifice, dating back to 1789, you will enjoy your stay in a refined decor. With its 32 newly renovated rooms and suites totaly equipped with luxuous bathrooms, it represents the art of living in Paris, with a typical Parisian charm.

A business center is available in the private living room.

Address: 3, rue de Bourgogne, Paris 75007.
Phone: +33 1 45 51 20 22
Fax: +33 1 45 56 11 98
Email: b.montana@bourgogne-montana.com
Web site: http://www.bourgogne-montana.com/
Room Rates: 150–240 ¤
Suite Rates: 305–320 ¤
Suite Rates: 26
No. of Suites: 6
Attractions: The Bourgogne & Montana Hotel**** is located at the heart of the most prestigious quarter in Paris, facing the Palais Bourbon, near the courtyard of the Invalides and close to the Concorde.
Services & Amenities: The art of reception, a certain idea of tradition, a beautiful residence, resolutely turned towards elegance and refinement, which shines forth a home feeling. All rooms are air-conditioned with TV, mini-bar, hair-dryer and safe.
Restaurant: Paris is a gastronomic city. Our reception team will be pleased to inform you about the best restaurants aroud the hotel.
Sports Facilities: Yes
Spa Facilities: Yes
Location: Palais Bourbon, Invalides

HOTEL DES TUILERIES

The Hotel des Tuileries is situated in the heart of Paris near the Louvre, the Orangerie Museum, and the Orsay Museum. Once an 18th-century palace, the Hotel is breathtaking in its beauty and history.

Guests enter into a lobby of rich wood and light walls, displaying lovely artwork. Attentive staff members will greet guests and whisk them away to their relaxing accommodations. On the way, guests will walk upon intricate Oriental rugs as the daylight filters through the central atrium. Plush carpets, antique wood furniture, and paintings complement the guestrooms, whose light hues create a welcoming atmosphere where guests will enjoy luxurious beds and sofas. The French décor and the expansive brick archways of the lounge offer a sophisticated meeting place.

Excitement and grandeur are only moments away from the Hotel, inviting guests to walk down the bustling streets while shopping in Paris' many boutiques and sampling the delicious foods of France. Culture abounds in downtown Paris where guests can sample various ethnic foods and music before spending an afternoon in sublime peace at Notre Dame. For a spectacular end to an exciting day, guests can indulge in a breathtaking sunset atop the Eiffel Tower and arrive back at the Hotel within minutes to enjoy an exquisite dinner.

The Hotel des Tuileries will enrapture guests with its sophisticated atmosphere and ensconce them in refined comfort.

Address: 10, Rue Saint-Hyacinthe, Paris F-75001
Phone: 33-1-42-61-04-17
Fax: 33-1-49-27-91-56
Email: hotel-des-tuileries@wanadoo.fr
Web site: http://www.hotel-des-tuileries.com
Room Rates: € 170–250
No. of Rooms: 26
No. of Suites: 0
Attractions: Near the Louvre, The Orangerie's Museum, The Orsay's Museum, Shopping at the famous Faubourg Saint-Honore's shops, Place Vendome's jewellers and Galeries Lafayette department stores
Services & Amenities: Sitting room, Antique rugs, Rooms filled with art, Air conditioning, Parking, Mini bar, Private deposit box, Hair dryers, New Lift directly to Breakfast Room
Restrictions: Children under 12 stay free with parents, Smoking allowed, Pets welcome 10 ?.
Room Service: Room service
Location: In the heart of Paris

MADISON HOTEL

The view upon the Saint-Germain-des-Prés church is unique. In the heart of the Latin Quarter, the living space of this residence is decorated with furnishings and old paintings. The convivial atmosphere of the delightfully joyful rooms and the warmth of the welcome illustrate all the charm of Paris.

Every morning, a splendid Saxe porcelain rooster beckons you to a generous buffet.

The welcome at the reception desk is thoughtful. The concierge is prepared to care for all of your needs: restaurant reservation, car rental or train/plane tickets. . .

Address: 143 Boulevard Saint Germain, Paris 75006.
Phone: +33 1 40 51 60 00
Fax: +33 1 40 51 60 01
Email: welcome@hotel-madison.com
Web site: http://www.hotel-madison.com/
Room Rates: 155 – 320 ¤
Suite Rates: 320 – 390 ¤
Suite Rates: 53
No. of Suites: 1
Attractions: The Madison hotel is surrounded by art galleries, museums, antique shops as well as the most prestigious shops. Ideally located in the heart of Saint-Germain-des-Prés, just a few steps from the shore of the Seine, the hotel Madison is an assurely eminent
Services & Amenities: Amenities : lift, safe, bagage handling Rooms : Air-conditioning, hair dryer, telephone, mini-bar, TV satellite Pets are allowed (subject to conditions)
Restaurant: A lot of good restaurants are located in the distict of St Germain des Prés. The concierge will be able to help you in your choice.
Sports Facilities: Yes
Spa Facilities: Yes
Location: Saint Germain des Prés, Latin Quarter

ST. NICOLAS BAY HOTEL

St. Nicolas Bay is set in its own secluded world overlooking the coastline of Mirabello Bay. Nestled amongst olive, lemon and orange trees, the resort's airy and spacious bungalows and suites are the perfect place for couples seeking total seclusion.

All of the rooms have been designed in the traditional Cretan style with whitewashed walls and dark wooden furniture, as well as marble bathrooms featuring an aerospa bath. Many of the suites boast a private pool and a terrace which overlooks the bay.

Beautiful lush gardens immediately surround St. Nicolas Bay and during the warmer months guests can enjoy a sumptuous meal al fresco style in one of the hotel's restaurants overlooking the gardens.

The St. Nicolas Bay revels in old fashioned tradition of service and hospitality, treating all of its guests as VIPs.

Address: PO Box 47, Aghios Nikolaos G-72100
Phone: +30-28410-25041
Fax: +30-28410-24556
Email: stnicolas@otenet.gr
Web site: http://www.stnicolasbay.gr
Room Rates: € 130–300
Suite Rates: € 180–415
Suite Rates: 60
No. of Suites: 47
Attractions: Dining in Aghios Nikolaos at the Cretan Stars – an exclusive deluxe restaurant in an old mansion overlooking the harbour and terraced garden eith bougainvillea, orange and lemon trees.
Services & Amenities: Mini Club, playground, laundry, babysitting, private beach, 2 outdoor seawater pools, room service, video games, table tennis, billiards, boutique, dry cleaning Rooms – a/c, phone, satellite tv, some with aerospa bath and private pool
Concierge: Yes
Room Service: Yes
Restaurant: 5 – Amongst the most popular restaurants are the Blue Bay which serves lunch along the water's edge, the Kafenion which offers a la carte menus and the Minotaure with innovative cuisine.
Bar: Astra Bar, Club House, Blue Bay 11–12pm
Conference Rooms: Yes, 3 rooms 20-180 persons
Sports Facilities: Watersports, Scuba Diving
Spa Facilities: 1 indoor fresh water pool, jacuzzi, sauna, steam bath, fully equipped gym, massage, aromatherapy, moisturizing treatments
Location: Beachfront, East facing, Quiet

SEA VIEW HOUSE

The stately Sea View Hotel is set amidst lush gardens, rimming the shores of Bantry Bay, and when guests enter, they are gently lulled into another time. Set in well-tended gardens, it has cozy lounges with turf fires and comfortable, pleasantly decorated bedrooms.

The 25 spacious bedrooms are individually decorated, those at the front of the house having views of Bantry Bay through the trees. If guests are looking for extra-roomy accommodations, request one of the very reasonably priced family rooms with two bathrooms. All bedrooms are ensuite and include direct-dial telephone and TV. A new wing of bedrooms has just been added to the Hotel. These 9 rooms and suites are large with seafacing views and king sized beds.

The sitting room décor is pleasant and with shades of green and rust and light oak furniture. There are plenty of places to sit and, for those in search of peace and quiet, there is library/tv room.

The hotel caters to the fishing and golfing enthusiast and is also a good touring base for West Cork and Kerry. Explore the most beautiful parts of Ireland, from beautiful Killarney, in County Kerry to the North, to Kinsale a little further south. And don't miss Glengarriff and the world famous Garinish Island, where seals bask on the rocks with their pups. Other fun activities include watersports, cycling, golf, painting, horseback riding, and hiking.

The restaurant has won numerous awards including the AA Rosettes and Bord Failte Awards of Excellence. Along with lunch and dinner, morning coffee and afternoon tea are available. Although seafood is their specialty, vegetarian meals are available upon request. A new conservatory has been added to the Dining Room offering even more seating for the fabulous restaurant.

There is nowhere better to sample Irish hospitality than at this delightful country house.

Address: Ballylickey, Bantry
Phone: 353-27-50073
Fax: 353-27-51555
Email: info@seaviewhousehotel.com
Web site: http:// www.seaviewhousehotel.com
Room Rates: €140–170
Suite Rates: € 170
No. of Rooms: 25
No. of Suites: 3
Credit Cards: Visa
Attractions: West Cork, Kerry, Gougane, Barra Skibbereen, Glandore, Garnish Island, French Armada Center, Mizen Head
Services & Amenities: Library, Gardens, Car parking, 220/240 voltage, Baby-sitting service, Laundry service, TV, Satellite TV available, Direct-dial from bedroom, Open parking available, Hairdryer
Restrictions: Small pets allowed, Disabled facilities and public rooms
Concierge: Yes
Room Service: Room service
Restaurant: Restaurant and a conservatory – A.M. coffee available; Afternoon tea available, Lunch available, Last dinner available at 9:30 p.m., Vegetarian meals available
Bar: Bar lunch available, Cocktail Lounge
Sports Facilities: 2 excellent golf courses nearby
Location: 5 kilometers from Bantry, 11 kilometers from Glengarriff on N71

VILLA GAIDELLO CLUB

The Azienda Agricola Il Gaidello is a vast agricultural estate situated in the fertile Po River valley just outside the town of Castelfranco Emilia. The complex of 250-year-old farmhouses is located in an oasis of tranquillity and promises a delightful Italian experience.

The Villa Gaidello has been divided into three complete apartments, each named after one of the sisters who own the estate. The Adriana Lc is located where the original stable once was. The manger area is now the main bedroom, and it has open beam ceilings throughout. In the Paola Giovanna apartment, beautiful antiques and rich colors combine to create serene elegance. The Chiara Maria has high ceilings and a warm ambiance, reminiscent of times past. The apartments, furnished with 1800s antiques, also highlight local artists, from the hand-decorated walls to the wrought iron sconces. In addition, several farmhouses on the Gaidello estate have been restored and converted into guest apartments.

The fields surrounding the family estate produce rich red tomatoes used in the Gaidello's pasta sauces, onions for pickling in balsamic vinegar, walnuts used to make liquor called Nocino, and rows of moscato grapes for guests to pick and eat. Near the small lake by the Casa Padronale, there is a small orchard of wild fruit trees.

The restaurant, Il Gaidello, is a converted stable where guests can enjoy delicious food prepared by the rezdore (skilled countrywomen). Paola Bini closely supervises the cooking and adds finishing touches to every dish. Most of the meals are eaten family style at massive wooden tables and served with local wines and Nocino. For a real treat, try the Gaidello's Antipasto - Crescentine, Salami, Proscuito, Mortadella, Onions in Balsamic Vinegar and Artichokes in Olive Oil. Delicious!

For a true taste of Italy, don't miss the Villa Giadello.

Address: Via Gaidello 18/20, Modena, Castelfranco Emilia I-41013
Phone: 39-59-926806
Fax: 39-59-926620
Email: gaidello@tin.it
Web site: http://www.gaidello.com
Room Rates: € 65–93
Suite Rates: € 86–263
No. of Rooms: 2
No. of Suites: 7
Credit Cards: Visa
Attractions: From here one can easily visit the beautiful cities of Bologna, Modena, Ferrara, Ravenna and Parma. Other smaller but equally interesting cities nearby are Nonantola, Vignola, Castelvetro, and Dozza Imolese.
Services & Amenities: Modern kitchenettes available, Antiques, Beautiful views, 3 acres of lovely grounds, swimming pool nearby, archery area, lake with swans.
Restrictions: No pets allowed, No smoking
Restaurant: Villa Gaidello, Open from Tuesday through Sunday afternoon, reservations required.
Business Facilities: Can be reserved for business purposes
Conference Rooms: Meeting room, capacity 80
Sports Facilities: Mountain bikes for relaxing rides in the countryside, Nearby tennis courts and swimming pool.
Location: Near Castelfranco Emilia between Bologna & Modena – region Emilia Romagna

HOTEL LA VECCHIA CARTIERA

What is now called La Vecchia Cartiera (the Old Paper Mill) was once a valuable paper factory active since 13th Century. The old structure, located in the center of Colle Val d'Elsa, has become a comfortable, luxurious hotel after a careful restoration. The façade, characterized by harmonious arched windows, is typical of the architecture of paper mills from times past.

Bright, serviceable rooms and discreet attention make guests feel spoiled yet right at home. There are 38 well-appointed guest-rooms with private baths, direct telephones, air conditioning, refrigerator-bars, and color TVs. Nicely equipped conference and meeting rooms, a delightful reading room and a parking garage make La Vecchia Cartiera an ideal location for business.

Relive the distant past with all the modern amenities at La Vecchia Cartiera.

Address: Via Oberdan, 51719, Colle Val d'Elsa (Siena) I-53034
Phone: 39-577-921107
Fax: 39-577-923688
Email: cartiera@chiantiturismo.it
Web site: http://www.chiantiturismo.it
Room Rates: € 103–121
Suite Rates: € 106–125
No. of Rooms: 38
No. of Suites: 0
Attractions: Tuscany countryside filled with nature and tradition, breathtaking landscapes like the famous "Crete" of Siena and the Chianti region; nearby find other centre full of art and history like Siena, San Gimignano, Monterrigioni, Colle Val d'Elsa, Florence
Services & Amenities: Garage, Reading rooms, Buffet Breakfast 12.00 Euro, Direct telephone, Air conditioning, Refrigerator-bar, Color TV
Restrictions: No pets allowed, cradles not available
Bar: Full service bar
Business Facilities: Conference and meeting rooms
Location: The center of Coll Val d'Elsa

VILLA GIULIA

If you are looking for a true Italian holiday in Central Italy away from the tourist masses and by the sea, Villa Giulia is the best choice: it joins the natural hosting rule of an ancient aristocratic family together with the charm of the history, the fascinating guestrooms and the mediterranean landscaped gardens overlooking the sea!

Although it is called a villa, this spacious country residence is more like the equivalent in the Italian Marches of a French stately home with its tower, the Chapel and the long wide terrace looking towards the sea.

Getting to Villa Giulia is like opening a history book and witnesses of the old owners of the Villa, like Prince Eugêne de Beauharnais, Napoleon's stepson, are everywere. The lounges and the bedrooms are fully furnished with antique original furniture and all around there are the books and the objects of daily use from the past!

Guests have the run of the whole house, the frescoed salons, the terrace and the gardens, while a path through the Olive Grove leads to the swimming pool. The frescoes of the bedrooms have all been expertly restored or executed by your hostess, the charming and enterprising Countess Passi whose family has owned this magnificent summer home for generations and who now lives here all year round. The villa is furnished with family antiques and the fabrics are Spanish and French in yellows, pinks and greens.

The landscaped gardens surrounding the Villa are full of attractive places: in fact Villa Giulia is a perfect set for a romantic Honeymoon!

The ancient olive grove of the Family's Farm produces a good and healthy olive oil.

Distances from the main Italian cities: Rome 140 miles, Venice 130 miles, Florence 130 miles, Ancona 30 miles, Bologna 80 miles, Milan 160 miles.

Address: via di Villa Giulia – localitñ San Biagio, 40, Fano
Phone: 39 0721 823159
Fax: 39 0721 823159
Email: info@relaisvillagiulia.com
Web site: http://www.relaisvillagiulia.com
Room Rates: € 80–140
Suite Rates: € 100–230
No. of Rooms: 4
No. of Suites: 11
Attractions: Wide sandy beaches. Sightseening to the most important Central Italy cities of art, unspoiled little medieval walled villages and Natural Parks. Delicious regional foods and wines. Great relaxation!
Services & Amenities: The Villa Giulia's guests will be able to choose among charming suites and bedrooms with a delicious breakfast or cosy self-catered apartments. In-room refrigerator with refreshments, robes & toiletries, hairdrier. Free parking.
Restrictions: Dogs are welcome!
Concierge: Yes
Restaurant: Wake up to the aromas of a delicious deluxe italian breakfast! Corner bar in the ancient lemon greenhouse and exquisite candlelit dinners in the terrace overlooking the sea.
Bar: Yes
Sports Facilities: Panoramic swimming pool. Beaches, horse riding and tennis court in the neighbourhood.
Location: Overlooking the sea, 600 metres from the beach

HOTEL VILLA DEL SOGNO

In a splendid position sloping down towards the Lake, Villa del Sogno is a romantic "fin de siêcle" Villa surrounded by a large centuries-old park, planted with tall trees and flowering gardens with a superb Terrace overlooking the azure water of Lake Garda that has always enchanted travellers from all over the world. Built in 1904 by the Viennese silk industrialist Maximilian Heydweiller in a neoclassical style, today it is an exclusive and welcoming location in which the rooms and the suites, all furnished in different ways, offer the most modern comforts. The Villa has a Restaurant for unforgettable dinners by candlelight, an American Bar for extremely enjoyable moments of relaxation on the Terrace, a Garden Bar, the open-air swimming pool, tennis court, private car park, sauna, solarium and whirlpool.

Address: Via Zanardelli 107, Lago di Garda
Phone: 39 0365 290181
Fax: 39 0365 290230
Email: info@villadelsogno.it
Web site: http://www.villadelsogno.it/
Room Rates: 300–500 US $
Suite Rates: 500–600 US $
No. of Rooms: 30
No. of Suites: 3
Attractions: Lake Garda Tours – Arena di Verona – Venezia
Services & Amenities: Buffet Breakfast on the Terrace – American Bar – Garden Bar at Pool – Outdoor Swimming-Pool – Tennis court – Private parking – Sauna, solarium and Jacuzzi – Laundry service – Courtesy shuttle bus service
Concierge: Yes
Room Service: Yes
Restaurant: Candle-light cosy atmosphere, exquisite creativity cuisine, attentive first class service characterize the ambiance of the Restaurant "Villa del Sogno"
Bar: American bar on the Terrace
Sports Facilities: Tennis court – Swimming pool

ALBERGO VILLA MARTA

The Hotel Albergo Villa Marta is a nineteenth-century hunting lodge which has recently been restored. The hotel is located at the foot of the renowned Monti Pisani, only 5 km from the historic town of Lucca.

The Hotel Albergo Villa Marta is located in the heart of a typical Mediterranean landscape, where verdant hills and cool woods offer an alternative to the traditional and geometric olive groves typical of the area.

The villa is surrounded by a spacious Renaissance Lucchese garden, where guests can enjoy unique serenity. On the facing hillside is an impressive view of the peaceful Convent of San Cerbone, still in use today.

The Hotel Albergo Villa Marta, with its elegance and crystal-clear swimming pool, promises an unforgettable holiday for those looking for relaxation, warm Tuscan hospitality and culture.

Similarly, for those travelling on business, Hotel Albergo Villa Marta is the ideal place to relax from the stresses and strains of the day.

The exclusive site includes a small, private neo-classical chapel, the ideal location for an intimate and romantic wedding.

Hotel Albergo Villa Marta has double rooms and double deluxe; each room has its own character, created with a combination of elegant furnishings, subtle colour schemes and simple architecture.

Our aim is to make your stay unforgettable and satisfy your every need.

All the rooms (some of them connecting) are spacious, well-lit and equipped with the most modern amenities including air-conditioning, telephone, desk, TV sat, minibar and hair dryer. Everything is designed to satisfy all your needs. You can choose from different room types: some have marvellous frescoed ceilings, and all offer a magnificent view over the surrounding countryside.

Disabled access is also provided, in rooms on the ground floor of the villa.

Guests at the Hotel Albergo Villa Marta are invited to enjoy an extensive buffet breakfast served in summer in the villa's garden and in winter in the comfortable and elegant Breakfast Room with its welcoming open fire.

Address: Via del Ponte Guasperini, 873, Lucca 55100
Phone: +39.0583.370101
Fax: +39.0583.379999
Email: info@albergovillamarta.it
Web site: http://www.albergovillamarta.it
Room Rates: 156–197 US $
Suite Rates: 170–262 US $
No. of Rooms: 11
No. of Suites: 2
Credit Cards: Visa
Attractions: The hotel is located near the beautiful town of Lucca, which still preserves its romantic and mysterious fascination. In the surrounding area there are ancient gardens, castles, churches and historical places to visit, as for example Puccini's house.
Services & Amenities: Wine & Oil Tasting, Art Gallery, Transfer Service, Traditional dinner on request, Conference Organization Tours, Painting Course, Cookery Course, Swimming Pool, Chapel, Bicycles, Safe box, Internet, point in communal areas, Babysitting service.
Room Service: Room service and laundry service are available on request
Restaurant: Typical tuscan and italian cuisine are provided. Personalized menu. In the good season is possible to taste the special flavor of our dishes by sitting outside in the big garden.
Bar: Lounge bar, open lounge bar .
Business Facilities: Fax Service, conference organization
Conference Rooms: The hotel has 1 meeting room with a capacity range of 10 to
Sports Facilities: Nearby health club, tennis courts, Jogging track
Location: Only 5 km from the historical town of Lucca.

CA' P'A

Our history

As we sailed along the coast 9 years ago, we discovered this old ruin. The physiognomy of the construction was fascinating as it stood isolated amidst a wide-open space, slightly sloped towards the sea. The land around the ruin was unique for the area and flowed into a rocky coastline, which appeared to be less steep and rough than the land preceding or following it.

Retaining something of the original impression of the place became quite a challenge. At first, we envisioned it as being a holiday home, but once all the rooms had been laid out with their own bathrooms, we realized we could not keep the place all to ourselves. So we set out to make it accessible to our friends.

The most difficult aspect was preserving the quality and charm of the original structure. In the end, we manage to make the ruin habitable.

One of the main topics of concern was air conditioning. After countless discussions, we decided it was better to keep the distinctive sensation of a hot night than to cool the place artificially like everybody else would. As for experiencing the cold, we had other thoughts: We definitely decided to install a heating system in order to make the house tolerable during the colder months.

The product of our musings is the Ca' P'a —*una casa privata.*

The Rooms

There are just 6 rooms in Ca' P'a: 2 suites and a double room on the 1st floor, and 3 double rooms and a large terrace on the 2nd floor. The suites are comprised of two connected rooms, whereby one is positioned in the centre of the house and therefore a little darker and cooler. Every room is 4.30 meters high with a domed ceiling, stone floor and a view of the sea. Real-Life Picture Postcards—*Positano*—peek out from behind a rocky outcrop. The sky and sea change by the minute while the Faraglioni di Capri remain unchanged at the centre of the picture with the Isole dei Galli on their left.

In the centre of each room you will find a glass bookcase cube holding around 130 volumes. Each of the 6 rooms has its own library that focuses on a different field of interest: art, architecture, nature, history, philosophy and psychology.

Address: Via Rezzola 41, Praiano 84010
Phone: +39 3341000348
Fax: +39 089871153
Email: info@casaprivata.it
Web site: http://www.casaprivata.it/
Room Rates: € 160–180
Suite Rates: € 230–250
No. of Rooms: 4
No. of Suites: 2
Attractions: The most beautiful Coast in the world – the Amalfi Coast. The view: Positano on the right, The Faraglioni di Capri in the middle and the Isole dei Galli on the left.
Services & Amenities: 5000 square metre garden areal, sea-water swimming pool, private beach, open-air rooms – each guest also has a room in the garden.
Restrictions: Many stairs on the Coast
Room Service: available
Bar: Self-service
Business Facilities: Conference and meeting possible
Location: Amalfi Coast

PARKHOTEL SOLE PARADISO

The Parkhotel Sole Paradiso enjoys a wonderful setting in an open meadow, embraced by the woods of San Candido and fringed by the imposing Baranci peaks.

Guests have an opportunity to appreciate the warmth and expertise of the Ortner Family, who have taken exquisite care of their visitors for over four generations.

Guests will relish the attention, impeccable taste and panache manifested in every detail. The hardwood floors are inlaid with stylish and original designs, which create an incomparable atmosphere.

Each of the 42 comfortable rooms and suites have private bathrooms and come equipped with hair-dryers, mini safes, telephones, and color TVs. The accommodations fall within four categories: Standard, Standard with balcony, Superior, Superior with balcony, Royal and Royal with balcony. Each is unique in its décor and variations include late 19th century, the 1920s, and modern designs.

Amenities are numerous. A heated indoor swimming pool is surrounded by a Solarium, which includes a sauna, bodybuilding facilities and massages. There is also table tennis, billiard, tennis courts, citybikes and boccia ball. For moments of repose, relax in the Tyrolean reading room. If business is a must, the hotel has a bright conference hall, Internet point and fully equipped meeting rooms.

In the midst of the charming Dolomites, the area is a well-known winter and summer vacation resort. In the winter, skiing abounds, with 70 miles of cross-country slopes, ski races, excursions on horse-drawn sleds, ice skating and curling.

In the summer enjoy winding woodland paths, lush meadows and breathtaking scenery.

After a long day of fun, retire to the dining room where the marvelous dishes of resident chef Markus Auer await. The Parkhotel Sole Paradiso is proud of its renowned cuisine, which is characterized by fresh ingredients and natural flavors.

Address: Via Sesto, 13, San Candido I-39038
Phone: 39-474-913120
Fax: 39-474-913193
Email: info@soleparadiso.com
Web site: http://www.soleparadiso.com
Room Rates: € 120–258
Suite Rates: € 180–290
No. of Rooms: 43
No. of Suites: 10
Credit Cards: Visa
Attractions: Dolomites, San Candido (10 minutes on foot), Cortina d'Ampezzo (30 km), Venice (200 km)
Services & Amenities: Garden/park, car park, Solarium, Ski bus stop in front of hotel, Satellite Color TV, Telephone, Wall safe, Hair dryer, Home cinema
Restrictions: Non-smoking reading and dining room
Concierge: Yes
Room Service: Yes
Restaurant: 3 restaurants with local and international cuisine, Banquet and reception rooms
Bar: Yes
Business Facilities: Fully equipped meeting rooms enjoying ample natural light
Conference Rooms: 4 rooms, capacity 10 – 100
Sports Facilities: Indoor swimming pool, Downhill and cross-country skiing, Tennis, Bocce Ball, Bikes, Bodybuilding
Spa Facilities: Finnish sauna, Turkish steam bath, Bodybuilding facilities, Massages, Solarium
Location: In an open meadow, embraced by the woods of San Can Candido

HOTEL VILLA DUCALE

Set in the most exclusive and unspoiled part of Taormina, Villa Ducale is a small charming luxury hotel immersed in nature and offering breathtaking views over the sea. A recent refurbishment program has provided the hotel with the classical grace of an ancient aristocratic Sicilian villa. Quiet elegance and intimate Italian charm are reflected by the antiques and keen attention to detail throughout the hotel. Ideal spot for honeymoons and anniversaries. All rooms have a balcony overlooking the sea, air conditioning, TV, radio, safe, minibar, phone, Internet connection. Most rooms have Jacuzzis and large panoramic patio. Mediterranean garden with open air Whirlpool, 24 hours room service, bar and wine bar with local pasta and hot snacks. Free Internet point in the lobby.

Villa Ducale is proud to be a member of the prestigious Italian hotel collection named "The Five Senses Hotels."

Address: Via Leonardo da Vinci, 60, Taormina I-98039
Phone: +39-0942-28153
Fax: +39-0942-28710
Email: info@villaducale.com
Web site: http://www.villaducale.com
Room Rates: € 130–250
Suite Rates: € 250–440
No. of Rooms: 11
No. of Suites: 6
Attractions: Visit Taormina, Volcano Mount Etna, Eolian Islands, Siracusa, Greek and Roman temples and ruins, enjoy the best Mediterranean beaches with all water sports from April to October.
Services & Amenities: Library, golf, free Internet point, open air large whirlpool and spa.
Restrictions: Children welcome, smoking allowed, small pets welcome
Concierge: Managed 24 hours
Room Service: 24 hours
Restaurant: In our wine bar we serve hot local dishes, fresh pasta , salads and great Sicilian wines and spirits all day.
Bar: Bar
Business Facilities: Internet connection in rooms
Spa Facilities: Jacuzzi open air spa in the garden during the summer.
Location: Taormina near the centre

IS MORUS HOTEL

The Is Morus Relais has a truly superb setting on the southern coast of Sardinia. Only a one-hour flight from Rome and Milan, Sardinia is one of the most beautiful islands of the Mediterranean. The Is Morus Relais is located in a wonderful park on the shore of the magnificent green-blue sea.

An elegant house in natural surroundings, the Is Morus has 85 rooms and suites in both the main building and luxurious villas. They provide all the comforts one would expect in a elegant hotel. All contain air conditioning, mini bars, telephones, and televisions.

Activities abound. Swimming, tennis, water sports, and mountain biking are right on-site, and there is a playground and baby-sitting available. The Golf Club Is Molas, 18 holes of spectacular golf, is only 10 minutes away, as is the Is Morus Ranch where guests can horseback ride at their leisure. Or, if relaxation is the order of the day, sunbathe on a private sandy beach. Massages, manicures, and hairdressers are available upon request.

The ancient town of Nora provides a beautiful change of pace. Visit the exquisite mosaics or attend an exhibition of textiles by local craftspeople. There are several excursions by boat, which highlight the beauty of the Mediterranean.

Located on a sea-view terrace, the Is Morus Relais' gourmet restaurant offers refined regional and national cuisine, prepared with the most discriminating tastes in mind.

Although the Is Morus Relais is a deluxe resort, a friendly, home-like ambiance prevails.

Address: S.S. 195 – Km. 37,400, Santa Margherita di Pula, Sardinia I-09010
Phone: 39-70-921171
Fax: 39 070 921596
Email: ismorusrelais@tin.it
Web site: http://www.ismorus.it
Room Rates: € 520
Suite Rates: € 1,028
Suite Rates: 85
No. of Suites: 12
Attractions: Private beach, 2 Golf Clubs, Ancient town of Nora, Boat excursions
Services & Amenities: Air conditioning, minibar, telephone, TV, Beauty services (available upon request),
Restrictions: 2 rooms handicap equipped, Reduced rates for children, Small pets allowed in Villa or cottage
Concierge: Available
Room Service: Gourmet restaurant, 7:30–10
Restaurant: Central Bar 10:30 a.m.-midnight, Beach Bar 10:30 a.m.-5 p.m.
Bar: Conference facilities for up to 120 people capacity
Conference Rooms: Swimming pool, Tennis, Water sports, Mountain biking, Minigo
Sports Facilities: One hour flight from Milan and Rome on the island of Sardinia

CEIBA DEL MAR SPA RESORT

Escape to Paradise. Immerse your body and spirit in ancient rejuvenating techniques blended with modern amenities to energize and beautfy you from the inside out. Enter the unspoiled world of the Mayan Riviera and the tropical relaxation of the elegant Ceiba del Mar Spa Resort. Nestled on more than a half-mile stretch of sandy beach, bathed by turquoise Caribbean waters, Ceiba del Mar isn't for everyone . . . just those expecting exceptional service in tropical splendor.

Beautifully appointed rooms and suites, rooftop Jacuzzi, sundeck bar atop your villa, your personal host-concierge providing butler services, award-winning architectural splendor, gourmet dining with complete SPA menu, and a 9,000 square-foot full service Spa to pamper the most sophisticated guest. Traditional Swedish massage, Holistic massage and restoring Shiatsu performed by skilled spa personnel using natural vegetable base and organic essentials oils specifically customized for your body chemistry. Unique to CDM is the Aztec Temazcal ancient ritual performed on the beach at sunset inside a torch-lit terra cotta hut. Hot volcanic rocks enchanced with aromatic herbs cleanse the body, renew the mind and spirit, in this purifying and meditative experencience.

Twenty minutes south of Cancun International airport, Ceiba del Mar provides undiscovered splendor in the perfect location for exploring the Mayan culture yet close enough to enjoy either Playa del Carmen or Cancun.

For the ultimate interlude your deserve, step into the paradise called Ceiba del Mar.

Address: Puerto Morelos, Cancun 77580
Phone: 52-998-872-8060
877-545-6221
Fax: 52-998-872-8061
Email: info@ceibadelmar.com
Web site: http://www.ceibadelmar.com
Room Rates: 369–462 US $
Suite Rates: 424–1320 US $
No. of Rooms: 120
No. of Suites: 6
Credit Cards: Visa
Attractions: Visit the nearby Mayan communities, archeological sites of Tulum and Coba,Reservation of Si'an K'an, Rappel in Aktun Chen, snorkel the pristine Cenote (fresh water holes) or enjoy magnificent marine life at the 2nd larget reef in the world.
Services & Amenities: Personalized services, A la Carte menus. Free work shop on stress management, various seminars offered throughout the year.
Restrictions: No children under 15
Concierge: Available
Room Service: 24 hours
Restaurant: 3 Restaurants: The Xtabay, International menu, the Arecife, offers Mexican Specialties, from 6 p.m. to 10 p.m. Yaché Seaside Palapa specialize in fresh seafood with Asian flavor
Bar: Arrecife, 10 am to 5p.m., Xtabay, 4p.m. to 11p.m.
Business Facilities: One business center with 2 computers with Internet and 24 hour access.
Conference Rooms: 2 Conference centers, Small Executive Boardroom for up to 35
Sports Facilities: Full equip gym, one tennis court, Complete fitness program, yoga, Aquafit, Pilates, power walk
Spa Facilities: Holistic healing, private consultation with our in-house specialist.

VILLA DEL SOL

Villa del Sol, a member of the prestigious Small Luxury Hotels and voted one of the "Top 25 Small Hotels in the World" by *Condé Nast Traveler*, is located in a sheltered picturesque bay on Mexico's Pacific coast. Builder-owner Helmut Leins came under the spell of the sleepy fishing village of Zihuatenejo and its glistening ocean beach in 1969. Today his vision of an intimate beachfront inn, framed by lush tropical gardens, is a reality. 72 rooms and suites, individually designed, tastefully appointed and air-conditioned, now comprise Villa del Sol.

The Mexican-style rooms feature large canopied beds and comfortable, attractive built-in sitting areas. Private terraces, fans and hammocks add to the relaxing Villa lifestyle, an ambiance born of hospitality and a touch of romanticism. The resort consists mostly of suite rooms. The Lagoon Suites offers spacious one-bedroom suites with lake view and partial ocean views, separate sitting area and terrace with outdoor minipool. The Garden Suites are two-bedroom, two-bath with large terrace and outdoor minipool. The Beach Suites, directly on the beach, uniquely designed with extensive amenities. And, the Presidential Suite, overflowing with amenities, is in the most privileged beachfront spot with a fantastic 180 degree view of the entire Zihuatanejo bay.

The chefs combine their talents to prepare the finest international cuisine. Start at Orlando's Bar with their famous margaritas. And then whichever your choice of restaurant . . . feast! At La Villa Restaurant you will delight Pacific-Mexican cuisine with an emphasis on only the finest local seafood. A special Mexican Fiesta with a large buffet and live entertainment is generally held each Friday night. If your choice is La Cantina Bar & Grill enjoy great Mexican fair for lunch and dinner in a casual and fun setting at the bar, outside on the large wooden deck or inside by the open kitchen.

Be as energetic as you want with water sports, tennis, swimming, parasailing, and fishing. Or simply relax on the beach and absorb the tranquil beauty of this Mexican paradise.

Address: P.O. Box 84, Playa La Ropa S/N, Zihuatanejo 40880
Phone: 52-755-55 5 55 00
888-389-2645
Fax: 52-755-55 4 27 58
Email:
reservation@hotelvilladelsol.net
Web site: http://
www.hotelvilladelsol.net
Room Rates: 275–330 US $
Suite Rates: 450–1400 US $
No. of Rooms: 37
No. of Suites: 35
Attractions: Small boutique area in Ixtapa and Zihuantanejo, Magnificent beaches. Be as active as you wish; swim, sail, water ski, go snorkeling or scuba diving, windsurfing, sportsfishing, parasailing, horseback riding or play golf at the 2–18 golf courses.
Services & Amenities: Welcome cocktail, Daily morning coffee served on your terrace, Valet service, Garage and parking, Car hire, Gift shop, Day Spa, Massage, Currency exchange, Laundry, Doctor on call, Baby-sitting service, Art Gallery, Boutique, Cable TV, Tour Desk.
Restrictions: Small pets allowed, Children accepted in Garden Suite & large Beach Suites only
Concierge: 7 a.m.-11 p.m.
Room Service: 8 a.m.-10:30 p.m.
Restaurant: La Villa Restaurant, 8 a.m.-10:30 p.m., La Cantina Bar & Grill, 12 p.m.-10:30 p.m.
Bar: La Barca, 4 p.m.-11 p.m.
Business Facilities: Message & admin. assistance, E-mail, Copiers, Fax, Internet
Conference Rooms: 1 room, capacity 30
Sports Facilities: 4 outdoor swimming pools, Fitness Center, Tennis courts, 2 18-hole golf courses & Water activities
Spa Facilities: The Spa facility offers a range of personal treatments including Massages, Facials, Aromatherapy, Reflexology as well as Manicures and Pedicures.
Location: Only 2 kms from downtown & 10 kms from the airport

DAR AYNIWEN VILLA HOTEL

Dar Ayniwen, a sanctuary of peace and tranquillity in its 5 acre park, is at last revealed in all its splendour.

Built as the owner's family home, after 20 years a house with seven bedrooms became too big and four years ago it was turned into a luxury guest house, all of the very highest quality, now run by father and son.

The majestic old residence with its charming and peaceful garden stands proudly in the heart of the Marrakech palm grove, facing the snow-covered Atlas Mountains.

You will be enchanted by all that it has to offer, whether for a weekend, a formal lunch, or a candle-lit dinner in a veranda by the pool or one of the saloons. What a way to discover Marrakech!

Described by previous visitors as a positive mirage and a place of everlasting wonder, the Dar Ayniwen villa hotel is there to fulfill your every wish. You can take your time to relax, enjoy the hamam (steam bath) and sauna, or sunbathe by the palm-bordered swimming pool. It is also possible to taste the delights of Moroccan and international cuisine.

Dar Ayniwen: an eternal kingdom, fit for a prince . . . .

Dar Ayniwen is ideal for renting in its entirety for a special occasion and is a great location for a party, although rooms are also available individually.

Address: nslm. Lazrak – Rue Hassan Ben M'Barek, Marrakech
Phone: 212 44 32 96 84/85
Fax: 212 44 32 96 86
Email: infos@dar-ayniwen.com
Web site: http://www.dar-ayniwen.com/
Suite Rates: 220–500 US $
No. of Rooms: 0
No. of Suites: 7
Attractions: Fun!Fun!Fun! Skiing and mountain climbing, this is serious . . . but also, Golf, Tennis, Horse and Camelback riding, biking. The jamel Fnaa spectacle and the snake charmers are a Marrakech special. Belly dancers, Musicians and/or Folklore possible.
Services & Amenities: We are a staff of 19 to make your dream vacation come true! Cable TV, DVD player, sound system, safe, mini bar in every room. Afternoon mint tea, moroccan pastries and roses are traditions.
Restrictions: Pets Welcome
Concierge: Trilingual
Room Service: 24hr
Restaurant: Our à la carte service allow our customers to pick directly from our numerous cooking books. (Moroccan and international cuisine)
Bar: 24hr
Business Facilities: Modem, Fax, Phone
Conference Rooms: 14 Pax
Sports Facilities: Heated swimming pool/Hamam/Sauna/Ping Pong table
Spa Facilities: Hammam (Steam Bath) Sauna (dry heat) Massage and gommage (black soap rubbing)
Location: Marrakech Palm Grove (Palmeraie)

MONTE DO CASAL

Monte do Casal is in a protected preservation area close to the ancient hill village of Estoi, yet only 15 minutes from the airport, 25 minutes from Quinta do Lago, Vale do Lobo and the world famous golf courses and beaches.

Monte do Casal is not grand and neither is it pretentious, but probably it is somewhere that you have been looking for and most likely for some time. It has taken 20 years to evolve from an old manor house and now it is ready for you to experience and enjoy,. And hopefully, give you the best holiday in your life and one you will always treasure. Most good things in life take time to mature. Monte do Casal has become one of the world's classic small luxury country house boutique hotels and is now a member of "The Small Luxury Hotels of the World."

Monte do Casal is a beautiful old 18th century Country house boutique hotel offering a high degree of privacy with an emphasis on comfort, personal service and first class food in a very special atmosphere of total relaxation.

But the greatest endorsement are the sheer number of guests who return year after year. They create a wonderful atmosphere, at times they give the feeling of a house party. Often there is spontaneous and stimulating after dinner conversation.

There are nineteen individually designed and decorated spacious bedrooms and suites with their own private terraces. The luxury breakfast is brought in the morning onto your large terrace by your personal maid, discreetly and directly without bothering you. Once the table is set, complete with flowers, she announces quietly that breakfast is ready.

The Villa at Monte do Casal has seven luxury bedrooms and is a leisurely three minute walk through the gardens to the Restaurant. Perfect for small parties to enjoy the exclusive use of the villa. Private dinner parties with butler service by the pool. Complete privacy and security within the walled garden if required.

I look forward to personally welcoming you to Monte do Casal and I will be delighted to give you lots of advice on the best areas to visit.

Bill Hawkins, Managing Owner

Address: Cerro do Lobo, Faro, Estoi P-8005-436
Phone: 00-351-289-991503
Fax: 00-351-289-991341
Email: bill.hawkins@montedocasal.pt
Room Rates: 120–210 ¤
Suite Rates: 150–385 ¤
Suite Rates: 19
No. of Suites: 6
Credit Cards: Visa
Attractions: Estoi Palace. Estoi and Milreu Archaeological Roman site. Museums. Cacela Velha ancient village.Carnival in February. Beautiful beaches and Ilha Deserta. stunning inland countryside. Walking. World famous golf. Saville-Monuments, Flamingo, Sta Cru,Tapas.
Services & Amenities: Luxury Continental breakfast on private terrace. Room CD with complimentary specially prepared CD. Complimentary Anywhere wireless Internet access. Two heated swimming pools, two whirlpools for hydromassage. Waterfalls, rock pools, Koi. Croquet.
Restrictions: No children under 16 yrs. No dogs or pets. No smoking in restaurant.
Concierge: Front desk 8am until ??
Room Service: Breakfast, Lunch and Dinner
Restaurant: Modern Cuisine with House specialities. French based, influenced by Portuguese and Thai cuisine.
Bar: Cocktail bar and terrace
Business Facilities: Fax, and secretarial services. Complimentary wireless internet.
Conference Rooms: By previous arrangement
Sports Facilities: 2 heated swimming pools, 2 whirlpools, croquet and putting green. Nearby world class golf courses
Spa Facilities: Aromatherapy. Reflexology. Massage Therapies. Luxury Whirlpool with hydromassage in six different positions.
Location: Estoi, Algarve, Portugal

DUQUESA DE CARDONA

Located in the heart of Barcelona, close to the Ramblas, in a historic building of the mid19th century, home of nobility and refuge of kings, the hotel has been remodelled to adapt the advanced technology to the flavor, tradition and hospitality which make it an example of the personalized service every customer deserves.

In the center of culture and historic district of a cosmopolitan city, the hotel is a haven of peace and tranquility for the visitor.

Located in front of Port Nautic, the hotel has the benefit of Mediterranean light. From the rooms and the extensive solarium terrace one can enjoy a magnificent, panoramic view of the gothic district, the hill of Montjuic and the Colombus statue across to the Olympic port.

Address: Paseo Colon, 12, Barcelona 08002
Phone: 0034 93 268 90 90
0034 93 268 90 90
Fax: 0034 93 268 29 31
Email: info@hduquesadecardona.com
Web site: http:// www.hduquesadecardona.com/
Room Rates: € 165–265
Suite Rates: € 295–345
No. of Rooms: 43
No. of Suites: 1
Attractions: Visit the gottic district of Barcelona, Picasso museum, Gaudi Houses (Batlo House . . .), the Rambla, the famous Boqueria Market. Go to the hill of Montjuic or to the beach
Services & Amenities: Services included: bathroom equiped with hair-dryer, mirror, bathrobe, slippers. Direct phone line, Safe and desktop facilities. Flat panel television with parabolic antenna. Individual air conditioning control. Connecting rooms available.
Concierge: Reception
Room Service: 24 hours
Restaurant: Restaurant "La Duquesa." The terrace "Brisa del mar" on the last floor of the hotel with a Barcelona Port panoramic view. The terrace "La Marina" on the Paseo Colon (Entry of the hotel).
Bar: 2 terraces during Spring and Summer seasons
Business Facilities: Yes
Conference Rooms: 2 meeting rooms
Sports Facilities: Outdoor small swimming pool
Location: City center – Barcelona Olympic port

TORRE DEL REMEI

Torre del Remei is a unique hotel establishment standing in the midst of an extensive private area. While many mansions are converted into hotels, this magnificent country estate sets itself apart from the ordinary with a high level of comfort and exceptional quality of services. Their beautiful surroundings and idyllic lifestyle will undoubtedly mesmerize guests at this unique turn-of-the-century getaway.

The original structure and style of the mansion have been carefully preserved, though its interior has been refurbished. Styling and technology have joined hands to ensure guests of the most enjoyable stay possible. The hotel's floor plan was created with ease and elegance in mind. The main lobby, whose ceiling is crowned by a domed skylight, leads to the dining room, which is lit through tall windows offering a memorable view. A small and charming reading room lies to the right inviting guests to relax and relish the silence of their own thoughts. The grand stairway leads guests to the floors above and exquisite guestrooms.

The eleven guestrooms of the hotel are located on three different levels and each offers an individual style and layout. Specially designed furniture paired with luxurious amenities create an elegant and comfortable atmosphere. All bathrooms feature whirlpool baths, towel dryers, hair dryers, wall sockets and heated floors. Other special touches include panoramic views, embroidered linens, fully equipped bar cabinets, television and VCR's, safes, under-floor heating and night lighting.

In addition to the unique surroundings and luxurious accommodations, the Torre del Remei offers fine cuisine prepared by chef Josep-Maria Boix. Josep has given more than sufficient proof of his mastery of the difficult art of creating original dishes of genuine quality. A private spring of water and a kitchen garden add to the colorful array of Josep's European cuisine.

With its peaceful setting, elegant accommodations and fine dining, Torre del Remei beckons a return time and again.

Address: Cami Reial, Bolvir E-17539
Phone: 34-972-14-0182
Fax: 34-972-14-0449
Email: info@torredelremei.com
Web site: http://
www.torredelremei.com
Room Rates: 260–312 US $
Suite Rates: 416–754 US $
No. of Rooms: 13
No. of Suites: 7
Attractions: Kitchen garden and private 5 acre park, Segre River, Natural reserve of Cadí-Moixeró, Pyrenees Mountains, Puigcerda nearby with ancient monuments and buildings, Walk to the lake ringed with elegant mansions, Beautiful panoramas, the rutes of Cathares.
Services & Amenities: Parking, Air conditioning, Heating, Reading room, Videotheque, Spanish & international newspaper, Medical service, Television with VCR, Telephone, Radio alarm clock, In-room safe, Bar cabinet, Night lighting, Whirlpool bath, Hair dryer, Towel dryer
Restrictions: Pets welcome, handicap access
Room Service: Avalaible 24 hours
Restaurant: Our restaurant opens every day from 13h–16h and from 20:30h–22:30h (weekend until 23h). Any special request please contact Marc Ruiz, our restaurant manager.
Bar: Wine cellar
Business Facilities: Yes
Conference Rooms: 1 room, capacity 10-30
Sports Facilities: Swimming pool, Putting greens, Gym & Sauna, close to Puigcerda Golf Course, Glider flying
Spa Facilities: At this beginning of year, we inaugurated our gym room equipped with modern machines ultra stepper, bicycle elliptic, bicycle of working and running. Our small corner gym is also equipped with a s
Location: Land of Cerdanya, Segre Valley thru Toses or the tunnels of Cadi Mountains

HOTEL REINA CRISTINA

The Hotel Reina Cristina is in what used to be the Rosales family house, and where the poet Federico Garcia Lorca spent his last days. The owners of the hotel have made every effort to keep the building the same as it was when the Rosales lived there.

The building, in typical Andalusian style with patios and fountains, remind us of the poet and surrounded by the commercial and social center of Granada. The Hotel Reina Cristina is a place where guests are treated with friendliness and respect, which in turn, makes guests feel as if at home.

The exquisitely decorated interior and the hotel's facade are due to the Jimenez family's expertise in the hospitality field, especially in restoration. All the rooms, whether double or individual, are individually decorated with all the amenities and facilities meet every need.

Address: Calle Tablas numero 4, Granada CP-18002
Phone: 34-9-58-253211
Fax: 34-9-58-255728
Email: clientes@hotelreinacristina.com
Web site: http://www.hotelreinacristina.com
Room Rates: € 94
Suite Rates: 43
No. of Suites: 0
Credit Cards: Visa
Attractions: Granada is the cultural capital of Spain, 500 year old University, Music, Theatre, Restaurants and artisans. There are monuments marked by the Arab and Christian presences over the years.
Services & Amenities: Safe, Maid service, Laundry service, Parking, TV and video room, Fully equipped private bathrooms with hair dryer, Telephone, TV, Music, Minibar, Air conditioning and central heating, Internet connection
Restrictions: Children under 2 free with parents, children 2-12 50% rate
Concierge: 24 hours
Room Service: 7:30am-midnight
Restaurant: El Rincon de Lorca, serving typical Spanish cuisine, was selected as the best restaurant in Granada last year. It is open from 12:30pm-4pm and 8pm-11:30pm. The hotel also offers a tapasbar.
Bar: Cafetería Reina Cristina 07,30-midnight
Location: In the commercial and social center of Granada

CLARIDGE HOTEL TIEFENAU

Perfectly located right in the city center, yet very quiet, just off main theaters and museum of fine art; within walking distance of the city's main attractions, shopping & business districts.

The charming business Boutique Claridge Hotel Tiefenau is often mentioned in travel magazines as a boutique hotel with a very special turn of the century style that succeeds in being both a business and a leisure hotel with a most modern infrastructure. The 31 spacious and elegantly furnished rooms in the style of the French kings feature hairdryer, TV, mini- & cosmetic-bars, high-speed wireless LAN and modems and voicemail in every room. Other hotel facilities include the famous Orson's Bar with its sun terrace and the Orson's Restaurant with its garden restaurant. A private parking lot is available. Hotel shuttle to and from the Airport.

Zurich's charming old town with a long history hosts many museums, churches and art galleries and is only at a few minutes' walking distance. The famous Bahnhofstrasse is an exclusive shopping area in the city center and has many fine cafes, restaurants and bars. The Niederdorf area on the east bank of the river is a good area for bars and nightlife. Museums include the fairytale Swiss National Museum with fine collection of work depicting Swiss cultural history, the Kunsthaus (just next to the Hotel), which houses many modern works including paintings by Picasso and Monet. Other places of interest include the Opera House and Grossmunster and Fraumunster churches. Guided tours of the city are available. The parks around the Zurichsee feature shows by street entertainers.

Deluxe junior suite with very comfortable sitting area with color TV, minibar, bathroom with scale/hair dryer/bath gown, in-room shopping, writing desk with business center with highspeed wireless LAN, in-room fax, voicemail, modem hook-ups, copier.

All rooms equipped similar to the one above are in the style of French King Louis XV. We offer superior double bed suites (or deluxe singles) or deluxe bedsitting rooms (twin beds) and junior suites.

Address: Steinwiesstrasse 8-10, Zurich CH-8032
Phone: 41-44-267-8787
Fax: 41-44-251-2476
Email: info@claridge.ch
Web site: http://www.claridge.ch
Room Rates: 199–420 CHF
Suite Rates: 450–540 CHF
No. of Rooms: 31
No. of Suites: 8
Credit Cards: Visa
Attractions: Lake of Zurich, Uetliberg-mountain, Opera & Musicals, Art Galleries, Shopping, Excursions to Lucerne & Berne, to Mt Titlis / Säntis / Rigi / Pilatus / Jungfraujoch, Rhine Falls & Schaffhausen, Round trip along the lake, sightseeing by old tramways & buses
Services & Amenities: Awarded the "QQ" for outstanding service quality. Parking, Airport Shuttlebus, Elevator, Beauty Salon, Laundry, Fax, voice mail, copier & modem hook-ups & highspeed wireless LAN in each room, Babysitting, Children's menus, Cribs, 24 hour room service
Restrictions: Children welcome (up to 6 years old free with parents), smoking allowed, pets welcome
Concierge: Yes
Room Service: Yes
Restaurant: Fine local and Swiss-Asian fusion dining at Orson's Restaurant, lounge & bar with bar-terrace and garden restaurant.
Bar: Orson's Bar & Longe with sun terrace
Business Facilities: Business Center (PC/Printer/Fax/Copier), 4 different modem hook-ups and high speed wireless.
Conference Rooms: 8 to 15 persons
Sports Facilities: Massage, Garden/park, Nearby: fitness center & Riding school, Jogging path into the forest of Zürich
Spa Facilities: Massage in guestrooms available – spa & fitness centers nearby
Location: Quiet surrounding right in the City Center

TONGSAI BAY COTTAGES & HOTEL

The land of Tongsai Bay is undoubtedly one of the most beautiful in Thailand. The cottages were built around the beauty and kept as much of what Mother Nature gave them as possible. Their philosophy is "living in harmony with nature."

In order to appreciate nature, guests need to be in open space; not just watching from inside an air-conditioned box. The concept of great outdoor living then followed. There are spacious outdoor spaces for all suites and villas all overlooking the sea. First you can start with the bathtub on the balcony for bathing with a seaview. Then you can eat, take a bath with a view, and even sunbathe and sleep (mosquito netting provided) all in open space while you are safe with the knowledge that you only have to step inside for air-conditioning and cover if it is too hot or if it rains.

If that isn't enough, there is Prana Spa which consists of 3 private cottages with unique relaxation techniques combined with a variety of original herbal recipes that help relieve stress. The massages offer their own effective but harmless techniques that combine the traditional Thai massage with the scientific study of the human body.

If you never want to leave your suite, room service is available all day. But do venture out, because the restaurants are superb. Chef Chom's Thai Restaurant by the Lobby offers spectacular views out over the bay with an International Breakfast Buffet and Thai dinner. Try the Tongsai Thai Salad, a mixture of King prawns, fresh fruits and vegetables. Floyd's Beach Bistro on the Beach offers open-air international cuisine for lunch and dinner. The Butler's Restaurant on the hillside just a few minutes walk from the Grand Villas, specializes in European food with a menu created for each day of the week.

This resort has thought of everything to renew and restore your mind, body and soul. You may never want to go home.

Address: 84 Moo 5 Bophut, Ko Samui, Suratthani 84320
Phone: 66-77-245-480
Fax: 66-77-425-462
Email: info@tongsaibay.co.th
Web site: http://www.tongsaibay.co.th
Suite Rates: 11,000–52,000 ¤
No. of Rooms: 0
No. of Suites: 83
Credit Cards: Visa
Attractions: Scuba diving, Deep sea fishing nearby, 25 acres of gardens, Private beach
Services & Amenities: Car rental, Taxi service, Gift shop, Minibar, DVD/CD & VCD library, IDD telephone, Safety box, Hairdryer, Coffee & tea making facilities, Sea views, Open-air terraces, Satellite TV, DVD/VCD/CD player, and "Sip" Internet Cafe
Restrictions: The hotel will be entirely closed for renovations between 16 October to 15 December 2005.
Room Service: 7 a.m.-midnight
Restaurant: Chef Chom's Thai Restaurant – 7-10:30 am breakfast, 7-10 pm dinner; Floyd's Beach Bistro on the Beach – Lunch, Dinner, Supper 11 am-Midnight; The Butler's Restaurant – Dinner 7-10 pm
Bar: Floyd's Beach Bar – 11 – 2 a.m., Lobby Lounge Bar – 10 a.m.-Midnight
Sports Facilities: Swimming pools, wading pool & Jacuzzi, Exercise, Tennis court, Non-motorized watersports
Spa Facilities: Prana Spa opens 11 a.m. – 10 p.m. with 3 private spa cottages each with herbal steam, floral bath, treatment and massage beds and either a rainfall or waterfall shower.
Location: Northeastern coast of Samui Island in the Gulf of Thailand